English poetry in the first half of the seventeenth century is an outstandingly rich and varied body of verse, which can be understood and appreciated more fully when set in its cultural and ideological context. This student *Companion*, consisting of fourteen new introductory essays by scholars of international standing, informs and illuminates the poetry by providing close reading of key texts and an exploration of their background. There are individual studies of Donne, Jonson, Herrick, Herbert, Carew, Suckling, Lovelace, Milton, Crashaw, Vaughan, and Marvell. More general essays describe the political and religious context of the poetry, explore its gender politics, explain the material circumstances of its production and circulation, trace its larger role in the development of genre and tradition, and relate it to contemporary rhetorical expectation. Overall the *Companion* provides an indispensable guide to the texts and contexts of early-seventeenth-century English poetry.

THE CAMBRIDGE
COMPANION TO
ENGLISH POETRY
~
DONNE TO MARVELL

Cambridge Companions to Literature

THE CAMBRIDGE
COMPANION TO
ENGLISH POETRY
~
DONNE TO MARVELL

EDITED BY

THOMAS N. CORNS

University of Wales, Bangor

CAMBRIDGE
UNIVERSITY PRESS

Published by the Press Syndicate of the University of Cambridge
The Pitt Building, Trumpington Street, Cambridge CB2 1RP
40 West 20th Street, New York, NY 10011–4211, USA
10 Stamford Road, Oakleigh, Melbourne 3166, Australia

© Cambridge University Press 1993

First published 1993
Reprinted 1994, 1995, 1997

Printed in the United Kingdom at the University Press, Cambridge

A catalogue record for this book is available from the British Library

Library of Congress cataloguing in publication data

The Cambridge companion to English poetry, Donne to Marvell / edited by
Thomas N. Corns. (Cambridge Companions to Literature)
p.   cm.
Includes index.
ISBN 0 521 41147 5 (hardback) – ISBN 0 521 42309 0 (paperback)
1. English poetry – Early modern, 1500–1700 – History and criticism.
1. Corns, Thomas N.
PR541.C36 1993 93–44508
821′.309–dc20 CIP

ISBN 0 521 41147 5 hardback
ISBN 0 521 42309 0 paperback

CONTENTS

CONTENTS

CONTRIBUTORS

Thomas N. Corns, University of Wales, Bangor
Alastair Fowler, University of Virginia, Charlottesville
Donald M. Friedman, University of California, Berkeley
Achsah Guibbory, University of Illinois at Urbana-Champaign
Richard Helgerson, University of California, Santa Barbara
Elaine Hobby, University of Loughborough
David Loewenstein, University of Wisconsin, Madison
Anthony Low, New York University
Leah S. Marcus, University of Texas, Austin
Arthur F. Marotti, Wayne State University
Jonathan F. S. Post, University of California, Los Angeles
Brian Vickers, Swiss Federal Institute of Technology, Zürich
Helen Wilcox, Rijksuniversiteit Groningen
Michael Wilding, University of Sydney

PREFACE

The purpose of this collection of new writing is to make it easier and more pleasurable to read English poetry of the first part of the seventeenth century. The term *Companion* carries its usual implications; we would be your associates in the process of exploring an extraordinarily varied and accomplished period of the English literary tradition.

The poets who constitute the subjects of the second part of this book may seem decidedly unvaried. All are male; most were born into the gentry class or more prosperous echelons of London society; nearly all were educated at Oxford or Cambridge, the only English universities of the time; many were associated in some way with the courts of James I or Charles I or both, and were beneficiaries of royal patronage. They are heirs to a common literary and cultural inheritance. Yet despite these shared characteristics their writings are very diverse. In part, such differences reflect abilities and temperament. But they reflect, too, the fissured and changing nature of the English cultural establishment and the opening up, in extraordinary fashion, of the scope and range of English poetry, and particularly of non-narrative poetry.

The poetic idiom of all these poets, even the young Milton, is primarily lyric; poems, typically, are short, indeed sometimes very short. Telling a story, however heroic or elevated, rarely attracts these writers. Their poems are intense in expression and often in sentiment, the distilled spirit, the hard liquor of the English literary tradition. Devotional poetry comes of age, engaging a range of religious belief and sensibility, from incipient puritanism through the mainstream of the Church of England to Catholicism, and from a rationalist sort of faith, through a range of piety, to mystical experience. Political verse finds a new role as the ground slips away beneath the old hierarchical assumptions. Panegyric becomes suffused with nostalgia or tinged with criticism; blame as well as praise enters the poet's repertoire; the certainties of the declarative and epideictic modes are joined by the expression of doubts and the rationalization of and ratiocination about profound changes in the political order. Love poetry was the finest achievement of the high Elizabethan poets. Spenser, Sidney, and Shakespeare have qualities rarely found in Jacobean and Caroline verse. But the poets from Donne, through Carew and Lovelace, to Marvell have qualities of their own, reflecting new continental influences, admitting a fresh union of literary impulse and sexual excitement, incorporating a new intellectualism and a new libertinism with impulses towards both elegance and depth of expression. Love poetry develops to carry a new freight of cultural and even political values. Robert Herrick coined the phrase 'Time's trans-shifting', aptly capturing the spirit of his own age; the poets this volume celebrates deeply reflect the fissuring and the mutations of the cultural milieu they inhabited.

I had wondered how best to organize the volume. My original inclination was to begin with the chapters on individual poets and to conclude with the more general chapters on larger aspects of context, moving from the specific to the general. I was persuaded to do otherwise by the argument that all the contributors probably believe that the experience of reading one poet is deeply enriched by an awareness of the cultural, political, economic, and literary system within which that individual worked. Hence the present ordering. How should you use the book? Certainly it is a volume that may be dipped into for individual guidance on an author or an aspect of context. The essays are self-contained. Each addresses a discrete topic. None is premissed on the content of another, and they may be read in your own order of choosing. But the value of the volume, I should like to maintain, is greater than the sum of the parts. Taken together, they provide a thorough grounding in understanding the cultural phenomenon of English poetry from Donne to Marvell. Moreover, in terms of critical method and theory, they represent a cross-section of the most fruitful approaches to the study of the English literary renaissance of the last twenty-five years.

Finally, a note on the editions quoted and cited. In the case of a number of writers several alternative editions are available, and contributors were encouraged to select, quote from, and refer to whichever seemed to them most appropriate for their purposes. Titles, however, have been modernized both in the text of the essays and in the index to the volume.

ABBREVIATIONS

ELH	*Journal of English Literary History*
ELR	*English Literary Renaissance*
HLQ	*Huntington Library Quarterly*
JEGP	*Journal of English and Germanic Philology*
JWCI	*Journal of the Warburg and Courtauld Institutes*
MP	*Modern Philology*
PBA	*Proceedings of the British Academy*
PMLA	*Publications of the Modern Language Association of America*
RES	*The Review of English Studies*
SEL	*Studies in English Literature*
TLS	*The Times Literary Supplement*

CHRONOLOGY

1572	Birth of John Donne
	Birth of Ben Jonson
1573	Birth of William Laud, future Archbishop of Canterbury
	Birth of Michelangelo Merisi da Caravaggio
	Birth of Inigo Jones
1575?	Birth of Cyril Tourneur
1577	Birth of Robert Burton
	Birth of Peter Paul Rubens
1579	Birth of John Fletcher
1580?	Birth of John Webster
1584	Birth of Francis Beaumont
1586	Death of Sir Philip Sidney
1588	Birth of Thomas Hobbes
	Destruction of Spanish Armada
1591	Birth of Robert Herrick
1593	Birth of George Herbert
	Birth of Thomas Wentworth, Earl of Strafford, statesman
1594	Birth of Nicolas Poussin
1595?	Birth of Thomas Carew
1596	Birth of René Descartes
1598	Birth of Giovanni Lorenzo Bernini
1599	Birth of Oliver Cromwell
	Birth of Sir Anthony Van Dyck
	Death of Edmund Spenser
1600	Birth of the future Charles I
1603	Death of Elizabeth I
	Accession of James I
1605	Birth of Sir Thomas Browne
	Publication of Sir Francis Bacon's *Advancement of Learning*
1608	Birth of John Milton

1609	Birth of Sir John Suckling
1610	Birth of Henrietta Maria, future Queen of England
1610	Death of Caravaggio
1611	Publication of Authorized Version of the Bible
1612	Birth of Thomas, third Baron Fairfax
	Birth of Anne Bradstreet
1613?	Birth of Richard Crashaw
1616	Publication of Ben Jonson's *Works*
	Death of William Shakespeare
	Death of Francis Beaumont
1618	Rebellion of Bohemia against the Holy Roman Empire initiates the Thirty Years War, in which the Empire, most German states, Denmark, Sweden, the United Provinces, and France become involved Frederick, Elector Palatine and son-in-law to James I, accepts the Bohemian crown and with it assumes a major role in opposition to the Holy Roman Empire; initiation of recurrent English policy of avoiding being drawn into continental conflict
1620	Battle of the White Mountain (Imperial victory ending the Bohemian rebellion; rout of Frederick, Elector Palatine)
	The Pilgrims establish a colony in New England
1621	Birth of Andrew Marvell
	Publication of Burton's *Anatomy of Melancholy* (numerous extended editions published later)
1622	Birth of Henry Vaughan
	Completion of Banqueting House at Whitehall, designed by Jones (Rubens's ceiling paintings installed 1635)
1623	Birth of Margaret Cavendish, Duchess of Newcastle
	Publication of Shakespeare's *Comedies, Histories and Tragedies* (First Folio)
1625	Death of James I
	Accession of Charles I
	Death of John Fletcher
1625?	Death of John Webster
1626	Birth of Richard Cromwell
	Death of Bacon
	Death of Cyril Tourneur
	Battle of Lutter, Germany (Imperial victory forcing Denmark's withdrawal from the war)
1628	Birth of John Bunyan
	Assassination of George Villiers, Duke of Buckingham, politician and court favourite

1630	Birth of the future Charles II
1631	Death of John Donne
	Birth of John Dryden
	Sack of Magdeburg (Imperial victory)
	Battle of Breitenfeld, Germany (victory for Sweden under Gustavus Adolphus over Imperial forces)
1632	Birth of Katherine Philips
	Birth of John Locke
	Battle of Lutzen, Germany (victory for Sweden over Imperial forces, but Gustavus Adolphus is killed)
1633	Publication of Donne's *Poems*
	Death of George Herbert
	Publication of Herbert's *The Temple*
	Birth of the future James II
	Laud appointed Archbishop of Canterbury
1634	Performance of Carew's masque *Coelum Britannicum*
	Performance of Milton's *Masque* (*Comus*)
	Judicial mutilation and incarceration of William Prynne, Puritan activist
	Battle of Nordlingen, Germany (Imperial victory over Sweden)
1637	Death of Ben Jonson
	Judicial mutilation and incarceration of Prynne, Henry Burton, and John Bastwick (Prynne was in prison already)
	Publication of Milton's 'Lycidas' in *Iusta Eduardo King*
	Publication of Descartes's *Discourse on Method*
1638	Judicial flogging and incarceration of John Lilburne, Puritan activist
1640	Publication of second edition of Jonson's *Works*
	Death of Carew
	Publications of Carew's *Poems*
	Convocation of Long Parliament
	Birth of Aphra Behn
	Death of Rubens
1641	Execution of Strafford
	Death of Van Dyck
1642	Death of Suckling
	Beginning of English Civil War
	Battle of Edgehill (stalemate)
	Closure of London theatres
	Death of Galileo
	Publication of Thomas Browne's *Religio Medici* (authorized edition, *1643*)
	Birth of Isaac Newton

1644	Battle of Marston Moor (Parliamentarian victory)
	Publication of Milton's *Areopagitica*
1645	Publication of Milton's *Poems ... both English and Latin*
	Battle of Naseby (Parliamentarian victory)
	Execution of William Laud
1646	Publication of Suckling's *Fragmenta Aurea*
	Publication of Crashaw's *Steps to the Temple* (second edition *1648*)
1647	Birth of John Wilmot, second Earl of Rochester
	Putney Army Debates between Levellers and Cromwell and his officers
1648	Publication of Herrick's *Hesperides* (including *His Noble Numbers*)
	Siege of Colchester (Parliamentarian victory)
	Colonel Pride's purge of Long Parliament
	Treaty of Westphalia concluding the Thirty Years War
1649	Execution of Charles I
	Proclamation of the English Republic
	Death of Crashaw
	Mutiny at Burford, Oxfordshire, of Levellers within the New Model Army (suppressed by Cromwell)
	Establishment by Diggers led by Gerrard Winstanley of short-lived agrarian commune on St George's Hill, near Cobham, Surrey
	Publication of Lovelace's *Lucasta*
	Publication of Milton's *Eikonoklastes*
	Massacres of Drogheda and Wexford (Parliamentarian victories)
1650	Publication of Vaughan's *Silex Scintillans* (second edition, *1655*)
	Battle of Dunbar (Parliamentarian victory)
	Death of Descartes
1651	Battle of Worcester (Parliamentarian victory)
	Publication of Hobbes's *Leviathan*
1652	Inception of First Anglo-Dutch War
	Death of Inigo Jones
1653	Long Parliament, already purged, dismissed by Cromwell
	Cromwell declared Lord Protector
	Publication of Cavendish's *Poems and Fancies*
1654	Conclusion of First Anglo-Dutch War
1657?	Death of Lovelace
1658	Death of Oliver Cromwell
	Richard Cromwell becomes Lord Protector
1659	Resignation of Richard Cromwell
	Publication of Lovelace's *Lucasta*[:] *Posthume poems*

PART ONE

THE CONTEXT

THE CONTEXT

I

DAVID LOEWENSTEIN

Politics and religion

The poets of early modern England, from Donne to Marvell, were deeply engaged and stimulated by the period's political antagonisms and rich diversity of religious experience. Indeed, in their age politics and religion were thoroughly interconnected: as Sir Francis Bacon observed, 'Matters of religion and the church ... in these times are become so intermixed with considerations of estate.'[1] Since the time of Henry VIII's Protestant Reformation, which rejected papal authority, the king of England had assumed the supreme headship of the English Church and thus governed both state and church: this was true for the Stuart kings of our literary period – James I (1603–25) and Charles I (1625–49) – whose absolutist power was reinforced by the ecclesiastical hierarchy. As James I succinctly put it, 'No bishops, no king, no nobility'; and his son, Charles I, fully agreed, observing that in the kingdom 'religion is the only firm foundation of all power'.[2] The purpose of this essay, however, is not only to explore the intimate connections between politics and religion as essential background for appreciating earlier seventeenth-century poetry: the aim is to highlight, using select examples from poems of the age, some of the ways its leading poets responded imaginatively to the political conflicts, ideologies, and religious currents of early-modern England up to the tumultuous years of the Civil War and Interregnum, when both the Stuart monarchy and Church of England were disrupted by revolution and Puritan opposition. We shall see, for example, how the language of political absolutism, characteristic of the theory of Stuart kingship, finds anxious expression in Donne's love poetry; the ways the languages of both Protestant theology and kingly power find expression in the restlessness of Herbert's devotional performances; how Vaughan poignantly responds in verse to the destruction of the traditional Anglican Church during the Civil War; and how Marvell's verses imaginatively recreate the responses of Puritan exiles to religious persecution and explore the dynamics of power and politics in the Interregnum.

Our period was an age when politics, religion, and literary culture intersected. The poets of early modern England were themselves often directly engaged in serving or writing on behalf of the state and church: Donne, who had considerable political ambitions, became Dean of St Paul's in 1621; Jonson, the author of lavish court masques praising Stuart kingship, believed the poet had an essential role to play in the state; Herbert and Herrick both served as priests in the Anglican Church; Crashaw wrote extravagant poetry displaying his high-church sympathies; Lovelace 'was imprisoned twice by Parliament during the Civil War for his pro-royalist activities; and both Milton and Marvell served in the position of Latin Secretary under Oliver Cromwell, while Marvell also served as a Member of Parliament for Hull. The author of some of the age's most vehement pamphlets attacking the Anglican clergy and Stuart monarchy, the Puritan Milton considered himself 'church-outed by the prelates': his own visionary poetry, he hoped, would serve 'to deplore the general relapses of kingdoms and states from justice and God's true worship'.[3] Given that such intimate links existed between poets and the civic and ecclesiastical worlds, we should expect their poetry to interact with and represent the conflicting political ideologies and religious controversies of their age.

STUART MONARCHS, POWER AND POETRY

'The kings of the earth are fair and glorious resemblances of the king of the heaven; they are beams of that sun, tapers of that torch, they are like gods, they are gods': so observed John Donne in a sermon preached near the end of James I's reign.[4] Donne's notion here that kings are essentially gods on earth was thoroughly compatible with the theory and myth of Jacobean kingship. King James himself famously articulated the absolutist assumptions behind Stuart power in his printed *Works of the Most High and Mighty Prince, James* (1616): 'God', he announced in a sonnet encapsulating the argument to *Basilikon Doron*, 'gives not Kings the stile of *Gods* in vaine, / For on his Throne his Scepter doe they swey'[5]; and in a speech delivered at Whitehall in 1609, he asserted that 'Kings are justly called Gods, for that they exercise a manner or resemblance of Divine power upon earth ... if you will consider the Attributes to God, you shall see how they agree in the person of a King' (p. 529). According to James, then, regal power comes directly and solely from God: the king was thus an anointed, semi-divine figure who ruled by divine right, a belief shared as well by his son Charles I.[6] Indeed, such a view, James claimed, was supported by scripture, where, as he noted, 'Kings are called Gods by the propheticall King *David*' (James I, p. 194); numerous biblical texts like 1 Samuel 8:9–20 or Psalm 72:1 ('Give thy Judgements to the King, O God, and thy Righteousnesse to the Kings

Sonne') only helped to buttress the claim for divine sanction (pp. 196–7, 549). Absolutist monarchs like James and Charles thus magnified royal power so that the king was above the restraint of human law and Parliament, limited only by the laws of God: he alone in the kingdom possessed political power.[7] As a writer who eagerly wished to win the favour and support of his king, Donne himself concurred in 1610, observing that the people 'cannot contract nor limit [the king's] power'.[8]

When the poet Donne let himself imagine, in the following year, 'all coherence gone ... and all relation', his extravagant vision of social disintegration meant that 'Prince, subject, father, son, are things forgot' (*The First Anniversary*, lines 213–15). The cult of Stuart monarchy was supported by a hierarchical order which configured the king's absolute authority in patriarchal terms: the king was '*Parens patriae*, the politique father of his people',[9] just as Adam himself had been both the first father and first king to whom God had granted an unlimited monarchy. Great power was concentrated in this patriarchal head of the state, an authority to be obeyed and never to be resisted actively by his subjects. As God's lieutenant on earth, the Stuart monarch thus had power over Parliament – which he could summon as he wished – and over the ecclesiastical order. Given the patriarchal emphasis on obedience to political authority in the earlier seventeenth century, it seemed highly unlikely that before 1640 a Cromwell might emerge who would altogether disregard the 'antient Rights' of kings and dare, in Marvell's famous words, to 'cast the Kingdome old / Into another Mold' ('An Horatian Ode', lines 38, 35–6).[10]

Major poets of the period both promoted and were stimulated by the Jacobean myth of royal power and divinity. As the leading professional court poet of the age, Ben Jonson saw himself contributing to it through his imaginative writing, including his non-dramatic verse. Publishing his *Works* (1616) in the same year that James I published his, Jonson, in his polished epigram 'To King James', suggested that poetry (which James himself had written) plays a central role in the service of a great royal state:

> How, best of Kings, do'st thou a scepter beare!
>   How, best of *Poets*, dost thou laurel wear!
> But two things, rare, the *Fates* had in their store,
>   And gave thee both, to shew they could do no more.
> For such a *Poet*, while thy dayes were greene,
>   Thou wert, as chiefe of them are said t'have beene.
> And such a Prince thou art, wee daily see,
>   As chiefe of those still promise they will be.
> Whom should my *Muse* then flie to, but the best
>   Of Kings for grace; of *Poets* for my test?[11]

5

Jonson is essentially conservative in his political ideology: recognized by James as the poet laureate of his age, this author of royal entertainments and court masques projecting the power and magic of his monarch certainly knew how to 'sing / The glories of [his] *King*'.[12] In praising ideal kingship in James – whom he treats as both the 'best of Kings' and the 'best of *Poets*' in his epigram – Jonson develops one of his numerous analogies between poets and princes: 'I could never thinke the study of *Wisdome* confin'd only to the Philosopher: or of *Piety* to the *Divine*: or of *State* to the *Politicke*', he writes in his *Discoveries*. 'But that he which can faine a *Common-wealth* (which is the *Poet*) can governe it with *Counsels*, strengthen it with *Lawes*, correct it with *Judgements*, informe it with *Religion*, and *Morals*; is all these.'[13] The Jonsonian poet, in his diverse roles, is essential to a strong monarchy because he can help to sustain the king's authority by offering counsel, advice, praise, and blame; by shaping political values and perceptions; and by creating powerful fictions (including masques in which kings appear like gods) in the service of the state. So Jonson often places the poet in the midst of the world of power and aristocracy, as he does in 'To Penshurst', where the Sidney family receives him as warmly as they receive royalty (lines 65–88): 'all is there; / As if thou, then, wert mine, or I raign'd here'. But even as he praises the nobility, which James considered essential to his absolutist hierarchy, a discriminating Jonson does not hesitate to offer criticism and tactful warning, such as when he contrasts the more modest Sidney country estate (itself an ideal microcosm of the commonwealth) with 'Those proud, ambitious heaps' (line 101) displayed by other Jacobean lords.

Although he never regarded himself as a professional Jacobean court poet, Donne reveals in his poetry a fascination with the world of Stuart politics and kingship,[14] as well as a sense of unease about that world of seemingly unlimited power which he himself was never able fully to participate in. Indeed, more flamboyantly than any other poet of the age, Donne appropriates the extravagant language of kingship, power, and absolutism (which, we have noted, he himself used in his public discourse) and brings it right into the private world of his love poetry. There is plenty of evidence to indicate that the restless Donne himself was at times highly ambitious and eager to advance at James I's court[15] – a public ambition thwarted by the disaster following his clandestine marriage to Ann More, the daughter of a social superior, in 1601. But if Donne could never obtain a central and secure place at court in the real world of power, he could nevertheless imagine, in the exuberant love poetry of his *Songs and Sonets*, a world of power that rivals that of the Stuart court and state:

> Ask for those kings whom thou saw'st yesterday,
> And thou shalt hear, All here in one bed lay.

> She'is all states, and all princes, I,
> Nothing else is.
> Princes do but play us; compared to this,
> All honour's mimic.   ('The Sun Rising', lines 19–24)

In one sweeping gesture, Donne in 'The Sun Rising' obliterates the external world of politics: the lovers' intensely private new world *is* that real world of politics, with its states and princes – 'Nothing else is.' In Donne's extravagant vision, where the lovers can assume the role of powerful monarchs, 'All' (one of Donne's favourite words) in the world of power is merely an imitation of this new private realm. In an age where politics and theatricalism are often inseparable, Donne can imagine for a moment that 'Princes do but play' them. Donne has taken the hyperbolic language of absolutism, given new emphasis in the age of James I, and wittily focussed it on the bedroom: if 'The State of MONARCHIE is the supremest thing upon earth', as James insisted in his *Works* (p. 529), then the all-powerful institution of kingship in Donne's extravagant imagination can be contracted into the bedroom which itself assumes that supreme 'State of MONARCHIE'. In Donne's own poetry, then, we find this urgent insistence on the lovers themselves becoming all-powerful – Donne's way of giving a particular intensity to their private, mutual relationship.

Yet in a poem like 'The Anniversary', where Donne sets the mutual world of the two lovers against the dazzling world of kings and courtiers, he becomes less exuberant and more anxious as he contemplates death: 'Alas, as well as other princes, we, / (Who prince enough in one another be,) / Must leave at last in death' (lines 13–15). Being 'prince enough' is not quite the same thing as boldly asserting that 'She'is all states, and all princes, I.' The lovers' desire to possess absolute and unconstrained power here and now on earth ('we are kings, and none but we / Can be such kings', lines 23–4) is strengthened by their recognition that in heaven there will indeed be a levelling of such political hierarchy ('then we shall be throughly blessed, / But we no more, than all the rest', lines 21–2): no longer will they resemble monarchs with their unlimited power and supremacy. Yet the suggestion that 'True and false fears' could lead to 'Treason' in the lovers' earthly kingdom (lines 25–7), adds, in the final stanza, a darker note to the poem's political language of mutuality: even as Donne appropriates the analogy of kingly power to characterize the intensity of a mutual relationship, he can also register unease with the analogy's more treacherous implications.[16]

If the reign of James I encorauged a perception of kingly power as absolutist, so did the rule of his son Charles, who also firmly believed that monarchy was the true pattern and image of divinity. Like his father he believed that church and state should be modelled on the divinely ordered

7

hierarchy.[17] Yet an increasingly absolutist King Charles was also a less able politician than his father: a ruler who was aloof and intolerant of political disagreement, Charles refused to play the role of a limited monarch during his years of Personal Rule when he governed without Parliament from 1629 to 1640. His austere and reserved temperament, his devotion to a Catholic queen, Henrietta Maria, and his controversial alliance with William Laud, the powerful Archbishop of Canterbury who promoted religious cere-monialism under Charles (discussed below), gradually helped to isolate the king and his court. With the summoning of the Long Parliament in Novem-ber 1640 and especially with the Civil War erupting in the summer of 1642, the Stuart king's exceptional powers and mystique were increasingly under-mined. Indeed, with the powers and mystique of Stuart kingship sharply challenged during the Civil War years, one radical observer was prompted to remark: ''Tis true the kings have been instruments to cast off the Pope's supremacy, but we may see if they have not put themselves into the same state.'[18]

The republican revolution of 1648–9 not only abolished monarchy and the House of Lords, but culminated in the daring public trial at which Charles was sentenced to death in January 1649. With the execution of the Stuart king, the world of royal power, absolutism, and hierarchy was now turned upside down. Indeed, pleading the 'antient Rights' could no longer protect the king's authority nor his person; the revolution had challenged the king's claim that he was answerable only to God. No poet of the period captures better than Marvell the king's theatricalism on that extraordinary political occasion of his execution:

> *He* nothing common did or mean
> Upon that memorable Scene:
>   But with his keener Eye
>   The Axes edge did try:
> Nor call'd the *Gods* with vulgar spight
> To vindicate his helpless Right,
> But bow'd his comely Head,
> Down as upon a Bed.
>
> ('An Horatian Ode', lines 38, 57–64)

Charles's bearing at his trial (where he challenged the authority of the special Parliamentary court to try him) and at his execution – 'that memor-able Scene' – was dignified.[19] In a political poem where the energy and forces of history all seem to be on the side of the active revolutionary who casts 'the Kingdome old / Into another mold', Marvell's lines acknowledge the grace, as well as the theatrical power, of Charles's final act – a historical moment when the claim to royal power by divine right was rendered 'helpless'. Here the king has become the tragic actor in the final royal masque performed at Whitehall. The Stuart monarchs of our period believed that their power and mystique were inseparable from role-playing and theatrical-ism, 'That a King is as one set on a stage, whose smallest actions and ges-tures, all the people gazingly doe behold' (James I, p. 180). For King Charles, Marvell suggests, such was the case in life as well as in death.

The Civil War, then, released forces destructive to the very foundation the monarchical order with its authoritarian hierarchy and patriarchal values. Indeed, royalist poets found themselves disoriented and deeply unsettled 'In this our wasting Warre' (Herrick, 'Upon the Troublesome Times', line 12).[20] Nevertheless, during the tumultuous years of the 1640s, the Cavalier poets rallied around the king, exploring in their verse issues of loyalty, gallantry, honour, and defiance in the midst of political crisis and royalist defeat. Even in prison, the royalist poet – unvanquished in his spirit and liberated in his soul – refused to relinquish his ideal of a once all-powerful and paternal monarch:

> When (like committed Linnets) I
>   With shriller throat shall sing
> The sweetness, Mercy, Majesty,
>   And glories of my KING;
> When I shall voyce aloud, how Good
>   He is, how Great should be,
> Inlarged Winds that curle the Flood
>   Know no such Liberty.
>   (Lovelace, 'To Althea, From Prison', lines 17–24)[21]

Like Ben Jonson, this Cavalier poet sings the glories of his king, though with a 'shriller throat', conveying the urgency of maintaining the traditional royalist vision of kingship in a radically unstable political world. Yet by singing not only 'how Good / He is' but also 'how Great' his king 'should be', Lovelace painfully acknowledges that in this age of revolution and poli-tical upheaval, Stuart kings, with their contracted power, no longer seem like gods 'adorned and furnished', as the absolutist James I had so assuredly put it, 'with some sparkles of the Divinitie' (James I, p. 500).

RELIGION AND POETRY

Seventeenth-century poets responded to the complexity of religious beliefs in an age that produced exceptionally diverse and rich religious verse: the Laudian and anti-Calvinist poetry of Crashaw was strikingly different from the Calvinist verses of the Protestant Donne or from the anti-Laudian and prophetic poetry of Milton. The religious beliefs which shaped and were articulated by this poetry were themselves often closely interconnected with the world of politics and state power. Thus Laudianism, with its new and controversial emphasis on ceremonial religion, was promoted by the court of Charles I in the 1620s and 1630s. In this section, I want to highlight, using select examples from the period's poetry, some of its principal religious currents, including two conflicting religious movements within the English Church that heightened tensions in earlier seventeenth-century Protestant England: Calvinism and Laudianism.

In the early seventeenth century, Calvinist theology was by and large the orthodox creed of English Protestantism: it dominated the Church of England and, indeed, James I himself was Calvinist, though his son, we shall see, would be influenced in the 1620s and 1630s by conflicting and hostile religious developments. The popularity of the Geneva Bible (1560), which went through at least thirty-nine quarto editions printed in England between 1579 and 1615,[22] and the enormous influence of Calvin's own sermons, biblical commentaries, and especially his *Institutes of the Christian Religion* (1536; 1559; translated 1561), contributed to the dominance of Calvinism in Elizabethan and Jacobean England. Calvinism emphasized God's eternal decrees, along with his initiative and irresistible grace enabling man's salvation; consequently it downplayed, as Luther did, the efficacy of the works of sinful man and denied that his free will played any role in matters of salvation or damnation. Most significantly, it stressed absolute divine sovereignty and power and the notion of divine predestination (see, for example, *Institutes* 3.21.5) whereby elevation to Heaven (as one of the elect) or reprobation to Hell depends solely on the will of God: as number 17 of the Thirty-Nine Articles (1563), the English confession of faith, read, 'predestination to life is the ever-lasting purpose of God, whereby ... he hath constantly decreed by his counsel, secret to us, to deliver from curse and damnation those whom he hath chosen in Christ out of mankind'.[23] Calvinist divines suggested, however, that the number of the elect was very few and that most men, women and children would perish: 'Some think one of an hundred, some but one of a thousand shalbe saved.'[24]

The starkness of Calvinist theology, with its persistent emphasis on human depravity and sinfulness, could generate acute anxiety, doubt, and restlessness. For one thing, Calvinism expelled intermediaries between an omnipotent, often inscrutable God and man's soul: the Protestant Reformation emphasized justification by faith alone, and neither the church nor the sacraments nor religious ceremonies could provide divine grace needed to assure one's salvation. With this emphasis on the individual's personal relation to God, Protestantism could thus make God seem more awesomely distant and yet also bring him more awesomely close.[25] Donne's agonistic and intensely introspective *Holy Sonnets* offer powerful examples of his Calvinistic terror of damnation and sense of sinfulness as he confronts his personal and awesome God; thus at one moment an anxious Donne can become contentious with God as he envies the rest of creation:

> If poisonous minerals, and if that tree,
> Whose fruit threw death on else immortal us,
> If lecherous goats, if serpents envious
> Cannot be damned; alas, why should I be?

But then, recognizing the all-powerful nature of this Protestant God who can forget Donne's human sins, the poet retreats from his quarrelsome posture: 'But who am I, that dare dispute with thee / O God?' Indeed, Donne's awesome heavenly monarch possesses a power not unlike that which James I attributed to kings: 'they make and unmake their subjects: they have power of raising, and casting downe: of life, and of death' (James I, p. 529). So in the sonnet 'Batter my heart', Donne's Calvinistic God – capable of making and unmaking his sinful, helpless subject – becomes, in the poem's three successive quatrains, a metal worker, a warrior-king, and a male lover as the resistant Donne himself, paradoxically, demands God to apply his violent force:

> Batter my heart, three-personed God; for, you
> As yet but knock, breathe, shine, and seek to mend;
> That I may rise, and stand, o'erthrow me, and bend
> Your force, to break, blowe, burn and make me new.

The alliteration and forceful verbs of line 4 (God's spirit blows rather than breathes, his face burns rather than shines) convey the divine power and violence needed to break Donne's resistance and make him anew, especially when he is 'betrothed' – as he is in the third quatrain – to God's enemy, Satan. After all, with its deep conviction of human sin, Protestantism simultaneously increased the sense of the enormous and potentially irresistible powers of Satan – that 'prince and God of this world' as John Knox called him.[26] Since Donne is betrothed to Satan (though he dearly loves God), Donne urges God's sexual assault and penetration: 'Divorce me, untie, or break that knot again.' For Donne, however, God's enthralment paradoxically enables Donne's freedom, just as God's ravishment paradoxically enables Donne's chastity: 'for I / Except you enthral me, never shall be free / Nor ever chaste, except you ravish me'. The dazzling paradoxes, the vivid tropes suggesting God's great force and Donne's complete inadequacy, the imperative mode of Donne's dramatic address – all convey, in a highly individualistic and flamboyant way, intense emotional pressure and the urgent need for God to apply his full power and grace to remake the sinful Donne.

Although less flamboyant than Donne, the Protestant Herbert, with his emphasis on the religion of the heart, also often focusses on the agony within. Using the Bible as his chief source of imaginative expression, Herbert in 'Sion', for example, contrasts the glorious artifice and architecture of Solomon's Temple (2 Chronicles 3–4) – which hardly seems to affect God – with the architecture of the New Testament temple found within the individual's heart (see 1 Corinthians 3:9, 16; 1 Peter 2:5):

> There thou art struggling with a peevish heart,
> Which sometimes crosseth thee, thou sometimes it:
> The fight is hard on either part.
> Great God doth fight, he doth submit.
> All Solomons sea of brasse and world of stone
> Is not so deare to thee as one good grone.[27]   (lines 13–18)

In Herbert's interior world of arduous spiritual battle between God and the Protestant sinner, 'one good grone' – that simple pained utterance and emission from the heart – is far more effective and spontaneous as an expression of devotion than any ornate or lavish external form of worship. To be sure, Herbert's poetry often refers to the external features and rituals of the Anglican Church (to which he was devoted), but he tends to transform them inwardly so that the altar becomes his heart, its monuments become his flesh, its lock becomes his sin, its marbled floor becomes the basic virtues, and so on. That is precisely the kind of inwardness that the Protestant Herbert emphasizes at the end of 'The Church-floor': 'Blest be the *Architect*, whose art / Could build so strong in a weak heart' (lines 19–20). But then if God is the powerful artist who creates strong spiritual virtues within the feeble heart of the Protestant individual and poet, what about Herbert's own artistic contribution and mortal agency? This issue is a source of considerable tension in Herbert's work: for as he uses his fallen human art to praise God's transcendent power and art, the Protestant poet, fully aware of his own sinfulness, is indeed often uneasy that he may go too far in his display of artifice and 'weave [him] self into the sense' (Jordan (II)', line 14).

Herbert, moreover, will sometimes characterize the restless relationship between the individual speaker and his omnipotent Protestant God in language reminding us of the close interconnections between politics and religion in earlier seventeenth-century England. For example, Herbert will dramatize that relationship in terms of an unworthy subject serving a powerful king, so that the inner self now becomes the principal site of political power and struggle. In 'Affliction (I)', he begins by writing about God's enticing and 'gracious benefits' and then asks, hoping for a life of mirth without grief, 'What pleasures could I want, whose King I served ...?' (lines 6, 13–14). But once Herbert's speaker encounters strife, sorrow, and sickness, he then becomes rebellious and restless: 'Well, I will change the service, and go seek / Some other master out' (lines 63–4). Elsewhere Herbert complains that this powerful divine monarch frustrates his intentions and will ('things sort not to my will, / Ev'n when my will doth studie thy renown: / Thou turnest th' edge of all things on me still, / Taking me up to throw me down'), prompting the poet to highlight the pain and contradictions of serving an omnipotent God: 'A my deare Father, ease my smart! / These contrarieties crush me: these crosse actions / Doe winde a rope about, and cut my heart' ('The Cross', lines 19–22, 31–3). And when the fiercely rebellious, unruly speaker of Herbert's religious poetry wants to highlight his feelings of rage as a result of his unrequited appeals, he can employ the language of a frustrated courtier: 'Shall I be still in suit?' (line 6) he impatiently asks at the beginning of 'The Collar'. Herbert's awesome God of power, however, is also a benign God of love who can use his penetrating, intimate gaze to rejuvenate the restless, sinful heart: 'If thy first glance so powerfull be ... What wonders shall we feel, when we shall see / Thy full-ey'd love!' ('The Glance', lines 17, 19–20). When the poet anticipates a visit from his heavenly superior ('The harbingers are come. See, see their mark'), he is glad that the approaching monarch's servants leave him his 'best room, / Ev'n all [his] heart, and what is lodged there'; Herbert's God, indeed, is a powerful king capable of taking over Herbert's poetic powers, as well as his interior self: 'My God must have my best, ev'n all I had' ('The Forerunners', lines 1, 7–8, 18).

Given Herbert's painful question in 'The Temper (I)' – 'Will great God measure with a wretch?' (line 15) – we may ask whether all Anglican poets of the period convey an equally strong Protestant sense of anxiety about inherent human weakness and sinfulness. In an age of diverse religious expression, this is by no means always the case. Thomas Traherne, like Herbert and Vaughan, was devoted to the Anglican Church; yet his poetry and prose, with their emphasis on the visionary and divine powers of childhood, deny original sin and corruption as hereditary: 'Misery proceedeth ten thousand times more from the outward Bondage of Opinion and Custom, then from any inward corruption or Depravation of Nature: And ... it is not our Parents Loyns, so much as our Parents lives, that Enthrals and Blinds us'.[28] As an infant free of inward guilt, Traherne writes in his poem 'Innocence', 'I felt no Stain, nor Spot of Sin' (line 4). How different this is from Donne who keenly feels our paradoxical spiritual state which begins the very first minute of our life 'in our mother's womb' when 'we become guilty of Adam's sin done 6000 years before'; for then the image of God and original sin coincide: 'Powers, that dwell so far asunder, as Heaven, and Hell, God and the Devil, meet in an instant in my soul.'[29] According to Traherne, however, it is the evil customs and devices of society and men that cause depravity and prevent us from enjoying the radiant pleasures of a paradisal vision:

> Cursd and Devisd Proprieties,
>   With Envy, Avarice
> And Fraud, those Feinds that Spoyl even Paradice,
>   Fled from the Splendor of mine Eys.
>
> ('Wonder', lines 49–52)

Although Traherne's poetry continually reminds us that evil does exist, it conveys a much more optimistic sense (than, say, does Vaughan's religious poetry) that the visionary poet can truly regain a state of innocence and a paradise within.

One Anglican poet sympathetic to Laudian ceremonialism, Robert Herrick, even deflates the Calvinist notion of divine predestination itself; for him, it hardly seems like a terrifying concept at all, as his little epigrammatic poem by that name makes clear: 'PREDESTINATION is the Cause alone / Of many standing, but of fall to none.' Even Herrick's religious poetry from *His Noble Numbers* (1647) most explicitly evoking a sense of spiritual helplessness and doubt hardly conveys the same level of terror, fear, and emotional pressure we associate with Donne's tormented Calvinistic verse in poems like the *Holy Sonnets*; as Herrick writes in his 'His Litany, to the Holy Spirit':

> When (God knowes) I'm tost about,
> Either with despaire, or doubt;
> Yet before the glasse be out
>   Sweet Spirit comfort me!
>
> When the flames and hellish cries
> Fright mine eares, and fright mine eyes,
> And all terrors me surprize,
>   Sweet Spirit comfort me!   (lines 33–6, 41–4)

Herrick's petitionary refrain – 'Sweet Spirit comfort me!' – in this litany focussed on last things, emphasizes the relief rather than the terrifying anguish of his predicament. How different this emotional response is from Donne's!

The most powerful challenge to Calvinism in the age came from the highly controversial figure of William Laud (1573–1645), who became

Bishop of London in 1628 and Archbishop of Canterbury in 1633. Supported by his patron Charles I, he in effect ruled the Church of England until he was impeached by the Long Parliament in 1640. Indeed, the policies of Charles and Laud were themselves deeply intertwined: 'the church and state are so nearly united and knit together', Laud observed in 1626, 'that . . . they may be accounted but as one'.[30] Laud's principal innovation was his new emphasis on the role of ceremony and ritual in religious practice. His sacramentalism stressed the formal and outward aspects of worship: it placed emphasis on the holiness of church buildings, on the sanctity of the altar (which was to be raised and railed off), on confession to the priest, on set forms of prayer (as opposed to preaching), on the belief that salvation came through the church and the sacraments. As Laud himself put it, he was concerned 'that the external worship of God in this church might be kept in uniformity and decency, and in some beauty of holiness'.[31] This was clearly a challenge to the Protestant belief that the supremacy of the individual conscience and the individual response to the holy scriptures are much more important than the correct performance of church ceremonies. Under Laud, priests were elevated to a position of privilege and power, while bishops, he claimed, acted by divine right. We might at first think of Laud as a conservative reactionary in matters of religious policy, but as Patrick Collinson has more accurately put it, he is best seen 'as the principal *agent provocateur* of religious revolution'.[32]

Laud was in fact rejecting major aspects of the Reformation, including Calvinist predestinarianism. His innovations were often associated with so-called 'Arminianism', the name applied to those thought to follow the Dutch theologian Jacobus Arminius (died 1609), who had allowed that men could participate in the scheme of salvation by exercising their free will. Such a belief only infuriated orthodox Calvinists (however, Milton who hated Laudianism but valued free will would later assume a kind of radical Arminianism). For Arminians, salvation was especially made possible through the rituals and sacraments of the church, and through the mediation of the clergy. Given the new emphasis Laud placed on ceremonies and ritualized worship, as well as on the authoritarian hierarchy of the church, his counter-reforming policies generated fear and horror among many Protestant Englishmen who believed that he was subverting religious liberties and assuming 'an absolute and unlimited power'.[33]

For an Anglican royalist poet like Herrick, however, the Laudian emphasis on ceremonialism was clearly appealing. Singing of maypoles and maying in his collection of verses, *Hesperides* (1648), Herrick reveals his sympathy with the renewed emphasis on ritual, festivals, and recreations promoted by Charles I and Laud. His 'Corinna's going a Maying' is a spirited holiday poem that refers in its second stanza explicitly to the controversial *Book of Sports* issued by James in 1618 and then reissued by Charles himself in 1633, a proclamation that officially sanctioned various traditional Sunday and holiday pastimes:[34]

> Can such delights be in the street
> And open fields, and we not see't?
> Come, we'll abroad; and let's obay
> The Proclamation made for May,
> And sin no more, as we have done, by staying;
> But my *Corinna*, come, let's goe a Maying.   (lines 37–42)

With the proclamation of the *Book of Sports*, both the church and king associated themselves with old festival culture and traditional customs: indeed, for royalist sympathizers maypoles themselves became symbols of release from godly reformation of the church encouraged by Puritanism (see below). Of course, Laudian ritualism and the protection of rural sports and revels only incensed sabbatarian reformers who thought that such activities appealed to what was unregenerate and undisciplined in men.[35] Yet for Herrick, the poet of mirth and pleasure, such cultural conflicts are not particularly troubling; what is important for him is the licensed festivity and May games made possible by this proclamation issued by the church and state – a proclamation that condones the festive even as it encourages obedience to the traditional political and ecclesiastical authorities with which Herrick himself was aligned.

Those Protestants hostile to Laudian ceremonialism frequently linked it with popery and Catholicism. Indeed, the poet whose extravagant, ornate verse perhaps most exemplifies such Laudian church tendencies is Richard Crashaw who sought refuge, during the mid-1630s, from religious and political controversies in the Laudian sanctuary of Peterhouse, Cambridge. Crashaw wanted a religion that put on 'A majestie that [might] beseem thy throne' ('On a Treatise of Charity', line 20):[36] he would have found that at Peterhouse whose chapel was elaborately decorated with stained-glass windows, a marble altar, gilded candlesticks, a large crucifix, a wooden statue of Peter and the crossed keys, among other ornaments. This religious enclave, however, offered seclusion from the upheaval of civil war only until 1643 when Crashaw was expelled from Cambridge by Puritans hostile to Laudian innovations. For Crashaw the exile from the cloistered, protected world of Laudian Peterhouse was, as he wrote in his one surviving letter, nothing less than 'a dislocation of my whole condition'.[37] Fleeing to the continent, he entered the Roman Catholic church in 1646: the Protestant emphasis on spiritual doubt, introspection, and inward struggle that we associate with poets like Donne, Herbert, and Vaughan clearly did not appeal to Crashaw's Counter-Reformation sensibility and imagination, which focussed on saints, sacraments, the cult of tears, and the worship of the Holy Name of Jesus. His religious and creative sensibility was much more attracted to the world of elaborate church ritual and sacramentalism that we have associated with the Laudian milieu he encountered in Cambridge during the 1630s and early 1640s.

While strikingly different from much of the Protestant verse we have been looking at, Crashaw's poetry can reveal its own extreme intensity of emotion as he writes, for example, about Mary Magdalene's tears or about the martyrdom, spiritual ecstasy, and burning piety of St Teresa of Avila, the sixteenth-century Spanish mystic and key figure of the Catholic Counter-Reformation. Mary Magdalene's tears in 'The Weeper' are so plentiful, as well as sensual, that a cherub in heaven can feed upon them:

> Every morn from hence
> A brisk Cherub somthing sippes,
> Whose sacred influence
> Addes sweetnes to his sweetest Lippes.   (lines 25–8)

Laudian and Counter-Reformation in his religious sensibility, Crashaw can imagine a cherub mediating between heaven and Mary Magdelene, whose bubbling and nourishing stream of tears rises upwards in this poem. Crashaw's poetics of excessive emotion and extravagant adoration reaches a climax in his veneration of St Teresa's mystical and sensuous death:

> O how oft shalt thou complaine
> Of a sweet and subtile paine?
> Of intollerable joyes?
> Of a death, in which who dyes
> Loves his death, and dyes againe,
> And would for ever so be slaine!
>   ('In memory of ... Teresa', lines 97–102)

Crashaw indeed felt compelled to write a further poem defending his verses on St Teresa against the anti-Catholic and anti-Spanish sentiments of his Protestant countrymen: 'O 'tis not spanish, but 'tis heav'n she speaks!' ('An Apology', line 23). Crashaw's point, of course, is that such religious devotion, and the creative sensibility it inspires, transcends national boundaries; nonetheless his strongly Laudian, anti-Puritan, and Counter-Reformation aesthetics articulate, with a distinctive poetic voice, what was in England one of the more extreme (but far from insignificant) forms of High Anglican devotional expression in an age remarkably full of diverse and contradictory religious beliefs. Indeed, the religious sensibility represented by Crashaw's poetry and Laudian orientation generated great hostility, especially among Puritans.

RELIGIOUS CONFLICT: PURITANISM AND THE ENGLISH CHURCH

Every good Christian believer, Milton observed in one of his anti-prelatical tracts, is 'more sacred than any dedicated altar or element'.[38] Indeed, Puritans (a term not always easy to define with precision in seventeenth-century England) were those vanguard English Protestants who most strongly opposed the sacramental elements of worship and vigorously wished to eliminate what they considered vestiges of popery from the church. In the 1630s they viewed the ceremonialist Charles with mistrust and considered Archbishop Laud a dangerous popish innovator in his religious policies. Attempting to live their lives according to God's Word, Puritans elevated preaching, the authority of scripture, and the individual conscience above the sacraments, church ritual, and priestly intervention. (The term Puritan itself was frequently an abusive epithet referring to Protestant religiosity.) Puritans were often associated with Calvinist doctrine (especially after the 1620s), though Milton himself chose to dissent from Calvinist orthodoxy in his passionate belief in human free will. Seeing themselves at war with the ungodly world, Puritan saints formed communities of the godly and tended to highlight the doctrine of divine providence. Puritanism was not necessarily subversive of the established order, though in the Civil War years the appeal to scripture and the liberty of conscience unleashed forces – some of them quite militant – that challenged constraining authorities in the state and church: 'this license of interpreting the Scripture', Thomas Hobbes observed, 'was the cause of so many sects, as have lain hid till the beginning of the late King's reign, and did then appear to the disturbance of the commonwealth'.[39] Two poems of the period – Marvell's 'Bermudas' and Vaughan's 'The British Church' – can illustrate important elements of the Puritan imagination as well as the religious conflicts it generated during the English Civil War.

Marvell's 'Bermudas' dramatizes the emotional and spiritual experience of the persecuted Puritans fleeing a stormy England at the height of Laud's power in search of an earthly paradise and a safe haven where episcopal worship is no longer enforced:

> Where the remote *Bermudas* ride
> In th'Oceans bosome unespy'd,
> From a small Boat, that row'd along,
> The listning Winds receiv'd this Song.

What should we do but sing his Praise
That led us through the watry Maze,
Unto an Isle so long unknown,
And yet far kinder than our own?
Where he the huge Sea-Monsters wracks,
That lift the Deep upon their Backs.
He lands us on a grassy Stage;
Safe from the Storms, and Prelat's rage,
He gave us this eternal Spring,
Which here enamells every thing;
And sends the Fowl's to us in care,
On daily Visits through the Air.
He hangs in shades the Orange bright,
Like golden Lamps in a green Night.
And does in the Pomgranates close,
Jewels more rich than *Ormus* show's.
He makes the Figs our mouths to meet;
And throws the Melons at our feet.
But Apples plants of such a price,
No Tree could ever bear them twice.
With Cedars, chosen by his hand,
From *Lebanon*, he stores the Land.
And makes the hollow Seas, that roar,
Proclaime the Ambergris on shoar.
He cast (of which we rather boast)
The Gospels Pearl upon our Coast.
And in these Rocks for us did frame
A Temple, where to sound his Name.
Oh let our Voice his Praise exalt,
Till it arrive at Heavens Vault:
Which thence (perhaps) rebounding, may
Eccho beyond the *Mexique Bay*.
Thus sung they, in the *English* boat,
An holy and a chearful Note,
And all the way, to guide their Chime,
With falling Oars they kept the time.

Besides reflecting an interest in the discovery of the New World (the Bermudas had been discovered in 1515 and the English had colonized them in the seventeenth century), Marvell's poem nicely conveys the experience of a group of English Puritans, the tiny community of the godly, in exile and responding to a providential universe. It is likely that Marvell wrote the poem after July 1653 when he was living in the house of a Puritan divine, John Oxenbridge, who had fled to the Bermudas during the Laudian persecution of the 1630s; for it was then that the Archbishop of Canterbury had fiercely opposed the Puritans with what the religious exiles of Marvell's poem call his 'Prelate rage'. Indeed, for attacking the Laudian church and its popery during the 1630s, the Puritan pamphleteers John Bastwick, Henry Burton, and William Prynne had famously suffered the consequences of that rage: they underwent the brutal punishment of having their ears cropped. The Puritans Marvell has imagined in his 'Bermudas' have escaped such harsh repression and offer a song of thanksgiving to God and a vision of an unspoiled paradise awaiting them – an island 'far kinder than our own'.

The central portion of Marvell's poem (lines 5–36), the Puritan paean of praise and gratitude conveying an inner assurance of salvation, is itself modelled on the biblical psalms: it captures the Puritan understanding of God's role in the drama of history, as well as the post-Reformation emphasis on God's sovereignty and immediate providences.[40] Puritan providentialism, a major force in English life and politics from 1620 to 1660, included the sense that God intervenes continually in the world (with signs of his presence) and the sense that Israelite history serves as a parallel to English experience.[41] Marvell's poem conveys the sense of the godly community having been led by providence – God having rescued these latter-day exiles and 'led [them] through the watry Maze' to a promised land. Consequently the Puritans' song conveys a vision of the workings of divine purpose with God as the agent, presenting him repeatedly as the active subject of its main verbs: 'He lands us on a grassy Stage'; 'He gave us this eternal Spring'; 'He makes the Figs our mouths to meet'; 'he stores the Land'; and so on. Although these exiles travel in 'a small Boat' on a vast ocean, having been cast out of one potential paradise, they have faith that God is indeed guiding them towards a new one. The fact that their song mixes verb tenses as it describes God's numerous providential acts only further underscores the sense of divine control in both the past and present. The providential universe, then, is by no means indifferent to the needs of these Puritan pilgrims who flee the intolerance of a hostile, ungodly world – the Arminian England of Laud and Charles I. To the contrary, the catalogue of natural delights reveals the kind of earthly paradise and rewards God's power might provide for those Puritan believers who have faith.

That God 'did frame' a temple for their worship among the rocks of their new land is no less significant for understanding the Puritan sense of the way providence has provided for their spiritual needs. Unlike Laud, who had emphasized the holiness of church buildings, these Puritan exiles have no need for any kind of elaborate ecclesiastical structure, nor for any kind of ceremonial religion with set forms of prayer and rituals. Rather, their song of praise is spontaneous and they can worship anywhere – even the rocks of this newly found paradise will serve perfectly well as their temple. Moreover, they clearly hope that their 'chearful' song will not only reach heaven but 'perhaps' reach 'beyond the *Mexique Bay*', thus encouraging the godly reformation of religion in other parts of the Roman Catholic New World as well. Of course, the fact that Marvell has set off this song and vision of unspoiled paradise with four lines at the beginning and four at the end – with both framing passages in the third person – gives the central section of the poem a particularly dramatic quality. Marvell often creates dramatic voices, sometimes putting them in perspective with his own narrative voice: the poet reminds us at the end that this godly community is still in its small '*English* boat' and not yet arrived at its paradisal garden. Through the exiles' song, he has recreated sympathetically the Puritan vision of providential order and history, but reminded us that it is sustained by, more than anything else, an unwavering faith in the power of God to provide the godly with both material and spiritual blessings.

Vaughan's 'The British Church', from his collection of religious verse *Silex Scintillans* (1650), offers an entirely different response to the rise of Puritanism in this period. His poem poignantly expresses the response of an Anglican poet to the terrible plight of the Church of England under the revolutionary Puritans during the 1640s. An Anglican royalist educated in Oxford and London, Vaughan returned to his native Wales at the outbreak of the Civil War in 1642; anti-Puritan in his sentiments – he had little sympathy for Protestant sectaries – and deeply shocked by the royalist defeat, he lamented the destruction of the national church caused by the conflicts of the Civil War. His powerful poem, in which he imagines the impassioned response of the Bride of Christ, conveys a profound sense of loss and anxiety over the disappearance of the traditional ecclesiastical order:

> Ah! he is fled!
> And while these here their *mists*, and *shadowes* hatch,
>   My glorious head
> Doth on those hills of Mirrhe, and Incense watch.
>   Haste, hast my dear,
>   The Souldiers here
>   Cast in their lots again,
>   That seamlesse coat
>   The Jews touch'd not,
>   These dare divide, and stain.
>
>   2.
>   O get thee wings!
> Or if as yet (until these clouds depart,

And the day springs,)
Thou think'st it good to tarry where thou art,
Write in thy bookes
My ravish'd looks
Slain flock, and pillag'd fleeces,
And hast thee so
As a young Roe
Upon the mounts of spices.

O Rosa Campi! O lilium Convallium! quomodo nunc facta es pabulum Aprorum![42]

In dramatizing the Bride of Christ – here the Anglican Church – passionately addressing her 'deare' Christ during the darker years of the war, Vaughan's poem differs considerably from Herbert's poem of the same title, which explores the *via media* of the matriarchal Church of England in relation to the wanton Church of Rome and the naked Calvinist Church of Geneva. (But then Herbert, the religious poet from whom Vaughan learned most, was not of course writing during the chaotic and tumultuous years of the English Revolution.) Vaughan alludes in the first stanza to the soldiers, who serve under Pontius Pilate, casting lots for the seamless coat of the crucified Christ in John 19:23–4: here the soldiers of the gospel become the Parliamentary soldiers of the English Civil War who would not only stain Christ's clothing but devastate his church.

The sense of urgency of Vaughan's poem continues in the second stanza with the ravaged Bride's dramatic address to Christ ('O get thee wings!') and with her explicit reference to the destruction brought on by the Civil War and the Parliamentary forces ('My ravish'd looks / Slain flock, and pillag'd fleeces'). Here again Vaughan refers to a biblical passage – this time from the Song of Solomon 8:14 – to highlight the poignancy of the Bride's address to her Bridegroom: 'Make haste, my beloved, and be thou like to a roe or to a young hart upon the mountains of spices.' The Bride thus implores her spouse's swift return (since 'he is fled' in these dark days) at the Second Coming in order to save his desolated Bride. The Latin motto at the end provides a particularly powerful and graphic conclusion to this haunting poem lamenting the devastation suffered by the English Church under the revolutionary Puritans: 'O rose of the field! O lily of the vallies! how have you now become the food of wild boars!' Fusing Solomon 2:1 with Psalm 80:13 in this final passage, a pessimistic Vaughan suggests the wasteland that England has now become as a result of the chaotic destruction of this traditional institution: 'The boar out of the wood doth waste it, and the wild beast of the field doth devour it'. Like Milton or Marvell, then, the Anglican Vaughan could respond acutely to the religious and political upheavals of his time.

PROPHECY, POLITICS, AND REVOLUTION

The English Revolution stimulated poetry that fused religion and politics in new and sometimes radical ways, especially by employing, with greater urgency, prophetic language, and apocalyptic imagery. Indeed, a fairly conservative Jacobean court poet like Jonson, who used his literary talents to praise, counsel, and serve the Stuart aristocracy, was hostile to Puritan apocalypticism – the kind of prophetic strain noticeable in the visionary poetry of Milton's 'Lycidas' (1637), a passionately anti-clerical and anti-Laudian work. After all, the Protestant prophetic tradition in poetry could be transformed to encourage dynamic and even radical political and religious reform. For Protestant reformers, the prophetic Book of Revelation foretold the spectacular destruction of the Romish Antichrist; thus the vivid imagery and language of the Bible was capable of inspiring apocalyptic prophecies and revolutionary visions, especially during and after the upheaval of the 1640s. A brief look at 'Lycidas' and Marvell's Cromwellian poem, 'The First Anniversary of the Government under O. C.' (published 1655), can illustrate how two major poets creatively employed biblical prophecy in their occasional and politically engaged verses.

Milton's 'Lycidas' gives the language of politics and religion a strikingly new radical and prophetic inflection. Indeed, in order to make the political dimension of the poem more explicit, Milton added a telling headnote to 'Lycidas' when he published his 1645 *Poems*: 'by occasion' his prophetic poem 'foretells the ruin of our corrupted Clergy then in their height' – as if to anticipate the English Revolution itself. Even the poem's opening, 'Yet once more', alludes to the promise of apocalyptic judgement in Hebrews 12:26–7. The untimely death of one of the nation's young model pastors, Edward King, struck a deep chord in Milton prompting, through his use of the pastoral code, the poem's impassioned religious and political criticism. Having himself considered an ecclesiastical career, Milton felt 'church-outed by the prelats' and 'Lycidas', especially through the fiery apocalyptic voice of St Peter (lines 113–31), registers his profound disillusionment with the corrupt Anglican clergy during the 1630s, the years of Laud's authoritarian power when the bishops were exalted. Referring to the clergy's 'Blind mouths' (suggesting their rapacity and gluttony), Milton scornfully puns on the etymology of bishop (one who sees) and pastor (one who feeds). The inexplicable death of Lycidas seems even more unjust when the present clergy are such bad shepherds, their sermons nothing more than fashionable and superficial exercises ('lean and flashy songs'), the work of bad artists (they grate on 'scrannel Pipes of wretched straw') who cannot feed or satisfy their Christian flock. Milton's criticisms recall a biblical text like Ezekiel

34:2 ('Woe *be* to the shepherds of Israel that do feed themselves! should not the shepherds feed the flocks?'), giving biblical pastoral a radical Protestant inflection as he builds up to the climactic vision of judgement in which 'that two-handed engine at the door / Stands ready to smite once, and smite no more'. This ominous and resonant passage of promised retribution, a famous crux in Milton criticism (it seems to refer to, among other things, the 'two massy Keys' of St Peter earlier in the poem, and to the sharp two-edged sword issuing out of the apocalyptic Christ's mouth in Revelation 1:16 and 19:15), looks forward to the fierce 'two-handed' sword of the warrior-angel Michael which 'smites' Satan and his rebel forces in *Paradise Lost*'s apocalyptic battle in heaven for the territory of God (see 6.250ff.).

Less strident in its apocalypticism, 'The First Anniversary' by Milton's younger contemporary scrutinizes the arts of power and politics in the age of Oliver Cromwell. Marvell's celebratory poem explores the dynamic and creative political role of Cromwell in the Interregnum when 'heavy Monarchs' are associated with an old order no longer actively shaping the forces of history in England: ' 'Tis he the force of scatter'd Time contracts, / And in one Year the work of Ages acts' (lines 15, 13–14). Marvell is referring specifically to the anniversary of Cromwell becoming the Lord Protector of England (16 December 1653), an occasion when Cromwell assumed greater powers over the Commonwealth declared after the death of Charles I. Unlike 'An Horatian Ode' which depicts the restless Cromwell more as an iconoclast who destroys 'Pallaces and Temples' (line 22) as he recasts the kingdom into another mould, 'The First Anniversary' depicts Cromwell as the creative architect of a new political order – 'Here pulling down, and there erecting New, / Founding a firm State by Proportions true' (lines 247–8). Marvell indeed repeatedly highlights Cromwell's political achievements and talents in aesthetic terms, reminding us that the aesthetic and the political were themselves closely interconnected in this age. So Cromwell, in tune with the will of God, has 'tun'd the ruling Instrument' (line 68) – the Instrument of the Government, the constitution which invested executive authority in the Protector and a Council of State, while providing for triennial parliaments. Marvell's Cromwell is (in one elaborate conceit) like an inspired Amphion raising the walls of Thebes by playing his golden lyre (lines 49–67); moreover, as a highly skilful political architect, he has managed to construct a new edifice, a mixed state whose strength incorporates political tensions and opposing strains within it (lines 87–98), much as Milton's famous temple of God in *Areopagitica* (1644) incorporates religious differences – 'brotherly dissimilitudes that are not vastly disproportional' – to achieve its goodly symmetry.[43]

For Marvell, the creative and inspired Cromwell, then, is an instrument of providence ('an higher Force him push'd / Still from behind', lines 239–40), an identification the poet underscores with apocalyptic references. Repeatedly contrasting an active Cromwell with other earthly kings and princes – of whom his poem is often sharply critical – Marvell suggests that the apocalpytic events prophesied in Daniel (e.g. 7:18, 27, 10:14) and Revelation might indeed be fulfilled under this new dispensation: 'How might they under such a Captain raise / The great Designes kept for the latter Dayes!' (lines 109–10). Among princes and leaders, the divinely chosen Cromwell is alone in pursuing the fierce battle against the powers of Antichrist. Marvell's more hopeful, excited prophetic vision is nonetheless qualified by his more realistic sense that the apathy and sinfulness of his own unworthy and thankless countrymen prevent Cromwell from bringing about the approaching millennium, that period of utopian conditions on earth coinciding with the Second Coming of Christ: 'Hence that blest Day still counterpoysed wastes, / The Ill delaying, what th'Elected hastes' (lines 155–6).

But in endorsing the legitimacy and power of the Protectorate, Marvell's politically engaged poem condemns other, more radical forms of prophecy and political expression in the age: Marvell in any case tends to mistrust the extreme religious enthusiasm which erupted during the revolution. While he is critical of traditional and hereditary kingship, he is no less suspicious of the sectarian fervour of the revolutionary decades. Marvell's poem criticizes the Levellers or radical democrats of the age (lines 257–64) and it criticizes at length (lines 293–320) those radical Puritan sects – the Fifth Monarchists, Quakers, Ranters, among others[44] – which had opposed a politically more conservative Cromwell. In Marvell's poem, Cromwell's 'sober Spirit' (line 230) contrasts favourably with the 'frantique Army' of sectaries (line 299), 'The Shame and Plague both of the Land and Age' (line 294). Ten years earlier, Milton had been considerably more tolerant in *Areopagitica* of the sectarian excitement unleashed by the revolution; but for Marvell, whose political allegiances often resembled Milton's (both wrote in defence of the Protectorate), the extreme radicalism of the age only threatened to undermine the more moderate reforming spirit and social reconstruction of Cromwell's Protectorate.

Marvell's Cromwellian poem, then, attempts to steer deftly between political radicalism and political tyranny:

> 'Tis not a Freedome, that where All command;
> Nor Tyranny, where One does them withstand:
> But who of both the Bounders knows to lay
> Him as their Father must the State obey.   (lines 279–82)

Here Marvell redefines the symbolic appeal to patriarchal power that, as we saw earlier, was so closely aligned with the politics of Stuart kingship: in this new age, it is the Protector who is now the political 'Father' of the people and who provides true liberty by avoiding extreme political measures. Indeed, Marvell is careful to suggest that Cromwell is no monarch, despite his increased powers under the new regime. In order to stress the wondrous progress and renovation under Cromwell's animating power, Marvell introduces, in the final section of his poem, the reluctant praise of a foreign and potentially hostile monarch:

> 'He seems a King by long Succession born,
> And yet the same to be a King does scorn.
> Abroad a King he seems, and something more,
> At Home a Subject on the equal Floor.'   (lines 387–90)

Besides alluding to Cromwell's famous refusal not to be crowned, Marvell's lines convey the paradoxical nature of Cromwell's political role as Lord Protector: both a 'great Prince' (line 395) and an English 'Subject', he appears kingly and yet is no king at all.

By the end of the decade, however, the experimental Protectorate collapsed, despite the prophetic hopes of Marvell in 'The First Anniversary' and Milton in his visionary tract, *The Second Defence of the English People* (1654), which likewise depicted Cromwell as the mythic and dynamic architect of the state. The Stuart Restoration of 1660 meant that a true *regnum Christi* in England would be deferred yet once more. For those poets who challenged the ecclesiastical and civil powers of worldly monarchy during the revolution, one critical response after 1660 was to valorize a more spiritual, inward notion of power and kingship. Like Marvell's Cromwell, Milton's Jesus in *Paradise Regained* (1671) would also encounter the temptation of worldly kingship and yet scorn 'a Crown, / Golden in show'. Challenging the authority of worldly powers and institutions in the Restoration, his polemical and prophetic responses to his Tempter would reconceive the politics of kingship in a distinctly more interior way:

> Yet he who reigns within himself, and rules
> Passions, Desires, and Fears, is more a King;
> Which every wise and virtuous man attains:
> And who attains not, ill aspires to rule
> Cities of men, or headstrong Multitudes,
> Subject himself to anarchy within,
> Or lawlesse passions in him, which he serves.
>
>   (2.458–9, 466–72)

NOTES

1 Christopher Hill, *The Collected Essays of Christopher Hill*, vol. 2: *Religion and Politics in 17th Century England* (Brighton: Harvester, 1986), p. 17.

2 Christopher Hill and Edmund Dell (eds.), *The Good Old Cause: The English Revolution of 1640–1660*, 2nd edn (London: Cass, 1969), pp. 178, 173.

3 *John Milton: Complete Poems and Major Prose*, ed. M. Y. Hughes (Indianapolis and New York: Odyssey, 1957), pp. 671, 670; all quotations from Milton's poetry and prose are from this edition.

4 *John Donne*, ed. John Carey (Oxford University Press, 1990), p. 325. Quotations from Donne's poetry and prose are taken from this edition.

5 King James I, *The Works of the Most High and Mighty Prince, James* (London, 1616), p. 137; all parenthetic references are to this edition.

6 J. P. Kenyon (ed.), *The Stuart Constitution: Documents and Commentary*, 2nd edn (Cambridge University Press, 1986), p. 150.

7 J. P. Sommerville, *Politics and Ideology in England, 1603–1640* (London: Longman, 1986), pp. 35–6; James I, p. 203.

8 *Donne*, p. 192.

9 James I, p. 529; G. J. Schochet, *Patriarchalism in Political Thought* (Oxford: Basil Blackwell, 1975), passim.

10 Quotations from Marvell's poetry are from *The Poems and Letters of Andrew Marvell*, ed. H. M. Margoliouth, 3rd edn, rev. Pierre Legouis with E. E. Duncan-Jones (Oxford: Clarendon Press, 1971).

11 Quotations from Jonson's poetry and prose are from *Ben Jonson*, ed. C. H. Herford, P. Simpson, and E. M. Simpson, vol. 8 (Oxford: Clarendon Press, 1947).

12 See Jonson's 'Ode to himself' (lines 51–2) in *Ben Jonson*, vol. 6 (1938), p. 494.

13 *Ben Jonson* 8.595.

14 See Jonathan Goldberg, *James I and the Politics of Literature: Jonson, Shakespeare, Donne, and Their Contemporaries* (Baltimore: John Hopkins University Press, 1983); and David Norbrook, 'The Monarchy of Wit and the Republic of Letters: Donne's Politics', in Elizabeth D. Harvey and Katherine E. Maus (eds.), *Soliciting Interpretation: Literary Theory and Seventeenth-Century English Poetry* (University of Chicago Press, 1990), pp. 3–36.

15 John Carey, *John Donne: Life, Mind and Art* (London and Boston: Faber, 1981), pp. 60–130.

16 There is, moreover, increasing evidence that Donne was not an unequivocal absolutist and that he could at times maintain a more critical stance towards the world of courtly power and politics: see Norbrook, 'Monarchy of Wit' and Arthur F. Marotti, *John Donne: Coterie Poet* (Madison: University of Wisconsin Press, 1986).

17 Derek Hirst, *Authority and Conflict: England 1603–1658* (London: Edward Arnold, 1986), p. 165.

18 A. S. P. Woodhouse (ed.), *Puritanism and Liberty*, 3rd edn (London: Dent, 1986), p. 40.

19 Hirst, *Authority and Conflict*, p. 287.

20 Quoted from *The Poetical Works of Robert Herrick*, ed. L. C. Martin (Oxford: Clarendon Press, 1956); further quotations from Herrick's poetry are taken from this edition.

21 Quoted from *The Poems of Richard Lovelace*, ed. C. H. Wilkinson (Oxford: Clarendon Press, 1930).

22 Nicholas Tyacke, *Anti-Calvinists: The Rise of English Arminianism, c. 1590–1640* (Oxford: Clarendon, 1987), p. 2.

23 Quoted in Tyacke, *Anti-Calvinists*, p. 4.

24 See Arthur Dent's popular work, *The Plaine Mans Path-Way to Heaven* (London, 1601), p. 290.

25 Blair Worden, 'Providence and Politics in Cromwellian England', *Past and Present* 109 (1985): 55–99 (58).

26 Keith Thomas, *Religion and the Decline of Magic* (London: Weidenfeld and Nicolson, 1971), pp. 470–1.

27 Quotations from Herbert's poetry are from *The Works of George Herbert*, ed. F. E. Hutchinson (1941; rev. edn, Oxford: Clarendon, 1945).

28 From *The Third Century* in *Poems, Centuries and Three Thanksgivings*, ed. Anne Ridler (Oxford University Press, 1966), p. 268; further quotations from Traherne are from this edition.

29 From a sermon preached at Lincoln's Inn (1618) in *Donne*, p. 274.

30 Hill and Dell, *Good Old Cause*, pp. 171–2.

31 Kenyon, *Stuart Constitution*, pp. 148–9.

32 Patrick Collinson, *The Religion of Protestants: The Church in English Society, 1559–1625* (Oxford: Clarendon Press, 1982), p. 141.

33 Hill and Dell, *Good Old Cause*, p. 176; see also William Prynne, *Canterburies Doome* (London, 1646).

34 Leah S. Marcus, *The Politics of Mirth: Jonson, Herrick, Milton, Marvell, and the Defense of Old Holiday Pastimes* (University of Chicago Press, 1986), passim; and Hirst, *Authority and Conflict*, p. 76.

35 David Underdown, *Revel, Riot, and Rebellion: Popular Politics and Culture in England,1603–1660* (Oxford:Clarendon Press, 1985), pp. 274,276; and Christopher Hill, *The Century of Revolution, 1603–1714* (Edinburgh: Nelson, 1961), p. 85.

36 Quotations from Crashaw are from *The Poems*, ed. L. C. Martin, 2nd edn (Oxford: Clarendon Press, 1957).

37 *Poems*, p. xxx.

38 *Complete Poems and Major Prose*, p. 681.

39 *Behemoth: The History of the Causes of the Civil Wars of England*, in *The English Works of Thomas Hobbes*, ed. Sir William Molesworth, vol. 6 (London, 1840), p. 191.

40 Thomas, *Religion*, pp. 78–112.

41 See Worden, 'Providence and Politics', passim.

42 Quoted from Vaughan's *Works*, ed. L. C. Martin, 2nd edn (Oxford: Clarendon Press, 1957).

43 *Complete Poems and Major Prose*, p. 744.

44 Christopher Hill, *The World Turned Upside Down: Radical Ideas During the English Revolution* (London: Maurice Temple Smith, 1972), passim.

FURTHER READING

Ashton, Robert, *The English Civil War: Conservatism and Revolution, 1603–1649*, 2nd edn (London: Weidenfeld and Nicolson, 1989)

Collinson, Patrick, *The Religion of Protestants: The Church in English Society, 1559–1625* (Oxford: Clarendon Press, 1982)
  The Birthpangs of Protestant England: Religious and Cultural Change in the Sixteenth and Seventeenth Centuries (Basingstoke: Macmillan, 1988)
Coolidge, John S., *The Pauline Renaissance in England: Puritanism and the Bible* (Oxford: Clarendon Press, 1970)
Corns, Thomas N., *Uncloistered Virtue: English Political Literature, 1640–1660* (Oxford: Clarendon Press, 1992)
Cross, Frank L. and More, Paul E. (eds.), *Anglicanism: The Thought and Practice of the Church of England* (London: S.P.C.K., 1962)
Cust, Richard and Hughes, Ann (eds.), *Conflict in Early Stuart England: Studies in Religion and Politics, 1603–1642* (London: Longman, 1989)
Dubrow, Heather and Strier, Richard (eds.), *The Historical Renaissance: New Essays on Tudor and Stuart Literature and Culture* (University of Chicago Press, 1988)
Goldberg, Jonathan, *James I and the Politics of Literature: Jonson, Shakespeare, Donne, and Their Contemporaries* (Baltimore: John Hopkins University Press, 1983)
Hill, Christopher, *The Century of Revolution, 1603–1714* (Edinburgh: T. Nelson, 1961)
  The World Turned Upside Down: Radical Ideas During the English Revolution (London: Maurice Temple Smith, 1972)
  The Collected Essays of Christopher Hill, vol. II: *Religion and Politics in 17th Century England* (Brighton: Harvester, 1986)
Hill, Christopher and Edmund Dell (eds.), *The Good Old Cause: The English Revolution of 1640–1660*, 2nd edn (London: Cass, 1969)
Hirst, Derek, *Authority and Conflict: England 1603–1658* (London: Edward Arnold, 1986)
Hughes, Ann, *The Causes of the English Civil War* (London: Macmillan, 1991)
Judson, Margaret A., *The Crisis of the Constitution: An Essay in Constitutional and Political Thought in England, 1603–1645* (New Brunswick: Rutgers University Press, 1988)
Kendall, R. T., *Calvin and English Calvinism to 1649* (Oxford University Press, 1979)
Kenyon, J. P. (ed.), *The Stuart Constitution: Documents and Commentary*, 2nd edn (Cambridge University Press, 1986)
Lake, Peter, *Anglicans or Puritans? Presbyterianism and English Conformist Thought from Whitgift to Hooker* (London: Allen and Unwin, 1988)
Lamont, William M., *Godly Rule: Politics and Religion, 1603–1660* (London: Macmillan, 1969)
Lewalski, Barbara K., *Protestant Poetics and the Seventeenth-Century Religious Lyric* (Princeton University Press, 1979)
Marcus, Leah S., *Childhood and Cultural Despair: A Theme and Variations in Seventeenth-Century Literature* (University of Pittsburgh Press, 1978)
  The Politics of Mirth: Jonson, Herrick, Milton, Marvell, and the Defense of Old Holiday Pastimes (University of Chicago Press, 1986)
Marotti, Arthur F., *John Donne, Coterie Poet* (Madison: University of Wisconsin Press, 1986)
Norbrook, David, *Poetry and Politics in the English Renaissance* (London: Routledge and Kegan Paul, 1984)

'The Monarchy of Wit and the Republic of Letters: Donne's Politics', in *Soliciting Interpretation: Literary Theory and Seventeenth-Century English Poetry*, ed. Elizabeth D. Harvey and Katherine E. Maus (University of Chicago Press, 1991), pp. 3–36

Parry, Graham, *The Seventeenth Century: The Intellectual and Cultural Context of English Literature, 1603–1700* (London: Longman, 1989)

Russell, Conrad, *The Causes of the English Civil War* (Oxford: Clarendon Press, 1990)

Schochet, G. J., *Patriarchalism in Political Thought* (Oxford: Basil Blackwell, 1975)

Sharpe, Kevin and Zwicker, Stephen N. (eds.), *Politics of Discourse: The Literature and History of Seventeenth-Century England* (Berkeley: University of California Press, 1987)

Sommerville, J. P., *Politics and Ideology in England, 1603–1640* (London: Longman, 1986)

Stachniewski, John, *The Persecutory Imagination: English Puritanism and the Literature of Religious Despair* (Oxford: Clarendon Press, 1991)

Stone, Lawrence, *The Causes of the English Revolution, 1529–1642* (London: Routledge and Kegan Paul, 1972)

Summers, Claude J. and Pebworth, Ted-Larry (eds.), *'The Muses Common-Weale': Poetry and Politics in the Seventeenth Century* (Columbia: University of Missouri Press, 1988)

Thomas, Keith, *Religion and the Decline of Magic* (London: Weidenfeld and Nicolson, 1971)

Trevor-Roper, H. R., *Catholics, Anglicans and Puritans: Seventeenth Century Essays* (London: Secker and Warburg, 1987)

Tyacke, Nicholas, *Anti-Calvinists: The Rise of English Arminianism, c. 1590–1640* (Oxford: Clarendon Press, 1987)

Underdown, David, *Revel, Riot, and Rebellion: Popular Politics and Culture in England, 1603–1660* (Oxford: Clarendon Press, 1985)

Wedgwood, C. V., *Poetry and Politics under the Stuarts* (Cambridge University Press, 1960)

Wilding, Michael, *Dragons Teeth: Literature in the English Revolution* (Oxford: Clarendon Press, 1987)

Woodhouse, A. S. P. (ed.), *Puritanism and Liberty*, 3rd edn (London: Dent, 1986)

Wooton, David, (ed.), *Divine Right and Democracy: An Anthology of Political Writing in Stuart England* (Harmondsworth: Penguin, 1986)

Worden, Blair, 'Providence and Politics in Cromwellian England', *Past and Present* 109 (1985): 55–99

2

ELAINE HOBBY

The politics of gender

Although it is unarguably the case that governmental and other state structures have changed since the seventeenth century, sometimes it can be unthinkingly assumed that in another major site of power differences, that of gender roles, matters have remained largely the same. This has the result that whilst readings of Donne, or Vaughan, or Marvell might include an active consideration of the specifics of the status of Catholics in the early 1600s, or of the problematics of political alliances in the 1650s, it is still relatively common to find work on those same poets paying no heed to the particular contemporary limitations of femaleness and maleness. The result is a blurring of the specificity of the poetry and its concerns.

If the only evidence we had to go on when imagining the relationships between men and women in the seventeenth century was the most frequently anthologized male poetry of the period, we would gain a very distorted impression of the probable social realities. Whereas the legal and economic structures of seventeenth-century society ensured women's subordination to men, defending this through a panoply of ideological assertions, vast numbers of poems present the (would-be) mistress as all-powerful, able to kill her admirer with an angry glance, her will irresistible. In pursuit of his Julia/Celia/Corinna, the lover expends 'Sighs, tears, and oaths, and letters' (Donne, 'Lovers' Infiniteness'),[1] urging her to remember 'Time will not be ours, for ever' (Jonson, 'Song: To Celia'),[2] declaring,

> Thou art my life, my love, my heart,
> The very eyes of me:
> And hast command of every part,
> To live and die for thee.
> (Herrick, 'To Anthea, who may Command him Any Thing')[3]

The fact that we would not know how distorted this impression of female potency is, would also mean that our reading of the poetry itself would be at best inadequate. Recent work in women's and family history and research

31

that is uncovering the forgotten published writings of seventeenth-century women are presenting new questions to men's poetry of the period, making it seem in some ways more complicated than it might at first appear, and stranger. The newness of this research, however, also means that it is fragmentary: there are studies of remarrying widows in Abingdon[4] and of family structures in Ryton,[5] but no national, century-wide picture. Even once the statistics are all established, or established as far as they can be, this will be no more than a beginning: it is one thing to know that the median marriage age for women in the period was twenty-four, that of men twenty-eight[6]; it is quite another problem to work out how people felt about this, or how they organized their sexual lives in the long period between puberty and marriage, or why more women remained unmarried as the seventeenth century progressed.[7] The relationships between legal and economic structures, and people's knowledge of those structures and their ideas about them, are not simple or predictable. Whilst social history research presents questions to literary critics, writings of the period can also suggest what some of the answers to historians' questions might be.

To begin, though, with one of the most striking differences between social reality and poetic representation: the assertion of female omnipotence in male/female relationships. In fact, women's subordination to men was axiomatic in the legal and economic organization of society, and firmly reinforced in ideological formulations that insisted the subordination was natural; as inevitable, for instance, as the head's control of the body. This is a point frequently made in conduct books, sermons, and other explicitly ideological formulations of the day. Thomas Gataker asserts:

> the man is as the head, and the woman as the body ... And as it is against the order of Nature that the body should rule the head: so it is no less against the course of all good order that the woman should usurp authority to herself over her husband, her head.[8]

The legal and economic identity of a married woman was subsumed in that of her husband. This is succinctly expressed in *The Law's Resolution of Women's Rights*:

> In this consolidation which we call wedlock is a locking together. It is true, that man and wife are one person; but understand in what manner. When a small brook or little rivulet incorporateth with Rhodanus [the Rhone], Humber, or Thames, the poor rivulet loseth her name; it is carried and re-carried with the new associate; it beareth no sway; it possesseth nothing coverture. A woman as soon as she is married is called *covert*; in Latin *nupta*, that is, 'veiled'; as it were clouded and overshadowed; she hath lost her stream. I may more truly, far away, say to a married woman, her new self is her superior; her companion, her master.[9]

The significance of this loss of selfhood to possible readings of seventeenth-century poetry is made clear if we juxtapose it with some of the celebrations of the merging of lover and beloved. Amongst the most famous, and most admired, of these are found in the works of John Donne. In 'A Valediction: Forbidding Mourning', for instance, the lady is urged not to lament the poet's absence because their unity will be maintained despite physical separation:

> Our two souls therefore, which are one,
>   Though I must go, endure not yet
> A breach, but an expansion,
>   Like gold to aery thinness beat.
>
> If they be two, they are two so
>   As stiff twin compasses are two,
> Thy soul the fixed foot, makes no show
>   To move, but doth, if th'other do.
>
> And though it in the centre sit,
>   Yet when the other far doth roam,
> It leans, and hearkens after it,
>   And grows erect, as that comes home.
>
> Such wilt thou be to me, who must
>   Like th' other foot, obliquely run;
> Thy firmness makes my circle just,
>   And makes me end, where I begun.
>   (Donne, *Complete English Poems*, pp. 84–5)

What is striking is that the celebrated merger is not a union of equals: the lady's part in the relationship is to be the 'fixed foot' of the compasses, only moving when the roaming foot rotates. The conceit indicates, indeed, not mutuality but a power differential. To notice this is not, of course, to dismiss the poem, but it does raise some questions: is the poet here striving to invent an image of equality but failing to do so because of the limitations imposed on his imagination by the world he inhabits? A similar point might be made about Donne's 'The Anniversary' (Donne, *Complete English Poems*, pp. 41–2), where both lover and mistress are described as 'kings' and so equal; but a woman, of course, cannot be a king; and a queen is not, quite, equal to a king, and so that term is not an available alternative. The inappropriateness of the description, therefore, exposes the actual lower level of female power both within the relationship imaginatively depicted, and in the nation as a whole.[10]

Female contemporaries of John Donne's also worked to invent images of mutuality. In 'Friendship in Emblem, or the Seal: To my dearest Lucasia'

Katherine Philips reworks the compasses conceit, making it possible for the identity of the moving foot to alternate: 'Each follows where the other leans, / And what each does, this other means.'[11] In Philips's case the imagined interchangeability is made possible by the fact that the lovers are of the same gender: elsewhere she rejoices in Lucasia as 'My Joy, my Life, my Rest', explicitly preferring their delight to the crowing 'mirth' a bridegroom feels with a new bride.[12] Anne Bradstreet, on the other hand, writes a poem from the point of view of the wife left at home by the travelling husband. This opens describing him in conventional terms as 'My head', and ends acknowledging that she is 'Flesh of thy flesh, bone of thy bone', as Christian orthodoxy would require; but in between she wittily establishes both her own authority – he is her 'dearest guest', not her master – and her own intellectual powers as a poet.[13] As she plays with 'natural' imagery – the relationship of head to body, the changing of the seasons being dependent on the height of the sun in the sky – she demonstrates that argumentation based on such features is false: she is warmer, not colder, as the sun moves northward; head and body can both continue to live when severed. The reader is invited to speculate whether the 'natural' differences between men and women might also be open to question. The poem can be seen then, like Donne's, as enacting and exploring the contradictions of claiming a merged identity of two people divided by a power differential. He explores this from a male perspective, she from a female one:

> 'A Letter to her Husband Absent upon Public Employment'
> My head, my heart, mine eyes, my life, nay, more,
> My joy, my magazine of earthly store,
> If two be one, as surely thou and I,
> How stayest thou there, whilst I at Ipswich lie?
> So many steps, head from the heart to sever,
> If but a neck, soon should we be together.
> I, like the Earth this season, mourn in black.
> My Sun is gone so far in's zodiac,
> Whom whilst I 'joyed, nor storms, nor frost I felt.
> His warmth such frigid colds did cause to melt.
> My chilled limbs now numbed lie forlorn:
> Return, return, sweet Sol, from Capricorn:
> In this dead time, alas, what can I more
> Than view those fruits which through thy heat I bore?
> Which sweet contentment yield me for a space,
> True living pictures of their father's face.
> O strange effect! now thou are southward gone,
> I weary grow, the tedious day so long;
> But when thou northward to me shalt return,

I wish my Sun may never set, but burn
Within the Cancer of my glowing breast,
The welcome house of him my dearest guest.
Where ever, ever stay, and go not thence,
Till Nature's sad decree shall call thee hence:
Flesh of thy flesh, bone of thy bone,
I here, thou there, yet both but one.

The existence of poems like these rebuts the argument at one time advanced by historians that the fact that the spouse was chosen by family decision, not at the whim of individual emotion, led to seventeenth-century marriages being distant and affectionless. Both Bradstreet and Donne take it for granted that a long-term relationship involves deep emotional commitment, and whilst Donne's own marriage might have been impolitic and therefore seem to make his love poetry atypical in this respect, Bradstreet's marriage at the age of about fifteen was certainly to someone chosen by her parents.[14] It is the case, however, that whilst such relationships might have developed intimacy, they were undertaken as economic transactions, and during marriage a woman's right to hold property was largely removed by her husband: as T. E. phrased it, she 'possesseth nothing coverture'. Any love which might develop within the relationship did not undo the power differential between the partners involved.[15] A bride brought with her a dowry, or 'portion', in return for which she was promised support in the form of freehold tenancy in land, her 'jointure', should her husband predecease her. The fact that the level of portions increased by 300 per cent between 1600 and 1700 (in a period when general price inflation was just 50 per cent)[16] might also indicate that financial considerations increased in significance in the period. A sense of women's lack of influence even over men they might have married for love is voiced by Isabella in Middleton's *Women Beware Women*:[17]

Oh, the heartbreakings
Of miserable maids, where love's enforc'd!
The best condition is but bad enough:
When women have their choices, commonly
They do but buy their thraldoms, and bring great portions
To men to keep 'em in subjection.
. . . No misery surmounts a woman's:
Men buy their slaves, but women buy their masters.

It is scarcely surprising, given the interconnection between finance and marriage, that the love poetry of the day makes such frequent use of economic metaphors. The lady is praised for 'her store / Of worth'

(Crashaw, 'Wishes: To his (supposed) Mistress'[18]), called to 'unlocke' her 'mine of Pleasure' (Carew, 'To a Lady that Desired I Would Love Her'[19]), or threatened that she will be superseded: 'I must search the black and faire / Like skilfull Minerallist's that sound / For Treasure in un-plow'd-up ground' (Lovelace, 'The Scrutiny'[20]). The ending of a relationship is bemoaned as it 'lies now exhaust and spend, / Like summes of treasure unto Bankrupts lent' (King, 'The Surrender'[21]). A golden age is evoked where women were the common property of men, and sexual pleasure therefore freely available to the male sex:

> It was not love, but love transformed to vice,
>   Ravished by envious avarice,
> Made women first impropriate: all were free:
>   Enclosures men's inventions be.
> In the golden age no action could be found
>   For trespass on my neighbour's ground:
> 'Twas just with any fair to mix our blood.
> (Randolph, 'Upon Love Fondly Refused for Conscience's Sake')[22]

Within such fantasies lie implicit fears: if men were able 'with any fair to mix our blood' they could not be confident that their wives' offspring were legitimate heirs to their own property, and Randolph's poem ends invoking a time 'when time's colder hand leads us near home / Then let that winter-virtue come'. Such anxieties are also given voice in Donne's Elegy 'To his Mistress Going to Bed', where she is celebrated in terms which simultaneously assert that she is his possession and indicate male anxiety about the extent of that possession: the lady is 'my America, my new found land, / My kingdom, *safeliest* when with one man manned' (emphasis mine).[23]

The idolizing courtship of the desired mistress, then, is inviting her at best to a legal relationship where she has no independent existence but becomes a man's possession; this is encoded in the language adopted by the male poets. This was also a dynamic much commented on, often with irony, by their women contemporaries. In *Her Protection for Women* (1589) Jane Anger warns her woman reader, 'Their singing is a bait to catch us and their playings, plagues to torment us. And therefore take heed of them.'[24] Katherine Philips published a poem described as 'An Answer to Another Persuading a Lady to Marriage':

> I.
> Forbear bold Youth, all's Heaven here
>   And what you do aver,
> To others Courtship may appear,
>   'Tis Sacriledge to her.

2.

She is a publick Deity,
 And were't not very odd
She should depose her self to be
 A petty Houshold God?

3.

First make the Sun in private shine,
 And bid the World adieu,
That so he may his beams confine
 In complement to you.

4.

But if of that you do despair,
 Think how you did amiss,
To strive to fix her beams which are
 More bright and large than this.

(Philips, Poems, p. 155)

Many of the verses addressed by men to women in the period were courtship poems of the kind mocked here by Anger and Philips. More specifically, a large number, like Randolph's quoted above, call on women to abandon their 'coyness' and agree to sex. This is so common as a literary pattern that it is easy to forget that a real woman's choice in matters of sexual desire was not a free one. The central requirement imposed on seventeenth-century women was chastity: to be thought an honourable woman she must be a virgin on marriage, and thereafter be sexually faithful to her husband. In the poems the mistress is admonished for refusing sex with a would-be lover, but in the social world women were supposed to be chaste. At the same time, she would have been taught from childhood that hers was the gender with the more libidinal nature; that her sexual appetite was enormous, and must be kept under careful restraint. For women, these contradictions might have been a source of confusion, or of irony, or a site of potential resistance. In men's poetry of the period, these self-contradictory ways of thinking about female sexuality produce curious effects. For instance, male fearfulness about women's sexual capacity often lurks in the corners – or perhaps at the heart – of poems urging a reluctant mistress to agree to consummation. This is most famously dramatized in Donne's 'The Apparition' where the poet envisages his would-be mistress in bed with another lover:

And he, whose thou art then, being tired before,
Will, if thou stir, or pinch to wake him, think
 Thou call'st for more,
And in false sleep will from thee shrink.

(Donne, Complete English Poems, pp. 42–3)

His imagined punishment of her – that if she refuses him now, she will in the future be sexually rejected herself – barely masks a suspicion that once aroused, women might be difficult for men to satisfy. Aphra Behn was presumably responding to such masculine fears about sexual performance in her mischievous poem 'The Disappointment'. This opens with the 'amorous Lysander' urging his advances on 'fair Cloris', and her refusing them. Eventually, though, she is overcome by her own desire, and offers herself to him, at which he becomes instantly impotent and 'the o'er-ravish'd shepherd lies / Unable to perform the sacrifice'. Behn describes Cloris's disgust and her would-be lover's attempts to regain his erection in a detail that is agonizing for 'poor Lysander' and for the male reader:

> Nature's support (without whose aid
> She can no human being give)
> Itself wants the art to live;
> Faintness its slackened nerves invade:
> In vain th'inraged youth essayed
> To call its fleeting vigour back,
> No motion 'twill from motion take;
> Excess of love his love betrayed:
> In vain he toils, in vain commands;
> The insensible fell weeping in his hand . . .
>
> Cloris returning from the trance
> Which love and soft desire had bred,
> Her timorous hand she gently laid
> (Or guided by design or chance)
> Upon the fabulous Priapus,
> That potent god, as poets feign;
> But never did young shepherdess,
> Gath'ring of fern upon the plain,
> More nimbly draw her fingers back,
> Finding beneath the verdant leaves a snake
>
> Than Cloris her fair hand withdrew,
> Finding that god of her desires
> Disarm'd of all his awful fires,
> And cold as flowers bathed in the morning dew.
> Who can the nymph's confusion guess?
> The blood forsook the hinder place,
> And strewed with blushes all her face,
> Which both disdain and shame expressed:
> And from Lysander's arms she fled,
> Leaving him fainting on the gloomy bed.[25]

Where a woman's honour was dependent upon her sexual behaviour, a man's honour, by contrast, was associated with the reliability of his word and his physical bravery. In a rather banal way this difference is manifest in Lovelace's 'Song: To Lucasta, Going to the Wars', where he assures the mistress 'I could not love thee (Deare), so much, / Lov'd I not Honour more' (Lovelace, *Poems*, p. 18). More curiously, it is the distinction between the definitions of male and female honour – or, more accurately, a confusion of those definitions – that produces the terms of the opening lines of Carew's sexually explicit fantasy, 'A Rapture' (Carew, *Poems*, pp. 49–53). He urges her to join him in bravely defying 'The Gyant, Honour', and 'be bold, and wise'. Given the locus of the definition of women's honour, urgings in such terms as Carew uses here could not be expected to be effective: they entirely miss the point, from a seventeenth-century honourable woman's perspective. But they make possible an exploration of the nature of 'honour', and the way in which this concept relates to male understandings of the erotic:

> We shall see how the stalking Pageant goes
> With borrowed legs, a heavie load to those
> That made, and beare him; not as we once thought
> The seed of Gods, but a weake modell wrought
> By greedy men, that seeke to enclose the common,
> And within private armes impale free woman.
>   ... there I'le behold
> Thy bared snow, and thy unbraided gold.
> There, my enfranchiz'd hand, on every side
> Shall o're thy naked polish'd Ivory slide.

The connections between this poem and the one by Randolph quoted above are obvious: the rapturous state is one in which women are freely available to male sexual possession, and this is a common fantasy in male poetry of the period, found in many of Carew's other works, as well as, for instance, in Lovelace's masturbatory fantasy 'Love Made in the First Age: To Chloris' (Lovelace, *Poems*, pp. 146–8).

Another ubiquitous concern in the poetry of the period is with the mistress' physical appearance. The assumption is clearly made that a woman dresses not for warmth or comfort, but to attract a man. Both Jonson's 'Still to be Neat' (Jonson, *Poems*, pp. 291–2) and Herrick's 'Delight in Disorder' (Herrick, *Poetical Works*, p. 28), for instance, depend on the woman being there on display to the male gaze, gaining her definition and worth from her power to attract him. She is sternly warned that she can only please by presenting an image of unadorned simplicity. In Jonson's words, 'Such sweet neglect more taketh me, / Than all the adulteries of art.'[26] The point then is not to be 'natural', but to appear to be so in order to please the male observer. Herrick's poem precisely captures the contradictoriness of this desire: the woman must make an effort to appear to not be making an effort if she is to be a successful instigator of male desire. This 'sweet disorder' makes it possible for the clothes themselves, not the lover or his desired object, to be seen as the source of lust and the active party in love-making. It is her lace that is 'erring', the stomacher that 'enthralls' her, her petticoat that is 'tempestuous'. This relieves him of responsibility for his desire, and appears to relieve her of responsibility for it, too, as long as she is sufficiently careful in producing her impression of carelessness.

In a culture where connections were regularly drawn between people's external features and their inner qualities, it is not surprising that this preoccupation with the lady's looks also links to wider opinions or anxieties about her other characteristics. Such connections are commonplace, in particular, in the misogynistic polemics that reached a wide readership in the day, such as Joseph Swetnam's *The Arraignment of Lewd, Idle, Froward and Unconstant Women* (1615). He warns his male reader:

> Women have a thousand ways to entice thee and ten thousand ways to deceive thee and all such fools as are suitors unto them: some they keep in hand with promises, and some they feed with flattery, and some they delay with dalliances, and some they please with kisses. They lay out the folds of their hair to entangle men into their love; betwixt their breasts is the vale of destruction; and in their beds there is hell, sorrow, and repentance ... For take away their painted clothes, and then they look like ragged walls; take away their ruffs, and they look ruggedly; their coifs and stomachers, and they are simple to behold; their hair untrussed, and they look wildly. And yet there are many which lays their nets to catch a pretty woman, but he which getteth such a prize gains nothing by his adventure but shame to the body and danger to the soul ... Many women are in shape Angels but in qualities Devils, painted coffins with rotten bones.[27]

These views are crudely echoed in Herrick's 'Upon some Women', where the male reader is urged to 'Learne of me what Woman is':

> False in legs, and false in thighes;
> False in breast, teeth, haire, and eyes:
> False in head, and false enough;
> Onely true in shreds and stuffe.
>
> (Herrick, *Poetical Works*, pp. 76–7)

More challengingly, Richard Crashaw's 'Wishes: To his (supposed) Mistress' (Crashaw, *Complete Poetry*, pp. 479–83) longs for 'That not impossible shee ... that Divine / *Idaea*', a woman whose virtue is in part made evident by the fact that she does not make use of extravagant clothing or make-up: she has 'A face made up / Out of no other shop, / Than what natures white hand sets ope'. In part the concern here is, once again, an economic one: whilst the woman is supposed to be an adornment to her husband, an advertisement of his financial well-being, she is also often portrayed as a potentially dangerous spendthrift. Swetnam, explaining to his male reader the 'real' meaning of the idea that God created woman as a helpmeet to man, insists that 'she helpeth to spend and consume that which man painfully getteth' (Swetnam, *The Arraignment*, p. 1). What is implicitly at stake in this description of the perfect woman, though, is not only a question of money. The poem is a fantasy which invents a 'supposed', that is, imagined, mistress; a perfect woman who also has 'A well tam'd Heart' and whose highest desire, since 'her store / Of worth, may leave her poore / Of wishes', is to 'dare' to be worthy of this man's love:

> Her that dares bee,
> What these Lines wish to see:
> I seeke no further, it is shee.
>
> 'Tis shee, and heere
> Lo I uncloath and cleare,
> My wishes cloudy Character.
>
> May shee enjoy it,
> Whose merit dare apply it,
> But Modesty dares still deny it.
>
> Such worth as this is
> Shall fixe my flying wishes,
> And determine them to kisses.
>
> Let her full Glory,
> My fancys, fly before yee,
> Be ye my fictions; But her story.

Crashaw here makes explicit what is implicit in much of the writing on ideal women in the period: these are his fictions, his invention; but they are, nonetheless, to provide the pattern, the 'story', of her life. The desirable woman is the woman who wants her very identity to be defined by male desires. Most women are not like this: as the users of make-up and deceit, they are implicitly reproached in this praise of the exceptional mistress.

There is a curious irony in the fact that Crashaw's own mother died in childbed after giving birth to him, her first baby: her story in a literal sense ended with the beginning of his life. After her death, however, *The Honour of Virtue*, a collection of writings eulogizing her as the kind of perfect woman later reinvented by Crashaw, was published. The praise here, like the compliments to Crashaw's 'supposed mistress', is also implicitly derogatory of the general run of womankind who, it is said, do not achieve the same standard.[28] In the light of this dynamic – the 'perfect woman' being invented as a standard against which most women can be found wanting – one of the poems in *The Honour of Virtue* is particularly interesting. F. Smith of Cambridge describes her as:

> Mild, gracious, modest, comely, constant, wise,
> Matchless for piety and spotless fame:
> All words want force her merit to comprise,
> Complete in all Grace, Art, or Nature claim.
>
> An honour of her Sex: blest virtue's pride,
> True beauty's pattern, mighty nature's wonder.
> In her, Pandora-like, there did reside
> All Graces others do possess asunder.
> (Henderson and McManus (eds.) *Half Humankind*, p. 349)

At first glance, this poem simply says that the lady was exceptional because she united in her so many virtuous qualities, something most women fail to do. The reference to Pandora, however, introduces a profound ambiguity into the poem. Whereas Smith refers to her here as the site of 'all Graces', taking the literal Greek meaning of her name, 'all gifts'; the reader will have another point of reference. In myth, Zeus created Pandora to punish Prometheus for stealing fire from the gods and giving it to humanity. At her creation she was endowed by the gods and goddesses with special qualities such as beauty, grace, and dexterity. But upon her arrival on earth she opened a box given her by Hephaestus and let loose on the world suffering and disease. She also originated the race of women, who 'live with mortal men, and are a great sorrow to them, and hateful poverty they will not share, but only luxury'.[29] Within even the most perfect of women, the implication goes, is a source of evil and destruction, just as the praise of an individual woman is premissed on the assumption that in being virtuous, she is exceptional. In Swetnam's words, 'Many women are in shape Angels but in qualities Devils, painted coffins with rotten bones.'

The fear of female deviation from the male ideal revealed here is also manifest in much other writing of the time. In 1620 King James ordered church ministers 'to inveigh vehemently in their sermons against the insolence of our women and their wearing of broad-brimmed hats, pointed doublets, their hair cut short or shorn, and some of them stilettos or poniards, and such other trinkets of like moment'.[30] Whether or not many women actually cross-dressed in this way, certainly the belief was commonplace that some wished to do so, and that to allow such behaviour was to allow a threat to natural order. The best known attack on such unfeminine behaviour is found in a pamphlet published in the same year that King James expressed his own anxieties: *Hic Mulier: Or, The Man-Woman: Being a Medicine to cure the Coltish Disease of the Staggers in the Masculine–Feminines of our Times.*[31] This is particularly concerned that women who have financial independence are choosing to dress and behave like men, making them 'good for nothing' (that is, presumably, not useful as breeders of children):

> Such as are able to buy all at their own charges, they swim in the excess of these vanities and will be manlike not only from the head to the waist, but to the very foot and in every condition: man in body by attire, man in behaviour by rude complement, man in nature by aptness to anger, man in action by pursuing revenge, man in wearing weapons, man in using weapons, and, in brief, so much man in all things that they are neither men nor women, but just good for nothing.
>
> (Henderson and McManus (eds.), *Half Humankind*, p. 269)

It is worth remarking that these fears also reveal a feature that is often found in assertions about the 'naturalness' of gender difference: if the difference is so natural, why is it so threatening for women to behave in a way not given them by 'nature'; and, indeed, how is such 'unnatural' behaviour possible? The most famous poetic rendering of a man's concern about women cross-dressing appears in Donne's Elegy, 'On his Mistress' (Donne, *Complete English Poems*, pp. 118–19). The lover, who is off to war, urges his lady to abandon her plans to dress as a lad and go with him as his page. The details of his argument reveal how interlinked and, therefore, potentially fragile are the elements commonly presented as assuring gender difference. The lover in asking the lady to be his 'true mistress' recalls to her her proper role in his past courtship of her, when he won her 'remorse' through 'my words' masculine persuasive force'. The manipulativeness of such argumentation is revealed when he continues by urging her to 'feed on this *flattery*, / That absent lovers one in th'other be' (emphasis mine). If none of this succeeds in convincing her, he has a dirtier trick yet: she is threatened that her true femininity will shine through her clothes, and she will be the object of sexual advances wherever she goes; or that 'th'indifferent Italian' will happily rape her as a boy, anyway. It is better for her to stay at home and dream of him. Deliberately or not, the poem makes it clear that what is really being protected here is not the woman, but gender differentiation.

It may well be the debate about the man/woman, the cross-dressing woman, was based more on fears and fantasies than on the actual behaviour of particular individuals. There is evidence, though, of some women choosing to assume men's clothes for their own reasons. One of the most delightful explorations of the pleasures for a woman of abandoning female garb appears in the memoirs of Ann, Lady Fanshawe, a royalist who travelled widely with her husband during the Civil War and Commonwealth period. She recalls an episode in 1650 when, at the sighting of a Turkish warship, all the women on her ship were ordered by her husband to hide below deck, because 'if they saw women, they would take us for merchants and boord us':

> This beast captain had locked me up in the cabine. I knocked and called long to no purpose, untill at length a cabine boy came and opened the doore. I, all in teares, desired him to be so good as to give me his blew throm cap he wore and his tarred coat, which he did, and I gave him half a crown, and putting them on and flinging away my night's clothes, I crept up softly and stood upon the deck by my husband's side as free from sickness and fear as, I confess, from discretion; but it was the effect of that passion which I could never master. By this time the 2 vessels were ingaged in parley and so well satisfyd with speech and sight of each other's forces that the Turk's man-of-war tacked about and we continued our course. But when your father saw it convenient to retreat, looking upon me he blessed himself and snatched me up in his armes, saying, 'Good God, that love can make this change!' And though he seemingly chid me, he would laugh at it as often as he remembred that voyage.[32]

The terms in which this incident is described are as revealing as the forms of persuasion used in Donne's poem: she portrays herself as not rebellious but ruled by a 'passion' that we are required, through her husband's approving reaction, to read as love for her man. It is the ship's captain, not her husband, who is criticized as a 'beast' for locking her up. She wins the cabin boy over not with threats or with money, but with feminine tears. Rebellion, then, can be managed, and recorded, as long as it is written about as if motivated at its heart by properly feminine desire.

The wifely behaviour described and excused here by Lady Fanshawe is not at all the kind of thing commended by the ideologues of the day. If the nation, and the world as a whole, was to continue in an orderly fashion, women must accept their proper subservient position and display the required characteristics. It is no accident that an integral part of Jonson's harmonious vision in 'To Penshurst' is a good housewife who is also an honourable spouse:

> Thy lady's noble, fruitful, chaste withal.
> His children thy great lord may call his own:
> A fortune, in this age, but rarely known.
>
> (Jonson, *Complete Poems*, p. 97)

The fiction was that women's virtue, or their beauty, or, failing all else their class status or size of dowry would bring them security, and help ensure stability in the country. The reality, however, was that women were designed to be powerless whilst appearing to have control. The fact that this version of womanhood is an active social construction, and one invented by men in the interests of maintaining hierarchies, is displayed in Carew's 'A Married Woman':

> When I shall marry, if I doe not find
> A wife thus moulded, I'le create this mind:
> Nor from her noble birth, nor ample dower,
> Beauty, or wit, shall she derive a power
> To prejudice my Right; but if she be
> A subject borne, she shall be so to me:
> As to the soule the flesh, as Appetite
> To reason is, which shall our wils unite;
> In habits so confirm'd, as no rough sway
> Shall once appeare, if she but learne t'obay.
>
> (Carew, *Poems*, pp. 115–16)

The power of the husband is directly tied here to the structure of domination and subordination within the state: 'if she be / A subject borne, she shall be so to me'. It is also linked to the control of the mind or soul over the body: the man is reason/the soul, the woman is flesh/appetite. If she will give her 'free' consent, he will not be rough with her. Such vehement assertions, and explicit threats, contrast sharply with the reworking of these connections that is made by Bradstreet in her poem quoted earlier.

During the seventeenth century the asserted naturalness of these power structures came under increasing pressure as the focus of state power, the monarchy and national church, were first challenged and then overthrown.[33] Thomas Edwards, a presbyterian divine, attempted to persuade men against tolerating heterodox religious belief by reminding them that their own power as husbands and fathers was intimately related to the authority of the church and state:

> Oh! let the ministers, therefore, oppose toleration . . . possess the magistrates of the evil of it, yea and the people too, showing them how if a toleration were granted, they should never have peace in their families more, or ever after have command of wives, children, servants.[34]

That the distribution of power within the church and state mirrored that between the genders had long been asserted: James I, for instance, in his speech to Parliament on 21 March 1610 had justified his authority over the nation by comparing it to that of a father in the family.[35] The ubiquitous appearance of this parallel, and the fact that the economic basis of society was indeed partially dependent on the alliances and exchanges produced through marriage contracts, makes it unsurprising that poetry presenting itself as solely concerned with personal emotion sometimes also encoded a discussion of public political matters.[36] After 1629, when Charles I dismissed Parliament and ruled for eleven years without it, social tensions increased, and many poems appeared that long for an escape from such conflicts, sometimes linking this with a call to return to the 'peace' of loving relationships.[37] One of the most interesting of these was written by Sir Richard Fanshawe, the husband of the cross-dressing woman quoted above. In 'An Ode, upon Occasion of His Majesty's Proclamation in the year 1630: Commanding the Gentry to Reside upon their Estates in the Country', he images England as the sole locus of peace and harmony in a Europe erupting in war, urging the gentry to stay away from the political conflicts of London and live on their country estates. In presenting the sweetness of domestic life, he evokes a conventional image of romantic love, the nightingale; and in this moment is made manifest the difference between the actual power relations between the sexes, and the politically motivated poetic use of a mythology of loving contentment:

> There shall you heare the Nightingale
> (The harmelesse Syren of the wood)
> How prettily she tells a tale
> Of rape and blood.[38]

Although the nightingale is typically associated in male poetry with love, the classical myths which explain the nightingale's song, and to which Fanshawe refers here in unusual detail, shows the linking of this bird to romantic love silences the female perspective on what it can mean to be desired by a man. Philomela, the woman who was metamorphosed into the nightingale, was raped by her brother-in-law Tereus, who then cut out her tongue to prevent her betraying him. To see the family as a centre of loving harmony that can be contrasted to public discontent, one has to forget the inequality of power that could be made manifest in rape. Even whilst Fanshawe presents romantic love as a centre of harmony, the terms in which he does this betray the underlying social reality. As the author of *The Law's Resolutions of Women's Rights* sharply reminded his reader, if a woman resisted the advances of her aspiring 'lover' he could take her by force:

When sweet words, fair promises, tempting, flattering, swearing, lying will not serve to beguile the poor soul, then with rough handling, violence and plain strength of arms they are, or have been heretofore, rather made prisoners to lust's thieves than wives and companions to faithful honest lovers. So drunken are men with their own lusts, and the poison of Ovid's false precept, 'Vim licet appellant, vis est ea grata puellis' ['You may call it force: that force is pleasing to girls'], that if the rampier [i.e., 'rampart'] of laws were not betwixt women and their harms, I verily think none of them, being above twelve years of age and under a hundred, being either fair or rich, should be able to escape ravishing.   (p. 377)

It is worth adding that once raped, she might be forced to marry her attacker rather than live dishonoured and unmarriageable. Alice Thornton's autobiography records her relief that Jerimy Smithson's plot to rape her and thereby force her to marry him was revealed in time for it to be foiled.[39] It is also the case that it was quite legal for a man to beat his wife: the nightingale's tale is indeed one 'Of rape and blood'.

It is the silencing of the nightingale, or of the abused woman that she can be seen to represent, that forms the final focus of this essay. One of the most marked features of male love poetry is the silence within it of the women it is supposedly addressed to: the woman is usually present as an object of desire, but not as a speaking subject. Indeed, as has frequently been commented upon, the very existence of the poetry often had little to do with the woman or women to whom it was ostensibly addressed: the writing of poetry was a social skill which brought acceptance within the upper echelons of male society, its subject-matter and tone dictated by the expectations of that grouping. It is for this reason, most of all, that the writings by women of the period are precious: they demonstrate the limitations of the required male stances. Margaret Cavendish, Duchess of Newcastle, for instance, was fiercely critical of the cleverness of much male writing:

> The reason why men run in such obscure conceits, is because they think their wit will be esteemed, and seem more when it lies in an odde and unusual way, which makes their verse not like a smooth running stream; but as if they were shelves of sand, or rocks in the way, and though the water in those places goeth with more force, and makes a greater sound: yet it goeth hard and uneasy. As if to expresse a thing hard, were to make it better.[40]

Donne was criticized by Dryden for the fact that he 'affects the metaphysics, not only in his satires, but in his amorous verses, where nature only should reign; and perplexes the minds of the fair sex with the nice speculations of philosophy, when he should engage their hearts, and entertain them with the softnesses of love',[41] but this remark missed the point. The person who was expected to be impressed was not the lady, but other men.

The outbreak of civil war not only ended for ever the assumption that kings ruled by divine right and could not be challenged. It also released into print the voices of many women protesting against their confinement to roles of domesticity and/or desired lady. The first great outpouring of published women's writing is concerned not with love and courtship, but with the structures of the public world and, crucially, with women's right to voice opinions on such matters. This shift of perspective was put most eloquently by Hester Biddle as she lamented the return to 'business as usual' in the debauched Restoration court:

> Oh you high and lofty ones! who spendeth God's Creation upon your lusts, and doth not feed the hungry, nor cloath the naked, but they are ready to perish in the streets; both old and young, lame and blind lyeth in your streets, and at your Masse-house doors, crying for bread, which even melteth my heart, and maketh the soul of the righteous to mourn: did not the Lord make all men and women upon the earth of one mould, why then should there be so much honour and respect unto some men and women, and not unto others, but they are almost naked for want of Cloathing, and almost starved for want of Bread? and are you not all brethren, and all under the Government of one King? Oh repent! least the Lord consume you, and be ashamed, and cloath the naked, and feed the hungry, and set the oppressed free.[42]

NOTES

1 John Donne, *The Complete English Poems*, ed. A. J. Smith (Harmondsworth: Penguin, 1971, 1976), p. 64.
2 Ben Jonson, *The Complete Poems*, ed. George Parfitt (Harmondsworth: Penguin, 1975), p. 103.
3 *The Poetical Works of Robert Herrick*, ed. L. C. Martin (Oxford: Clarendon Press, 1956, 1963), p. 109.
4 Barbara J. Todd, 'The Remarrying Widow: A Stereotype Reconsidered', in *Women in English Society 1500–1800*, ed. Mary Prior (London and New York: Methuen, 1985), pp. 54–92.
5 Miranda Chaytor, 'Household and Kinship: Ryton in the Late 16th and Early 17th Centuries', *History Workshop Journal* 10 (1980): 24–60.
6 Lawrence Stone, 'Family History in the 1980s: Past Achievements and Future Trends', *Journal of Interdisciplinary History* 12.1 (1981): 58.
7 Lawrence Stone, *The Family, Sex and Marriage in England 1500–1800*, abridged edn (New York: Harper and Row, 1977, 1979), p. 40.
8 Thomas Gataker, *Marriage Duties Briefly Couched Together* (London, 1620), pp. 9–10.
9 T. E., *The Lawes Resolutions of Women's Rights* (London, 1632), p. 125. OED defines 'coverture' as 'the condition or position of a woman ... when she is by law under the authority and protection of her husband'.
10 Even Elizabeth I presented herself to her nation as a 'Prince' in order to enhance her status. See Allison Heisch, 'Queen Elizabeth and the Persistence of Patriarchy', *Feminist Review* 4 (1980: 45–56); Lisa Jardine, *Still Harping on Daughters: Women and Drama in the Age of Shakespeare* (Brighton: Harvester, 1983); Katherine Usher Henderson and Barbara F. McManus (eds.), *Half Humankind: Contexts and Text of the Controversy about Women in England, 1540–1640* (University of Illinois Press, 1985).

11 Katherine Philips, *Poems By the most deservedly Admired Mrs Katherine Philips The Matchless Orinda* (London, 1667), pp. 37–8. Repr. in *Minor Poets of the Caroline Period*, ed. George Saintsbury (Oxford: Clarendon Press, 1905). Selections in *Salt and Bitter and Good: Three Centuries of English and American Women Poets*, ed. Cora Kaplan (New York and London: Paddington Press, 1975), pp. 41–8; Moira Ferguson (ed.), *First Feminists: British Women Writers 1578–1799* (Bloomington: Indiana University Press, 1985), pp. 102–13; *Kissing The Rod: An Anthology of 17th Century Women's Verse*, ed. Germaine Greer, Jeslyn Medoff, Melinda Sansone, and Susan Hastings (London: Virago, 1988), pp. 186–203.

12 Philips, 'To my Excellent Lucasia, on our Friendship', *Poems*, pp. 51–2.

13 Anne Bradstreet, *Several Poems Compiled with great variety of Wit and Learning* (Boston: 1678), pp. 240–1. Modern facsimile intro. J. K. Piercey, *The Tenth Muse (1650) and, from the Manuscripts: Meditations Divine and Morall, Together with Letters and Occasional Pieces* (Gainesville: Scholars' Facsimiles and Reprints, 1965). Modern editions: *The Works of Anne Bradstreet*, ed. Jeannine Hensley (Cambridge, Mass.: Harvard University Press, 1967); *The Complete Works of Anne Bradstreet*, ed. J. R. McElrath and A. P. Robb (Boston: Twayne, 1981). Selections in Kaplan, *Salt and Bitter and Good*, pp. 27–39; Greer et al. (eds.), *Kissing the Rod*, pp. 119–40; *The Norton Anthology of Poetry*, 3rd edn, ed. A. W. Allison et al. (New York and London: W. W. Norton, 1983), pp. 322–6.

14 George Parfitt, *John Donne: A Literary Life* (London: Macmillan, 1989); *Works of Anne Bradstreet*.

15 Stone, *Family, Sex and Marriage*. For economic considerations in other classes, see Chaytor, 'Household and Kinship'.

16 Lawrence Stone, 'Marriage among the English Nobility in the 16th and 17th Centuries', *Comparative Studies in Sociology and History* 3 (1960–1): 189.

17 *Women Beware Women* 1.2.171–81, *The Selected Plays of Thomas Middleton*, ed. D. L. Frost (Cambridge University Press, 1978), p. 204.

18 *The Complete Poetry of Richard Crashaw*, ed. G. W. Williams (New York University Press, 1972), p. 482, lines 103–4.

19 *The Poems of Thomas Carew with His Masque of Coelum Britannicum*, ed. R. Dunlap (Oxford: Clarendon Press, 1949, 1964), p. 82, lines 35, 33.

20 *The Poems of Richard Lovelace*, ed. C. H. Wilkinson (Oxford: Clarendon Press, 1930, 1963), p. 27.

21 Henry King, 'The Surrender', in *The Metaphysical Poets*, ed. Helen Gardner (Harmondsworth: Penguin, 1957, 1972), p. 108.

22 Thomas Randolph, 'Upon Love Fondly Refused for Conscience's Sake', in *The Literature of Renaissance England*, ed. John Hollander and Frank Kermode (Oxford University Press, 1973), p. 604.

23 *Complete English Poems*, p. 125.

24 *Jane Anger her Protection for Women*, in Henderson and McManus (eds.), *Half Humankind*, p. 183. This pamphlet is one of several published by women in the late sixteenth and early seventeenth centuries to defend their sex against explicitly misogynistic attacks. See Henderson and McManus (eds.), *Half Humankind*; and Simon Shepherd (ed.), *The Women's Sharp Revenge* (London: Fourth Estate, 1985). On courtship language see also *The Case of Madam Mary*

Carleton, in Elspeth Graham, Hilary Hinds, Elaine Hobby, and Helen Wilcox (eds.), *Her Own Life: Autobiographical Writings by Seventeenth-Century Englishwomen* (London and New York: Routledge, 1989).

25 Aphra Behn, *Poems Upon Several Occasions: With a Voyage to the Island of Love* (London, 1684), p. 75. Repr. in Kaplan, *Salt and Bitter and Good*, pp. 51–5. Behn selection in Greer et al., *Kissing the Rod.*, pp. 240–60.

26 See also Suckling, 'Farewell to Love', in *The Poems, Plays and Other Remains of Sir John Suckling*, ed. W. C. Hazlitt (London: Reeves and Turner, 1892), pp. 45–7, where the no longer desired mistress is presented as monstrous because of her attempts to be attractive.

27 Joseph Swetnam, *The Arraignment Of Lewd, Idle, Froward, and Unconstant Women* (1615), pp. 15, 20. Repr. in Henderson and McManus (eds.), *Half Humankind*.

28 *The Honour of Vertue . . . Mrs Elizabeth Crashawe. Who dyed in child-birth and was buried in Whit-Chappell: Octob. 8. 1620. In the 24 yeare of her age*, excerpted in Henderson and McManus (eds.), *Half Humankind*, pp. 343–50.

29 Hesiod, *Theogony*, lines 592–3, trans. Richard Lattimore in *Hesiod* (Ann Arbor: University of Michigan Press, 1959), p. 158; quoted in Henderson and McManus (eds.), *Half Humankind*, p. 5.

30 See Louis B. Wright, *Middle-Class Culture in Elizabethan England* (Ithaca: Cornell University Press, 1958), p. 493. The report of James I's order appears in a letter from John Chamberlain dated 25 January 1620.

31 *Hic Mulier*, excerpted in Henderson and McManus (eds.), *Half Humankind*, pp. 264–76.

32 *The Memoirs of Anne, Lady Halkett and Ann, Lady Fanshawe*, ed. John Loftis (Oxford: Clarendon Press, 1979), pp. 127–8. On cross-dressing, see Rudolf Dekker and Lotte van de Pol, *The Tradition of Female Transvestism in Early Modern Europe* (London, Macmillan, 1989).

33 See Elaine Hobby, *Virtue of Necessity: English Women's Writing 1649–1688* (London: Virago, 1988).

34 Thomas Edwards, *Gangraena* (1646), Part 1, p. 156.

35 Extract in *Seventeenth-century England: A Changing Culture*, vol. 1: *Primary Sources*, ed. Ann Hughes (London: The Open University, 1980), pp. 28–9.

36 Arthur Marrotti, *John Donne, Coterie Poet* (Madison: University of Wisconsin Press, 1986); Achsah Guibbory, '"Oh, Let Mee Not Serve So": The Politics of Love in Donne's *Elegies*', *ELH* 57 (1990): 811–33.

37 See George Parfitt, *English Poetry of the Seventeenth Century* (London and New York: Longman, 1985, 1992).

38 Richard Fanshawe, 'An Ode, upon occasion of His Majesties Proclamation in the year 1630', in Gardner (ed.), *The Metaphysical Poets*, p. 173.

39 Alice Thornton, *The Autobiography of Mrs Alice Thornton* (London: Surtees Society, 1875), p. 47n.

40 Margaret Cavendish, *The Worlds Olio* (1655), p. 10.

41 Quoted in *A Selection from John Dryden*, ed. Donald Thomas (London: Longman, 1972), p. 14, from Dryden's *A Discourse concerning the Original and Progress of Satire* (1693).

42 Hester Biddle, *The Trumpet of the Lord* (London: 1662), p. 12.

FURTHER READING

Fraser, Antonia, *The Weaker Vessel: Woman's Lot in Seventeenth-Century England* (London: Methuen, 1985)

Graham, Elspeth, Hinds, Hilary, Hobby, Elaine, and Wilcox, Helen (eds.), *Her Own Life: Autobiographical Writings by Seventeenth-Century Englishwomen* (London and New York: Routledge, 1989)

Greer, Germaine, Medoff, Jeslyn, Sansone, Melinda, and Hastings, Susan (eds.), *Kissing The Rod: An Anthology of 17th Century Women's Verse* (London: Virago, 1988)

Parfitt, George, *English Poetry of the Seventeenth Century* (London and New York: Longman, 1985, 1992)

Prior, Mary (ed.), *Women in English Society 1500–1800* (London and New York: Methuen, 1985)

Usher Henderson, Katherine and McManus, Barbara F., (eds.), *Half Humankind: Contexts and Text of the Controversy about Women in England, 1540–1640* (Urbana and Chicago: University of Illinois Press, 1985)

3

ARTHUR F. MAROTTI

Manuscript, print, and the social history of the lyric

In the English Renaissance, poetic texts were related to their social contexts both in their original conditions of production and in their subsequent history of reception through the media of manuscript and print. Since lyric poems, in particular, were primarily occasional, composed in specific circumstances for known audiences, factors of class, gender, patronage, kinship, friendship, political partisanship, and religious allegiance were inseparable from aesthetic issues in such works. Poets were acutely conscious of the social contexts of their work, and, especially when their poems were disseminated in manuscript, readers were able to appropriate poetic artefacts and adapt them to their individual needs. In the course of the seventeenth century lyrics were in the process of changing their status from that of ephemeral productions transmitted in manuscript within restricted social environments to that of durable artefacts widely distributed through the medium of print. While most lyric poetry first circulated in manuscript to family members, friends, colleagues, and patrons had specific social uses, print culture began to highlight the aesthetic features of poems, recontextualized their meanings, and preserved them for readerships beyond their original audiences. Throughout the seventeenth century, however, *two* systems of literary transmission thrived and interacted. In the manuscript system, the social history of the lyric is more visible; but printed verse was also socially positioned and both media were part of a process of cultural change that shaped the modern institution of literature.

In the Renaissance lyric poems served as instruments of social intercourse: they could be passed personally to friends and family members, performed in social gatherings, sent as verse epistles or as accompaniments to prose letters. Poems were used to celebrate births, commemorate deaths, pursue a courtship, seek benefits from a patron or patroness, or express gratitude for favours received, present (or serve as) gifts at New Year, cement the bonds of friendship, attack or answer the attacks of rivals or enemies, engage in literary competition, commend the writings of others, mock or satirize social inferiors, equals or superiors, and share private devotional exercises with others.[1]

Take, for example, the poetry of Ben Jonson. Although he was interested in the ways in which print could preserve and monumentalize texts and he published a carefully designed folio volume of plays and poems in 1616 as his *Works*, he wrote basically occasional verse that was connected with his ongoing social relationships. In the *Conversations with Drummond*, we learn, for instance, about the circumstances in which Jonson composed one of the lyrics gathered in the folio, 'Song: That Women are but Men's Shadows' (*Forest* 7):[2] 'Pembrok and his Lady discoursing the Earl said the Woemen were mens shadowes, and she maintained them, both appealing to Johnson, he affirmed it true, for which my Lady gave a pennance to prove it in a Verse, hence his epigrame.'[3] William Herbert, Earl of Pembroke, to whom Jonson dedicated his *Epigrams* in the 1616 volume, was a friend and patron, only one of several members of the extended Sidney family Jonson addressed in his poems: the poet wrote 'To Penshurst' (*Forest* 2) for Sir Robert Sidney and encomiastic verse for such other family members as Lady Mary Wroth and Elizabeth, Countess of Rutland,[4] the last of whom, we also learn in the *Conversations*, was accused by her jealous husband of having 'keept table to poets' (line 358). The *Conversations* also names the occasion of Sir John Roe's epistle to Jonson, 'The State and men's affairs are the best plays':[5] 'Sir John Roe loved him & when they two were ushered by my Lord Suffolk from a Mask, Roe wrott a moral epistle to him, which began that next to plays the Court and the State were the best. God threatneth Kings, Kings Lords & Lords do us' (lines 155–9). The same document also indicates that Jonson's private satiric poem on the close friend of the Countess of Bedford, Cecelia Bulstrode, 'An Epigram on the Court Pucelle [i.e. slut] (*Underwood* 51) 'was stolen out of his pocket by a Gentleman who drank him drowsie & given Mistress Boulstraid, which brought him great displeasur' (lines 646–8). Jonson, Donne, Sir Thomas Roe, and other writers and wits shared in the social, intellectual, and literary recreations of the Bedford–Bulstrode circle, but the piece was obviously not intended for the eyes of its subject.[6]

Jonson wrote to friends, patrons, and patronesses with specific purposes – for example, to reaffirm social bonds or to signal his clientage and needs – but he generally used the occasions of addressing particular individuals as opportunities for setting forth his social, intellectual, and moral values. In the encomiastic verse, he instructed others by means of praising them, a strategy he adopted also in the court masque. He developed also what he came to call the 'Tribe of Ben' (*Underwood* 49), surrounding himself with friends and disciples who appreciated his poetry and his witty conversation.

Though he was eager to exploit the medium of print in order to reach a larger audience, he continued to hold his select coterie audience as a model for the behaviour of those unknown readers who were less under his control.

In the socially restricted confines of manuscript circulation, Jonson could be more casual about his work than he could in print, even, on occasion, opening the door to co-creative participation by others. In one of his poems 'To John Donne' (*Epigrams* 96) he refers to his sending the poet his epigrams for criticism and comment. Professing to care more for the critical attention of a respected poet/intellectual than for the general approval of a popular audience, Jonson idealizes Donne as a reader and welcomes his contribution to the process of rewriting the text. Within the confines of private circulation Jonson views his epigrams as revisable, not only by himself, but also by trusted friends. By contrast, when published in his 1616 *Works*, they were presented as the perfected texts meant to be fixed by print and preserved for posterity.

Although it is almost impossible to lay hold of specific evidence about the particular social occasions for which John Donne composed most of his lyrics, it is not difficult to see how many of his poems were associated with particular social milieux or occasions: early pieces like 'Community', 'Confined Love', 'Love's Usury', and 'The Indifferent' would have suited the social environment of the Inns of Court, where Donne functioned from about 1592 to 1596; 'The Paradox', 'Negative Love', and 'The Ecstasy', were probably written in poetic competition with his friend Sir Edward Herbert; some pieces utilizing the conventions of poetic compliment – 'The Funeral', 'A Fever', and 'Twickenham Garden', for example – were probably composed in the context of his relationship to Lucy, Countess of Bedford, his patroness for several years. And, of course, poems were associated with Donne's relationship with the woman he married, both before and after they were wed; it is obvious that at least some of his valedictions, for example, were written on the occasion of bidding farewell to Ann More Donne before his journey to the continent in 1605. Later, 'A Hymn to Christ, at the Author's last going into Germany' was written on the occasion of Donne's leaving England to serve as chaplain on the Doncaster embassy in 1619.[7]

Thomas Carew, who moved from Oxford, to the Inns of Court, to the court, and had a good appreciation of Donne's verse as coterie literature, composed basically occasional verse in the 1620s and 1630s within a court-centred coterie that included Jonson, Selden, Cotton, Digby, May, Davenant, Townshend, and Suckling'.[8] When his and other Cavalier lyrics left this setting, however, and found their way into the manuscript collections of university students and the provincial aristocracy, their social elitism was part of their attraction, but the texts became less courtly – read in more general terms as sophisticated wit set in opposition to middle-class and Puritan attitudes.[9] The posthumous 1640 edition of Carew's poetry broadened its audience still further.

Sometimes the social relations of amateur poets provided the occasion for the composition of verse: answer poems and competitive pieces on set themes were produced, for example, by John Donne and Sir Henry Wotton ('Sir, more than kisses, letters mingle Soules' is answered by Wotton's own epistle "Tis not a coate of gray or Shepheardes life');[10] by Ben Jonson and (his poetic son) Thomas Randolph (Jonson's 'Ode to Himself' (*Ungathered Verse* 53) and Randolph's 'An answer to Mr Ben Jonson's Ode to persuade him not to leave the stage');[11] by the Christ Church (Oxford) poets Richard Corbett, William Strode, and Jeramiel Terrant, who competitively composed poems on the preservation from iconoclasm of the stained glass windows of Fairford church;[12] and, most notably, by William Herbert, Earl of Pembroke and Sir Benjamin Rudyerd. In 1660, John Donne, Jr published poems by these last two writers in a poetical miscellany disguised as a Pembroke–Rudyerd collection: *Poems Written by the Right Honorable William Earl of Pembroke, Lord Steward of his Majesties Houshold, whereof Many of which are answered by way of Repartee, by Sir Benjamin Ruddier, Knight. With several Distinct Poems Written by them Occasionally, and Apart* (1660). Interestingly, their most famous poem-and-answer set, Pembroke's 'If her disdain least change in you can move' and Rudyerd's "Tis Love breeds Love in me, and cold disdain' (printed in the 1635–9 editions of Donne) was conflated into a single poem in the Pembroke–Rudyerd edition and some manuscripts attribute the pieces to Sir Henry Wotton and John Donne.[13] Throughout the seventeenth century, there are dozens of examples of poem-and-answer sets, or poetic parodies and imitations, of competitive versifying on set themes – all underscoring the social character of lyric verse.[14]

In this period, even what would seem to be the most private of lyric kinds, the religious lyric, was fundamentally social verse. Donne's harrowingly self-examining 'Goodfriday, 1613: Riding Westward', for example, was supposedly composed en route from Sir Henry Goodyer's estate to Sir Edward Herbert's Montgomery Castle and it was probably shared with both men.[15] Donne forwarded 'A Litany' to Goodyer with the explanation that it (like his other religious verse), was 'for lesser Chapels, which are my friends'.[16] He sent the *La Corona* sonnets to Magdalen Herbert with a dedicatory poem; the Earl of Dorset was given six of his holy sonnets. George Herbert, a more private religious poet than Donne, committed *The Temple* to Nicholas Ferrar, leaving it to his judgement whether to destroy it or (as Herbert undoubtedly wished) to publish it more widely for the edification of a general readership. Richard Crashaw dedicated *Carmen Deo Nostro* (1652) to his patroness, the Countess of Denbigh, in the hope that it might help convert her to Roman Catholicism. Thomas Traherne composed his *Centuries of Meditations* within the context of the pious social circle gathered around Susanna Hopton.[17] Henry Vaughan, whose religious verse is a sign of sociopolitical alienation during the Civil War and Interregnum, formulated private religious experience as a response to public events. During this period religious poetry was inescapably political.[18]

The social character of seventeenth-century lyric verse was reinforced by its circulation in manuscript. Of those who wrote lyric poetry in the period between Donne and Marvell, the majority preferred to restrict their work to manuscript circulation, many first functioned within a system of manuscript transmission and then organized their work for publication, and very few took a direct route from private composition to typographical presentation of their work to a large public. John Donne, Francis Beaumont, John Hoskins, Sir John Roe, Sir Henry Wotton, William Herbert (Earl of Pembroke), Sir Benjamin Rudyerd, Richard Corbett, William Strode, Thomas Carew, Thomas Randolph, Sir John Suckling, and Andrew Marvell confined their work to coterie circulation. Ben Jonson, Robert Herrick, Richard Crashaw, Henry Vaughan, Henry King, Edmund Waller, and Richard Lovelace first allowed their texts to be passed about in manuscript and then to be printed. George Herbert's and John Milton's work did not get distributed widely in manuscript but took a fairly direct route from the private papers of the author to the pages of a book.

Given the fact that print had been working its large-scale cultural transformations for well over a century, it is surprising to discover how vigorous was the system of manuscript transmission and compilation in seventeenth-century England. Peter Beal notes that the high-water mark for the production of such texts was the 1620s and 1630s, a time one would expect print to have replaced the older system of literary transmission.[19] The lyric, of course, as the most occasional of the literary kinds (with the exception of the personal letter), was slower to make the transition from manuscript culture to print culture than such other forms as prose fiction, poetic romance or epic, or drama. But, as least as far as English texts are concerned, one must look both to general and specific reasons why writers and audiences favoured the manuscript environment for lyric poetry for so long.

The system of manuscript transmission, which was essentially an elitist practice, had a remarkable durability through much of the seventeenth century, continuing to foster group solidarity among academic, professional, and upper-class coteries as well as embattled minorities such as recusant Catholics. During the pre-Civil War, Civil War, and Commonwealth and Protectorate periods, for example, dozens of manuscript miscellanies were produced in connection with Oxford University and royalist households: these preserve the work of such poets as Corbett, Strode, Herrick, Carew, and Randolph, along with that of an earlier generation of writers such as Ralegh, Donne, and Jonson. Such collections contain a large number of encomiastic poems, elegies, and epitaphs addressed to or written about members of the royal family, the Duke of Buckingham, the Earl of Strafford, and others close to James I and Charles I, but also anti-Puritan and anti-Parliament satiric verse. They preserve poems either that would have been dangerous to disseminate in print or that spoke to the partisan and private concerns of their compilers and their immediate audiences. In addition to the obscene verse that would have been censored in the medium of print (as three of Donne's elegies were from the 1633 edition), these poems include (illegal) poetical libels, political satires and protest poems, and other pieces commenting on contemporary public events and personages, including the monarchs. Much of this material did not get into printed anthologies until the last few years of the Interregnum. Some manuscript collections run to several hundred poems and constitute possibly the most underused body of social-historical evidence for the study of the literature of the time. Because modern literary history has been based, for the most part, on a canonizing process taking place within print culture and textual scholars have utilized these documents for very limited purposes, the *socioliterary* history implicit within the manuscript system has largely been ignored.

Since it was more obviously tied to social occasions and social relations, the surviving manuscript miscellanies and poetical anthologies contain some interesting traces of the conditions of production, transmission, and reception of texts and groups of texts. Sometimes manuscripts preserve (or fabricate) specific social occasions for poems, that, in print, have a more general meaning. For example, the Carew poem that appeared in the 1640 printed edition of that poet's work under the title 'Secrecy Protested', was given a very specific context in Nicholas Burghe's manuscript collection, 'A gentle man that had a Mistress, and after was constrayned to marry a nother, the first was afrayd that hee would reveale to his new wyfe, their secret Loves whereuppon hee wrights thus to her' (Bod. MS Ash. 38, p. 25).[20] The printed text comes across as a conventional promise of secrecy in love, while the manuscript version has a much more specific (fictional or real) social context. BL MS Sloane 1446 provides for Henry Harington's poem, 'Reade and pittie as you goe', the following explanatory title: 'Mr H: Harington to the Countess of Bedford hee beinge her kinseman and in prison for debt; his freends neglecting him for feare of displeasing her in reguard of her distasting and beinge angry at some of his unthriftie courses' (fol. 46r). The situation of a young spendthrift appealing to a powerful relative for assistance would have interested a whole class of individuals similarly dependent on the system of kinship and patronage.

The material workings of the system of manuscript transmission throw light on the social history of the texts being disseminated. The transmission of poems in loose sheets and booklets generally preceded the transcription of pieces in miscellanies or poetical anthologies.[21] Since such documents are the most perishable of literary records, there are very few surviving examples of this practice: most of those that we have were bound into the larger unit of the manuscript book, although, for example, poems in letters and in loose family papers have been preserved. In her study of the circulation of the verse of John Donne and Henry King, Margaret Crum speculates that the former's search in 1614 for his scattered verse resulted in a compilation of loose sheets and booklets of poems that were in circulation and that King's papers used by scribes collecting that poet's verse in their manuscript anthologies were similar documents.[22] Mary Hobbs points to good evidence that Carew's poems circulated first in a manner similar to that of Donne's and King's.[23] The 1640–1 (second) folio of Jonson's works contains Sir Kenelm Digby's explanation of why some portions of the ten-poem sequence to Venetia Digby were missing: 'A whole quaternion in the middest of this Poem is lost'[24] – that is a small four-leaf section made from a single folded sheet got separated from the rest of the booklet and was not recovered.

Some surviving manuscripts, bound either in their own time or subsequently, constitute gatherings into larger units of loose papers or fascicles. Many of these throw light on the transmission processes that precede deliberate collecting efforts. For example, Bod. MS Eng. Poet. c. 53, connected with the Lingard-Gutherie family, represents the gathering together of pages of folded correspondence into one collection.[25] BL MS Add. 23229, part of the larger collection of papers of Viscount Conway,[26] has many pages of folded correspondence, some containing poetry. One of the verses transmitted is a bawdy poem followed by a note on the other side of the paper from the transcriber: 'pray my Lord tell nobody from whom this Song comes, for I am ashamed to owne it' (fol. 43r–v). BL MS Add. 11743 is a composite volume of verse written by or related to members of the Fairfax family,[27] containing much folded correspondence and incorporating papers of different sizes. Nicholas Burghe's folio manuscript (Bod. MS Ash. 38) opens with a distinct bifolium containing three items: a poem identified as Donne's ('Fairwell yee guilded follies, pleasing troubles'), Bacon's 'The

World's A Bubble', and a piece beginning 'she that will eate hur breakfast in hur bed'. The remains of the wax stamped with someone's personal seal are on one of the sides of the paper (which is itself of smaller size than the sheets following). Bod. Rawl. Poet. MS 26 has several different units bound together, some bifolia, some regular folio booklets, tipped in quarto pages, and so on. One of the items seems to reproduce the form in which the piece was sent in correspondence: Corbett's encomiastic poem to the Duke of Buckingham, 'When I can pay my Parents, or my Kinge', is transcribed on fol. 6or with the subscription 'Yor Lor[rdship's] most humble servant to command. Rich[ard] Corbet ... Christs-church, this present New-yeares day 1621'. Written sideways in the margin is the note 'To the Duke of Buckingham. L[or]d George Villiers'.

At the other extreme from those collections that are gatherings of loose sheets and independent quires of writing are those blank books or 'table books' that were designed as pre-bound receptacles for the prose and poetry individuals wished to transcribe. These ranged from small pocket-size books that students and others could use for notes and jottings to quarto and folio volumes that would have made handsome presents and served the needs of more deliberate and serious collectors of texts. One of the items for sale from the pack of Autolycus in Shakespeare's *The Winter's Tale*, incidentally, is a 'table book' (4.4.601), the sort of gift the poet in Shakespeare's Sonnet 77 mentions having given to the young man.

Manuscript papers, miscellanies, and poetical anthologies might include information about the particulars of the transmission of the texts they contain. In Bod. MS Mal. 19, for example, the poem beginning 'Christ rode some 7 yeares since to Court' is introduced with the heading, 'Verses found in a box sealed, found at the Court, & delivered to the kinge' (p. 145). There is a note in Bod. MS Rawl. Poet. 26 about the poem. 'Who doubts of Providence, or God denyes', 'Mr Thomas Scott sent these verses by the hand of Dr John White to Sr Walter Raleigh; upon the setting forth of his Booke of the History of the World' (fol. 6v). The passing of manuscript collections *to* and the borrowing of them *from* others sometimes were noted within the documents themselves. In BL MS Sloane 396, for example, at the start of a transcription of Matthew Bacon's poems, there is a personal note: 'Brother Vessy Matt Bacon desires you to send this up againe to his mothers, when you have sithen usd it, or writt it out. J[eramiel?] T[errent?]' (fol. 2r). In Bod. MS Eng. Poet. c.50, a large folio collection of the mid-seventeenth century in which many hands are represented, there is a note at the end, apparently by one of the transcribers, to someone to whom the volume was being lent: 'the manuscript of Judge dodridge will shew you more. vale' (fol. 133v.).[28]

One can detect some of the connections between poetry and other aspects of compilers' intellectual and social lives in those miscellanies in which poems are found in the company of other written material. In personal commonplace-book miscellanies one is as likely to find recipes for brandy, household accounts, copies of correspondence, medical information, and business calculations as poetical texts of various kinds. For example, the miscellany of Simon Sloper (Bod. MS Eng. Poet. f. 10),[29] who was educated at Oxford, starts with a transcription of Bacon's essay 'Of Great Place' (fol. 2r), 'the catalogue of nobilitie' (fols. 3–5v), sheets on each of the colleges of Cambridge, a list of twenty-six English bishoprics, a table of the reigns of all English kings through to Charles I, notes on scriptural commonplaces, other passages from Bacon's essays, only beginning its poetical selections on fol. 84r, including the transcription of a series of numbered poetical extracts (fol. 87r), before returning toward the end of the manuscript to prose, 'Wittie Apothegms or Speeches' (fol. 123r–v) and medical receipts (fols. 125v–130v). Poetry, then, constitutes a minor feature in a miscellany in which a wide range of the compiler's intellectual and social interests is visible. The Interregnum manuscript kept by Sir Edward Dering (Hunt. MS HM 41536) contains a diary from October 1656 in the first part and poetry at the back of the volume in reverse transcription. BL MS Sloane 739 is basically a medical commonplace book in which extracts from Carew's poems are found on fols. 103vff. BL MS Egerton 4064 contains a large business diary, models of legal and financial documents and then, on fols. 231r–99v, forty-seven poems by Donne in a miscellaneous poetical collection whose items are numbered from 1 to 95. The commonplace-book collection of John Ramsey (Bod. MS Douce 280)[30] contains not only transcriptions from printed literature such as Spenser's 'Mother Hubbard's Tale', 'Tears of the Muses', and 'The Visions of Petrarch', songs from published books of songs and madrigals, Francis Sabie's *The Fisherman's Tale* (published 1595) and its continuation, *Flora's Fortune* (published 1595), individual poems by the Earl of Essex, Robert Southwell, and Ramsey himself, but also 'A Rule to find the golden or prime number', a discussion of the organization of and admissions to Cambridge University, a translation of one book of Caesar's *Commentaries*, medical receipts, lists of the offices of England, of the Kings of England since the Conquest, of Lords, Knights, Captains, Bishoprics, and Counties of England, and comments on theology and on English history and politics. It also has more personal items: a partial autobiography, a family genealogy, the copy of Ramsey's will, a reading programme, instructions to his son and heir, and the family coat of arms. Poetry is, of course, a minor feature of this miscellany, but it is certainly embedded in a context of the compiler's intellectual, political, and familial, as well as literary interests.

The social environments with which manuscript collections of verse were connected include the university, the Inns of Court, and aristocratic and middle-class households. The majority of such documents from the sixteenth and seventeenth centuries developed in university settings, the great period for university anthologies starting about 1620 and running through the mid-1640s. Of these surviving manuscripts, an extraordinary number originated at Oxford, at Christ Church. Mary Hobbs, who has studied the relationships among these manuscripts, has traced the influence of practices of verse-composition encouraged at Westminster School, which educated many Christ Church poets, and of such individual poets as George Morley, Brian Duppa, Richard Corbett, William Strode, and William Cartwright on the development of circulating groups of poems that entered into the expanding collections of this period. She suggests that William Strode and George Morley, who were both at Christ Church for long periods, allowed pupils to copy poems from their personal anthologies and that this may partly account for the large number of surviving manuscripts from that Oxford college.[31] The title page of Folger MS V.a.262, for example, labels the collection 'Divers Sonnets & poems compiled by certaine gentil Clerks and Ryme-Wrights', testifying to the shared practices of poetical anthologizing at the University. Folger MS V.a.345 is written in many different hands, signalling a group effort at anthologizing. Compilers of poetic anthologies were associated with other Oxford colleges, especially New College[32] and St John's, but Christ Church was the social centre of this activity. Many Oxford anthologies not unexpectedly contain verse of local, topical interest, especially short satiric poems on deceased, disgraced, or ridiculous university figures, but they also have an eye on the larger sociopolitical world. It is interesting that the full title of the 1656 printed anthology *Parnassus Biceps* refers to the poems it contains as 'Composed by the best wits that were in both the Universities before their Dissolution', signalling that the verse came from the time before the complete victory of Parliamentary forces in the Civil War. The fall of Oxford as the king's headquarters on 24 June 1646 was a significant date in this reckoning.

Since students at the university came from different levels of the social hierarchy, it is fair to say that in this environment the practices of manuscript transmission most dramatically cut across social classes. Nevertheless, one of the obvious reasons for the persistence of the manuscript system of literary transmission through the seventeenth century was that it stood opposed to the more democratic medium of print and it allowed those who participated in it to feel that they were part of a social as well as an intellectual elite. For example, a short poem found on the first page of a large, collaborative Christ Church anthology was obviously composed by a student who was not a member of the moneyed classes, someone who identified himself as a scholar:

> My wits my wealth, my learning is my lands
> My gownes my goods, my bookes for buildings stand,
> Arts are my acres, tongues my tenements,
> Pens are my ploughes, my writings are my rents.
>
> (Folger MS v.a.345, fol. [*]r)

This piece suggests much about the social status of the students who participated in the system of manuscript transmission: their social and political conservatism might have been more a sign of their sociopolitical aspirations than the defensive gestures of a privileged class. Whether or not they were from the ranks of the gentry, Oxford and Cambridge students who compiled miscellanies and poetical anthologies were engaging in the leisure activities of educated gentlemen.

Many university students who started manuscript miscellanies or poetical anthologies continued to add items to their collections when they entered new environments. One of the most typical movements was from the university to the Inns of Court. Rosenbach MS 1083/15 from the last decade of the sixteenth through the first quarter of the seventeenth century is a large poetry collection connected with both Oxford and the Inns.[33] Robert Bishop's commonplace book (Rosenbach MS 1083/16) reflects the compiler's Oxford and Inns of Court background: entitled 'Miscellanies, or a Collection of Divers witty and pleasant Epigrams, Adages, poems, Epitaphes &c: for the recreation of the overtraveled Sences 1630', this anthology of 396 poems is a fine representative of the university and Inns of Court compilations of the period.[34] Bod. MS Eng. Poet. e.14 has many Oxford associations, beginning with a transcription of Richard Corbett's 'Iter Boreale', a long political poem that recurs in a surprising number of manuscript collections, but the volume also has signs of being used in an Inns milieu: it contains, for instance, two poems 'On Charles the Porter of Lincoln's Inn' (fols. 11r and 13v–14r). BL MS Sloane 1446 has both Christ Church pieces and Inns of Court material.[35] This collection is a good example of the social diffusion and conflation of verse from different sources, starting with the group of poems derived from the local circulation of manuscript material at Oxford and moving to works associated with the more politically charged environment of London.

Other manuscripts were probably begun at the Inns of Court, a social and cultural milieu in which both political consciousness and literary activity were quite high, especially at the end of the sixteenth and at the beginning of the seventeenth centuries.[36] Bod. MS Don. c.54 is a miscellany of verse and

prose owned by Richard Roberts, identified by Robert Krueger as a Welsh-
man who became a judge and was part of a Jacobean social circle of legal
professionals among whom verse was circulated.[37] His manuscript compilation is unusual in that it includes a long final section of poems in Welsh from
friends back home. It contains politically sensitive libels against such figures
as Edward Coke (fol. 6v), Robert Cecil (fol. 20r), and Robert Carr, Earl of
Somerset (fol. 22v) and poems by such authors as Ralegh, Jonson, Joshua
Sylvester, Davies, and Donne. BL MS Add. 22601 looks like a collection compiled in both Inns of Court and courtly settings in the early years of the
seventeenth century. Its courtly and political focusses are striking: it contains letters that deal with the political situation at the start of the Jacobean
era, including such matters as the early petitions to the king, the pressure
from Puritans, the arrest and trial of Ralegh, and poems by King James,
along with various ballads, song, and love lyrics.[38]

Another important environment with which manuscript compilation of
poetry was associated was that of the houses of the nobility and gentry.
Many seventeenth-century family miscellanies and poetical anthologies have
survived. For example, Bod. MS Eng. Poet. f. 9, a very large collection of
Donne poems mixed with the verse of such other authors as Jonson,
Wotton, Ralegh, Ayton, Pembroke, and Rudyerd, has its owner's name and
social rank on the first page ('1623. me posidett Hen: Champernoune De
Dartington in Devonina: generosus' – that is, 'This book belongs to Henry
Champernoune of Dartington in Devon, gentleman'). It also contains a
comical epitaph by one of Champernowne's relatives, 'Edward Champernowne'.[39] BL MS Add. 25707 is a miscellany associated with the Skipwith
family of Cotes, Leicestershire: it incorporates the verse of at least three
family members (William, Henry, and Thomas Skipwith).[40] Some of these
manuscripts contain fragments of family history: Bod. MS Rawl. Poet. 209, a
verse miscellany partly compiled after 1646 by John Peverell,[41] is one
example: fols. 28–9 have information about the compiler's family background. Of course, a blank book or table book in a family's possession
might start out being used for miscellaneous contents and then incorporate
poetical selections or, conversely, begin as a poetry collection and get used
subsequently for other purposes. Hunt. MS 46323, a manuscript associated
with the Calverley family in the Caroline period,[42] is an example of the
latter: the volume looks like it began as an anthology of verse and then,
later, a new hand added a legal treatise and other prose.

Given the demographic facts of literacy and cost of paper and of blank
table books, it was unlikely that the practices of manuscript transmission
and collection of verse extended very far below the ranks of the gentry,
but there are some surviving manuscripts from the middle class that

demonstrate the downward reach of this cultural practice. BL MS Egerton 2230 is a verse anthology kept by one 'Richard Glover', a London pharmacist (the first page announces 'E. Libris Richardo Glovero pharmacopol. Londonieni . . . 1638').[43] The compiler of BL MSS Harl. 6917–18, Peter Calfe, seems to have been a London apothecary, identified by Mary Hobbs as the son of a Dutch merchant and an acquaintance of Thomas Manne, who was one of Henry King's amanuenses.[44] Hunt. MS HM 93 is a commonplace book of poetry and prose, 'Dayly Observations both Divine & Morall / The First part. by Thomas, Grocer, Florilegius' – a decidedly middle-class commonplace book full of proverbial wisdom and pithy knowledge, the bourgeois counterpart of the poetical anthologies of the upper classes, with some contents, such as Herrick's poems (pp. 4–27), lifted from the elite tradition. The collection contains several sermons, along with such other works as Winstanley's *Muses' Cabinet* (pp. 109–15), May's epigrams (pp. 116–19), selections from Dubartas (pp. 129–49), Fletcher's piscatory eclogues (pp. 150–67), Richard Fleckno's poems (pp. 158–60), selections of Fletcher's *Purple Island* (pp. 160–5) and Wotton's *Remains* (pp. 183–6), and 'Dr Aglets poems' (pp. 209–10). The compiler's tastes reflect the religious, moral, and utilitarian biases of his class, but the practice of this grocer–florilegist is one borrowed from his social superiors.

Since a fair number of surviving miscellanies and poetical anthologies can be associated with Catholic families and individuals, it is fair to suggest that, in a period in which Catholics, especially recusant Catholics, were a persecuted minority, since the censored public sphere of print was not especially receptive to Catholic poetry and prose, they found the older manuscript system of transmission especially congenial.[45] The mid-seventeenth-century manuscripts associated with the Astons of Tixall, for example, contain a rich record of private manuscript circulation of verse and prose correspondence within an extended Catholic family.[46] The manuscript compiled by Constance Aston Fowler between 1635 and 1640 (Hunt. MS HM 904) preserves the courtship verse of the compiler's brother Herbert Aston and his wife-to-be Katherine Thimelby as well as an anthology of other poetry by friends and family members along with selected work of more well-known writers such as Robert Southwell, Henry King, Ben Jonson, and Richard Fanshawe (the last, a family friend).[47] One of the family poets included in the Aston family manuscripts, Edward Thimelby, refers to 'our soft-pend Crashaw', contrasting this Catholic author with those Cavalier 'toyling witts'[48] within the mainstream secular tradition.

Although the keeping of commonplace books was taught to males in grammar schools and the practice of compiling miscellanies and poetical anthologies flourished in all-male social worlds like the universities and the

Inns of Court, some women contributed to and/or owned poetical collections. They were the recipients of individual poems, groups of poems, and whole manuscript collections. In great houses and in courtly circles, they had access to and sometimes added poems to manuscript collections. Margaret Ezell has argued that, because it has focussed primarily on print culture and largely ignored women's participation in the coterie circulation of work in manuscript, feminist scholarship has drastically underestimated the literary activities of Renaissance women.[49] As producers of writing, women, of course, were much more involved in the system of manuscript transmission than with print. In addition to Constance Fowler, women who have been identified as owners of manuscript collections include Eleanor Gunter, sister of Edward Gunter of Lincoln's Inn (Bod. MS Rawl. Poet. 108),[50] Lady Ann Southwell (Folger MS v.b.198), Henrietta Holles (BL MS Harl. 3357), and Margaret Bellasys (BL MS Add. 10309), identified as the daughter of Thomas, Lord Fauconberg (1577–1653), a royalist turned Cromwell supporter.[51]

One can trace both the specific and general social, political, and religious interests of compilers in the manuscript collections they assembled, especially if one looks at the kinds of poems that were most often copied in these documents. The poetical tastes and the social functioning of the men and women involved in the manuscript transmission of verse were interrelated. The poems that recur frequently in manuscript collections might be classified in three groups: (1) model epitaphs, elegies, and epistles for either social superiors, equals, or inferiors; (2) poems that express general cultural beliefs and/or moral truisms; (3) poems celebrating the lifestyle and shared values of a social or intellectual (usually royalist) elite.

In the first category, there are some epitaphs and elegies that were repeated in the manuscript collections not only because they are especially eloquent expressions of their kind, but also because they delineated social relations in a hierarchical system clearly and embodied attitudes that had widespread appeal. Manuscript collections of verse are preoccupied with death, even more than with sex and politics. There are hundreds of serious elegies and epitaphs about both prominent and less-known adults and children as well as comic and satiric epitaphs and elegies about political enemies, social inferiors, and other figures of scorn. Like verse letters to social superiors, many elegies established or affirmed ties of social, political, or economic patronage; others were composed to declare in-group allegiances of various sorts – to family, to a network of friends and/or colleagues, to a political faction. In both serious and comical elegies and epitaphs class is usually an important factor. Despite the production of published volumes of commemorative verse and the appearance of elegies

and epitaphs in both anthologies and editions of the work of particular
authors, much of this verse was confined to the manuscript system, where
the restriction of audience suited the social exclusiveness of much of this
work. Among the most notable of these poems are Juxon's epitaph on
Prince Henry ('Nature waxing old'); William Browne of Tavistock's epitaph
for the Countess of Pembroke ('Underneath this sable hearse'); a beautiful
epitaph on a dead infant, 'Within this marble casket'; Henry King's elegy for
his wife, 'The Exequy', which celebrates the values of companionate marriage; Wotton's elegy for James I's daughter, Elizabeth, Queen of Bohemia,
'You meaner beauties of the night'; Beaumont's elegies for the Countess of
Rutland ('Madame, so may my verses pleasing be') and Lady Markham ('As
unthrifts groan in straw for their pawn'd beds'); and William Browne of
Tavistock's epitaph on the six-year-old Mistress Anne Prideaux, 'Nature in
this small volume was about'.[52] The poems about social superiors accept the
structure of the social hierarchy and the system of patronage it entails; the
poems about deceased children permit their author to express socially con-
descending sentimentality; the comic epitaphs are recreational trivia and
forms of social bonding.[53]

Poems that express general cultural beliefs include several of Ralegh's
lyrics – 'What is our life?', 'Even such is time', 'Like to a hermit poor', and
'The Lie' ('Go soul the bodies guest'). The first two express the traditional
attitude of *contemptus mundi*, but have currency because they were associated with Ralegh's fall and execution. 'The Lie' takes a satiric stance with
which those whose sociopolitical ambitions are frustrated could identify. In
a more seventeenth-century mode, Wotton's 'The Character of a Happy
Life' articulates a stoic ideal especially attractive in times of political conflict
and the anonymous poem 'Farewell, ye gilded follies' enacts a moral rejection of secular desires. Wotton's 'O Faithless world' responds to betrayal in
love from a male point of view.

In the third category of popular poems, I would place those pieces that
are witty trivia. These include Sir John Harington's bawdy epigram 'A
virtuous lady sitting in a muse', Randolph's 'On a deformed Gentlewoman
with a Sweet voice' ('I chanced sweet Lesbias voice to hear'), Walton Poole's
'If shadows be a picture's excellence', Corbett's 'To the Ladies of the New
Dress' ('Ladyes that weare black cypresse vailes'), William Browne of Tavistock's 'On one drowned in snow' ('Within a fleece of silent waters
drowned'), Henry Reynolds's 'A Blackamoore Maid wooing a fair Boy'
('Stay lovely Boy, why fly'st thou mee'), and Henry King's 'The Boy's
answer to the Blackamoore' ('Black Mayd, complayne not that I fly'), the
anonymous poem 'Of a Lady with one eye which brought forth a Child with
one' ('A one eyed boy born of a half blind mother'),[54] and two enormously

popular Carew poems, 'A Fly that flew into my Mistress's eye' ('When this flye liv'd, she us'd to play') and 'Ask me no more whither do stray', the second of which had an extraordinary life in the manuscript system of transmission, partly because it invited imitation. Carew's 'The Rapture', which has been discussed as a royalist poem by Kevin Sharpe,[55] ought also to be mentioned, given the fact that it is found in a large number of manuscripts. Herrick's 'Welcome to Sack' and 'Farewell to Sack' were popular probably because, as Lois Potter has pointed out, drunkenness was used as a royalist code during the Civil Wars and Interregnum.[56]

For political and social reasons, the manuscript system of transmission remained vigorous throughout most of the seventeenth century, though, at the same time, lyric poetry was gradually being absorbed into the literary institution shaped by print culture. Printed poetry itself, however, often had clear social and political coordinates, despite the efforts to separate literature from other forms of discourse. One of the things to remember in examining the components of the printed book in the early modern period – for example, the frontispiece, the title page, the dedicatory epistles to patrons, the addresses to readers, and the commendatory poems – is that each feature was a site of contestation and negotiation. In the format of printed publications, despite the illusion of stable monumentality created by the appearance of some published texts, the ideological and social assumptions of different restricted socioliterary environments often clash with the democratizing force of print and the commercial commodification of texts in print culture. Every party to the literary transaction – author, publisher, printer, dedicatee, reader – had to be relatively positioned. At stake were the sociocultural authority of writers and patrons; the property rights to texts to be claimed variously by authors, publishers, and consumers; the control of interpretation by authors or readers; the relationship of classes and subgroups in the society in which printed volumes transported texts over social boundaries; and the stability or instability of the literary institution being shaped by the print medium. Given this situation, we should pay especial attention to the 'front matter' of early printed texts, since such features as frontispieces, title pages, dedications, epistles, and commendatory verse historically mediate texts in revealing ways.[57]

There were (at least) four important moments in the publication history of English lyric verse that deserve especial attention: those of the appearance of Tottel's *Miscellany* (1557); of the 1591 Newman edition of Sidney's *Astrophil and Stella* and Ponsonby's 1598 folio of Sidney's collected works; of Jonson's 1616 *Works*; and of the 1633 editions of the poems of John Donne and George Herbert. These books, spread over some seventy-five years, each had a marked impact on the relationship of lyric poetry to print culture and together worked to make print the normal and preferred medium for such verse – this despite the fact that the manuscript transmission of lyrics continued as a widespread practice throughout the seventeenth century.

Throughout most of the sixteenth century (and much of the seventeenth), because of the 'stigma of print', men of rank and others who had pretentions to gentility either deliberately avoided print or, usually with the cooperation of a publisher, tried to maintain the illusion that they only reluctantly allowed their work to be printed.[58] Even more then the mid-century poetical anthology printed by Richard Tottel, the landmark (posthumous) publication of Sidney's *Astrophil and Stella* in the early 1590s went a long way towards providing the necessary sociocultural legitimation for printing of lyric verse. It was not merely Sidney's adroit mastery of the sonnet form but also his status as a kind of culture hero that stimulated the widespread imitation of his sonnet sequence. He made poetical pamphlets more socially acceptable and thus paved the way for such poets as Daniel, Drayton, and Jonson to print their poems.[59] In addition, the practice of producing prestigious folio volumes of the collected works of Chaucer, and then of contemporary writers like Sidney, Spenser, Daniel, Jonson, and Shakespeare invested printed literature and literary authorship with higher prestige, influencing the willingness of writers to see their work in various lyric forms appear in print.

While the phenomenon of the folio printing of individual writers' collected works continued to flourish, there were relatively few editions of individual poets' lyrics or of poetical anthologies between the time of Jonson's 1616 *Works* and that of the appearance of the first editions of John Donne's and George Herbert's poetry in 1633. Editions of Michael Drayton's *Poems*, which were finally produced in a folio edition in 1619, of Lady Mary Wroth's *Urania* (which included her sonnet sequence) in 1623, of works like Wither's *Juvenilia* (1622), and of *The Golden Garland of Princely Pleasures and Delicate Delights* (1620) were published in this period, but compared, for example, to the previous fifteen or so years, there was clearly a drop in the production of new editions of lyric poetry: single authors' works and anthologies[60] were reprinted, but very few new titles came on the market. From the mid Jacobean period through the first seven years of the reign of Charles I, lyric verse tended to remain within the system of manuscript circulation.

The virtually simultaneous, posthumous publication of Donne's *Poems* and Herbert's *The Temple* in 1633, however, was a watershed event that changed the relationship of lyric poetry to the print medium, helping to normalize within print culture the publication of individual authors' collected poems. As successive editions of both Donne's and Herbert's verse continued to appear through the pre-Civil War and Civil War periods and the Interregnum, they became part of a process by which courtly and royalist poets were installed in the literary institution taking shape within print culture. After the publication of Donne's and Herbert's poems, and certainly after the appearance of the numerous volumes of individual authors' verse whose publication was partly authorized by the Donne and Herbert editions, lyric poems themselves were perceived less as occasional and ephemeral and more as valuable artefacts worth preserving in those monumentalizing editions that were among the most prestigious products of print culture.

Apart from the text of the verse, the Cambridge University Press edition of Herbert's *The Temple* contains only Ferrar's short prefatory biography of the poet and an index of the titles of the poems (to facilitate their use for devotional purposes). The author's life is made to serve as an index to meaning, but also, because the author function has become important in printed literature, it is a locus of authority to be highlighted within the print medium, in its own way a substitute for the social presence of the poet in the environment of private manuscript circulation. Justified, then, as serious religious writing by a saintly, learned parson whose exemplary life could edify readers, presented by the press of the university with which he was formerly affiliated, published in the handy portable form of the duodecimo, *The Temple: Sacred Poems and Private Ejaculations, By Mr George Herbert* had no need for apology as a printed volume of lyrics. Posthumously glorifying its humble author through the print medium, it offered a model other religious writers of lyric verse could, and did, follow. Herbert's *The Temple* spawned, for example, not only Richard Crashaw's imitative *Steps to the Temple* (1646), a volume issued in the same duodecimo format, and the editions of Henry Vaughan's religious lyrics, but also Christopher Harvey's *The Synagogue* (1647), a duodecimo pamphlet Philemon Stephens sold bound with Herbert's collection.[61] After Herbert, print was the proper medium for the dissemination of the religious lyric – one sign of the way in which print culture paradoxically both made the private public and demarcated private life itself more clearly as a social space. Donne's *Poems*, on the other hand, were valued as the collected miscellaneous pieces of a deceased ecclesiastical figure whose prominence in Stuart culture contrasted with the relative privacy of his verse, a body of work formerly available only through the network of manuscript transmission. What was important is that such coterie poetry was transferred to a different medium and encouraged similar work to be published. The Donne and Herbert editions made the way for the publication of the work of other poet-ecclesiastics such as Richard

Corbett (1647 and 1648), Robert Herrick (1648), William Cartwright (1651), and Henry King (1657).

As posthumous editions, the 1633 Donne and Herbert volumes continued a tradition of posthumous collected editions of writers' works: the 1568 Skelton, *The Whole Works of G. Gascoigne: Compiled into one Volume* (1587), the 1598 Sidney folio, the 1611 collected Spenser, the 1623 First Folio of Shakespeare, Daniel's 1623 *Whole Works* are all memorials to esteemed authors as well as compilations of their works. The collected editions of living authors – the 1605 Daniel, 1616 Jonson folio, the 1619 Drayton *Poems* – are the exceptions rather than the rule. Greville's 1633 collected works, though prepared by the author with a long introduction that serves both as a biography of Sir Philip Sidney and as an autobiographical defence of Greville's career, appeared posthumously. Many of the editions of poets that followed over the next two decades were also posthumous publications: the 1638 Randolph (prepared by his brother and printed by the University Press at Oxford), the 1640 *Poems* of Thomas Carew, two editions of Suckling's works (*Fragmenta Aurea* (1646) and *The Last Remains* (1659)), the two (poorly produced) collections of Richard Corbett's poetry in 1647 and 1648, and Lovelace's *Lucasta: Posthume Poems* (1660). Robert Herrick's *Hesperides* (1648) is presented as a kind of pre-posthumous collection. In this period of political conflict, however, posthumous poetry, like funeral elegies, offered the opportunity to reinforce the political partisanship of poets, publishers, and readerships. In particular, from the mid-1640s through the 1650s, collected editions of poets' works as well as poetical anthologies were largely a manifestation of royalism. While, especially during the Interregnum, the published religious lyrics of clergymen and devout laymen could, as Lois Potter suggests, be valued for their authors' association with high-church Anglicanism and royalist politics, printed secular lyrics were also a sign of royalist partisanship.[62] In effect the aristocratic and conservative associations of poetry within the manuscript system carried over into the medium of print when lyric texts moved from one medium to the other in the middle third of the seventeenth century.

Donne and Herbert, then, were influential not simply because of the aesthetic impact of their printed work – but also because they came to be associated with the publication of royalist and high-church authors in the period of the Civil Wars and Interregnum. In an era in which conservative authors and readers felt embattled, print could have anti-democratic function (and thus lose some of its social stigma for members of the social and educational elites). This may account for the willingness of someone like Dudley, Baron North to publish his occasional writings in 1645 as *A Forest of Varieties*: he indicates that, despite what he calls the 'prostitution of the Presse', he found it necessary to overcome his scruples in publishing his private writings: 'meeting with this plundering age, if they venture not to undergoe the Presse, they are obnoxious [i.e. liable] to a sodain destruction' (sig. A3r). Margaret Cavendish, Duchess of Newcastle, also found it desirable and possible to print her own verse and prose in 1653. The medium of print was thus converted from a potential embarrassment to royalist writers to a safe haven for their work and a sign of political resistance to Puritan hegemony. In the hands of a satirist like John Cleveland, whose work also circulated in manuscript, the individual volume of verse could appear as a species of royalist journalism – hence use of the title *The Character of a London Diurnal* in 1647 for the small selection of that author's poems, some six editions of which appeared in that year. The nineteen or so editions of Cleveland's verse that were published before the Restoration are an obvious example of royalist poets' free resort to the print medium.

One publisher in particular, Humphrey Moseley, exploited the potential royalist market for such publications in producing more collections of lyric poetry than any of his competitors. He was responsible for printing the poems of Quarles (1642), Milton (1645), Waller (1645), Crashaw (1646 and 1648), Shirley (1646), Suckling (1646, 1648, and 1658), Cowley (1647 and 1655), Carew (1651), Cartwright (1651), Stanley (1651), and Vaughan (1651 and 1654). In a commendatory poem to Moseley's edition of Cartwright's *Comedies, Tragedies and Other Poems* (1651) John Leigh praised the publisher for having brought before the public the 'high Atchievments' of 'Noble Souls' that 'wrote Wit', urging him to 'gather up all / Those precious Lines which brave Wits have let fall' (including the poems of Cleveland and Cowley), 'For times approach wherein Wit will be dear.'[63] In the midst of the austere Commonwealth/Protectorate period, Moseley served to preserve the courtly and royalist aesthetic. By the time of the Restoration, thanks partly to Moseley, the single-author edition of lyric poetry was a familiar phenomenon in the world of publication, though many verse collections appeared posthumously and few authors took the kind of care in seeing their work into print that Robert Herrick did in compiling his work for the 1648 *Hesperides*.

Although most published lyric verse was produced for an educationally and socially elite readership whose values were conservative, the very fact of publication broadened the audience for such work. This process is most visible, perhaps, in the poetic anthologies and, especially, in the courtesy books published in the century's middle two decades. Works like the often revised and expanded *Wits' Recreations* (1640), *The Harmony of the Muses* (1654), *Musarum Deliciae* (1655), *Parnassus Biceps* (1656), and *Wit Restor'd* (1658), and the two anthologies banned by the Cromwell's government,

Choice Drollery (1656) and *Sportive Wit* (1656), all manifest royalist nostalgia, intellectual snobbery, upper-class exclusiveness, and anti-Puritan sentiments (as do other types of publication, such as single-author editions): they were all royalist texts directed at a partisan readership antagonistic to middle-class, Puritan values. Other books containing collections of lyrics were, however, obviously aimed at a broader, and more varied readership.[64]

Given the steady market for self-improvement books in print culture, it is not surprising that some texts appealed more obviously to a middle-class readership and clientele. One such work is a courtesy book that included verse among its contents: *The Mysteries of Love & Eloquence, or the Arts of Wooing and Complementing; As they are manag'd in the Spring Garden, Hide Park, the New Exchange, and other eminent places. A Work, in which are drawn to the Life, the Deportments of the most accomplisht Persons, the mode of their Courtly Entertainments, Treatments of their Ladies at Balls, their accustom'd Sports, Drolles and Fancies, the Witchcrafts of their perswasive Language, in their Approaches, or other more Secret Dispatches. To Compleat the young Practitioners of Love and Courtship, these following conducing Helps are chiefly insisted on. Addresses, and set Forms of Expressions for imitation. Poems, pleasant Songs, Letters, Proverbs, Riddles, Jeasts, Posies, Devices, A la mode Pastimes, A Dictionary for the making of Rimes, Four hundred and fifty delightful Questions, with their several answers. As also Epithets, and flourishing Similitudes, Alphabetically connected, and so properly applied to their serveral [sic] Subjects, that they may be rendered admirably useful on the sudden occasions of Discourse or Writing. Together, with a new invented Art of Logick, so plain and easie by way of Questions and Answers; that the meanest capacity may in short time attain to a perfection in the wayes of Arguing and Disputing* (1658). In terms of the processes of literary institutionalization at work in the English Renaissance, this work is a retrogressive one, recontextualizing poetry in the environment of the social life of the upper classes and stripping it of its growing association with the modern conception of authorship. Combining a strong snob appeal with its strategies of vulgarization, this text exploits the democratizing potential of the print medium, advertising itself as superior to the manuscript miscellanies of the elite as a source of imitable style. Attempting to reverse the traditional social inferiority of print to manuscript, the editor, Edward Phillips, claims this collection is better than those found in private commonplace books (sig. A5r). He argues that, with the right sources for imitation, any one might best his or her social betters: addressing 'the Youthful Gentry', he claims: 'I have known a wench of fourteen, with a few Dramatic *Drayton* and *Sidney* Quillets [i.e. quibbles], put to the *nonplus* a Gallant of thirty ... I have heard such a Lass defeat a

Gentleman of some years standing at the Inns of Court' (sig. A5r). In this formulation Drayton's and Sidney's poems lose their dignity as literary monuments and become, as was literature in an earlier system, a treasury of language open to any needy user. At the same time, as the epistle dedicatory explains, the book so successfully demystifies the 'mysteries' of love that it serves a curative function for those victimized by it, as exemplified in the story of the 'mad lover' (sig. a1r) who supposedly was quickly disabused of his live illusions by perusing the text. The world of civility envisioned by this text is one from which both romantic illusions and the 'inspirations' of Puritan 'Enthusiasts' (sig. a2v) are purged.

Another self-improvement book, however, John Cotgrave's *Wits' Interpreter* (1655), which also includes a selection of poetry, had attacked the vulgarizing potential of such works as *The Academy of Complements* (1640) – a book that had fifteen editions by the year 1795 – publications that appealed to a '*Chambermaid* to make her beleive [sic], she may be easily compleated with *offensive* and *defensive* terms of Language, so to manage her Wit as if she were at a prize' (sig. A3v). This text, whose frontispiece enshrines a series of writers and political figures including 'Spencer', 'Shakespeare', 'Johnson', 'Randolph', 'Sr. T. Moore', 'Ld. Bacon', 'Sydney', '[The Earl of] Strafford', '[Cardinal] Richilieu', and 'Dubartas', is addressed to 'the *wiser Reader*' (sig. A3r), to an intellectually elite audience that can value high-quality poetry and learning. Cotgrave claims to have taken great pains to secure previously unavailable texts, 'from the private Papers of the choicest Wits ... from which Manuscripts of theirs ... I crossed out whatsoever I could hear had been formerly publisht' (sig. A4r). He treats the authorial manuscripts and the printed texts derived from them with the kind of respect fostered by print culture. And, to produce this text, he claims the full cooperation of many of the authors: 'the *English Tongue* was never honored with a larger or a more *Accurate Collection* ... those Honorable Persons which furnisht me with many of these Admirable *Peeces*, were in a readiness to speak the worth of those *Copies* to the publication wherof they so freely gave their Consents' (sigs. A4r–v). The publisher Nathanial Brooke associates the question of textual accuracy ('these sheets of paper, some whereof are printed from [the authors'] own Manuscripts' (sig. A5r) and the elevated status of literature within print culture ('these inestimable Monuments (sig. A5r)) with royalist nostalgia and politics ('the Reliques of the dead are not esteemed amongst the reformed of the Nation' (sig. A5r)), associating the worth of the texts with the symbolic value of a lost monarchy in calling the items 'Fragmenta Regalia Aurea & Sacra' (sig. A5r). Despite the way in which the collection is presented, it is actually a hodge-podge in its contents, mixing a treatise on logic, miscellaneous examples of wit and humour (including practical jokes and tricks) before presenting (in a newly paginated section) the main collection of poetry, an anthology of (largely unascribed) serious and frivolous poetry running from the time of Ralegh to the mid seventeenth century.

If one compares the contents of the mid-century printed anthologies and miscellanies containing lyric verse with surviving manuscript collections, however, one is struck by the richer contents of the latter. For example, Nicholas Burghe's manuscript collection (Bod. MS Ash. 38) contains a remarkably varied gathering of the work of both older and contemporary poets such as Jonson, Donne, Drayton, Constable, Ralegh, Campion, Alabaster, Carew, King, Herrick, Randolph, Shirley, and Corbett – over 400 poems in all, some obviously transcribed from printed copies, but most derived from the continuing tradition of manuscript transmission. Next to a large anthology such as this, the 'drolleries'[65] and mid-century witty collections look thin and shoddy. They contain, along with the work of skilled mid-century poets, a lot of clumsy political songs and ballads, satiric doggerel and witty trivia. Both the manuscript and printed anthologies of the period, however, mark poetic anthologizing as an elitist activity, largely a socially and politically conservative act (features that, to some extent, characterize the practice up to the present time), though, of course, there are significant differences between the assumptions implicit in the two systems of literary transmission.

Although the Restoration resulted in a marked increase in the publication of poetical texts, practices of manuscript transmission and collection continued among the upper classes, partly because of the higher social prestige of the earlier system. For example, Jacobite groups after the Glorious Revolution, like royalists in the Interregnum, turned to manuscript compilation and transmission of verse, supporting at least one anachronistic scriptorium to produce texts for their particular purposes.[66] Manuscript transmission not only still retained its social appeal but also continued to serve as a safe harbour for texts that might have been somewhat dangerous to set forth in the public realm of the typographical. Print culture, however, finally assumed clear dominance in the eighteenth century, as the definitions of authorship, reader roles, and textuality that we associate with the modern conception of 'literature' were solidified. As the new practice of *literary* history developed and literature itself came to be regarded as a self-enclosed discourse, those social contingencies that affected the composition, transmission, and reception of texts were ignored or obscured.

NOTES

1 See my essay on 'The Transmission of Lyric Poetry and the Institutionalizing of Literature in the English Renaissance', in *Contending Kingdoms: Historical, Psychological, and Feminist Approaches to the Literature of Sixteenth-Century England and France*, ed. Marie-Rose Logan and Peter L. Rudnytsky (Detroit: Wayne State University Press, 1991), pp. 21–41. See also J. W. Saunders, 'The Social Situation of Seventeenth-Century Poetry', in *Metaphysical Poetry*, ed. Malcolm Bradbury and David Palmer, Stratford-upon-Avon Studies, no. 11 (London: Edward Arnold, 1970), pp. 236–59.

2 *The Complete Poetry of Ben Jonson*, ed., intro., notes, and variants by William B. Hunter, Jr (1963; repr. New York: Norton, 1968), p. 93. Citations of Jonson's poems are from this edition.

3 *Ben Jonson*, vol. 1, ed. C. H. Herford and Percy Simpson (Oxford: Clarendon Press, 1925), p. 142 (lines 364–7). I cite this edition of the *Conversations* and use Herford and Simpson's line numbers.

4 See *Epigrams* 79; *Forest* 12; *Underwood* 28.

5 This poem is printed in *The Poems of John Donne*, vol. 1, ed. Herbert J. C. Grierson (Oxford University Press, 1912), pp. 414–15.

6 For an interesting discussion of this social circle, see *The 'Conceited Newes' of Sir Thomas Overbury and His Friends*, facsimile repro. of ninth impression of 1616 of *Sir Thomas Overbury His Wife*, with commentary and textual notes on the 'Newes' by James E. Savage (Gainesville: Scholars' Facsimiles and Reprints, 1968).

7 See my discussion of the social context of Donne's poetry in *John Donne, Coterie Poet* (Madison: University of Wisconsin Press, 1986).

8 See *The Poems of Thomas Carew*, ed., intro. and notes by Rhodes Dunlap (Oxford: Clarendon Press, 1949), p. xxxiii.

9 Although BL MS Add. 53723 (Henry Lawes's folio autograph manuscript), which has 38 Carew poems with musical settings, might be considered a courtly collection, Bod. MS Ash. 38 (with 18 Carew poems), Boc. MS Eng. Poet. f. 27 (with 16), BL MS Harl. 3511 (with 26), BL MS Harl. 6917 (with 33), and BL MS Sloane 1446 (with 22) are non-courtly anthologies. For a discussion of the Carew manuscripts and for information on most of the manuscripts cited in this essay I am greatly indebted to Peter Beal (compiler), *Index of English Literary Manuscripts*, vol. 1 (in two parts) (London: Mansell, 1980), vol. 2 (part 1 only) (1987). The Carew manuscripts are discussed in 2.1.39–46.

10 See Ted-Larry Pebworth and Claude J. Summers, '"Thus Friends Absent Speak": The Exchange Verse Letters Between John Donne and Henry Wotton', *MP* 81 (1984): 361–77.

11 *The Poems of Thomas Randolph*, ed. G. Thorn-Drury (London: Etchels and Macdonald, 1929), p. 82.

12 For the text of Corbett's 'Upon Faireford Windowes', see *The Poems of Richard Corbett*, ed. J. A. W. Bennett and H. R. Trevor-Roper (Oxford: Clarendon Press, 1955), p. 87. For Strode's 'On Fayrford Windowes', see *The Poetical Works of William Strode*, ed. Bertram Dobell (London: Dobell, 1907), pp. 25–7. Terrant's poem is found in Bod. MS Eng. Poet e.97, p. 33 and BL MS Sloane 542, fol. 59 (attributed to Corbett).

13 See, for example, Bod MSS Rawl. Poet. 117, fol. 199v and Rawl. Poet. 147, p. 81;
Rosenbach MS 240/2, pp. 13–17.

14 For a good discussion of answer-poetry see E. F. Hart, 'The Answer-Poem of the
Early Seventeenth Century', *RES* ns 7 (1956): 19–29.

15 See Marotti, *Donne*, pp. 266 and 345 n267.

16 *Letters to Severall Persons of Honour (1651)*, a facsimile repro., intro.
M. Thomas Hester (Gainsville: Scholars' Facsimiles and Reprints, 1977), p. 33.

17 See the discussion of this in Graham Parry, *Seventeenth-Century Poetry: The
Social Context* (London: Hutchinson, 1985), pp. 116–17.

18 See Helen Wilcox, 'Exploring the Language of Devotion in the English Revolution', in *Literature and the English Civil War*, ed. Thomas Healy and Jonathan
Sawday (Cambridge University Press, 1990), pp. 75–88.

19 Beal, *Index*, 1.1.246.

20 *Ibid.* 2.1.40 has identified Burghe as a royalist captain in the Civil War. In tran-
scribing texts, I modernize i/j, u/v and expand most contractions.

21 See J. W. Saunders, 'From Manuscript to Print: A Note on the Circulation of
Poetic MSS in the Sixteenth Century', *Proceedings of the Leeds Philosophical and
Literary Society*, 6.8 (1951): 507–28. See also Harold Love's discussion of the
movement from single-sheet circulation of individual pieces to larger groupings
in 'Scribal Publication in Seventeenth-Century England', *Transactions of the
Cambridge Biographical Society* 9.2 (1987): 143 and Germaine Warkentin's discussion of the bifolia circulation of verse in 'Sidney's *Certain Sonnets*: Speculations on the Evolution of the Text', *The Library* 6th ser., 2 (1980): 430–44.

22 Margaret Crum, 'Notes on the Physical Characteristics of some Manuscripts of
the Poems of Donne and of Henry King', *The Library* 4th ser., 16 (1961): 121–32.

23 *The Stoughton Manuscript: A Manuscript Miscellany of Poems by Henry King
and his Circle*, circa *1636*, facsimile edn, intro. and indexes by Mary Hobbs
(Aldershot, England: Scholar Press, 1990), p. xviii.

24 *Complete Poetry*, p. 256.

25 This contains twenty-three originally folded folios. See Beal, *Index* 2.1.554.

26 See *ibid.*, 1.1.247–8.

27 See *ibid.*, 1.2.526.

28 *DNB* identifies Sir John Doderidge (1555–1628) as a member of the Society of
Antiquaries and an MP who went on to a long judicial career.

29 See Beal, *Index* 1.2.134.

30 In the *Register of Admissions to the Honourable Society of the Middle Temple:
From the Fifteenth Century to the year 1944*, comp. Sir Henry F. MacGeagh and
H. A. C. Sturgess (London: Butterworth & Co., 1949), p. 86, Ramsey's admis-
sion is listed for 23 March 1605/6 and he is identified as the son of William
Ramsey of Charlwood, Surrey. He should not be confused with the more famous
Scots John Ramsey, an important Jacobean courtier.

31 See Mary Hobbs, 'An Edition of the Stoughton Manuscript (An Early Seventeenth-Century Poetry Collection in Private Hands Connected with Henry King
and Oxford) Seen in Relation to Other Contemporary Poetry and Song Collections', D.Phil. Thesis, University of London, 1973, pp. 152–5; and 'Early Seventeenth-Century Verse Miscellanies and their value for Textual Editors', *English
Manuscript Studies 1100–1700*, vol. 1, ed. Peter Beal and Jeremy Griffiths
(Oxford: Basil Blackwell, 1989), pp. 189–210. See also Raymond A. Anselment,

'The Oxford University Poets and Caroline Panegyric', *John Donne Journal* 3 (1984): 184, 185–6. One can number among these Christ Church anthologies such manuscripts as BL MSS Add. 30982 and 58215, Egerton 2421, Sloane 1792; Bod. MSS Eng. Poet. e.14 and e.30; Folger MSS V.a.97, V.a.170, V.a.262, V.a.345, and V.b.43; Rosenbach MSS 239/22 and 239/27; and Westminster Abbey MS 41.

32 Hobbs, 'An Edition', p. 55, says this college, with close ties to Winchester School, which encouraged the writing of vernacular verse, also fostered poetic composition and compilation.

33 See James Sanderson, 'An Edition of An Early Seventeenth-Century Manuscript Collection of Poems (Rosenbach MS 186)', Dissertation, University of Pennsylvania, 1960.

34 See David Coleman Redding, 'Robert Bishop's Commonplace Book: An Edition of a Seventeenth-Century Miscellany', Dissertation, University of Pennsylvania, 1960.

35 See Beal, *Index* 1.2.278 and Hobbs (ed.), *Stoughton Manuscript*, p. xv; and 'An Edition', pp. 135–9.

36 See Philip Finkelpearl, *John Marston of the Middle Temple: An Elizabethan Dramatist in His Social Setting* (Cambridge, Mass.: Harvard University Press, 1969), pp. 3–80; and Wilfred R. Prest, *The Inns of Court Under Elizabeth I and the Early Stuarts* (London: Longman, 1972).

37 See *The Poems of Sir John Davies*, ed. Robert Krueger, with intro. and commentary by the editor and Ruby Nemser (Oxford: Clarendon Press, 1975), p. 438.

38 See Krueger and Nemser (eds.), *Davies*, p. 435, where the manuscript is defined as written for someone at court; see also Beal, *Index* 1.2.135.

39 See Beal, *Index* 1.2.252, 466.

40 See Hobbs, 'An Edition', pp. 119–29; and Beal, *Index* 1.1.252. In a letter published in *TLS* 10–16 June 1988, Mary Hobbs asserts that, in this manuscript, five separate collections are bound (p. 647).

41 See Beal, *Index*, 1.2.271.

42 See *ibid.*, 1.2.15 and 2.1.557.

43 See *ibid.*, 1.1.255, where it is dated around 1630.

44 Hobbs (ed.), *Stoughton Manuscript*, pp. xv and 309.

45 See Nancy Pollard Brown, 'Paperchase: The Dissemination of Catholic Texts in Elizabethan England', *English Manuscript Studies 1100–1700*, vol. 1, ed. Peter Beal and Jeremy Griffiths (Oxford: Basil Blackwell, 1989), pp. 120–43.

46 See the edition of poetry from the Aston family manuscripts, *Tixall Poetry: With Notes and Illustrations*, ed. Arthur Clifford (Edinburgh and London: James Ballantyne & Co., 1813).

47 See Jenijoy La Belle, 'The Huntington Aston Manuscript', *The Book Collector* 29 (1980): 542–67, for an interesting analysis of this manuscript and the related treatment of the Constance Fowler–Herbert Aston relationship in her 'A True Love's Knot: The Letters of Constance Fowler and the Poems of Herbert Aston', *JEGP* 79 (1980): 13–31 (which prints a transcription of some of Herbert Aston's poems). This particular manuscript was not included in Clifford's edition of *Tixall Poetry*.

48 Clifford (ed.), *Tixall Poetry*, p. 40.

49 Margaret Ezell, '"To Be Your Daughter in Your Pen": The Social Functions of Literature in the Writings of Lady Elizabeth Brackley and Lady Jane Cavendish', *HLQ* 51 (1988): 281–96.

50 See, Beal, *Index* 1.2.391.

51 See *ibid.*, 1.2.452.

52 In compiling the lists of poems that were popular in manuscript transmission, I have used Beal's *Index*; Hobbs, 'An Edition', p. 210; and Redding, 'Robert Bishop's Commonplace Book', pp. lii–liii; *First-Line Index of English Poetry 1500–1800 in Manuscripts of the Bodleian Library Oxford*, 2 vols., ed. Margaret Crum (New York: MLA, 1969); and my own research.

53 See Joshua Scodel, *The English Poetic Epitaph: Commemoration and Conflict from Jonson to Wordsworth* (Ithaca: Cornell University Press, 1991), pp. 140–62.

54 See Crum (ed.), *First-Line Index*, A179, A324, F53, H142, T2227 for different versions of this found in Bodleian MSS.

55 Kevin Sharpe, *Criticism and Complement: The Politics of Literature in the England of Charles I* (Cambridge University Press, 1987), pp. 118–22.

56 Lois Potter, *Secret Rites and Secret Writing: Royalist Literature, 1641–1660* (Cambridge University Press, 1989), pp. 134–40.

57 See Richard Helgerson, *Self-Crowned Laureates: Spenser, Jonson, Milton, and the Literary System* (Berkeley: University of California Press, 1983). See also my discussion of some of these issues in two essays: 'Shakespeare's Sonnets as Literary Property', in *Soliciting Interpretation: Literary Theory and Seventeenth-Century English Poetry*, ed. Elizabeth D. Harvey and Katharine Eisaman Maus (University of Chicago Press, 1990), pp. 143–73; and 'Poetry, Patronage, and Print', *The Yearbook of English Studies* 21 (1991): 1–26.

58 See J. W. Saunders, 'The Stigma of Print: A Note on the Social Bases of Tudor Poetry', *Essays in Criticism* 1 (1951): 139–54.

59 See my essay '"Love is Not Love: Elizabethan Sonnet Sequences and the Social Order', *ELH* 49 (1982): 396–428.

60 For example, *England's Helicon* was reissued in 1614 and *A Poetical Rhapsody* in 1621.

61 See T. A. Birrell, 'The Influence of Seventeenth-Century Publishers on the Presentation of English Literature', in *Historical and Editorial Studies in Medieval and Early Modern English*, ed. Mary-Jo Arn and Hanneke Wirtjes (Groningen: Wolters-Noordhoff, 1985), p. 164.

62 Potter, *Secret Rites*, pp. 115–16.

63 This is quoted in an important study by John Curtis Reed, 'Humphrey Moseley, Publisher', *Oxford Bibliographical Society Proceedings and Papers*, 2.2 (1927–30): 61–142 (65–6).

64 I have profited from reading in manuscript an essay by Ann Baynes Coiro now published as 'Milton and Class Identity: The Publication of *Areopagitica* and the 1645 *Poems*', *Journal of Medieval and Renaissance Studies* 22 (1992): 261–89. In it, Coiro discusses the mid-century printed miscellanies, especially *Wits' Recreations* and *The Academy of Complements*.

65 See Courtney Craig Smith, 'The Seventeenth-Century Drolleries', *Harvard Library Bulletin* 6 (1952): 40–51.

66 See W. J. Cameron, 'A Late Seventeenth-Century Scriptorium', *Renaissance and Modern Studies* 7 (1963): 25–52.

FURTHER READING

Eisenstein, Elizabeth L., *The Printing Press as an Agent of Change: Communications and Cultural Transformations in Early-Modern Europe* 2 vols. (Cambridge University Press, 1979)

Loewenstein, Joseph, 'The Script in the Marketplace', *Representations* 12 (Autumn 1985): 101–14

Love, Harold, 'Manuscript Versus Print in the Transmission of English Literature, 1600–1700', *Bibliographical Society of Australia and New Zealand* 9 (1985): 95–107

Marotti, Arthur F., 'John Donne, Author', *Journal of Medieval and Renaissance Studies* 19 (1989): 69–82

Newton, Richard C., 'Jonson and the (Re-)Invention of the Book', in *Classic and Cavalier: Essays on Jonson and the Sons of Ben*, ed. Claude J. Summers and Ted-Larry Pebworth (University of Pittsburgh Press, 1982), pp. 31–55

'Making Books from Leaves: Poets Become Editors', in *Print and Culture in the Renaissance: Essays on the Advent of Printing in Europe*, ed. and intro. Gerald P. Tyson and Sylvia S. Wagonheim, preface by S. Schoenbaum (Newark: University of Delaware Press, 1986), pp. 246–64

Sharpe, Kevin, *Criticism and Complement: The Politics of Literature in the England of Charles I* (Cambridge University Press, 1987)

Sullivan, II, Ernest W. (ed.), *The First and Second Dalhousie Manuscripts: Poems and Prose by John Donne and Others, A Facsimile Edition* (Columbia: University of Missouri Press, 1988)

Wall, Wendy, 'Disclosures in Print: The "Violent Enlargement" of the Renaissance Voyeuristic Text', *Studies in English Literature* 29 (1989): 35–59

4

ALASTAIR FOWLER

Genre and tradition

The relation of genre to tradition in the seventeenth century was not simple. For one thing, tradition itself was composite; being intricately divided into pagan-antique and Christian strands, the Christian into Protestant and Catholic, and the Protestant further split by sect. For another, whereas emphasis on genre seems to imply engagement with a stable body of literature, the period itself was one of radical social changes, rapidly changing valuation of literary textuality, and deliberate literary innovation. The complexity was such that several stories about genre probably need to be disengaged. One of them might narrate how epigram came to dominate the literary scene, determining its minutest operations. Another, how georgic, after being exiled from poetry, was at last welcomed back and thought its most refined, consummate representative. A third story could tell of promotions and demotions in the hierarchy of kinds. In a fourth, changes in the concept of genre itself would be the theme: changes responding to alterations in the practice of imitation.

EDUCATION FOR SYLVA

Anyone trying to make sense of seventeenth-century genres encounters a large initial difficulty: how to account for the presence of classical (and therefore pagan) genres in a literature that addressed, often quite explicitly, a Christian muse. Doubtless classical genres might be excused during the early Renaissance; but after the Reformation, in the heyday of Puritanism, why were they tolerated? How could the author of *Samson Agonistes* bring himself to meddle with a genre so pagan as tragedy?

The answer may depend on elusive relations between Renaissance and Reformation – relations much studied during the last few decades. Many historians would now agree in seeing the Renaissance as itself a movement of reform, even a movement with monastic origins (for example Abbot Trithemius and Desiderius Erasmus). Renaissance humanists embraced classical culture not in any recrudescence of paganism, but for its usefulness to the movement to raise standards, technically and morally (the latter through careful selection, for example, or presentation in *a fortiori* arguments). With this in mind, they entered on a vast programme of naturalizing the best of ancient literary culture: a programme conceived rhetorically as the imitation of classical genres. To such an extent did this programme become institutionalized, that the classical genres were seen as antimedieval: they were identified with reformist ideology, whether Protestant or Roman Catholic.[1] For British humanists such as Roger Ascham, in consequence, and even for Thomas Nashe, imitating classical genres was reformative, and almost distinctively Protestant; whereas writing romances (a genre guilty by association with the Middle Ages) was unreformed, and best left to 'abbey-lubbers'. By the seventeenth century, such ideological stances had crystallized into hardened formations, so that ancient genres were often taken to be satisfactorily anti-Scholastic.

From the start, reform operated from an innovative educational base. The northern Reformation could only be as thorough as it was, because it had a coherent programme of education in schools, and even, to some extent, in universities. The new learning meant imitation of Cicero and other classical models, conveniently grouped in their genres by humanist printers.[2] Daily assignments (far too large for detailed textual study) suggest that the focus was on larger, generic features. Such wholesale, single-minded reconstruction of the *paideia* might well have proved ideologically stifling – as indeed sometimes happened. (Have C. S. Lewis's criticisms of sixteenth-century humanism ever been satisfactorily answered?) But fortunately the new education was saved from total disaster by the variety of classical literature – perhaps, too, by the need to find imaginative ways of accommodating unacceptably pagan features. And there is the additional consideration that grammar schools taught creative writing.

For schoolchildren not only learned to translate, parse, and scan classical poetry, but to imitate it in verse composition – even (at least with a master like Alexander Gill) English verse composition. Officially, all the main classical genres were learned. For example Richard Wills, in his *Poematum Liber* for Winchester School, offers models in a wide variety of kinds and devices and shapes – echo, eclogue, elegy, elogium, encomium, epicede, epitaph, epithalamium, and so on. But, understandably, the models are mostly very short. What the scholars of Winchester learned to write, in fact, was a variety of different types of epigram. (This could have been justified by appeal to Robortello's doctrine that epigrams were miniaturizations of larger kinds.) Such a curriculum would inevitably inculcate habits of epigrammatic composition. Because there were so many recognizable subgenres of epigram, poets were able to bring classical tradition to bear in a criticism of modern life. When the effects of the new education were disseminated through the writing community – by the 1590s, say – they strongly encouraged a taste for epigrams, and for consequential transformations of other kinds. The epigram madness, comparable in some ways with tulipomania, was beginning.

Up to the 1590s and the first decades of the seventeenth century, epigram collections – for example, Timothy Kendall's (1577), Thomas Bastard's (1598), John Weever's (1599), Francis Thynne's (1600), John Owen's (1615), and Sir John Harington's (1615, written much earlier) – mostly imitated the Latin epigram of Martial: moral, satiric, hard-boiled.[3] Typically they consisted of short, wittily compressed poems with a single 'point', fully revealed only in the closure, the structure's centre of gravity or levity. Their compression left little room for tropes or foregrounded rhetoric, so that their style was usually plain: they were 'with little art composed' (John Dryden, translating Boileau). (Aptly, this description itself puns: the epigram's art was an art of little.) In J. C. Scaliger's analysis, the epigram had five emotional tonalities, to which he attached culinary labels: *fel, acetum, sal, mel*, and *foetidas*. These can be thought of as emotional stances. *Fel* (gall) is angry, 'bold, licentious, full of gall' (Ben Jonson), as in 'To My Lord Ignorant' (*Epigrams* 10). *Acetum* (vinegar) is 'sharp, and toothed withal', as in 'On Something that Walks Somewhere' (11). *Sal* (salt) is witty or funny, although perhaps with a suggestion of *sal sapientiae*, as in 'To Pertinax Cob' (69). *Mel* (honey) is erotic, or written out of friendship or admiration, as in 'To William Roe' (128) – and here Catullus was more often the model. *Foetidas* (disgusting foulness, or sometimes 'lewd, profane, and beastly phrase') was counselled against, yet often practised to an extent far beyond modern limits of permissibility, as in 'On the Famous Voyage' (133). Ringing the changes on these ingredients promised piquant variety.

So far only the secular Latin model has been mentioned. But there was another tradition altogether: that of the sacred epigram, Latin and Greek, which had been almost continuously active since patristic times, and to which such seventeenth-century masterpieces as Richard Crashaw's *Steps to the Temple* and George Herbert's *The Temple* and *Lucus* notably contributed. There were also important ancient Greek models. From early in the sixteenth century, these were active in continental epigram; and they became significantly more so after Estienne's publication of the *Anacreontea* (1554) and the *Planudean Anthology* (1556), a part of the great *Greek Anthology*. Finally, from around 1600, copies of the more inclusive Palatine manuscript of the *Anthology* began to circulate – just when the epigram vogue was entering its excited state, and when Greek models in all genres were becoming attractive. A critical mass, as it were, was reached; and an amazing burst of creative activity ensued.

The Greek epigram was distinctive in at least two ways. First, it was often ekphrastic, that is, descriptive – particularly of art objects – as in such poets as Christodorus (*Palatine Anthology* 2) and Paulus Silentiarius. Directly or indirectly, this Greek model lies behind the epigrams accompanying Renaissance emblems; behind Edmund Spenser's accounts of tapestries and sculptures in *The Faerie Queene*; and behind countless seventeenth-century poems participating in the *paragone*, or rivalry, between visual and literary art. (In this direction no British poet, however, rivalled Giambattista Marino (1569–1625), whose *Galeria* is an entire volume composed of ekphrastic epigrams.) Secondly, the Greek epigram was more often *mel*, and this in a special, emotionally intense way, unlike the Latin. If the Latin form underlies Jonson's epigrams, it is the Greek of Anacreon that resounds in Herrick's.

Lawrence Manley suggests that around 1600 the epigram passed from Inns of Court gentlemen to professional writers.[4] But professionals were at work earlier; and university wits continued much later to produce epigrams in prodigious quantities. They supplied a great part of the contents of the miscellanies, manuscript and printed – *Wits' Recreations*, *Parnassus Biceps*, and the like – that kept presses busy throughout the seventeenth century. In any event, the epigram transformation has to be thought of as beginning at least as early as 1590.

Arguably the most significant feature of the Renaissance epigram was a negative one: that it had no specified generic subject. One could make an epigram about anything; so that the form was ideally suited to meet the challenges of a time of exploration and information explosion in every direction, inward as well as outward. There were epigrams on fashions and on philosophy; on Pythagorean diets and fat men; music and masturbation; novas and nipples; wet farts and diarrhoea; lawyers and sewage disposal. This freest of forms might almost have been destined for mastery of the new worlds of the seventeenth century. Moreover, situated as it was at the bottom of the paradigm of kinds, it could afford to be intimate and informal. Jonson even claimed it was free from social hierarchies –

> May none, whose scattered names honour my book,
> For strict degrees of rank or title look:
> 'Tis 'gainst the manners of an epigram:
> And, I a poet here, no herald am.
>
> (*Epigrams* 9, 'To All, to Whom I write')

– although this may be an expression of his idiosyncratic republican gall.

Was the epigram, then, a new, non-traditional form? By no means. For its 'spontaneous' novelty itself belonged to a generic tradition. From Martial, Quintilian, Statius, and others, Renaissance poets knew of the antique *sylva* ('forest'; 'material'), a collective genre assembling deliberately spontaneous, uniformly varied epigrams under the guise of a miscellany.[5] Jonson called two of his epigram collections *The Forest* and *Underwood*, in allusion to the ancient genre, and Dryden made even more explicit acknowledgement in his title *Sylvae* (1685). Miscellany, however, need not mean random miscellany. (When Andrea Alciati called his collection of emblem epigrams a farrago, he probably meant, modestly, medley or hotchpotch; but a farrago was also 'collected and gathered' (Sir Matthew Hale): it was a 'made dish'.[6] For Jonson in *The Forest*, sylva meant an elaborately structured symmetrical array. And this possibility was taken much further by George Herbert in *The Temple* (1633), a connected, even graduated exploration of a human heart turning to God, as highly structured as any sonnet sequence.[7] Robert Herrick's calendrically coherent *Hesperides* (1648) is an obvious major achievement in a similar direction.[8] But other sylvas, too, need to be examined structurally, and may well disclose similar organization.

EPIGRAMMATIC TRANSFORMATION

The epigram could be modulated throughout the entire gamut of poetry, by transposing it to the tonality of other genres. Alternatively, it could operate actively on the others, forcing on them its own qualities. And what seventeenth-century genre was not affected in this way? For the epigram's points 'overwhelmed Parnassus with their tide' (Dryden). But this flood was not always destructive. Indeed, it left the fertile sediment of concision; sharp wit; ambiguity; the Augustan couplet (epigram distich in disguise); and an altered difficulty and scale of the literary model, with individual words now for the first time regularly making themselves felt. All this argues a high degree of consciousness of genre. But epigrammatists were nothing if not self-conscious. Jonson (imitating Martial in this) has five epigrams about his own use of the genre; while Herrick (not always a great intellectual) has more than a dozen. Sir John Harington's 'Comparison of the Sonnet and the Epigram' contrasts the sugar of the one with the salt of the other; punning in the closure 'Yet let my verse have salt to make it last.'

Of all kinds, epigram mixed most easily with the sonnet. Both, after all, were structured on a 'turn'. According to one theory, the sonnet was merely a vernacular imitation of *mel* epigram. By 1600, sonnet sequences were ranging over a wide variety of topics and moods, not unlike those of sylvae. Injection of epigrammatism, then, was relatively painless. It could be variously managed, in ways that ranged from a toughening of stance (as, occasionally, in Petrarca himself) to outright dialogue, or even confrontation, of distinct 'parts' of the poem. A mannerist pace-setter in deliberate mixture was Sir Philip Sidney's *Astrophil and Stella* (1591; 1598), where high- and middle-style rhetoric (personifications, apostrophes, metaphorical figures) commingled arrestingly with the intimate, colloquial low style of epigram: 'Desire still cries "Give me some food"' (71) or 'But that which once may win thy cruel heart, / Thou art my Wit, and thou my Virtue art' (64) – where the 'thou' is too intimate for the decorum of the middle style. In Shakespeare's *Sonnets*, the sourness latterly predominates, as if winning out over sonnet sweetness. But epigrammatism was there from the beginning of the sequence in many couplets – plain, unfigurative, epigram distichs – that contrast with the richly metaphoric quatrains before them: 'If this be error and upon me proved, / I never writ nor no man ever loved.' Sir John Davies in his *Gulling Sonnets* and Michael Drayton in *Idea* went in for similarly explicit confrontations of genres.[9] Thomas Sebillet theorized about this possibility with characteristically French extremity; prescribing exactly where in a sonnet epigrammatic 'points' should be interpellated.

Less artificially, sonnet–epigram mixture could be an effort of realism: switching grids of selection might let through more of the complexity of experience. Or sometimes its fascination may have lain in the interactions: confrontations of Christian–Romantic sonnet values and the sceptical–rational values of sour epigram. Non-amorous sonnets continued to be composed well into the seventeenth century, as when William Drummond of Hawthornden realized their religious, and Milton their occasional possibilities; both, in this, taking up Italian traditions.

The kind most profoundly transformed by epigram was probably elegy, a directly contrasting lyric genre characterized by deep feeling, emotional repetition, and often by gradual, reflective insight or change of heart. Ancient Greek elegy, differentiated chiefly by its metre, was not always mourning poetry, but might have other reasons for sadness. Latin elegy, while keeping the elegiac metre, tended to treat themes of love. Early in the Renaissance, classical elegy was recovered by Bernardo Tasso, Ariosto, Garcilasso, and others, and in English there were experiments with quantitative elegiac metre. But the genre was hardly naturalized before it metamorphosed. Milton's 'Lycidas', the first great funeral elegy in English, did not appear until 1638; but already in Donne's 'A Funeral Elegy' in *An Anatomy of the World* (1611) each couplet had its 'point':

> And can she, who no longer would be she,
> Being such a tabernacle, stoop to be
> In paper wrapped; or, when she would not lie
> In such a house, dwell in an elegy?

Donne, whose classic epigrams were comparatively undistinguished (he lacked anger, or else preferred not to show it), was brilliant at mixtures like epigram-elegy. He gave to love elegy a new acuteness of thought and economy of diction, so that he is often intellectually challenging – something that Dr Johnson, who was sometimes averse to mixed forms, disliked in him. Thus Donne's Elegy 19 begins 'Come, Madam, come, all rest my powers defy, / Until I labour, I in labour lie.' This has the repetitions of elegy; but they are not repetitions of quite the same thing. 'Labour' changes meaning, so that by a witty superimposition elegiac *repetitio* has become also epigrammatic *traductio* or pun. As Joseph Spence put it (though with disgust) 'the majority of [Donne's] pieces are nothing but a tissue of epigrams'. Sometimes through the mixture one can detect the particular subgenre of epigram intended – as in 'A Valediction: Of My Name in the Window', where the emblem-description type shows through. In many seventeenth-century elegies, epigrammatic closure takes the form of a *sententia* or adage, or else an inset epitaph, on the pattern of Ovid's *Amores* 2.6.

It is a similar story with the ode, of which the Italian theorists considered the sonnet a short form. Just as with elegy and other forms, mixed variants (anacreontic sonnet; epigram-ode) appeared in the north almost before the pure. (The same happened in the Netherlands, with the mixed genres of Christiaan Huygens and the Dutch mannerists.) In part this was doubtless due to different phasing of the northern Renaissance; in part it may have resulted from the educational pattern mentioned earlier. At any rate, the full range of Michael Drayton's magnificent classical *Odes* did not appear until 1619; whereas Spenser's anacreontics in *Amoretti and Epithalamion*, and his sonnets based on exploits of Cupid, came out in 1595, while Sidney blended similar *genera mista* earlier still. In the seventeenth century, epigrams that amounted to miniature anacreontic odes became exceedingly popular: *festivitas*, early identified as a characteristic of epigram, meant not only 'humour' but also 'conviviality'. Besides anacreontics on drinking and on life's fleeting mutable sweetness (favourite subjects, or apparent subjects, of Herrick's) there were many on small creatures – although here a vernacular tradition intermediated, as several *capricci* in Marino's *Galeria* illustrate. Richard Lovelace, Abraham Cowley, and others imitated Anacreon's grasshopper poem, and Donne's 'The Flea' was part of an endemic infestation.

On a larger plan, even in Jonson's great Cary–Morison Ode the epigrammatic mode can be heard, for example in its metaphysical compression: 'mad'st thy mother's womb thine urn'. Here, Jonson attempts the strophes of the classical Pindaric ode; but usually in English these became stanzas – as with the many fine epithalamia of the period, like Spenser's, Donne's, and

Jonson's. But the possibilities of the ode were most clearly grasped, early in the century, by Drummond, who mediated classical and European poetic ideas to his less-well-read contemporaries Jonson, Drayton, and others. Even the young Milton imitated an ode of Drummond's, in 'On the Morning of Christ's Nativity'. By mid-century, Cowley was achieving truly Pindaric effects of heightening in poems like 'The Praise of Pindar in Imitation of Horace His Second Ode, Book Four'. Soon, however, the finest odes were to be seen as those of Dryden: the Augustan poets took as their vernacular model the measured, less exalted enthusiasm of such poems as the 'Song for St Cecilia's Day', 'Mrs Anne Killigrew', and 'Threnodia Augustalis'. Dryden avoided obvious epigrammatic mixture, yet retained the new scale of economic compression.[10]

PASTORAL AND GEORGIC

Turning to genres of middle size, one finds the main plot of the seventeenth century to be a bold revaluation of classical georgic, the rustic description or manual of an art. The georgic sector of the *rota Vergiliana* had in one way or another accounted for much of medieval literature: treatises, prologues, seasonal poetry, georgic sonnets. But in the sixteenth century many Renaissance Aristotelians (the leading cadre of literary theorists) questioned whether georgic should count as poetry at all, or even as literature.[11] For, as they pointed out, it was not fictive: it described what was actually the case. Thus, Sidney in his *Defence of Poesy* despises georgic as merely imitative: the georgic poet 'takes not the course of his own invention'. In the seventeenth century, however, a shift of theory, a turning away from Aristotle and Cicero, allowed revaluation of *ekphrasis* and the descriptive kinds. By the end of the seventeenth century, Joseph Addison was able to popularize the idea of the *Georgics* as Virgil's consummate achievement. His 1697 Preface to Dryden's Virgil can be seen as having set the scene, indeed, for georgic's domination of Augustan literature.

The rise of georgic has been related to a so-called 'georgic revolution' in agriculture, or to a 'revolution' of the Country party (white hats against an evil Court). On Anthony Low's thesis, georgic was 'belated' in England because English aristocrats disdained physical labour and hated Virgilian georgic's work ethic, preferring the indolent *otium* of pastoral.[12] But dispassionate study – some of it Low's own – has found more practitioners of georgic among royalists such as Robert Herrick and Sir John Denham than among the Commonwealth men. (Many Puritans had little interest in secular poetry.) As for English georgic's belatedness, that too has been subjected to revisionist questioning.[13] It seems that the georgics exist all right, but have remained unnoticed. Imitation of longer forms naturally tended to be looser, so that identification may now be far from easy. But one can be sure that the impulse to georgic was strong in Spenser's introduction of seasons in *The Shepheardes Calender*; in the agricultural imagery of authorial interpositions in *The Faerie Queene*; and in his descriptively specific catalogues of nature. A decisive turning-point may have been Drayton's *Poly-Olbion* (1612; 1622), where the digressiveness of georgic was carried to heroic lengths; allowing room to naturalize the classical form by interweaving British antiquities from William Camden and John Selden. Drayton's meanderingly digressive river-wanderings (to say nothing of Spenser's spousals of Thames and Medway) made the flow of national destiny a characteristic theme of English georgic (*Cooper's Hill*; *Windsor Forest*) and allowed the genre to engage some of the age's most serious aspirations. Another turning-point was probably Chapman's *Hesiod's Georgics* (1618). The fact that Virgil's *Georgics* was juxtaposed with Hesiod and other didactic models ensured that the seventeenth-century genre was looser, more capacious, and more heuristic than that of later neoclassicists.

Others may refer the georgic impulse to philosophical antecedents such as the ideas of Seneca (especially Seneca on retirement or on landscape, as in *Epistle* 90); or to political and social circumstances, such as the rise of landscape gardening, or the forced retirement of gentry and clergy from about 1630 to 1660. The seclusion of the Happy Man was a topic of Hesiod's *Georgics*; and one sees even Donne – urban and courtly as he was – feeling the attraction of its diction, if not of the country itself. In 'To Mr Roland Woodward' we are told to be 'farmers of ourselves'; and he urges Woodward 'manure thyself'.[14]

Georgic and pastoral often contrast with one another, as can be seen from the direct confrontations of lifestyles in *As You Like It*, or from Drayton's Sixth Nymphal (a *paragone* of shepherd, fisherman, and georgic woodsman). But modern confusion of the two is nevertheless understandable, in view of their already being mixed, if not exactly confused, in the English Renaissance. This doubtless had to do with the fact that England was the chief wool producer in Europe. Sheep were connected with so many familiar trades (at least sixteen of them) that pastoral could scarcely have, for the English, quite the same aura of simplicity, innocence, and ease. Robert Hooker the theologian and pastor kept literal sheep. Spenser's shepherds were not all ignorant and guileless. Before long, the Spenserian William Browne (1590?–1645?), a member of Drayton's circle, was practising a thoroughly blended genre, full of realistic rustic detail, that predicted Wordsworthian pastoral, and can be taken for granted, even now, as nature poetry. The opening of the Second Song of his *Britannia's Pastorals* (1616) is

as crisply, georgically descriptive as anything in seventeenth-century
literature:

> The Muses' friend (gray-eyed Aurora) yet
> Held all the meadows in a cooling sweat,
> The milk-white gossamers not upwards snowed,
> Nor was the sharp and useful steering goad
> Laid on the strong-necked ox; no gentle bud
> The sun had dried; the cattle chewed the cud
> Low levelled on the grass; no fly's quick sting
> Enforced the stonehorse in a furious ring
> To tear the passive earth, nor lash his tail
> About his buttocks broad; the slimy snail
> Might on the wainscot (by his many mazes'
> Winding meanders and self-knitting traces)
> Be followed, where he stuck, his glittering slime
> Not yet wiped off. It was so early time
> The careful smith had in his sooty forge
> Kindled no coal; nor did his hammers urge
> His neighbours' patience; owls abroad did fly,
> And day as then might plead his infancy.

Such writing is often simply called pastoral; but of course shepherds never
hear a blacksmith's hammer: the ox and the stallion are farmyard animals:
and details like the steering goad or the snail's trace are quite outside the
descriptive range of idealizing, generalizing pastoral. Browne found inspiration in the *Georgics* of Virgil, not in his *Pastorals*. The delicacy of
Browne's modulation, however, may be gauged by the fact that the hammer
is still silent, and the snail, in its way, idle enough.

Nevertheless, it would not be true to call pastoral a sixteenth-century
form, and say that its political function was taken over in the seventeenth
century by the less covert georgic.[15] For pastoral continued popular – so
much so that it actively affected many other genres, appearing in romances;
in masques; in Beaumont and Fletcher's dramatic *genera mista*; in songs by
Nicholas Breton, George Wither, and countless others; and in moral fables
like Dryden's *Baucis and Philemon*. Again, outspoken pastoral satire, in
works like Wither's *Shepherds' Hunting* (1615), stood in the humanist tradition of Petrarca, Baptista Spagnuoli, and Spenser. Later in the century,
however, Dryden construed Spenser's contribution in a different way. He
initiated a return to purity or singleness of genre; so that he praises Spenser's
pastoral for returning to ancient origins: 'Spenser, being master of our
northern dialect, and skilled in Chaucer's English, has so exactly imitated
the Doric of Theocritus, that his love is a perfect image of that passion . . .

before it was corrupted.'[16] A similar tendency can be seen in the rigorous simplicity of Alexander Pope's *Pastorals*. The classical genre still had more to offer, if free imitation, subtilized by a century of fine-scale composition, would attend to its finer nuances.

It was in the seventeenth century that classical pastoral made its most fertile contribution, combining in this with the vernacular Sannazaro's *Arcadia*. Theocritus' piscatorial Idylls, in particular, offered valuable models, as can be seen not only in Drayton's Sixth Nymphal but in a wide variety of piscatorial eclogues and 'pastoral' lyrics and georgic passages, from Phineas Fletcher to William Basse and Pope's *Windsor Forest*. At however many removes, Izaak Walton's delicious *The Complete Angler*, the quintessential example of *genera mista*, perpetuates something of Theocritus' familiarity with real country life, as well as his retrospective idealization. In Walton, piscatorial eclogue in prose is developed symbolically, as a vehicle for allusive treatment of meditation, happy life, retirement, and other georgic concerns.

NEW GENRES

But were there not also new genres in the seventeenth century? Perhaps this question is inappropriate. To contrast 'new' with traditional kinds is to misconceive how genre worked. For, in a myriad ways, ancient genres functioned precisely as institutions of renovation and renewal.[17] The Renaissance was like a literary *renovatio*, in which the classical genres were 'new' beside the old inherited medieval ones, and provided fresh strategies for 'reforming' them. Simply to naturalize a classical form was to innovate; as when Drayton achieved the *translatio* of ode into local Derbyshire terms. Alternatively, striking innovations could be produced by selecting an untried range of classical models. Thus, in the early seventeenth century, after fifty years of 'fat' Virgilian–Ciceronian genres, imitation turned to 'thin' or pithy forms based on Callimachus, Seneca, and Persius; the novelties of Jonson, Herrick, and Marvell eventuated. ('Upon Appleton House' has been called a heroically enlarged estate poem; but from another viewpoint it could be seen as a brief Callimachian epic, using the digressions of georgic as occasions for tricky insets and perspective effects.) Indeed, the whole taste for small forms can be construed as a turning from classical to Hellenistic models.

Or, a poem could be novel through direct *recusatio* (refusal) of a classical or vernacular generic tradition. So Milton decisively rejected chivalric epic 'not sedulous by nature to indite / Wars, hitherto the only argument / Heroic deemed'.[18] But even so, even if one allows for such possibilities,

surely it remains true that new genres abounded in the seventeenth century
– doubtless invented in response to *nova reperta*? Poems about landscapes;
estates; buildings; topography; science; paintings (whether in the form of a
paragone or of advice to a painter): what have such as these to do with
traditional genres?

It is easy now to think of the landscape poem as a distinct genre with a
definite subject. As such, it was a type as new, in the seventeenth century, as
the Dutch *landschap* that was contemporaneously emerging. Viewed in
another light, however, the landscape genre was descriptive, and continued
the late-Elizabethan vogue for ekphrastic poetry, that is, vivid description of
art objects. In the 1590s, the ekphrastic element in Ovid entranced Elizabethan poets.[19] Arthur Golding offered description as a main attraction of
his Ovid: 'Moreover thou mayst find herein descriptions of the times: / with
constellations of the stars and planets in their climes: / The sites of countries, cities, hills, seas, forests, plains and floods: / The natures both of
fowls, beasts, worms, herbs, metals, stones and woods'[20]; Marlowe's *Hero
and Leander* is a tissue of *ekphraseis*; *The Faerie Queene* puts the tapestries
of Ovid's *Metamorphoses* 6.70–102 to new uses; and Chapman's *The Shield
of Achilles*, an extended *ekphrasis*, was published out of sequence in 1598,
among his earliest essays in translating Homer, doubtless to arouse readers'
interest in the project. Descriptive writing may have found support of
another sort in the popularity of epigram; since that genre turned attention
away from fiction, and towards actual objects of imitation. Had not Martial
himself rejected the *vana ludibria* (vain fabrications) of story? Finally, in the
setting of seventeenth-century georgic and widespread landscape and estate
improvement, the urge to describe took a new direction. Once conceived as
a medium of agricultural and horticultural art, landscape became a fit
subject for *ekphrasis* – and even for writing (and painting) direct from
'nature'. Direct, that is, but for the mediating interposition of literary precedents. Given the ambience that in other spheres brought on the Royal
Society and institutionalized scientific research, value increasingly attached
to exact description in literature too. But, empirical as the impulse was, it
needed schemata and rhetorical models, valued topics and standards of
achievement; all of which were found in georgic literature. Poets ransacked
Hesiod, Virgil, and Lucretius; neo-Latin georgic of the continental Renaissance (Giovanni Pontano, for example, and Angelo Poliziano in *Rusticus*
mood); and, at a popular level, Du Bartas-Sylvester.[21]

Seventeenth-century landscape poems thus belong to genres within the
georgic or descriptive mode, whether or not mixed with the ekphrastic. One
may find them labelled as 'perspective' or prospective poems, like Denham's
Cooper's Hill – what is now often called topographical. Or they may be

ekphraseis – again, perhaps, called 'perspective' – of landscape paintings or imaginary scenes, whether realistic, or, like George Daniel's 'The Landscape' and Margaret Cavendish's 'A Landscape', symbolic.[22] Or, occasionally, they are harder to group – more 'original' – like William Strode's 'The Great Tree'. But all are georgic, as their digressive structures and authorial viewpoints soon show. The country-house poem, often treated as an independent new genre, similarly turns out on examination to belong in a close-knit group of subgenres with interrelated topics: the estate poem (Jonson's 'To Penshurst'); the park poem (Sir Edmund Waller's 'At Penshurst (I)'); the entertainment poem (Richard Leigh's 'On the Duke of Newburgh's Entertainment'); the welcome (Thomas Carew's 'To the King at His Entrance'); the invitation (Thomas Randolph's 'An Ode to Mr Anthony Stafford to Hasten Him into the Country'); the retirement poem (Lord Fairfax's 'The Solitude'); and the ideal day (Mildmay Fane's 'My Happy Life'). As I have argued elsewhere, these too are all georgic genres, as are such essay poems as Cowley's 'Of Solitude'.[23] Fuller understanding of such connections is likely to come through discourse analysis of their topical rhetoric. What relates and distinguishes them, after all, is largely their occasions, or speech-act contexts, in ceremonies of hospitality and duties of the land. They have similar, closely related, yet distinct, domains of association.

In the erotic mode, similarly, 'new' genres are said to have abounded. But here, too, if vernacular as well as classical traditions are taken into account, the novelty may come to seem more apparent than real. The lustiness or sourness of Jacobean love poetry was often simply a disguised, epigrammatic modulation of Elizabethan sweetness. Gone, it is true, were the old *blasons* – the tinctures of virtues adumbrating neo-Platonic images of a sonnet fair. Jacobean and Caroline mistresses might be black, or yellow, or ugly, or deformed; calling in question, in one way or another, the significance, even the objective existence, of beauty. Gone, too, or much reduced, were the endless complaints about virtuous cruelty. In the new moral climate, sexual cruelty was a sin. Poets like George Daniel could even be cynical about what 'neo-Platonism' might amount to in actual courtly behaviour. For, as if to subvert neo-Platonic assumptions further, countless erotomachic poems praised – or, in rebuttal, dispraised – either 'fruition' (coitus), or, its ostensible opponent, 'platonique' love. The issues were becoming less exclusively concerned with the granting of grace to the lover. To desire a compliant mistress was perhaps now to wish for a not altogether impossible she. But whether or not this considerable slide of the emotional landscape actually occurred outside milieux of wish-fulfilment and of the whorehouse, one can say with some assurance that it was far from marking a wholly new age in the literature of love. Many traditions of love poetry continued to thrive vigorously, not so much rejected as renovated. Consummated love, after all, was hardly unknown in classical erotic poetry. And Petrarchan, even Petrarchist, topics were highly susceptible to fresh statement – recoloured, perhaps, in more acid flesh-pinks, or luridly inverted and perverted. This was not just a matter of contingent intertextualities, borrowings, thefts – although of course these continued, to an accompaniment of smart or brazen denials of indebtedness. It was also that the new love poets used traditional devices of rhetoric as a regular part of their *imitatio*.

IMITATION

When the history of *imitatio* comes to be written, it is likely to describe the period from Donne to Dryden as divided into two overlapping or interfering phases. The first of these saw Renaissance humanist reinvention of the classical genres – pure, unmixed, unified, going by the book of Cicero and Aristotle – give way, from around 1585, to mannerist complication. Imitation became more exploitative or even transgressive, full of inversions, finesses, complex mixtures, contradictions resolved with difficulty. This complicating of the classical (and mostly classical Latin) tradition accelerated in the seventeenth century, with the tendency to prefer Hellenistic and silver Latin, or at least different classical models – Theocritus, Callimachus, and Hesiod; Seneca, Lucan, Statius, and Ausonius. But at the same time, continuity was preserved by a sustained reliance on the generic constructive types that all periods of classical and vernacular literature have shared.[24] In Elegy 19, for example, Donne uses not only epigram and elegy but also *blason*, or anatomical inventory – albeit a *blason* corrupted, after the manner of sixteenth-century French erotica.[25] (The personal features are rearranged to form a climactic progression of increasing intimacy.) In 'A Valediction: Forbidding Mourning', besides epigram and emblem, he adapts the rhetorical form known as *propemptikon*, or *valedictio*, whose topics of leave-taking have been addressed for thousands of years, with varying degrees of awareness and competence.[26] Many similar constructive types – for example *ekphrasis*, *recusatio* (rejection of subjects), and *priamel* (structured selection)[27] – continued to be used throughout all the innovations of the period. Indeed, they have continued since, as part of an unwritten craft tradition, which would repay much further study. As for Donne's valedictions, what is remarkable about them, and about many metaphysical or mannerist poems, is not so much large-scale generic innovation (the Tribe of Ben could do that better), and certainly not poetic art; but rather rhetorical energy.

The second phase brought a return to *imitatio* of golden-age authors. But the method was not quite that of the Renaissance; poets now tried to naturalize the fine detail of classical genres. Educational reform, or perhaps changes in the scale of the poetic model – readers' expectations of poetry – had apparently gone far enough for allusion and close stylistic imitation to commence. Even the taste for Greek had had its reforming aspect; bound up as it was with a theological return to primitive doctrine and the Greek Fathers. Now the new *imitatio* adopted a principle of Thorough that might lead to rational reform.

Milton's disciplined return to Christian humanism, rejecting Jacobean freedom, is the paradigmatic example of this stricter imitation. In *Samson Agonistes* he speaks of imitating 'tragedy, as it was anciently composed ... tragedy coming forth after the ancient manner'. But this is not to be put down to Milton's Puritan rage for reform. Those Puritans who had an interest in poetry seldom went in for correct classicism. Besides, equally prominent instances of pure classicism are seen in Denham, Dryden, and other King's Men. Herrick and Cowley, indeed, with their minutely classical generic effects, are better instances even than Milton. All reached out to an Augustan classicism: an ideal of reform through *renovatio* of reapplication of socially relevant classical genres. Of such *imitatio*, one of the most influential practitioners was John Oldham (1653–83), whose satires do not merely engage with ancient models through structural mimicry (in any event a difficult thing to do in the case of this genre), but by inventing in the spirit of Juvenal, and finding exactly equivalent modern targets. In this way, genre was for Oldham a means of discovering the moral structure of his own world. Sixteenth-century satire had assumed a good deal of doctrinal agreement: it was enough to point to the abuse and the offender. Now, however, satire had to analyze and persuade; and in this the classical satirists were useful guides. Lampoon and satire consequently began to be distinguished, as for example they are in Sir Thomas Blount's *De Re Poetica* (1694).

Even here, however, vernacular generic traditions remained lively. In 'A Satire: The Person of Spenser is Brought in, Dissuading the Author from the Study of Poetry ... ', in the very midst of imitating Juvenal, Oldham alludes to romance convention: he delays naming Spenser's ghost, in the manner of *The Faerie Queene* itself. The sequence of English satire exhibited in such ways a fluctuating but nevertheless distinct trend towards refining the scale of its effects. This can be seen as one scans the genre from Chaucer and Langland to Skelton, bold Wyatt, angry Joseph Hall, Donne with his guarded generalities, Oldham, and Rochester. Even the theory and perfected practice of Dryden was not minutely enough considered for Pope. In this sequence, changing generic concepts played a large part. Pope's *rifa-*

cimento of Donne's *Satires* introduce nuances and fine rhythms that the earlier poet had not thought to attempt. But the roughness Pope and Spence disliked in Donne was not altogether the result of incompetence and negligence. Donne and his contemporaries thought that satires (which they spelled 'satyres') should be rough like a satyr's pelt. This was false etymology, and false doctrine out of Renaissance Italian genre theory; Dryden, with his improved knowledge of the classics, corrected it.

PARADIGMS OF GENRES

Broader conceptions of the interrelations between genres also derived in large part from classical sources. The ancient systems had of course undergone much diachronic change; but Renaissance theorists depended selectively on Cicero, Quintilian, Diomedes, and relatively few other authorities.[28] Mainly on the basis of three ordering principles (metre, style height, and rank or value), the principal genres were arranged in paradigms or sequences of a dozen or less. Quintilian's version is *Epic | Pastoral | Elegiac | Satiric | Iambic | Lyric | Comic | Tragic* – where iambic may imply, besides the iambic metre, the genre of epode: poems of friendship, moralizing, or vituperation. In sixteenth- and seventeenth-century paradigms, epic, tragedy, hymn (the highest lyric form), and genres like metamorphosis using heroic metres, generally headed the list; while epigram might come last, or count as lowest.

Vernacular kinds like the sonnet were not easy to accommodate within such paradigms. This difficulty gave rise to much theorizing, and even to some innovative categories – notably Sir John Harington's 'amatory', in a paradigm of eight genres. The great quantities of popular verse at the base of literature's pyramid seldom won recognition; but Edward Phillips's 'epoinetic' genre may possibly have included popular bacchanalian verse besides Anacreontic odes. For in the seventeenth century generic paradigms were seldom rigid. On the contrary, they often give an incomplete, provisional impression; as in Dudley North's imaginative analogy: 'Music hath its anthems, pavans, fantasies, galliards, corantos, airs, sarabands, toys, chromatics, etc. And verses have their hymns, tragedies, satires, heroics, sonnets, odes, songs, epigrams, distichs, and strong lines, which are their chromatics.'[29] But, however unsystematic North's catalogue may seem, it has hymn, or high lyric, in first place; whereas low epigram comes last. His grouping of sonnet with the 'sung' genres ode and song probably implies the doctrine (of Antonio Sebastiano Minturno and others) that sonnet and ode are subtypes of *carmen* – a doctrine also reflected in the labelling convention in scribal manuscripts, whereby 'sonnet' means 'set to music'.[30]

Apparently, North still takes for granted the standard classical paradigm; although his inclusion of the fashionable 'strong lines' of epigrammatic wit glances at changes on the way.

North does not include georgic in his paradigm; nor do Sidney, Harington, or Francis Meres in theirs – unless it is subsumed under their pastoral, as an impurity or minor ingredient. But a new emphasis, didactic and empirical, can be seen in such mid-century lists as Philomusus' (T. C.'s), in his complimentary verses before Thomas Philipott's *Poems* (1646). Philipott's volume is said to contain

> Wit's curious tapestry
> Hymns, pastorals, elegies,
> Observatives, divinity,
> Philosophic scrutinies;
> It may be called a florilege for all
> That have not time for studies general.

Here 'florilege' may approximate to 'sylva'; but other of the terms are more exploratory. And soon georgic received explicit recognition. By 1665 Robert Boyle is calling 'the style of [Virgil's] *Georgics* as well noble . . . as that of his *Aeneids*'.[31] In Edward Phillips's paradigm of 1675, pastoral significantly makes way for bucolic, a term (from *boukolos*, cowherd) inclusive of rustic poetry at least, if not synonymous with georgic.[32] The way is open for Addison's 1797 elevation of georgic.

It was a similar story with satire and epigram. Even Dryden's 1683 translation of Boileau's *Art Poétique* (1674) paid fealty to the new tyrant epigram; and by 1704 Thomas Brown could write in *Praise of Poverty* that 'an epigrammatic poem is more charming than Homer or Virgil'. In such ways, adjustments to the classical paradigm provided a means whereby seventeenth-century theorists might take account of changes in poetic taste. The paradigm, while it served as a benchmark, was by no means immutable.

Even allowing for theory's inevitable belatedness, however, seventeenth-century movements of the classical paradigm can seem inexplicably random, if the generic atoms are conceived as hard-edged billiard balls. But the changes make more sense if one thinks of the genres as (at least in part) familial literary contexts, clusters or domains of relevant associations. When genre is viewed in this way, the classical paradigm shows up as vitally challenging throughout: ever exerting its pressure for reform or aspiration, constantly exerting newly varied restraints.

How this worked can perhaps be traced in seventeenth-century epic, a genre of which it is sometimes said merely that it became impossible to write. Until Spenser, heroic poems were either Virgilian epics or Ariostan romances; although shorter, Callimachian forms (epyllion; brief epic) were also becoming possible, as *Orchestra* (1596), *Hero and Leander* (1598), and other *epyllia* and biblical narratives show. But all this changed, in ways that may have had to do with agricultural improvements, visions of England as a garden, revaluations of landscape, and a new enthusiasm for classical georgic. Chapman translated Hesiod, Drayton carried through the adventure of his heroic georgic *Poly-Olbion*, and Cowley prematurely attempted a georgic epic, *Davideis* (probably written before 1645; printed 1656), with passages on retirement and on an institution for scientific study. One classical genre seems thus to have been used to modify another, in accordance with new requirements of relevance. Another procedure was to switch classical models: after the French civil wars, *Pharsalia*, Lucan's epic on contemporary history, attracted great interest. This issued not only in Thomas May's translation (1627) but in Cowley's *The Civil War*, and other less brilliant historical epics, like Sir John Beaumont's *Bosworth Field* (1629). As for Milton's *Paradise Lost*, it is not Virgilian epic either, but a complex assimilation and critique of many epic forms, with georgic (itself anciently given to epic excursions) predominating at strategic points. Georgic stands out in such passages as the descriptions of Eden and of creation, but may also be said to work unobtrusive furrows throughout. It was only the martial, aristocratic, chivalric epic that Milton parodied and subtilized into obsolescence. Georgic epic, on the contrary, flourished after his heroic gardening, and was to dominate eighteenth-century poetry up to James Thomson's *Seasons*, James Beattie's *The Minstrel* and William Wordsworth's *The Prelude*. Milton's comprehending of different forms of epic in *Paradise Lost* may be compared with Joyce's epitomizing of narrative forms in *Ulysses*. As Joyce stood between Victorianism and modernism, so Milton returned, perhaps, to classical humanism in order to signal a new onset in the age-long *querelle* of Ancients and Moderns.

All the most fruitful innovations and generic changes in seventeenth-century poetry seem to have been worked out through dialogue with classical and medieval tradition. And one may hazard the guess that something analogous is true of the centuries following, up to the decline of classical education in our own. Think of Whitman's heroic georgic *Song of Myself*, or Pound's First Canto drawing on Andreas Divus's neo-Latin *Odyssey*. Perhaps only in our own time has this gearing with long-term tradition been threatened. Apprehension about the results, if contact is lost, must arouse profound disquiet.

NOTES

1 Rosalie L. Colie, *The Resources of Kind: Genre-Theory in the Renaissance*, ed. Barbara Keifer Lewalski (Berkeley, Calif.: University of California Press, 1973), pp. 3ff.; see also R. R. Bolgar, *The Classical Heritage and Its Beneficiaries* (Cambridge University Press, 1954).

2 Colie, *Resources*, p. 4; Bolgar; Charles Martindale, *John Milton and the Transformation of Ancient Epic* (London: Croom Helm, 1986).

3 Besides partial translations or imitations of Martial, STC lists two Latin editions (1615 and 1633) and two translations (Vachan's, 1571; May's, 1629). Wing has nine Latin editions and four translations.

4 See Laurence Hanley, 'Proverbs, Epigrams, and Urbanity in Renaissance London', *ELR* 15.3 (1985): 26.

5 See Alastair Fowler, 'The *Silva* Tradition in Jonson's *The Forrest*', in *Poetic Traditions of the English Renaissance*, ed. Maynard Mack and George de Forest Lord (New Haven: Yale University Press, 1982), pp. 163–80. On the epigram generally, see Hoyt H. Hudson, *The Epigram in the English Renaissance* (Princeton University Press, 1947).

6 Ben Jonson, *Magnetic Lady* 1.7.

7 See Colie, *Resources*, pp. 57ff., on the *schola cordis* or School of the Heart.

8 See Alastair Fowler, 'Robert Herrick', Warton Lecture, *PBA* 66 (1980): 243–64.

9 See Ann Baynes Coiro, *Robert Herrick's 'Hesperides' and the Epigram Book Tradition* (Baltimore: Johns Hopkins University Press, 1988), p. 32; Alastair Fowler, *Kinds of Literature* (Cambridge, Mass.: Harvard University Press; Oxford: Clarendon Press, 1982), p. 185.

10 See Carol Maddison, *Apollo and the Nine* (Baltimore: Johns Hopkins University Press, 1960); G. W. Pigman III, *Grief and English Renaissance Elegy* (Cambridge University Press, 1985); Ruth C. Wallerstein, *Studies in Seventeenth-Century Poetic* (Madison: University of Wisconsin Press, 1950).

11 Colie, *Resources*, p. 9.

12 Anthony Low, *The Georgic Revolution* (Princeton University Press, 1985).

13 See Alastair Fowler, 'The Beginnings of English Georgic', in *Renaissance Genres*, ed. Barbara Kiefer Lewalski (Cambridge, Mass.: Harvard University Press, 1986), pp. 105–25.

14 See Maren-Sofie Røstvig, *The Happy Man*, 2 vols. (rev. edn; Oslo: Norwegian University Press, 1962, 1971).

15 On the disguised politics of earlier pastoral, see Helen Cooper, *Pastoral: Medieval into Renaissance* (Ipswich: Brewer; Totowa, N.J.: Rowman and Littlefield, 1977); and (for a more new historicist view) Annabel Patterson 'Reopening the Green Cabinet: Clément Marot and Edmund Spenser', *ELR* 16.1 (1986): 44–70.

16 Dedicatory Epistle before *Pastorals* (1697).

17 See William H. Race, *Classical Genres and English Poetry* (London: Croom Helm, 1988), chapter 1.

18 *Paradise Lost* 9.27.

19 See Race, *Classical Genres*, chapter 3.

20 'To the Reader', lines 199–202; ed. W. H. D. Rouse (London: Centaur, 1961), p. 19.

21 P. A. F. van Veen, *De Soeticheydt des Buyten-Levens* ... (The Hague: Van Goor

Zonen, 1960); Lisa Vergara, *Rubens and the Poetics of Landscape* (New Haven; Yale University Press, 1982); and Peter C. Sutton, ed., *Masters of Seventeenth-Century Dutch Landscape Painting*, Exhibition Catalogue. (London, Herbert Press, 1987) have all shown the pervasive intertextual effects of Virgil's *Georgics* in Netherlandish painting and poetry.

22 *The New Oxford Book of Seventeenth Century Verse*, ed. Alastair Fowler, nos. 611, 695. See James Turner, *The Politics of Landscape* (Cambridge, Mass.: Harvard University Press, 1979), pp. 42–8.

23 See Fowler, 'The Beginnings'.

24 Francis Cairns, *Generic Composition in Greek and Roman Poetry* (Edinburgh University Press, 1972); Race, *Classical Genres*, Fowler, *Kinds of Literature* and 'The Future of Genre Theory: Functions and Constructional Types', in *The Future of Literary Theory*, ed. Ralph Cohen (London: Routledge, 1989).

25 D. B. Wilson, *Descriptive Poetry in France from Blason to Baroque* (Manchester: Manchester University Press, 1967). On the origins of the *blason* in classical tradition, see Race, *Classical Genres*, p. 80 n5.

26 See Cairns, *Generic Composition*, with many examples.

27 To list some of the topics of William Race's excellent study *Classical Genres*.

28 See further in Fowler, *Kinds of Literature*, chapter 12.

29 *Forest of Varieties*, cit. Colie, *Resources of Kind*, p. 6.

30 On this convention, see *English Manuscript Studies 1100–1700* 1 (ed. Peter Beal and Jeremy Griffiths) (1990): 194.

31 Preface to *Occasional Reflections upon Several Subjects*.

32 Cf. the categories of Blount's *De Re Poetica* (1694), where bucolic and pastoral, ploughman and shepherd, are lumped together.

FURTHER READING

Chalker, John., *The English Georgic* (London: Routledge and Kegan Paul; Baltimore: Johns Hopkins University Press, 1969)

Colie, Rosalie L., *Shakespeare's Living Art* (Princeton University Press, 1974)

Durling, Dwight L., *The Georgic Tradition in English Poetry*, Columbia University Studies in English and Comparative Literature, no. 121 (New York: Columbia University Press, 1935)

Ettin, Andrew V., *Literature and Pastoral* (New Haven: Yale University Press, 1984)

Fry, Paul H., *The Poet's Calling in the English Ode* (New Haven: Yale University Press, 1980)

Greg, W. W., *Pastoral Poetry and Pastoral Drama* (London: Bullen, 1906)

Ide, Richard S. and Wittreich, Joseph (eds.), *Composite Orders: The Genres of Milton's Last Poems*, Milton Studics, no. 17 (University of Pittsburgh Press, 1983)

Lerner, Laurence, *The Uses of Nostalgia: Studies in Pastoral Poetry* (London: Chatto and Windus, 1972)

Lewalski, Barbara Kiefer, *'Paradise Lost' and the Rhetoric of Literary Forms* (Princeton University Press, 1985)

   Milton's Brief Epic: The Genre, Meaning, and Art of 'Paradise Regained' (Providence: Brown University Press; London: Methuen, 1966)

   Renaissance Genres (Cambridge, Mass.: Harvard University Press, 1986)

Marinelli, Peter V., *Pastoral*, Critical Idiom (London: Methuen, 1971)

McClung, William A., *The Country House in English Renaissance Poetry* (Berkeley: University of California Press, 1977)

Murphy, Avon Jack, 'The Critical Elegy of Earlier Seventeenth-Century England', *Genre* 5 (1972): 75–105

Patterson, Annabel, *Pastoral and Ideology: Virgil to Valery* (Berkeley: California University Press, 1987)

Pigman, G. W., III., *Grief and English Renaissance Elegy* (Cambridge, Mass.: Harvard University Press, 1985)

Roche, Thomas P., Jr, *Petrarch and the English Sonnet Tradition* (New York: AMS, 1990)

Turner, James, *The Politics of Landscape: Rural Scenery and Society in English Poetry 1630–1660* (Cambridge, Mass.: Harvard University Press, 1979)

Williams, Raymond, *The Country and the City* (London: Chatto and Windus, 1973)

5

BRIAN VICKERS

Rhetoric

One of the great achievements of modern literary studies has been the rediscovery of rhetoric. Thanks to the work of such scholars as E. R. Curtius,
E. Faral, and B. Muntéano we now know that rhetoric was a great forma-
tive influence on writers of all kinds from Virgil and Ovid to the generation
of Goethe, Byron, and Stendhal. Although Romantic aesthetics programma-
tically rejected any external literary form in favour of spontaneous utterance, writers continued to use rhetoric, and its influence persisted well into
this century.[1] As a system teaching the art of composition and self-express-
ion, rhetoric profoundly influenced poetry, drama, non-fictional prose
works (history, philosophy, autobiography), religious poetry and prose
(prayers, sermons). As the first fully developed aesthetic system it also
affected ancient theories of art, and in the great period of its revival in early
modern Europe, from 1400 to 1800, it was very influential in the visual arts
(painting, sculpture, architecture), and in both the composing and perform-
ing of music.[2] For English literature its high point of influence was in the 150
years between the Elizabethan writers and the Augustans. A knowledge of
rhetoric is indispensable to understanding not only the forms taken by
literature in this period but also the motives behind composition, the
writer's attitude to both his material and his readers.

When rhetoric was first developed in Greece, about 450 BC, it was for
practical, civic purposes.[3] Citizens qualified to take part in Athenian public
affairs, whether political discussion or legal disputes, had to appear and
speak in person, and a demand soon arose for instruction, both theoretical
and practical. The Sophists, a school of philosophers devoted to the practicalities of social life, taught the art of persuasive oratory, while the legal,
ethical, and psychological aspects were brilliantly treated by Aristotle in his
Rhetoric (c.335 BC). Later Greek rhetoric-books dealt with purely literary
topics, such as composition or structure, modes of persuasion, and style,
analyzing in great detail all the rhetorical devices of language (the figures
and tropes). In Rome[4] rhetoric also began as a practical art in the face-to-

face confrontations of politics and law, but when political developments made democratic debate impossible it became the discipline dominating education,[5] literature, and literary criticism.[6]

By the first century BC the whole Roman educational system, lasting six to eight years, was based on rhetoric. The basis of western education up to the nineteenth century was already formed in the concept of the 'Seven Liberal Arts': the *trivium* (comprising grammar, rhetoric, dialectic), and the *quadrivium* (mathematics, music, geography, astronomy). Whereas the outstanding writer on rhetoric in the first century BC, Cicero, was a lawyer and politician, his counterpart in the first century AD, Quintilian, was a schoolmaster. His *Institutio oratoria* (AD 92–4) is the largest and most comprehensive classical treatise. Books 1 and 2 deal with the nature of rhetoric and how it should be taught. Books 3 to 7 are dedicated to the first two stages of composition, *inventio* and *dispositio*, the finding of arguments and their arrangement. Books 8 to 11 discuss *elocutio* or eloquence, including the remaining stages, *memoria* (all speeches in antiquity were delivered from memory), and *pronuntiatio* or *actio* (expressive gesture), while Book 12 delineates the complete orator.

The success that rhetoric enjoyed in public life in Greece and Rome was due to its power over human minds, its ability to change or reinforce a belief. Cicero, making explicit an insight found in Aristotle, described the orator's duties as threefold, *movere, docere*, and *delectare*: 'the proof of our allegations, the winning of our hearers' favour, and the rousing of their feelings to whatever impulse our case may require' (*De Oratore* 2.27.115). Of the three, the most important was *movere*, with the orator supposedly exercising complete power over his audience's emotions. The major resource for arousing the emotions was *elocutio*, persuasive language, without which, Quintilian wrote in a much-imitated sentence, all the other 'accomplishments of oratory are as useless as a sword that is kept permanently concealed within its sheath' (*Institutio oratoria*, 8.Pr.15–16). The primacy of *movere*, and the importance of *elocutio* in gaining power over the audience, were two key principles in rhetoric from its revival in the Renaissance up to the Romantics.[7] The main tools within *elocutio* were twofold, first the tropes, verbal devices which 'turned' the meaning of a word or phrase from one area of reference to another, including metaphor (known in Latin as *translatio*), allegory, irony, metonymy, and some twenty other devices. Secondly, there were the more numerous figures (numbering over two hundred in some handbooks), which achieved their effect by the placing or repetition of a word, at the beginning or end of a sentence, say, or repeated within it, or repeated but varied in form.

When rhetoric was taken over into literature the same aims and methods were validated. A poet, like an orator, was supposed to delight, to teach, and to persuade, three interlinked goals. He or she must arouse the listener or reader's emotions, take up a definite attitude to the subject being treated, holding the audience's attention all the while by the pleasure of reading. The flowering of Roman rhetoric runs parallel with the great ages of Latin poetry. Throughout this period, from Virgil to Juvenal, it was axiomatic that the poet must use all the resources of language that the orator employed, adding the further expressive powers of verse. In a well-known passage in *De oratore* (1.16.70) Cicero had expressly linked poetry and rhetoric. As Ben Jonson translated it, some 1,700 years later: 'The *Poet* is the neerest Borderer upon the Orator, and expresseth all his vertues, though he be tyed more to numbers; is his equall in ornament, and above him in strengths.'[8]

Juxtaposing Jonson and Cicero helps us to realize the massive continuity between ancient Rome and England in the sixteenth and seventeenth centuries. The Renaissance humanists' rediscovery of antiquity,[9] which started in Florence between 1370 and 1420, spread throughout Italy and to northern Europe a century later, decisively forming English education and English intellectual life. While Greek (and Hebrew) remained in this period the acquisition of a limited group of students, the main aim of grammar-school education was to achieve a fluent mastery of Latin, and a training in the ancient *trivium* of grammar, rhetoric, and logic.[10]

The principles of reading and writing in all English schools in this period derive from that indefatigable proponent of Renaissance humanism, Erasmus, in his *De Ratione Studii* (1511–12). John Colet adopted Erasmus' recommendations for St Paul's School almost immediately, and T. W. Baldwin has traced in great detail the way in which all grammar schools founded in England over the next century and a half modelled their curricula on that of St Paul's or some other great model, such as Winchester, Eton, or Westminster.[11] By 1575 there were about 360 grammar schools, each practising a curriculum based on the piecemeal acquisition of Latin words, phrases, grammatical constructions, rhetorical tropes and figures, reinforced by constant repetition and revision. Skill in rhetoric was acquired in three stages: first, over a hundred rhetorical figures and tropes were memorized, perhaps at the rate of four a week for three years; secondly, pupils identified them in every work they read, making notes in the margin (if they owned the book: some have survived) or copying them into their notebooks; thirdly, they used the figures in their own compositions, Latin and English.

Founders of grammar schools left nothing to chance or to a teacher's whim, specifying in the school's statutes exactly what was to be done. An account from the 1630s of the sixth form at Westminster (whose pupils included Jonson, Herbert, and Dryden) records the afternoon lesson from 1.00 to 3.00 pm as being on a major literary text, Greek or Latin, which 'was to be exactlie gone through by construing and other grammatical waies, examining all the rhetorical figures and translating it out of prose into verse, out of Greeke into Latin, or out of Latin into Greek', which they then memorized. After an hour's private study, 'betwixt 4 and 5 they repeated a leafe or two out of some booke of Rhetoricall figures or choice proverbs and sentences collected by the Master for that use'[12]. Boys attending school might start rhetoric at the age of eight; those educated by tutors at home would start much earlier, some – like John Evelyn's son Dick, who died at the age of five – had already mastered Latin grammar, and knew 'many figures & tropes'.[13]

It goes without saying that all the English poets in this period had a familiar acquaintance with Latin literature and rhetoric. Those from well-to-do families had private tutors (Donne, Herbert, Henry and Thomas Vaughan), others went on to grammar school (Herbert, Marvell, Traherne). All of them went to university, with the exception of Ben Jonson, who was partly educated at Westminster, and partly self-taught. A university education offered more training in philosophy and the other arts, but its first two years were an extension of the grammar-school curriculum, now using the treatises of Cicero and Quintilian at first hand, rather than some modern digest.

All the poets, like the dramatists of the popular theatre, knew and respected the whole range of classical rhetoric. Jonson did not go to university but had studied Quintilian closely, as we see from his (posthumously published) notebook *Timber, or Discoveries*, which includes many excerpts from the *Institutio oratoria*, Books 1 and 2, passages concerning language, style, decorum, imitation, with some excerpts from Book 8 on metaphor.[14] When Jonson visited Scotland in January 1619, the poet William Drummond of Hawthornden carefully gathered the scraps of advice and gossip that Jonson passed on to him: 'He recommended to my reading Quintilian, who, he said, would tell me the faults of my Verses as if he had lived with me', with the further admonition 'that Quintilianes 6. 7. 8. bookes, were not only to be read but altogether digested'.[15] In returning to the sources Jonson was only echoing what writers of vernacular treatises had long recommended. George Puttenham, in *The Art of English Poesy* (published 1589, but written probably up to twenty years earlier), described rhetoric as essential to poetry, since 'the chief prayse and cunning of our Poet is in the discreet using of his figures ... with a delectable varietie, by all measure and just proportion, and in places most aptly to be bestowed'. To write 'eloquently', he affirms, 'cannot be without the use of figures'.[16]

The rationale behind this intensive study of rhetoric was the same as in classical antiquity: mastery of language meant mastery over people, in secular or sacred contexts, as readers of poetry or spectators at a theatre. Sir Henry Wotton, who became headmaster of Eton in 1624, persuaded his pupils 'not to neglect *Rhetorick*, because *Almighty God has left Mankind affections to be wrought upon*: And he would often say, *That none despised Eloquence, but such dull souls as were not capable of it*'.[17] The affections (passions, emotions) were to be aroused or 'wrought upon' (the process of *movere*) by using the resources of *elocutio*, in particular the rhetorical figures. One large category of figures, the *figurae sententiae*, were widely regarded as the most effective way of arousing the passions.[18] In *The Garden of Eloquence* (1577; expanded 1593), the most thorough of the English Renaissance rhetoric-books, Henry Peacham described these as 'verie sharpe and vehement' figures, 'by which the sundrie affections and passions of the minde are properly and elegantly uttered (by a forme of outcrie)'. These figures 'do attend upon affections, as ready . . . to expresse most aptly whatsoever the heart doth affect or suffer'.[19] The justification for using such figures of repetition as *epizeuxis* (repeating a word with no other words intervening) or *anadiplosis* (where the last word of one clause or sentence becomes the first word of the one following), together with various forms of *exclamatio* (outcry), is psychological. Such devices, rhetorical theory observed, are naturally used in life by people in the grip of such an emotion; the writer who uses them both simulates that emotion and arouses it in his readers.

Although modern historians have been reluctant to acknowledge the fact, throughout its career from Virgil to Byron and after rhetoric had a coherent theory of rhetorical figures as psychologically created, pockets of emotional energy.[20] All the Latin rhetoric-books describe the emotional impact of the figures. The anonymous *Rhetorica ad Herennium*, for instance, says of *ploche* ('the repetition of one or more words for the purpose of Amplification or Appeal to Pity') that 'the reiteration of the same word makes a deep impression upon the hearer and inflicts a major wound upon the opposition – as if a weapon should repeatedly pierce the same part of the body' (4.28.38). Quintilian emphasizes that 'there is no more effective method of exciting the emotions than an apt use of figures' (9.1.21). He describes *anaphora* (beginning a sequence of clauses or sentences with the same word) as bringing 'force and emphasis' (9.3.30), and says of *asyndeton* (omitting connectives) that such figures of syntactic incoherence 'make our utterances more vigorous and emphatic and produce outbursts of emotion' (9.3.50, 54).

English rhetoricians of the sixteenth and seventeenth centuries expanded these descriptions of the figures' emotional impact. George Puttenham informed English poets that 'a figure is ever used to a purpose, either of beautie or of efficacie', that is, either it 'beautifieth or enforceth the sense' or 'it urges affection [passion]' (p. 202). In *The Garden of Eloquence* Peacham frequently insists that in figures of repetition the word(s) repeated must be 'of importance and effectual [effective] signification' (p. 41). Of the figure *epistrophe*, which repeats the same word at the end of succeeding clauses or sentences (as in St Paul's words: 'When I was a child, I spoke as a child, I understood as a child, I thought as a child': 1 Corinthians 13:11), Peacham writes that 'this figure ... serveth to leave a word of importance in the end of a sentence, that it may the longer hold the sound in the mind of the hearer' (p. 43). *Epanalepsis* 'should place a word of importance in the beginning of a sentence to be considered, and in the end to be remembered' (p. 46).

The 'importance' of the word is its signification in the context of the oration, poem, or play, depending on the genre concerned and the intentions of the user, to arouse pathos, grief, laughter, or whatever other reaction. In his *Directions for Speech and Style*[21] (c.1599), John Hoskins advised the budding writer that 'you may insert all figures as the passion of the matter shall serve' (p. 21). Some figures, such as *exclamatio*, are 'not lawful but in extremity of emotion' (p. 33), whereas *polyptoton* (which repeats a word while varying its ending) 'is a good figure, and may be used with or without passion' (p. 17). An often cited instance of a figure's flexibility is *aposiopesis*, the breaking-off of a sentence with the sense incomplete. Puttenham describes it as 'the figure of silence, or of interruption', and notes its aptness in several different psychological situations: we can 'interrupt our speech for feare', or 'for shame'; 'for anger or by way of menace'. It can also be used when someone is moderating their anger, but equally well for 'phantasticall heads' (daydreamers) and 'such as . . . lacke memorie' (pp. 166–7). In Shakespeare, for example, Polonius and Justice Shallow come into the last category; Iago and Edmund use it to insinuate slander; for King Lear it expresses his impotent threats of revenge against Goneril and Regan; and by its incompleteness it cuts off the dying words of Hotspur, and Cleopatra.[22] This single instance shows that the figures are polysemous and polypathic, so to speak: they can express many different meanings and many different feelings. The bounds of rhetoric are as wide as those of language itself. This flexibility can be expressed as a three-way relationship:

Form

Meaning   Feeling

The form is given, in the rhetorician's classification of verbal devices – the breaking-off of a sentence is always the same thing formally – but both meaning and feeling are infinitely variable. The relationship between them is fixed in each instance of writing by an individual. His or her use of *anaphora* or *epistrophe* will vary from occasion to occasion, according to the genre or mood of the work, and each individual's use of it may differ from others'. A rhetorical approach to poetry helps us to understand the expressive nature of language, and to reconstruct some of the artistic choices – whether deliberate or the result of sustained training, where certain relationships between form and feeling have been unconsciously absorbed – that go into the making of a poem.

Each of the major English poets uses rhetoric individually, according to genre, mood, purpose, adapting it to his own idiom and poetic style.[23] Ben Jonson told William Drummond that he detested all poetic forms except couplets, which he described as 'the bravest Sort of Verses, especially when they are broken',[24] that is, when the units of sense do not coincide with the unit of form but overrun. This asymmetrical movement gives Jonson's rhetorical figures a comparably irregular character, particularly in such satiric poems[25] as *Epigrams* 11, 'On Something, That Walks Somewhere':

> At court I met it, in clothes brave enough,
> To be a courtier; and lookes grave enough,
> To seeme a statesman.

There the asymmetrical verse disguises the symmetry of the rhetoric, in the figures *parison* (where the parts of succeeding clauses or sentences exactly correspond, noun to noun, verb to verb: here 'clothes : lookes'; 'courtier : statesman'), *epistrophe* ('enough' ending lines 1 and 2: not properly a rhyme) and *anaphora* ('To' opening lines 2 and 3). Jonson repeats a satiric effect by setting rhetoric against verse-movement in this brief (eight-line) poem's conclusion, where he asks this court-creature's name:

> A lord, it cryed, buried in flesh, and blood,
> And such from whom let no man hope least good,
> For I will doe none; and as little ill,
> For I will dare none. Good Lord, walke dead still.

The half-line dismissal there gathers more force from the jerky symmetries preceding.

But Jonson can also use the same figures (*anaphora*, *parison*) in celebratory poems, like his panegyric to William Camden, his teacher at Westminster: '*Camden*, most reverend head, to whom I owe / All that I am in arts, all that I know' (*Epigrams* 14). Camden was famous for his work on British history, and Jonson celebrates his learning by using the figures *anaphora* ('what' in six clauses) and *parison*:

> What name, what skill, what faith hast thou in things!
> What sight in searching the most antique springs!
> What weight, and what authoritie in thy speech!
> Man scarse can make that doubt, but thou canst teach.

There are other examples in Jonson of this contrast between a simple direct rhetoric used for celebration (*Epigrams* 27, 'On Sir John Roe'; 64, 'To Robert Earl of Salisbury'; 76, 'On Lucy Countess of Bedford'), and an energetically irregular rhetoric for satire, such as *Epigrams* 12, 'On Lieutenant Shift'. This dodgy character evades all debts with the phrase 'God payes', which is repeated at the end of ten successive couplets (*epistrophe*), until the dénouement, when a brothelkeeper he has cheated turns out to have 'Lent him a pockie whore. Shee hath paid him'. That pungent turning of the word (*polyptoton*: 'payes, paid') is typical of the scornful pressure Jonson puts on language in his satires. In *Epigrams* 28, 'On Don Surly', who, 'to aspire the glorious name / Of a great man ... / Makes serious use of all great trade he knowes', the ironic repetition of the word 'great' (*ploche*) alternates with its metamorphoses (*polyptoton*: 'greater, greatnesse, greatly') to call in question his pretensions, before dismissing them in the last line: such 'arts ... only can / Stile thee a most great foole, but no great man'.

Jonson's poetry sounds like a man speaking to men, and women, in tones of admiration or reproof at their virtues or vices. George Herbert's poetry[26] sounds like a man speaking to God, where admiration is due the deity, reproof to humanity, including the poet himself. Most of the 167 poems in *The Temple* are variations on this basic situation of a dialogue between the poet and God, in a range of tones from anguish to assurance, and a corresponding range of rhetoric. In what might be called single-minded poems, such as the prayers, where an appeal to God is uttered without self-conflict or division, figures of symmetry and balance can present a constant, harmonious mood, as in 'Trinity Sunday', which has 3 three-line verses, ending:

> Enrich my heart, mouth, hands in me,
> With faith, with hope, with charitie;
> That I may runne, rise, rest with thee.

The use of *parison* to create a parallelism between the three nouns (parts of the body) in line 1, the three nouns of line 2 (the Christian virtues) and the three verbs in line 3 (human activity), presents a settled and coherent universe. Similarly in 'The Call', where an even more carefully balanced technique (known as correlative verse) sets out three nouns describing Christ in line 1 of the stanza, each becoming the subject of the three following lines (giving the pattern: line 1, A B C, line 2, A; line 3, B; line 4, C). The last of the (again, three) stanzas elaborates a further symmetry by recalling all three nouns in the last line:

> Come, my Joy, my Love, my Heart:
> Such a Joy, as none can move:
> Such a Love, as none can part:
> Such a Heart, as joyes in love.

Here, too, the key word is placed last.

Such poems of harmony and assurance can be written when the subject-matter is God alone. When man enters the scene, condemned by Adam's original sin to a flawed and finite existence, our propensity to evil only redeemable by God's grace, Herbert's rhetoric is appropriately tortured, self-accusing. 'Sighs and Groans' recalls the permanence of the Fall as affecting all human beings: 'I have deserv'd' my condition as an eternal Adam, the poet writes,

> because my lust
> Hath still sow'd fig-leaves to exclude thy light:
> But I am frailtie, and already dust;
> O do not grinde me!

Each stanza begins and ends with an apostrophe to God:[27] 'O do not bruise me!'; 'O do not scourge me!'; 'O do not kill me!' Eight times repeated, this double-negative exclamation gives way in the final stanza to a positive appeal, with an unexpected rhetorical heightening:

> But O reprieve me!
> For thou hast life and death at thy command;
> Thou art both *Judge* and *Saviour, feast* and *rod,*
> *Cordiall* and *Corrosive*: put not thy hand
> Into the bitter box; but O my God,
> My God, relieve me!

That unpredicted repetition of 'My God' is the figure *epizeuxis*, which rhetoricians described as a device only to be used for moments of intense emotion.[28] Herbert's placing of it, inside the echoing appeal 'reprieve me . . . relieve me!' shows his full awareness of this figure's expressive potential.

Figures of repetition could also express the speaker's involvement with one specific idea. John Hoskins described the psychology behind it: 'as no man is sick in thought upon one thing but for some vehemency or distress, so in speech there is no repetition without importance' (p. 12). In 'Church-monuments' the word repeated seven times (echoing the Burial Service) is 'dust', for such structures 'intombe my flesh', and 'flesh is but the glasse, which holds the dust / That measures all our time; which also shall / Be crumbled into dust'. A very different poem, 'The Odour' (based on a biblical text, 2 Corinthians 2:15: 'For we are unto God a sweet savour of Christ ... ') repeats the words 'sweet', 'sweeter', 'sweetning', 'sweetly' throughout, as does 'The Banquet'. In 'Misery', a poem of reproof, not celebration, which begins, 'Lord, let the Angels praise thy name', the second line measures the gap between God and man with an unexpected repetition – 'Man is a foolish thing, a foolish thing' – as if the speaker were suddenly struck by our folly. A later stanza repeats the device:

> Man cannot serve thee; let him go,
> And serve the swine: there, there is his delight.

This notion of the gap between man and God, so important to the Christian concept of humility, is the inspiration for many of Herbert's greatest poems, and most powerful rhetoric. The figure *antimetabole*, repeating two or more words in inverted order, adds the appropriate 'vehemency or distress' to the appeal which concludes 'Affliction (I)':

> Ah my deare God! though I am clean forgot,
> Let me not love thee, if I love thee not.

The next poem in the sequence, 'Repentance', begins:

> Lord, I confesse my sinne is great;
> Great is my sinne.

The figure acts as a hinge around which the Christian's consciousness of his own unworthiness revolves, never-endingly.

Herbert uses a great variety of poetical and rhetorical techniques to embody this sense of the gap between the human and the divine. 'Justice (I)' has two stanzas, juxtaposing the ways of God and man. The first verse is organized around the figure *anadiplosis*, where a word in (or, more usually, ending) one clause or sentence is repeated in the one following:

> I cannot skill of these thy wayes.
> *Lord, thou didst make me, yet thou woundest me;*
> *Lord, thou dost wound me, yet thou dost relieve me:*
> *Lord, thou relievest, yet I die by thee:*
> *Lord, thou dost kill, yet thou dost reprieve me.*

There the whole paradoxical movement in Christian belief, from the Creation to the Fall to Redemption is expressed in the series of interlinked verbs the coherence of the rhetorical structure showing the coherence of God's underlying plan. The second verse, describing man's ways, uses a very different rhetoric:

> But when I mark my life and praise,
>   Thy justice me most fitly payes:
> For, *I do praise thee, yet I praise thee not:*
> *My prayers mean thee, yet my prayers stray:*
> *I would do well, yet sinne the hand hath got:*
> *My soul doth love thee, yet it loves delay.*
>   I cannot skill of these my wayes.

In our world there is no coherence: good intentions are unfulfilled, things give way to their opposite, the centre falls apart. The understated eloquence of this contrast between divine and human depends on the reader being able to recognize the difference between an organizing rhetorical figure and its absence, a significance comparable to the presence or absence of rhyme in other poems in *The Temple*.

Herbert often uses a rhetorical figure throughout a whole poem, to give it a coherent structure. In 'A Wreath' the figure is *anadiplosis* again, in its extended form (known as *gradatio* or *climax*, the ladder figure).[29] In 'Sin's Round' the opening lines use *ploche* to express the sinner's remorse:

> Sorrie I am, my God, sorrie I am,
> That my offences course it in a ring.

The 'round' or cyclical nature of human sins is expressed by repeating whole lines, the last line of the stanza 1 becoming the first line of stanza 2, and so on, until the last line of the poem repeats the first: there is no way out from human sin. In 'Bitter-Sweet' the dominant figure, already expressed in the title, is *synoeciosis* (or *oxymoron*), the union of opposites, repeated in seven of its eight lines ('dear angry Lord' ... 'My sowre-sweet dayes'), to represent the unhappy situation of fallen man. Although doomed to separation by the Fall, the Christian constantly strives towards God, and in 'Clasping of Hands' Herbert organizes the whole poem by *antimetabole* on the possessive pronouns:

> Lord, thou art mine, and I am thine,
> If mine I am: and thine much more ...

This dense interplay of the two terms throughout twenty lines culminates in another exclamatory appeal:

> O be mine still! still make me thine!
> Or rather make no Thine and Mine!

– In heaven there will be no more *meum* and *tuum*.

The climaxes of Herbert's poems, as every reader knows, are unusually important and dramatic (a technique he may have learned from Sidney's

Astrophil and Stella). The intricate and anguished movements give way to a reversal, a rejection, a resolution. In some of these climaxes Herbert even uses the figure *aposiopesis* (breaking off an utterance incomplete), a very rare device in lyric poetry, more usually met in drama. But as always in Herbert, the rhetoric is perfectly calculated to make a harmony between thought and style, for he uses this figure to express the vast distance between Christ's suffering and man's deserts. In 'The Thanksgiving' the poet recalls Christ's paradoxical titles, 'Oh King of grief!. .. / Oh King of wounds! how shall I grieve for thee . . .?' The disparity between what Christ suffered on the cross and how man benefits from it is summed up at one point in the figures *antithesis* (together with *polyptoton*) and *zeugma*, one verb serving two or more disparate objects:

> Shall thy strokes be my stroking? thorns, my flower?
> Thy rod, my posie? crosse, my bower?

How can a thoughtful Christian come to terms with such a discrepancy? 'As for thy passion', the poet says, but uses the rhetorical device of postponement ('But of that anon . . . '), until the end of the poem, when it can be postponed no longer:

> Then for thy passion – I will do for that –
> Alas, my God, I know not what.

The poet is at a loss, as any Christian must be, reflecting on that self-sacrifice.

The disparity is even more dramatic in 'Dialogue', a poem of four eight-line stanzas spoken alternately by man and God (in italic type). In the first verse the human speaker describes his soul as not 'worth the having', with God replying that the benefit '*in having thee*' can only be seen by '*he,* / *Who for man was sold*'. In the third stanza the human speaker reiterates his unworthiness, and abandons all hope – 'I disclaime the whole designe: / Sinne disclaims and I resigne.' God's reply, in the final stanza, is to reiterate what He had planned for '*my clay, my creature*', and to remind man of the tremendous gift by which He parted with His own son:

> *That as I did freely part*
> *With my glorie and desert*
> *Left all joyes to feel all smart –*
> Ah! no more: thou break'st my heart.

That must be the only instance in the representation of God in literature where he is not allowed to finish a sentence, as the poet's sense of shame at man's unworthiness becomes so strong that it invades the poem, taking over a verse that doesn't belong to it, to make the only possible response.

Aposiopesis, the figure of interruption, is used again for the climax of 'A true Hymn', one of those poems where Herbert discusses the nature of Christian poetry and the primacy of sincere belief over insincere eloquence (quietly appropriating for himself the category of sincere eloquence). The 'finenesse' of 'a hymne or psalme', he writes, is 'when the soul unto the lines accords'. Someone wanting only the highest, most intense expression ('all the minde, / And all the soul') might complain 'If the words onely rhyme'. The final stanza gives the true attitude:

> Whereas if th'heart be moved,
> Although the verse be somewhat scant,
> God doth supplie the want.
> As when th'heart sayes (sighing to be approved)
> *O, could I love!* and stops: God writeth, *Loved*.

There the human sense of inadequacy and incompleteness is cancelled, completed by God's laconic, one-word reply, placed at the absolute limit of the poem. Rhetoric was one of the expressive resources used by Herbert to show how 'the soul unto the lines accords'.

In Donne's love poetry[30] rhetoric serves to express and dramatize a whole range of feelings and attitudes towards its subject-matter. Affirmatory, celebratory love can use the symmetries produced by *anaphora* and *parison*, as in 'The Good-morrow':

> Let sea-discoverers to new worlds have gone,
> Let maps to others, worlds on worlds have shown,
> Let us possess one world, each hath one, and is one.

In such poems the interdependence of two lovers is best expressed through *antimetabole*: 'My face in thine eye, thine in mine appears'. Another celebratory poem is 'The Sun Rising', which uses similar figures of symmetry –

> Love, all alike, no season knows, nor clime,
> Nor hours, days, months, which are the rags of time

– and the same figure of interdependence, where the inverted word order pushes the two pronouns to the outer limits of the line, enclosing between them all that is of value:

> She is all States, and all Princes I,
> Nothing else is.

That example shows another striking feature of these affirmative love poems, that Donne's *persona* expresses the subjectively felt absolute value that each lover has for the other by using the trope *hyperbole*, deliberately excessive utterances through which, as rhetorical theory taught, exceptionally rare truths could be conveyed.[31] Related to that trope is the figure *antithesis*, as in this last example, juxtaposing the 'all' of the lovers with the 'nothing' of everything else. Similarly in 'The Anniversary', which uses the figures of *anaphora* and *parison* to build up an imposing list of people and things subject to time and change – 'All Kings, and all their favourites, / All glory of honours, beauties, wits, / . . . All other things . . . ' – against which the lover affirms their uniqueness: 'Only our love hath no decay.'

In other love poems lists can serve a very different function to express the mood of cynicism and rejection that Donne developed so originally. In 'The Indifferent' the cynical male affirms his ability to love any type of woman:

> I can love both fair and brown,
> Her whom abundance meets, and her whom want betrays . . .

and so on through ten clauses linked by the parallelism of *anaphora* and *parison*. This cynical list of the varieties of woman culminates in the couplet detonating the first stanza:

> I can love her, and her, and you, and you,
> I can love any, so she be not true.

Yet in this shocking declaration of promiscuity, the next stanza argues, man is only making a virtue of necessity, since it is really women who are inconstant. Men and women in Donne's love poems occupy extreme positions: they are either joined together by intense and uniquely strong feelings or are independent agents, indifferent to constancy or loyalty. Each extreme has the appropriate rhetoric. In 'Love's Usury' the list form expresses a male wish for total liberty of choice, as the speaker asks the 'Usurious God of Love' to let him enjoy the time of youth and high sexuality to the full –

> let my body reign, and let
> Me travel, sojourn, snatch, plot, have, forget,
> Resume my last year's relict . . .

– do anything he likes with women.

This bold challenge to the Petrarchan convention of helplessly adoring male, all-powerful female living off his dependence, applies the rhetorical list form to declare 'cela m'est égal'. Where some rhetoric theorists assigned different stylistic effects to a list using *asyndeton*, the absence of connective conjunctions (as in the last quotation: 'travel, sojourn, snatch'), as against one using many (*polysyndeton*), Donne's cynical *persona* applies both to the same end. So in 'Love's Diet' the first four verses describe how the lover has 'dieted' his love by reducing the sighs, tears, and other signs of affection that he would normally utter, while the final verse sums up his detachment:

> Thus I reclaim'd my buzzard love, to fly
> At what, and when, and how, and where I choose;
>   Now negligent of sport I lie,
>   And now, as other falconers use,
> I spring a mistress, swear, write, sigh and weep:
> And the game kill'd, or lost, go talk, and sleep.

Such complete self-control and independence marks an extreme point on the spectrum of love, those many phases of relationship between men and women brilliantly embodied in these poems. On the same negative side of the scale, expressing bitterness or indifference towards women, is 'A Jet Ring Sent', where the figure *epanalepsis* (the same word(s) beginning and ending a clause or sentence) gives an appropriately ring-like structure to the opening address to the ring:

>   Thou art not so black as my heart,
> Nor half so brittle as her heart, thou art.

If the structure of that clause symbolizes the ring, so does its semantic content, as the speaker invokes the qualities of the ring to diagnose a basic discrepancy between the lovers' 'properties': man's is 'Nothing more endless', woman's 'nothing sooner broke'. The bitterness or discord expressed by these symmetries emerges in the last line in the rare use in Donne (or in Renaissance lyric poetry) of the figure *exclamatio*, where the male speaker addresses the ring that he once gave the woman:

> Be justly proud, and gladly safe, that thou dost dwell with me,
> She that, oh, broke her faith, would soon break thee.

At the other end of Donne's spectrum, love can be celebrated as a totality which can only be properly described by the word 'all'. In 'Lovers' Infiniteness' this word is frequently repeated, the three stanzas developing a logical proposition. First:

> If yet I have not all thy love,
> Dear, I shall never have it all.

Second:

> Or if then thou gavest me all,
> All was but all which thou hadst then.

And third:

> Yet I would not have all yet,
> He that hath all can have no more.

Figures of repetition here, notably *ploche* ('all' occurs six times in the first stanza) and *anadiplosis* (the opening of stanza 2) have less their normal function of emotional emphasis than an intellectual one, focussing an experience that is all-absorbing. Having sustained the discussion for thirty witty lines, the conclusion (rather like Herbert's 'The Clasping of Hands') collapses the category altogether:

> But we will have a way more liberal
> Than changing hearts, to join them, so we shall
> Be one, and one another's, All.

From exchange or reciprocity to incorporation: that is the movement behind all Donne's affirmatory poems.

Yet the union of lovers, like all earthly things (and despite the magnificent assertions of 'The Anniversary'), is subject to decay. If the couple formed an all, the death of one reduces the other to nothing. In 'A Nocturnal upon St Lucy's Day', the first stanza uses *hyperbole* and *antithesis* once again to express the vast distance between the lover and the rest of the creation, only this time to create an extraordinary sense of loss. At this lowest point of the year, 'the year's midnight, and ... the day's', the sun is at its weakest, 'the world's whole sap is sunk', life itself

> is shrunk,
> Dead and interr'd; yet all these seem to laugh,
> Compar'd with me, who am their epitaph.

Where 'She' and 'I' were once 'all States, and all Princes', the rest of the world 'Nothing', now the scales have shifted, as the third stanza, with its insistent repetitions of 'all' (*ploche*, again), shows:

> All others, from all things, draw all that's good,
> Life, soul, form, spirit, whence they being have;
> I, by Love's limbeck, am the grave
> Of all that's nothing.

That absolute opposition of 'all' and 'nothing' (*oxymoron*) is taken a stage further, impossible though it might have seemed, in the fourth stanza: 'But I am by her death ... / Of the first nothing the Elixir grown'. This staggering hyperbole – if one could imagine such a thing as the 'quintessence of chaos' – shocks us into realizing the feeling of absolute deprivation that can come with the loss of a person who meant everything. The speaker justifies this deliberately excessive statement by a logical argument, which is given tremendous force and urgency by figures of repetition:

> Were I a man, that I were one   30
> I needs must know; I should prefer,
>   If I were any beast,
> Some ends, some means; yea plants, yea stones, detest,
> And love; all, all, some properties invest;   34

> If I an ordinary nothing were,
> As shadow, a light and body must be here.

We can identify the figures *antimetabole* (line 30: 'Were I . . . I were'), *anaphora* (lines 31: 'I . . . I'; 33: 'Some . . . some; yea . . . yea'), *epizeuxis* (line 34: 'all, all'), *ploche* (lines 33–4: 'some'). Knowing the names, and forms, helps us to see how Donne has mobilized the expressive potential of these figures of repetition, the resource of human passion. Further, he has orchestrated them into a climax at line 34, a movement which cannot be read (either aloud or silently) without a sense of urgency and acceleration to this point, evoking bafflement.

From that tortured series of conditional statements, reaching the paradoxical deduction that if he were 'an ordinary nothing' that would at least imply the presence of a body and light, the final stanza dies down to a resigned acceptance of his unique condition in the present tense, definite and irrevocable – 'But I am none; nor will my Sun renew'. In the characteristically affirmative poems of living love Donne presents his lovers as a unit, joined in the plural pronoun to an extent unique in English Renaissance love poetry.[32] So 'The Anniversary' celebrates 'we / (Who Prince enough in one another be)', and affirms:

> Here upon earth, we are Kings, and none but we
> Can be such Kings, nor of such subjects be,

(the pronouns 'we', 'us', and 'our' occurring ten times in the final stanza). In the third stanza of 'St Lucy's Day', by contrast, that 'we' form is in the past tense, a remembered unity –

> Oft a flood
> Have we two wept, and so
> Drown'd the whole world, us two

– where the echoing 'we two . . . us two' draws attention to that once happy state. But in the last stanza the unity is broken, the speaker accepts their now separated places among the living and the dead:

> Since she enjoys her long night's festival,
> Let me prepare towards her, and let me call
> This hour her Vigil, and her Eve, since this
> Both the year's, and the day's, deep midnight is.

The sense of release, of letting-go that the ending gives, is due in part to the speaker's acceptance of this new and irrevocable loneliness. But it also derives from the poem's rhetorical structure, where the last line repeats the first, an outer frame within which emotion is aroused and allayed by these ancient devices for representing human thoughts and feelings.

NOTES

1 See E. R. Curtius, *European Literature and the Latin Middle Ages*, trans. W. R. Trask (New York: Pantheon Books, 1953); E. Faral, *Les Arts poétiques du XIIe et du XIIIe siècle* (1924; Paris: Editions Champion, 1971); B. Muntéano, *Constantes dialectiques en littérature et en histoire* (Paris: Didier, 1967); P. W. K. Stone, *The Art of Poetry 1750–1820. Theories of Poetic Composition and Style in the late Neo-Classic and early Romantic Periods* (London: Routledge, 1967).

2 For an introductory account see Brian Vickers, *In Defence of Rhetoric* (Oxford: Clarendon Press, 1988), chapter 7.

3 On Greek rhetoric see George Kennedy, *The Art of Persuasion in Greece* (London: Routledge, 1963).

4 On Roman rhetoric see George Kennedy, *Quintilian* (New York: Twayne, 1969); *The Art of Persuasion in the Roman World (300BC–300AD)* (Princeton University Press, 1972).

5 For the place of rhetoric in classical education see H. I. Marrou, *A History of Education in Antiquity*, trans. G. Lamb (New York: Sheed and Ward, 1956); and S. F. Bonner, *Education in Ancient Rome: From the Elder Cato to the Younger Pliny* (London: Methuen, 1977).

6 See J. F. D'Alton, *Roman Literary Theory and Criticism* (London, 1931; repr. New York: Russell and Russell, 1962); and D. A. Russell and M. Winterbottom (eds.), *Ancient Literary Criticism: The Principal Texts in New Translations* (Oxford: Clarendon Press, 1972).

7 See Vickers, *In Defence of Rhetoric*, pp. 24, 31–2, 37, 50, 74–6, 276–86, 345–7, 357–8.

8 *Timber: or Discoveries; made upon Men and Matter; as they have flow'd out of his daily Readings ...*, a notebook first published in the second (posthumous) volume of Jonson's *Workes* (1640), quoted here from *Ben Jonson*, ed. C. H. Hereford, P. Simpson, and E. Simpson, 11 vols. (Oxford: Clarendon Press, 1925–52), vol. 8, p. 640.

9 For rhetoric in Renaissance humanism see R. R. Bolgar, *The Classical Heritage and its Beneficiaries* (Cambridge University Press, 1954); and Brian Vickers, 'Rhetoric and Poetics', in *The Cambridge History of Renaissance Philosophy*, ed. C. B. Schmitt and Q. Skinner (Cambridge University Press, 1988), pp. 715–45.

10 See the marvellously detailed (and too little known) study by T. W. Baldwin, *William Shakspere's Small Latine & Lesse Greeke*, 2 vols. (Urbana: University of Illinois Press, 1944, 1966).

11 *Ibid.* 1.75–463. Erasmus' treatise appears in a new and excellent translation by B. McGregor in the *Collected Works of Erasmus*, vol. 24 (University of Toronto Press, 1978).

12 Baldwin, *Shakspere's Small Latine* 1.359–60.

13 *The Diary of John Evelyn*, ed. E. S. de Beer (Oxford: Clarendon Press, 1959), p. 385.

14 *Ben Jonson* 8.570, 583, 587–8, 610, 613, 619, 622, with the authorship identified in the Commentary volume (11), pp. 210–94.

15 *Ben Jonson* 1.132, 136.

16 Quoted from the excellent modern edition by G. D. Willcock and A. Walker (Cambridge University Press, 1936, 1970); further quotations incorporated into the text.

17 Izaak Walton, *The Lives of John Donne, Sir Henry Wotton, Richard Hooker, George Herbert and Robert Sanderson* (London: World's Classics, 1927, 1956), pp. 130–1.

18 Vickers, *In Defence of Rhetoric*, pp. 323–4.

19 Quoted from the facsimile edition by W. G. Crane (Gainesville: Scholars' Facsimiles and Reprints, 1977); further quotations incorporated into the text.

20 See Vickers, *In Defence of Rhetoric*, chapter 6 (pp. 294–339).

21 Quoted from the edition by H. H. Hudson (Princeton University Press, 1935); further quotations incorporated into the text.

22 See Vickers, *In Defence of Rhetoric*, pp. 335–7.

23 For a specimen survey, see Brian Vickers, *Classical Rhetoric in English Poetry* (London, 1970; 2nd, rev. edn, Carbondale, Ill.: S. Illinois University Press, 1989), chapter 4, pp. 122–50.

24 *Ben Jonson* 1.132.

25 Quotations are from *The Complete Poetry of Ben Jonson*, ed. W. B. Hunter, Jr (New York University Press, 1963).

26 Quotations are from *The Poems of George Herbert*, ed. H. Gardner (Oxford University Press, 1961).

27 In *A Priest to the Temple, or The Countrey Parson, His Character, and Rule of Holy Life* (dated 1632), Herbert wrote that the preacher could make his sermon holy in several ways, including 'by turning often, and making many apostrophes to God': *The Temple and A Priest to the Temple*, ed. A. R. Waller (London: Dent, 1902), p. 227.

28 See Vickers, *In Defence of Rhetoric*, pp. 338–9.

29 For an analysis of this poem see Vickers, *Classical Rhetoric in English Poetry*, pp. 163–6.

30 Quotations are from *The 'Songs and Sonets' of John Donne*, ed. T. Redpath (London: Methuen, 1956).

31 See Brian Vickers, 'The *Songs and Sonnets* and the Rhetoric of Hyperbole', in *John Donne: Essays in Celebration*, ed. A. J. Smith (London: Methuen, 1972), pp. 132–74.

32 See *ibid.*, pp. 133–6, and, for the contrasting example of Shakespeare, Brian Vickers, '"Mutual render": *I* and *Thou* in the *Sonnets*', *Returning to Shakespeare* (London: Routledge, 1989), pp. 41–88.

FURTHER READING

The best starting place for the detail of rhetorical devices is Sister M. Joseph, *Shakespeare's Use of the Arts of Language* (New York: Columbia University Press, 1947), which first gives Renaissance definitions of all the figures and exemplifies them with many quotations of Shakespeare. Useful reference works listing figures and tropes include L. A. Sonnino, *A Handbook to Sixteenth-Century Rhetoric* (London: Routledge and Kegan Paul, 1968); R. A. Lanham, *A Handlist of Rhetorical Terms: A Guide for Students of English Literature* (Berkeley: University of California Press, 1968); A. Quinn, *Figures of Speech: 60 Ways to Turn a Phrase* (Salt Lake City, Utah: Gibbs M. Smith Inc., 1982); B. Dupriez, *Gradus: Les procédés littéraires (Dictionnaire)* (Paris: Union générale d'éditions, 1980), trans. Albert Halsall as *Gradus: A Dictionary of Literary Devices* (University of Toronto Press, 1984).

For some of the relations between rhetoric and poetry see R. Tuve, *Elizabethan and Metaphysical Imagery: Renaissance Poetic and Twentieth-Century Critics* (University of Chicago Press, 1947); O. B. Hardison, Jr, *The Enduring Monument: A Study of the Idea of Praise in Renaissance Literary Theory and Practice* (Chapel Hill: University of North Carolina Press, 1962).

For the survival of rhetoric in modern literature see, e.g., B. Vickers, 'Rhetoric and Functionality in Hopkins', in *The Authentic Cadence. Centennial Essays on Gerard Manley Hopkins*, ed. A. Mortimer (Fribourg University Press, Switzerland, 1992), pp. 73–141, and Brian Vickers, *In Defence of Rhetoric* (Oxford: Clarendon Press, 1988), chapter 8. A valuable and wide-ranging journal, published quarterly, is *Rhetorica* (vol. 1: 1983–), produced by University of California Press for the International Society for the History of Rhetoric.

PART TWO

SOME POETS

6

ACHSAH GUIBBORY

John Donne

At the beginning of the seventeenth century, Donne's poems expressed a strong and independent spirit. For all their indebtedness to literary traditions and conventions, they took a sceptical stance toward many received ideas and seemed written in a 'new made Idiome'.[1] The importance of his innovation was recognized by Thomas Carew, who praised Donne as the monarch of wit who 'purg'd' 'The Muses garden', threw away 'the lazie seeds / Of Servile imitation ... And fresh invention planted'.[2]

Part of Donne's freshness comes from his intense analysis of important aspects of human experience – the desire for love, the desire to be purged of imperfection or sinfulness, and the longing to defeat mortality. He explores erotic love and human spirituality and the relation between them. Because his poetry speaks to needs and desires that seem to persist despite cultural and historical differences, Donne is accessible, compelling, and engaging. But his poetry is also difficult and complicated. Individual poems refuse to yield a single, unequivocal meaning, and his poetry exhibits considerable variety, defying readers' attempts to reduce it to a neat order. Whereas his contemporary Ben Jonson preferred to speak in a single, constant voice in his poems, avoiding masks as he praised virtue and castigated vice, Donne adopts different roles and postures – the libertine rake, the devoted and constant lover, the cynic who feels cheated by his experience in love, the despairing sinner fearing damnation, the bold suitor claiming his right to salvation. The poetry expresses radically contradictory views – of women, the body, and love.

One holy sonnet in particular provides insight into this quality of his poetry, for it suggests that contraries are Donne's distinguishing feature:

> Oh, to vex me, contraryes meete in one:
> Inconstancy unnaturally hath begott
> A constant habit; that when I would not
> I change in vowes, and in devotione.
> As humorous is my contritione

> As my prophane Love, and as soone forgott:
> As ridlingly distemperd, cold and hott,
> As praying, as mute; as infinite, as none.
> I durst not view heaven yesterday; and to day
> In prayers, and flattering speaches I court God:
> To morrow' I quake with true feare of his rod.
> So my devout fitts come and go away
> Like a fantastic Ague: save that here
> Those are my best dayes, when I shake with feare.

In this undatable poem, the speaker complains that inconstancy seems to be, paradoxically, his essential, unchanging nature. It is an inconstancy born of the conflict of contraries. He is pulled between a painful awareness of his 'humorous', changeable disposition (which he seems to take a certain pride in) and a strong desire for constancy and stability. The 'contraryes' which 'meete' in him define his identity; but they create a sense not of wholeness but of conflict and dis-ease. It is appropriate that the state of being vexed by unresolved contraries would be expressed by paradox – long recognized as an important feature of Donne's poetry – since paradox is self-contradicting, asserting that mutually contradictory statements are simultaneously true.

If Donne felt vexed by contraries, it should not be surprising to find that his poetry is too. Although the canon of his poetry is of a piece – it has a consistency or identity that allows us to recognize a poem as Donne's – it is also varied, full of complex poems exploring his sense of the contradictions at the heart of human experience and desire.

The body of Donne's poetry is not very extensive. He wrote five formal verse satires, fewer than twenty love elegies, some short epigrams, the long, unfinished poem *Metempsychosis*, some occasional poems and verse letters (including three epithalamions and two *Anniversaries* on the death of Elizabeth Drury) many of which were addressed to actual or prospective patrons, and thirty-five divine poems (including twenty-one religious sonnets and three hymns). The *Songs and Sonets* constitute his largest group of poems. Few of Donne's poems appeared in print during his lifetime. Instead, they circulated in manuscript, read by a select audience with whom Donne could assume a greater intimacy than would be possible for a more public writer.[3] Only after his death was an edition of his *Poems* published (1633). The conditions of the circulation of Donne's poetry, whereby he neither kept it to himself nor published it in print, mediate between competing desires for privacy and for a public voice.

Donne's poetry proved influential in the seventeenth century, though afterwards it was neglected until the nineteenth and, especially, twentieth centuries. The 'Cavalier' poets Thomas Carew, Richard Lovelace, and John Suckling were poetic sons of Jonson, but owed much to Donne in their treatment of erotic love. In the mid seventeenth century, we see Donne's influence in the funeral and valedictory poems of Henry King, possibly in the religious poet George Herbert, and markedly in the highly figurative poems of Abraham Cowley. Andrew Marvell's playful yet serious wit, his exploration of the relation of body and soul, and his fondness for arguing through images all suggest his reading of Donne. Donne's exalted descriptions of the union of lovers' souls were boldly adapted by Katherine Philips to celebrate 'female friendship'. Though by the end of the century Donne had gone out of fashion, the Restoration poets John Wilmot, Earl of Rochester, and Aphra Behn still found kinship in Donne's witty scepticism, libertine spirit, and insistence on the importance of the body and sexuality in human experience. Donne thus proved a rich poetic resource for both secular and religious poets, but none of these poets shared Donne's special, intense conjunction of spirituality and sensuality.

Love and salvation are not only the two great subjects of his poetry; they were also preoccupations that gave dramatic shape to his life. Donne was born into a Roman Catholic family, whose ancestors included Sir Thomas More and which had suffered persecution as those in power sought to make England a thoroughly Protestant country. At some point, though we are not sure when, Donne left Roman Catholicism for the Church of England. Contradictory impulses probably motivated his conversion. Ambition as well as the desire to escape persecution – the desire to have a comfortable place in his society in more than one sense – may have influenced his conversion. Intellectual and spiritual conviction, however, were also surely important factors, for Donne tells us he had read extensively in contemporary theological disputes. Perhaps more dramatic than his religious conversion was his marriage and its consequences. Having studied law at the Inns of Court and travelled in expeditions to Cadiz and the Azores, in 1597 he became employed as secretary to Sir Thomas Egerton, and subsequently fell in love with Egerton's young niece, Anne More. Though Donne's career until this point shows a practical concern with political advancement, Donne's eloping with Anne in December 1601 shows a romantic disposition careless, even contemptuous, of authority. Imprisoned briefly, Donne found himself barred from employment. Though for years he sought to attain a political position through influentiual patrons, he found secure employment only in 1615 when he took holy orders in the Church of England. His last years were spent as Dean of St Paul's, preaching powerful and dramatic sermons that applied personal experience to the public discussion of biblical texts, theological issues, and matters of faith.[4]

As even a brief sketch of his life suggests, Donne's poetry about love and about his relation to God invites connections with his personal life, yet it resists attempts to read it biographically. His seventeenth-century biographer, Izaak Walton, assigned the secular love poetry to the youthful Donne and the religious poetry to the mature priest. Embellishing on remarks Donne himself had made, Walton distinguished between Jack Donne, young-man-about-town, and Dr John Donne, the sober Dean of St Paul's, in effect simplifying Donne by constructing a conversion narrative in which Donne repented of his youthful errors.[5] But Walton's neat distinction between Donne's secular and sacred poetry was a misleading distortion, supporting his view of Donne's 'conversion' and effectively lessening the potential for complicated tensions between the sexual and the spiritual aspects of Donne. As Donne's Oxford editor Helen Gardner has argued, evidence indicates that a number of holy sonnets were probably written in 1609, and recently Dennis Flynn has suggested that an even earlier date is possible.[6] So Donne was writing religious poetry long before he took holy orders, perhaps even during the same period that he was writing 'secular' love poetry.

Moreover, the uncertainty of the dating and chronology of Donne's poetry compromises attempts to read his poetry biographically. In the case of most poems, we simply do not know when they were written. Probably most of the elegies and the five satires were written in the 1590s.[7] The two *Anniversaries* are datable by Donne's publication of them in 1611 and 1612, and the date of 'Goodfriday, 1613: Riding Westward' is identifiable by its title. But other religious poems cannot be dated with certainty. The *Songs and Sonets* pose the greatest difficulty in terms of dating but are also the most intriguing. The sheer variety and inconsistency of the attitudes toward love expressed in these poems entice readers to arrange them in some order that delineates a development from early to mature poems. But so long as our knowledge about the dating of Donne's poems, and about his life, remains limited and uncertain, any order we construct will be speculative. Indeed, to chart a progression in Donne's treatment of love risks minimizing, even erasing contradictions at the centre of his poetry.

For all the difficulty of discovering a clear development to Donne's poetry, and for all its variety, it is nevertheless characterized by a recognizable voice and 'personality', and by certain recurring preoccupations and stylistic features. Whether one is reading the *Elegies*, the *Satires*, the *Songs and Sonets*, or the *Divine Poems*, the poetry has an immediacy created by colloquial language and conversational tone and rhythms, but also heightened by its dramatic aspects. Many poems presume an occasion which has prompted the speaker's address, and some open with a dramatic outburst. Others are meditative. But many, perhaps most, poems combine meditative and dramatic elements as the intellect is brought to bear on human emotional experiences, desires, and fears. Never complacent, Donne is always analyzing. His lyrics combine passionate, emotional intensity with keen and active intelligence displayed in logical analysis and verbal wit, especially the extensive use of puns, equivocation, and the 'conceit' or extended metaphor – all features which in some sense work on a principle of contraries. Samuel Johnson in the eighteenth century noted Donne's fondness for conceits, which he called *discordia concors*, the 'discovery of occult resemblances in things apparently unlike'.[8] Sometimes 'conceits' or analogies bear the burden of conducting the poem's argument (as in 'A Valediction: Forbidding Mourning' or 'The Ecstasy').

Many of Donne's lyrics use logical argument; yet logic and the use of reason are often revealed to be arbitrary, imperfect, implicated in the speaker's motives. Perhaps the most famous example is the seduction poem 'The Flea', where the speaker uses a series of dazzling, witty arguments to convince a reluctant woman to go to bed with him. The speaker displays control, elegance, and power through verbal wit and argument, though the poem attributes an interesting independence and intelligence to the mistress who repeatedly frustrates his desire for conquest. His ability, indeed eagerness to reverse or switch his argument in order to answer her implied responses shows a speaker willing to argue almost any position in order to achieve his end.[9]

A similar use of logic and witty argument, sometimes verging on blasphemy, appears in the holy sonnets. Because these poems address God rather than a mistress, they raise special problems in interpretation. In the poem 'What if this present were the world's last night?' the speaker begins introspectively, looking into his own heart, examining the picture of Christ he finds, trying to determine whether to draw assurance or despair. In the last six lines, or sestet, he turns to address Christ, drawing a startling analogy between his flattering, persuasive addresses to his prophane mistresses and his present address to God:

> as in my idolatrie
> I said to all my profane mistresses,
> Beauty, of pitty, foulnesse onely is
> A signe of rigour: so I say to thee,
> To wicked spirits are horrid shapes assign'd,
> This beauteous forme assures a pitious minde.

Does Donne think God might appreciate his wit much as his 'prophane' mistresses did? Or is there anxiety and fear that this desire for verbal control, the desire to win the argument, might itself be a sin, a mark of his damnation? Are we to see the speaker as close to Donne? Or is there satirical distance between poet and speaker? In so many of the holy sonnets, reason and intellect are as essential to the poem's very existence as Donne believed they were to human nature, and yet the poems' arguments expose the failure or inadequacy of reason either to penetrate the mysteries of faith or to assure Donne of his personal salvation. In the poetry as a whole, an obvious delight with the exercise of reason, wit, and wordplay is crossed by a profound distrust of reason.

Wit, logic, equivocation, and dramatic immediacy all contribute to the central concern of Donne's poetry – the exploration of the individual's experience of love, mortality, and the divine. For Donne, the process of examining emotional experience inevitably produces poetry of contradictions.

His commitment to experience and discovery is announced in a famous passage about truth in *Satire 3*. Concerned about the difficulty yet necessity of finding the 'true religion' and having surveyed the existing Christian religious institutions, Donne's speaker resolves to continue his search:

> aske thy father which is shee,
> Let him aske his; though truth and falsehood bee
> Neare twins, yet truth a little elder is;
> Be busie to seeke her, beleeve mee this,
> Hee's not of none, nor worst, that seekes the best.
> To'adore, or scorne an image, or protest,
> May all be bad; doubt wisely, in strange way
> To stand inquiring right, is not to stray;
> To sleepe, or runne wrong, is: on a huge hill,
> Cragged, and steep, Truth stands, and hee that will
> Reach her, about must, and about must goe;
> And what the'hills suddennes resists, winne so;
> Yet strive so, that before age, deaths twilight,
> Thy Soule rest, for none can worke in that night. (lines 71–84)

The emphasis is on seeking, on process. Discovery is difficult yet necessary, and a sceptical mind plays an important part. 'Truth' is the goal, and life should be a journey toward it. It is perhaps impossible in this life fully to possess 'Truth', who stands on the summit of a 'huge hill'. Perhaps we will only experience an arduous, circuitous partial ascent of the hill as we 'about must, and about must goe' (line 81). Nevertheless, we must 'strive' now, inquire and make progressive discoveries. That it is possible to get pieces of truth is implied by the exhortation, 'Keepe the truth which thou has found' (line 89).

Though Donne is talking about religion and religious truth, his comments about the importance of discovery, process, and experience indicate the broad concern of his poetry.[10] Whether he is (as in the *Satires* and *Anniversaries*) anatomizing the corruption in his world, or (in the *Elegies* and *Songs and Sonets*) exploring the varieties and complexities of love, or (in the *Divine Poems*) meditating on sin, grace, and the anxious question of salvation, Donne is searching for a truth that will emerge from and fit his experience. His poems reveal a scepticism about social conventions and institutions, a sense that received opinions and beliefs may not fully accord with 'Truth' and must be tested against experience, and a conviction that the individual must seek truth for him- or herself.

Donne's interest in discovery links him with important concerns of his age. The sixteenth and seventeenth centuries were a time of exploration, both scientific and geographical. The New World was being explored, and astronomical observations by Copernicus, Kepler, and Galileo led to the discovery of a new order of the heavens. England also saw the emergence of modern, experimental science, which proposed to discover the true order of the physical world. Though Donne showed scepticism towards the new science in the *Anniversaries* and elsewhere, his poetry, with its emphasis on the process of active discovery, its sceptical stance towards received ideas and poetic conventions, and its sense of excitement at making fresh discoveries about human experience, is a poetic counterpart of the enquiry taking place in many fields in the seventeenth century.

Like *Satire 3*, Donne's poetry is as concerned with the process of seeking as it is with the attainment of truth. Donne often asks questions, many of which are never conclusively answered. 'Ends love in this, that my man, / Can be as happy'as I can; If he can / Endure the short scorne of a Bridegroomes play?' ('Love's Alchemy', lines 16–17). 'What if this present were the worlds last night?', 'Thou hast made me, And shall thy worke decay?' (holy sonnets). Moreover, the 'truths' the poems offer, though sometimes expressed definitely, often turn out to be provisional, partial – as they are either qualified by equivocations or hesitancies within the poem or contradicted by 'truths' offered in other poems. Taken individually, the poems enact an active process of discovery. Throughout a Donne poem there are shifts, changes of direction, reversals. Sometimes, as in 'The Flea', the speaker changes the tactics of argument. At other times, the audience addressed by the speaker changes. Some poems end at a very different place from their beginning, as speakers change their mind or reverse the views with which they started. The speaker in 'Air and Angels', for example, at first compares the woman he loves to an angelic presence ('So ... *Angells* affect us oft, and worship'd bee', lines 3–4) but concludes with a double analogy that seems to contradict the first lines by comparing himself to an Angel and the woman to the less 'pure' air which provides the 'sphere' for his love (lines 23–5).

Donne's wit involves surprise, a desire to startle readers, to make them look at things in a new, unconventional way.[11] He offers analogies that seem both unexpected and remarkably appropriate. Part of the pleasure and challenge his poems afford the reader comes from discerning the path of his logic, its complicated, subtle progressive discoveries. If Donne's poems enact a process of exploration, they demand a similar response from the reader who is asked to struggle with their difficult, knotty syntax, the concise, often elliptical phrasing, the direction and indirection of their arguments, to probe the equivocations and puns that change and complicate the meanings of poems.

The 'truths' Donne's poetry discovers in its exploration of human experience will be various, sometimes even contradictory, because experience is always in flux. Donne's persistent concern with change – as both subject and process in his poems – is not only part of his commitment to the ongoing discovery of truth, which requires an openness to change; it also embodies his personal sense that the universe is profoundly mutable and unstable. Almost everything is in the process of changing. *The First Anniversary*, identifying mutability with decay, anatomizes the degenerative changes, both physical and moral, that he finds throughout his world. Human inconstancy is part of the general instability of the universe. In the holy sonnet 'Oh, to vex me, contraryes meete in one', Donne laments his 'inconstancy' as if it were extraordinary, yet poems such as 'Confined Love' or the elegy 'Change' present inconstancy as the human condition. As he says in *The Second Anniversary*:

> You are both fluid, chang'd since yesterday;
> Next day repaires, (but ill) last daies decay.
> Nor are, (although the river keepe the name)
> Yesterdaies waters, and to daies the same.
> So flowes her face, and thine eies, neither now
> That saint, nor Pilgrime, which your loving vow
> Concern'd, remaines; but whil'st you thinke you bee
> Constant, you'are howrely in inconstancee.   (lines 393–400)

In a passage that strikingly anticipates Donne, the French essayist Michel Montaigne had similarly analyzed the human disposition to change: 'I find nothing more difficult to believe than man's consistency, and nothing more easy than his inconsistency ... What we have but now determined we presently alter, and soon again we retrace our steps; it is nothing but wavering and uncertainty ... We waver between different minds; we wish nothing freely, nothing absolutely, nothing constantly.'[12] If inconstancy is our nature, then contradiction will be our natural expression.

So far, we have looked at characteristics of Donne's poetry as a whole, despite differences of genre or audience. The rest of this essay discusses special concerns and achievements of the different kinds of poetry Donne wrote, in the process further defining the contrary impulses his writing reveals.

The *Satires* express an overwhelming sense of the degeneracy of late-sixteenth-century English society. In attacking this 'Age of rusty iron' (*Satire* 5, line 35), Donne recalls Roman satirists Juvenal, Persius, and Horace who similarly exposed the corruption of Rome, but he also emulates the biblical prophets moved by religious zeal who criticized the sinfulness and idolatry of Israel.[13] For all his independent spirit, Donne is here quite conservative, upholding old truths and values in a world that seems to be crumbling. There is a sense of frustration, for the satirist is compelled to expose what is wrong, but feels helpless to 'cure these worne maladies' (*Satire 3*).

Coming under scrutiny are the frivolous, materialistic values of his society (1), the legal system (2), religious institutions (3), the court and courtiers (4, 1), and the judicial system and structure of rewards in late Elizabethan England (5). The speaker of the *Satires* embodies qualities that oppose the viciousness of society: he is constant and scholarly (1), devoted to God and spiritual values, earnest and searching rather than complacent (3), preferring the 'meane' to either extreme (2), filled with hatred for vice (2) and vicious people in power (5) but moved by pity for humanity (3, 5). He presents himself as virtually alone in condemning the vices of his time – as if he were the last good man in a totally corrupt society. He criticizes not only the vices of his society but also the corruption of its institutions and systems. This opposition to the political establishment reappears in the *Elegies* and *Songs and Sonets*; and the accompanying feeling of isolation is seen in much of Donne's poetry, where there is little sense of fitting into a community.

The *Satires*, however, suggest contrary impulses, both outrage at this corrupt society, and a certain attraction to it. This conflict is suggested in *Satire 1*, in which the scholarly speaker, introverted and virtuous, and his inconstant companion, the ambitious and comically sycophantic would-be courtier, seem to represent conflicting, contrary aspects of Donne.[14] The relation between the speaker and his friend itself enacts the conflict, for the speaker is pulled in two directions – to stay at home, 'consorted' only with his 'bookes' (line 3), and to accompany his friend on a walk about town. That he goes with his friend, against the dictates of his conscience, indicates how difficult it is to stay away from the corrupt social world that repels him.

Satire 3 reveals a special aspect of Donne's complex feeling about the public world. This poem about the difficulty – yet necessity – of finding the true church (described in the Bible as the Bride (or spouse) of Christ) suggests the anxiety and alienation that Donne, born and raised a Roman Catholic, felt in a Protestant society that persecuted Catholics. The speaker surveys the various Christian religions one could choose (Roman Catholic, Genevan, Anglican), comparing each to a different kind of woman and suggesting a sceptical attitude toward all of them as well as criticizing those who select a particular religion (or wife) for the wrong reasons. That the speaker does not openly embrace any of the churches may indicate that he has no place in this world where he fits in. The poem concludes recognizing the dilemma the virtuous person faces: earthly authorities judge the seeker of truth by 'man's lawes' not God's, but social conformity may entail spiritual death. The best one can do is 'dwell' at the 'head' of 'Power['s]' 'streames' (lines 103–4) with God, even though that may not protect one's body from earthly punishment for religious nonconformity. Within the poem, we thus see both the desire to be part of the community, to have a secure place in society, and Donne's sense of isolation in the pursuit of truth which is a lonely, individual enterprise.

The sense of being at odds with society and its institutions and conventions also pervades Donne's Elegies, most of which, like the Satires, were probably written in the 1590s. They defy established, conventional authority (of parents, fathers, husbands) by flaunting illicit or socially disapproved relationships – affairs with a young girl ('The Perfume') or a married woman ('Jealousy' and 'Nature's lay Idiot'), or lesbian love ('Sappho to Phil- ænis'). Often the relations are described as secret, hidden from a dangerous public world.

In contrast to the Satires, with their public and political focus, the Elegies are concerned with the supposedly private sphere of love, but here, too, Donne's very choice of genre implies an oppositional stance to the court. In his Elegies, he turns to the example of the Roman poet Ovid, rather than imitating the Petrarchan, courtly love poetry popular during this period. Petrarch, adapting the conventions of courtly love which had flourished in the literature of the Middle Ages, had written a sonnet sequence in which an introspective speaker analyzed his fluctuating fortunes in love. Petrarch's poetry was enormously influential not only on the continent but in England. Particularly apt for expressing the complex relations between the superior, unattainable queen (source of all favour and rewards) and the subservient yet ambitious courtiers/suitors seeking rewards, courtly love became a 'dominant social and literary mode' of the Elizabethan court. Thus Donne's writing Ovidian elegies that mock courtly love suggests a critical, even oppositional, attitude toward the court.[15] But even here we see Donne pulled by contrary impulses since by circulating these elegies in manuscript he was adopting the practice of aristocratic courtiers who disdained to publish their poetry.

Ovid in his elegies reacted against idealization of love, insisting instead on a supposedly more 'realistic' analysis of love, based on the notion that human beings were natural, bodily creatures, possessing much in common with the animals. Donne draws on Ovidian situations and attitudes to reject the conventions of courtly and Petrarchan love poetry, with its chaste, beautiful, unattainable women, desired and sought by admiring, subservient, faithful male suitors. In Donne's *Elegies*, as in Ovid, love is very much of the body. The male speakers in these poems often frankly admit their interest in money and sex, and are moved by practicalities, not ideals. 'Love's Progress', for example, humorously defines the 'right true end' (line 2) and means of love in terms that reject the conventional postures of courtly lovers. The goal is sexual intercourse, and the best way to attain it is to take the path of least resistance.

In contrast to the faithful courtly lover, the men of the *Elegies* view constancy as 'subjection' and instead desire 'variety' and 'change' (Elegies 'Variety' and 'Change'). Where the Petrarchan lover is submissive and subservient, these lovers refuse 'to serve' (Elegy 'Oh, let mee not serve so'). They assert their superiority and control in relations with women, though power is more often desired than achieved since poems like 'Nature's lay Idiot' or 'Change' describe situations where the mistress seems very much out of the man's control. In the *Elegies* political language and analogies link the private sphere of love with the public world of politics, suggesting a desire for greater power in both spheres.

Though the *Elegies* are more of a piece than the *Songs and Sonets*, they vary in their attitudes toward women and sexual love. Some elegies present women as objects of revulsion and nausea and, for all the Ovidian emphasis on the naturalness of sex, reveal a distaste for the activity. Where courtly love exalts and idealizes the mistress, 'The Anagram' and 'The Comparison' parody Petrarchan conventions of (praising) female beauty by focussing on the lower parts of the female body, described in terms of excretions and disease. The 'best lov'd part' of his rival's mistress is like 'the dread mouth of a fired gunne, / Or like hot liquid metalls newly runne' or like 'an invenom'd sore' ('The Comparison', lines 38, 39–40, 44). In some poems, women are debased by comparison with animals, water, and land ('Nature's lay Idiot', 'Change', 'Oh, let mee not serve so') – things which are inconstant, mutable, or passive, and considered in the Renaissance to be 'naturally' meant to be under man's dominion. In other elegies, however, women and women's bodies are treated as immensely desirable. As 'Love's Progress' wittily and outrageously argues, her 'centrique part' is as infinite and worthy of love as the soul.

The best-known of the elegies, the witty seduction poem 'Going to Bed', celebrates sexual love and is less cynical than many of the other elegies. But even here we find conflicting valuations of woman and contrary impulses in love. As the male speaker urges his mistress to remove her clothes and inhibitions and asks her (like a monarch) to 'Licence' his 'roaving hands' (line 25) so he can explore her body (his 'America! my new-found-land', line 27), the poem moves between praising the mistress as source of all riches, joys, even 'grace' (line 42), and identifying her with land to be explored and possessed by man. Thus it expresses contradictory views of woman that were part of Renaissance culture in England, where the vogue of courtly love and the presence of a female monarch could glorify a woman as the source of all riches, favour, and grace, but political, legal, economic, and medical conventions and conditions defined woman as inferior and subordinate.[16] The poem's clever ending asserts the speaker's superiority as the master in love ('To teach thee I am naked first; why than / What needst thou have more covering then a man?' lines 47–8) and insists on what Petrarchan poetry, with its emphasis on the unattainable woman and unconsummated love, obscures – that the end of courtship is sexual intercourse. Sexual love itself, defined in this poem from the man's point of view as a process of seduction and conquest, engages and expresses his contrary desires for control and intimacy.

In insisting on the importance of sexual love, 'Going to Bed' not only counters Petrarchan poetry but also challenges Renaissance neo-Platonic ideas of love.[17] According to neo-Platonism, the object of love is properly the soul, and the body and senses must be left behind as the lover ascends to the spiritual in the process of loving. In contrast to this philosophy of love, Donne's glorifies the body and sexual love, which the speaker claims possesses spiritual significance: the unclothing of their bodies is analogous to the soul's divesting itself of the body in order to enjoy 'whole joyes' (line 35). This elegy's celebration of the private experience of sexual love as a supreme source of value marks what is one of the most important concerns of the *Songs and Sonets*.

The *Songs and Sonets* comprise Donne's most complicated exploration of love. Seemingly the most private of his poems, they are certainly the most varied, and were probably composed over a much greater period of time than the *Elegies* or *Satires*. The tensions and contradictions here are intense as Donne repeatedly attempts to define love by testing received ideas and conventions about love against the experience(s) of loving.

Like the *Elegies*, the *Songs and Sonets* often reject notions of love fostered by Petrarchan love poetry, even as they invoke conventions such as the aloof, distant mistress, or the suffering, submissive lover. In Petrarchan poetry, the mistress is chaste and remote (cool like ice, unmovable like a statue) and the male lover is constant in his devotion. But Donne sceptically challenges this formula of male/female relations. Sometimes he presents women as sexually inconstant, unfaithful, promiscuous ('Song. Goe, and catch a falling starre', 'A Jet Ring Sent'), and the male speakers often repudiate constancy, wanting to have all women ('Community'), refusing to be tied to 'dangerous constancie' ('The Indifferent', line 25; cf. 'Love's Diet'). But Donne challenges Petrarchan notions of male/female relations in yet another way, one that is at odds with his libertine emphasis on inconstancy. Many poems insist on the need for mutual love, finding unsatisfactory the frustrated longing and unreciprocated love that characterize Petrarchan formulations. As he writes in 'Love's Deity', 'It cannot bee / Love, till I love her, that loves mee' (lines 13–14). One of Donne's most important contributions to love poetry is thought to be his celebration of mutual, reciprocal love.

Donne praises mutual love as an experience of supreme value that opposes the transitory, material world and even transcends it. Whereas the *Elegies* in their political language and analogies often connect love and the political world, here there is a sharper opposition between the two spheres. The private little room of love (the microcosm) contrasts with the outside world of princes, explorers, lawyers, and merchants, who are all preoccupied with material concerns. The speaker of 'The Good-morrow' claims that his experience of mutual love gives him a new perspective from which the rest of the world looks insignificant:

> And now good morrow to our waking soules,
> Which watch not one another out of feare;
> For love, all love of other sights controules,
> And makes one little roome an every where,
> Let sea-discoverers to new worlds have gone,
> Let Maps to others, worlds on worlds have showne,
> Let us possesse one world, each hath one, and is one.
>
> (lines 8–14)

The world of love contains everything of value; it is the only one worth exploring and possessing. Hence the microcosmic world of love becomes larger and more important than the macrocosm. As the speaker in 'The Sun Rising' says:

> Nothing else is.
> Princes doe but play us; compar'd to this,
> All honor's mimique; All wealth alchimie. (lines 22–4)

Since the lovers in their bedroom contract all the world's riches, the sun can 'Shine here to us, and thou art every where; / This bed thy center is, these walls, thy spheare' (lines 29–30).

'She' is all States, all Princes, I' (line 21). As this famous line from 'The Sun Rising' suggests, Donne's description of 'mutual' love often assumes a degree of inequality between the lovers. Some poems seem attracted to the idea that love might diminish inequities and differences between the sexes – 'So, to one neutrall thing both sexes fit' ('The Canonization', line 25); 'Difference of sex no more wee knew, / Then our Guardian Angells doe' ('The Relic', lines 25–6). That the two lovers together create a whole (the two 'hemispheares' of 'The Good-morrow', line 17) suggests a kind of parity – the incompleteness of each without the other as well as the perfection of the lovers united. But other celebrations of mutual love assume conventional Renaissance hierarchical thinking about gender. Even Donne's portrayal of 'ideal love' is marked by contrary emphases on mutuality and disparity.

'The Canonization' defends the private world of mutual love against the public world, whose values are represented by the ambitious, materialistic person addressed in the opening lines. Attributing religious significance to what is clearly a sexual love, the speaker wittily argues (with a sense of the outrageousness of some of his arguments) that he and his mistress deserve to be canonized as saints. They oppose worldly greed, they have miraculously died and risen 'the same' (line 26; that is, orgasm has not diminished their vigour), they will die as martyrs in a hostile world, and finally their love will provide a 'patterne' (line 45) for others. In drawing an extended analogy between religious experience and sexual love, is Donne being humorous? blasphemous? serious? Conflicting possibilities are all suggested in this poem, as Donne examines the potential of human love to provide a redeeming grace.

With its spiritual powers, love seems enduring, constant, and capable of transcending the physical, mutable world. The poems of mutual love suggest that love may counter the process of change and decay that characterizes his universe. 'The Anniversary' claims that, though the world and everything in it including 'Kings' and their 'favorites' (line 1) is older by a year, true love is impervious to decay:

> All other things, to their destruction draw,
>   Only our love hath no decay;
> This, no to morrow hath, nor yesterday,
> Running it never runs from us away,
> But truly keepes his first, last, everlasting day.   (lines 6–10)

Similarly, 'The Good-morrow' ends with the hope that their love will defy the ordinary processes of time.

Remarkably, transcendence of the physical world and mortality is accomplished not by denial of the body but through its fulfilment. Whereas neo-Platonism taught that the lover could ascend to spiritual love only by leaving behind the impure body, Donne's poems sometimes insist that transcendent, spiritual love is also sexual, indeed, that lovers transcend the physical through embracing the body.[18] The fullest argument for the interrelation of body and soul and for the importance of the body in love appears in 'The Ecstasy'. The first half of the poem emphasizes transcendence and the spiritual nature of love as it describes how the lovers' souls have left their bodies and experienced an 'extasie' illuminating the mystery of their love as a mixture of souls. But love that leaves behind the bodies turns out to be incomplete. So the second half of the poem argues for the need to return to the body. Rejecting neo-Platonic, dualistic assumptions about the relation of soul and body, the speaker insists that the bodies are not 'drosse' but 'allay' (that is, alloy, line 56), the element that, though inferior, strengthens a metal and makes it more durable. Bodies make spiritual love more lasting. They are also the only means whereby two souls can fully unite. Souls can only 'flow' (line 59) into each other through the body, that is, through sexual love:

> So must pure lovers soules descend,
>   T'affections, and to faculties,
> Which sense may reach and apprehend,
>   Else a great Prince in prison lies.
>
> To'our bodies turne wee then, that so
>   Weake men on love reveal'd may looke;
> Loves mysteries in soules doe grow,
>   But yet the body is his booke.   (lines 65–72)

What a great stratagem for seduction. Perhaps 'The Ecstasy' is a seduction poem, and the speaker's seemingly high-minded arguments only a means to attain a carnal end. But, like many of Donne's poems. 'The Ecstasy' has built into it the potential for contradictory interpretations. Hence, it is entirely possible to read this poem as Donne's deeply serious attempt to define an integrative ideal of love and human nature that finds its ultimate sanction in the Incarnation of Christ.[19]

This kind of love cannot be experienced by many people. Donne presents his idealized lovers who embody wholeness and a spiritual grace as exceptional, unique, though also exemplary. As the analogy in 'A Valediction: Forbidding Mourning' suggests, they are the clergy of love. Their love is a holy mystery either kept secret from the 'layetie' (line 8) or possibly 'reveal'd' to another special person who has been 'refin'd' by love ('The Ecstasy', lines 70, 21).

The poems of mutual love are probably Donne's most well-known and admired poems, but they hardly represent the range of the *Songs and Sonets*, since others offer very different valuations of love, women, sexuality, and the body. The emphasis in the 'mutual love' poems on the spiritual dimension of love, and on the woman's special value as she enables the man to apprehend something of the divine, contrasts with those *Songs and Sonets* where love is defined simply as bodily appetite, where women are interchangeable, insignificant commodities that serve men's physical needs, and inconstancy seems the basic principle of all human experience.

'Community' argues that women are merely 'things indifferent' (line 3) which 'all' men may 'use (line 12). They have no moral value, let alone spiritual, and thus sexual love becomes a matter of physical appetite, and not an urgent one at that:

> they are ours as fruits are ours,
> He that but tasts, he that devours,
> And he that leaves all, doth as well:
> Chang'd loves are but chang'd sorts of meat,
> And when hee hath the kernell eate,
> Who doth not fling away the shell? (lines 19–24)

The misogyny evident in this poem surfaces in others too, where a disparaging attitude toward women is accompanied by revulsion from sexual intercourse. The speaker of 'Love's Alchemy' believes not only that love is purely physical and involves no marriage of 'mindes' ('Hope not for minde in women', lines 23, 19), but that even physical, sexual love is overrated. Going to bed with women is like having intercourse with a dead (though preserved) body – 'at their best, / Sweetness, and wit they'are, but, *Mummy*, possest' (lines 23–4)

Whereas the mutual love poems express longing for intimacy with another human being, the pull toward union that remedies 'defects of loneliness' ('The Ecstasy', line 44), these other poems exhibit a desire for emotional detachment, and for preserving a separate identity. 'The Indifferent' will love any woman so long as she is not interested in commitment. In 'Love's Diet' the speaker, trying to reduce the 'combersome unwieldinesse' (line 1) of his love and get it under control, thinks of love as a hunt, with women as his prey, where the goal is to enjoy the sport without emotional investment:

> Thus I reclaim'd my buzard love, to flye
> At what, and when, and how, and where I chuse;
> Now negligent of sport I lye,
> And now as other Fawkners use,
> I spring a mistresse, sweare, write, sigh and weepe:
> And the game kill'd, or lost, goe talke, and sleepe. (lines 25–30)

Both promiscuity and the devaluation of women and sexual pleasure are strategies in these poems for achieving detachment.

It is difficult to discuss Donne's various, contradictory explorations of the experience of love without implying some progression or development, such as from the cynical, libertine poems to the glorifications of a love that is both physical and spiritual. But one should be sceptical of assuming such a neat development – not only because of the uncertainty of dating but also because poems like 'Air and Angels' resist attempts to categorize them as either 'cynical' or 'celebratory'. Moreover, while 'Community' and 'The Indifferent' are often thought to be youthful poems exhibiting a cynicism that is the result of a limited range of experience, 'Farewell to Love' and 'Love's Alchemy' insist that disillusion has resulted from long experience. How can we say that 'Farewell to Love' and 'Love's Alchemy' were necessarily written before the celebrations of mutual love? Given what we know of Donne's unhappiness while living at Mitcham (1605–9), it is possible to imagine Donne writing cynical poems about love even after his marriage. Rather than constructing a progression in Donne's various treatments of love, perhaps we should see the variations and contradictions as expressing conflicting attitudes and contrary impulses that might characterize a full range of experience and desire.

That bitter disillusion may even accompany a continuing, intense, all-consuming experience of love is suggested by 'A Nocturnal upon St Lucy's Day', a poem sometimes associated with the death of his wife. As the speaker anatomizes his despair after the death of his beloved, who was like his soul, essential to his life, he explains with bitter, hyperbolic wit how he is 'every dead thing, / In whom love wrought new Alchimie' (lines 12–13). He is the 'quintessence' of 'nothingnesse' (line 15), the 'Elixer' of 'the first nothing' (line 29). Love 'ruin'd mee, and I am re-begot / Of absence, darknesse, death' (lines 17–18). Seen from one perspective, he is like the speakers for whom the experience of mutual love is all important, involving an exchange or union of souls, creating a private world that makes the external world unimportant. Seen from another perspective, his experience of despair, of being trapped in a state of living death now that his loved one has died, confirms the opinion of 'Love's Alchemy' and 'Farewell to Love' that love is the ultimate self-destructive experience. For all its obvious difference from those poems which devalue women as a group, 'A Nocturnal' shows the enormous cost of love, which is here paradoxically identified with death even as it survives the death of the beloved.

The *Songs and Sonets* explore man's relation with woman, seeing erotic love as one of the most important experiences of life – even, one could argue, in those poems that insist on its destructiveness. Donne's *Divine*

Poems explore man's relation with God, often describing it in terms of human love, and seeking to discover the true relation between man's love for woman and the love between God and man that promises salvation. Even in his *Divine Poems* exploring religious experience, Donne seeks to understand the relation between erotic and spiritual love.

Donne's *Anniversaries* on the death of Elizabeth Drury, daughter of his patron Sir Robert Drury, provide a link between the secular poems and the religious. As they eulogize the fifteen-year-old girl as the embodiment of virtue and see her death as having occasioned the death of the world, they recall 'A Nocturnal upon St Lucy's Day', which exalts the mistress as the soul of her lover and his world. But unlike those *Songs and Sonets* that suggest love integrates body and spirit as it transcends the physical, mortal world, the *Anniversaries* assume a dualistic division between body and soul. They exhort the reader to condemn the world, the body, and all earthly pleasures. The speaker counsels his soul to look upon his body as a poisonous 'small lump of flesh' that has 'infect[ed]' him 'with originall sinne' (*Second Anniversary*, lines 164–7) – a description that sharply contrasts with 'Air and Angels', where the body is necessary for the soul to function, or 'The Ecstasy' where sexual, bodily love becomes the way to touch the spirit. Focussing all our thoughts on heaven, we must 'forget this rotten world' (line 49) whose diseased state might be contagious (*First Anniversary*, lines 245–6).

The *Divine Poems* anatomize not the corruption in the outside world but corruption within. Like the love poems, these religious meditations are introspective, private, searching, always engaged in the process of discovery and revision. But their focus on sin, death, judgement, and resurrection, as well as their sense of the dualistic relation between body and soul, links them with the *Anniversaries*.

An overwhelming sense of sin and guilt leads to a deep uncertainty about salvation. The 'Hymn to God my God, in my sickness' is exceptional in its calm assurance that God is tuning him in the process of dying so he can join the 'Quire of Saints' (line 2) in heaven, and in its vision of being part of a community. More typically, Donne is disturbed by a painful awareness of his own sinfulness and inconstancy, which both isolate him (he is the worst of sinners) and make him part of the mutable world that he seeks to escape through love in some *Songs and Sonets*. His sins are so great that he asks God to delay Judgement Day so he can have enough time to repent ('At the round earths imagin'd corners').

Often the speaker feels helpless, passive, a pawn in the struggle between God and Satan. If he was created as God's 'Image', 'Why doth the devill then unsurpe' in mee? / Why doth he steale, nay ravish' what is God's 'right'

('As due by many titles', lines 7, 9–10)? Though he admits in this poem that he 'betray'd / My selfe' (lines 7–8), he emphasizes his passivity in the struggle between God and Satan for his soul. He may be responsible for his sins, but he is not responsible for his salvation. It is up to God to 'chuse' him (line 13), but so far he has no evidence that God has done so. Whatever Donne's actual theological views – and it is possible that the views in these poems are presented critically, with some distance between Donne and the speaker – these poems express a Calvinist sense of human depravity and the irresistible power of God's grace, which cannot be earned or merited.[20] They communicate what it feels like to be convinced of one's sin but also of the impossibility of doing anything to save oneself.

In Donne's *Divine Poems* the sense of sinfulness is so great that the speaker insists it will take extraordinary efforts on God's part to save him. Sin, which 'weigh[s]' him toward hell like a force of gravity, needs the irresistible power of God's 'Grace' which 'like Adamant' (the magnetic loadstone) alone can 'draw mine iron heart' away from the devil ('Thou hast made me, And shall thy worke decay?' lines 8, 13–14). It will take extreme 'Corrections' to discipline the proud 'I' and 'Restore' God's 'Image' ('Goodfriday, 1613: Riding Westward', lines 38–41). Just as the speakers in the *Songs and Sonets* often claim exceptional status, so the speakers in Donne's religious meditations present themselves as the worst of sinners. Their sense of passivity and helplessness contrasts with their insistent demands on God, their efforts to tell him what to do.

The demands for an intense, intimate relation with God – for an infusion of saving grace – are often couched in erotic language. Perhaps the most startling poem is the sonnet 'Batter my heart, three person'd God', in which the speaker says he is like a woman who loves one man (God) but is betrothed to another (Satan), and wants to be rescued, even by force:

> Yet dearely'I love you, and would be lov'd faine,
> But am betroth'd unto your enemie,
> Divorce mee,'untie, or breake that knot againe,
> Take mee to you, imprison mee, for I
> Except you'enthrall mee, never shall be free,
> Nor even chast, except you ravish mee.   (lines 9–14)

In this witty yet deadly serious plea for salvation, Donne highlights the unsettling implications that emerge when the biblical notion that Christ is the bridegroom (and the soul the bride) is conjoined to the Christian paradox that one is only free when bound to God. Metaphor and paradox are treated, for the moment, as if they were literally true, as Donne exploits analogies between sexual and religious love. Sometimes he tries to persuade

God to save him in much the same way as he addressed 'all my prophane mistresses' seeking their favours (as in 'What if this present were the worlds last night?'). In alternately adopting the conventionally 'feminine', passive role of bride and the aggressive 'masculine' role of suitor, Donne's religious poems exhibit contrary impulses that are curiously similar to those in his love poetry. For he both attempts to control God (thus preserving his individual separateness and autonomy) and seeks an intimate union with God that would erase his separate identity:

> Burne off my rusts, and my deformity,
> Restore thine Image, so much, by thy grace,
> That thou may'st know mee, and I'll turne my face.
> ('Goodfriday, 1613: Riding Westward', lines 40–2)

Repeatedly invoking analogies between human and divine love, Donne's *Divine Poems* suggest that erotic love is our only means, experientially, for apprehending our relation with God.

But if Donne draws an analogy between sexual and religious love, it is not without a sense of tension, for some poems suggest conflict or competition between human or 'prophane loves' and love of God. In 'A Hymn to Christ, at the Author's last going into Germany', the speaker claims that in leaving England he 'sacrifice[s] . . . all whom I lov'd there, and who lov'd mee' (lines 8–9) – as if the sacrifice is necessary for him to 'seeke God', 'the'Eternall root of true Love' (lines 12, 14). Though God does not 'controule, / The amorousness of an harmonious Soule' (lines 15–16), God places constraints on the object of man's love, demanding exclusive devotion. The allusion to God's commandment to Abraham to sacrifice his only son Isaac suggests both that God requires of us what is humanly impossible, and that the speaker's ties to earthly loves are still strong – which may be why finally he asks God to 'Seale then this bill of my Divorce to All' (line 22) so he will no longer be tempted.

The sonnet probably written on the occasion of his wife's death most painfully presents Donne's sense of anxiety and conflict about the value of human love:

> Since she whome I lovd hath payd her last debt
> To Nature, and to hers, and my good is dead
> And her Soule early into heaven ravished,
> Wholly in heavenly things my mind is sett.
> Here the admyring her my mind did whett
> To seeke thee God; so streames do shew the head.
> But though I have found thee, and thou my thirst hast fed,
> A holy thirsty dropsy melts mee yett.
> But why should I begg more Love, when as thou

> Dost woe my soule, for hers offring all thine:
> And dost not only feare least I allow
> My Love to Saints and Angels, things divine,
> But in thy tender jealosy dost doubt
> Least the World, fleshe, yea Devill putt thee out.

If he has 'found' God, who has 'fed' his 'thirst', why does he say that with Anne's death 'my good is dead'? He has 'found' God, yet still 'begg[s]' for 'more Love' – possibly a pun on Anne's maiden name, More, which suggests he still longs for her. Is God's love insufficient? Did God's jealousy cause her death? Loving this woman has led him to God ('so streames do shew the head'), yet toward the end of the poem she seems identified not only with forbidden objects of devotion ('Saints and Angels') but with 'the World, fleshe, yea Devill'. Does love for another person lead one to God, or is it yet another form of idolatry that leads to damnation and 'put[s]' God 'out'? The questions and contradictions are never finally resolved.

Perhaps the contrary impulses in Donne's poetry ultimately come from wanting to have it all. We see in the possible pun on his wife Anne's maiden name in the holy sonnet – in the desire to have 'more/More love' which is asserted even as it is denied – not only an admission of his continued longing for her but also a symbol of Donne's overwhelming desire to have it all, to possess the full range of love, not just part. He wants both human love and God's love, and though a number of the religious poems suggest a pressure to choose between them, they also suggest an unwillingness to give up those earthly ties, even a hope that those precious human loves will not be destroyed but actually included or contained in God, who is the 'root' or source of love ('Since she . . . ', 'Hymn to Christ'). Donne comes dangerously close to blasphemy in that holy sonnet on his wife by almost suggesting that God's love is, of itself, not sufficient to satisfy him. But that is what makes his poetry so humanly honest. Composed as he is of 'Elements' (the body) and 'an Angelike spright' ('I am a little world made cunningly'), he is pulled in different directions, yet is unwilling, perhaps by his very human nature unable, to give up the insistent demands of either body or soul.

Many of the tensions and contradictions in his poetry can be seen as deriving from wanting to satisfy conflicting human needs and desires. The demands of the body and sexuality are an important part of human nature, too important to 'forebeare' ('The Ecstasy', line 50), but the claims of the soul are equally insistent. Hence the coexistence of poems that see love as only sexual, poems that insist true love between people is a union of souls, and others that negotiate various interrelations of body and soul in human love. Some poems like 'The Indifferent' or 'Community' insist on male independence and autonomy in erotic relations. Others like 'The Sun Rising' or 'The Canonization' show a strong desire for intimacy. The pull between these conflicting desires gives focus to the *Songs and Sonets* as a group – and is brilliantly displayed in the single poem 'Air and Angels' – but it also surfaces in the religious poems as he examines his difficult relation with God. This desire for both autonomy and intimacy is not unrelated to Donne's desire, evident not only in the *Satires* and *Elegies* but in so much of his poetry, both to preserve his individuality, uniqueness, and satiric distance and to have a secure place in the world, to be part of the community.

Donne is vitally attracted to 'change', the 'fruitful mother of our appetite' (Elegy 'Variety'), as his many poems about promiscuity and unconfined love suggest. But there is also a deep longing for stability and permanence, evident in lyrics that celebrate exclusive, monogamous, mutual love. The excitement of sexual conquest vies with the comfort felt in a secure relationship where each partner is 'inter-assured' of the other ('A Valediction: Forbidding Mourning'). Several poems bring together the attraction to change and the desire for stability, exploring whether it is possible to have both in love. For though Donne dislikes mutability as it is a sign of mortality, he also seems to dislike stasis, which he identifies with stagnation. Poems like 'Love's Growth', 'Lovers' Infiniteness', and 'Lecture upon the Shadow' ask if love can be constant and yet grow, if love can include change without necessarily involving decay. Both in the experience of passionate love and in his anticipation of heaven, Donne wants the 'kind of joy [that] doth every day admit / Degrees of grouth, but none of loosing it' (*Second Anniversary*, lines 495–6).

Donne's poetry thus expresses the instability and infinity of human desire. For all its various attitudes, his poetry articulates a persistent desire to have everything, to experience an ever increasing 'joy' and fulfilment. This poignantly human characteristic of always wanting more than we presently have causes pain since we live in a world of limitation which disappoints and frustrates our desires. But what is so wonderful about Donne is that, for all his realistic assessment of those limits, and for all the admissions of guilt about his immoderate desires, he never gives up wanting – and asking for – more.

NOTES

1 'Valediction of the Booke', line 21, in *The Complete Poetry of John Donne*, ed. John T. Shawcross (Garden City, N.Y.: Doubleday, 1967). All quotations from Donne's poems follow the text of this edition.
2 'An Elegy upon the death of the Dean of Pauls, Dr John Donne', lines 25–8, in *The Poems of Thomas Carew*, ed. Rhodes Dunlap (Oxford: Clarendon Press, 1949).

3 On the manuscript transmission of Donne's poetry and the conditions of 'coterie' verse, see Arthur F. Marotti, *John Donne, Coterie Poet* (Madison: University of Wisconsin Press, 1986), especially pp. 3–24.

4 On Donne's life, see R. C. Bald, *John Donne: A Life* (Oxford University Press, 1970). John Carey emphasizes what he calls Donne's 'apostasy' in *John Donne: Life, Mind, Art* (Oxford University Press, 1981). See, however, Dennis Flynn's more sympathetic understanding of Donne's relation to Catholicism: 'Donne the Survivor', in *The Eagle and the Dove: Reassessing John Donne*, ed. Claude J. Summers and Ted-Larry Pebworth (Columbia: University of Missouri Press, 1986), pp. 15–24; and 'Donne and the Ancient Catholic Nobility', *ELR* 19 (1989): 305–23.

5 Izaak Walton, *The Lives of John Donne, Sir Henry Wotton, Richard Hooker, George Herbert, and Robert Sanderson*, intro. George Saintsbury (1927; repr. Oxford University Press, 1962), especially pp., 34, 47–8, 60–1.

6 Helen Gardner (ed.), *John Donne: The Divine Poems*, 2nd edn (Oxford: Clarendon Press, 1978), pp. xxxvii–lv. See also Dennis Flynn, 'Awry and Squint': The Dating of Donne's Holy Sonnets', *John Donne Journal* 7 (1988): 35–46.

7 Paul R. Sellin has argued for a much later date for *Satire 3*; see 'The Proper Dating of Donne's "Satyre III"', *HLQ* 43 (1979–80): 275–312.

8 Samuel Johnson, *The Lives of the Poets* (on Cowley), in *Selections from Samuel Johnson 1709–1784*, ed. R. W. Chapman (Oxford University Press, 1955), pp. 373–4.

9 On this quality of Donne's wit, see Judith Scherer Herz, ' "An Excellent Exercise of Wit that Speaks so well of Ill": Donne and the Poetics of Concealment', in *The Eagle and the Dove*, ed. Summers and Pebworth, pp. 3–14.

10 On Donne's concern with discovery and experience, see especially Joan Webber's book on Donne's prose, *Contrary Music* (Madison: University of Wisconsin Press, 1963).

11 Donne's concern with provoking readers to see things differently may owe something to Mannerist art. See Murray Roston's *The Soul of Wit* (Oxford: Clarendon Press, 1974). Other valuable discussions of the qualities of Donne's poetry include J. B. Leishman, *The Monarch of Wit*, 5th rev. edn. (London, 1962), and Arnold Stein, *John Donne's Lyrics: The Eloquence of Action* (Minneapolis: University of Minnesota, 1962).

12 Michel Montaigne, 'Of the Inconsistency of our Actions', in *The Essays of Montaigne*, trans. E. J. Trechmann, into. J. M. Robertson, 2 vols. (Oxford University Press, 1927), vol. 1, pp. 321–2. Tilottama Rajan, ' "Nothing Sooner Broke": Donne's *Songs and Sonets* as Self-Consuming Aritfacts', *ELH* 49 (1982): 805–28, sees both individual poems and the *Songs and Sonets* as a collection as self-consuming structures, grounded in assumptions about impermanence, inconstancy, and the insufficiency of human language to express truth.

13 See M. Thomas Hester, *Kinde Pitty and Brave Scorne: John Donne's Satyres* (Durham, N.C.: Duke University Press, 1982).

14 See Marotti's discussion of *Satire* 1 (in *Donne*, pp. 39–40). On the tensions in Donne's relation with the courtly system, see also Heather Dubrow, ' "Sun in Water": Donne's Somerset Epithalamium and the Poetics of Patronage', in *The Historical Renaissance*, ed. Heather Dubrow and Richard Strier (University of Chicago Press, 1988), p. 197–219. Carey, *Donne*, pp. 61–2, well observes that a

sense of separation or 'singularity' and a desire to overcome it, to become 'a part of the world' are 'contending features' of Donne's thought.

15 For an argument that Donne is writing within the Petrarchan tradition, see Donald Guss, *John Donne, Petrarchist* (Detroit: Wayne State University Press, 1966). But on the elegies as anti-Petrarchan and the political implications of his anti-Petrarchanism, see Marotti, *Donne*, pp. 44–66; and Achsah Guibbory, '"Oh, let mee not serve so": The Politics of Love in Donne's Elegies', *ELH* 57 (1990): 811–33.

16 See Ian Maclean, *The Renaissance Notion of Woman* (Cambridge University Press, 1980); Constance Jordan, 'Woman's Rule in Sixteenth-Century British Thought', *Renaissance Quarterly* 40 (1987): 421–51.

17 An important Renaissance statement of neo-Platonic ideas of love appears in Baldesar Castiglione, *The Book of the Courtier,*. trans. Charles S. Singleton (Garden City, N.Y.: Doubleday, 1959), The Fourth Book.

18 N. J. C. Andreasen, *John Donne, Conservative Revolutionary* (Princeton University Press, 1967), argues that Donne's idea of transcendent love is grounded in neo-Platonic philosophy; see especially pp. 19–20, 68–77, and 191–240.

19 See A. J. Smith's reading of 'The Ecstasy' in his *The Metaphysics of Love* (Cambridge University Press, 1985), chapter 3.

20 John Stachniewski, 'John Donne: The Despair of the "Holy Sonnets"', *ELH* 48 (1981): 677–705, argues for a Calvinist influence on these poems.

FURTHER READING

Andreasen, N. J. C., *John Donne, Conservative Revolutionary* (Princeton University Press, 1967)

Carey, John, *John Donne: Life, Mind, Art* (Oxford University Press, 1981)

Dubrow, Heather, '"The Sun in Water": Donne's Somerset Epithalamium and the Poetics of Patronage', in *The Historical Renaissance: New Essays on Tudor and Stuart Literature and Culture*, ed. Heather Dubrow and Richard Strier (University of Chicago Press, 1989), pp. 197–219

Flynn, Dennis, 'Donne and the Ancient Catholic Nobility', *ELR* 19 (1989): 305–23

Guibbory, Achsah, *The Map of Time: Seventeenth-Century English Literature and Ideas of Pattern in History* (Urbana: University of Illinois Press, 1986), chapter 3
'"Oh, let mee not serve so": The Politics of Love in Donne's *Elegies*', *ELH* 57 (1990): 811–33

Guss, Donald, *John Donne, Petrarchist* (Detroit: Wayne State University Press, 1966)

Hester, M. Thomas, *Kinde Pitty and Brave Scorne: John Donne's Satyres* (Durham, N.C.: Duke University Press, 1982)

Marotti, Arthur F. Marotti, *John Donne, Coterie Poet* (Madison: University of Wisconsin Press, 1986)

Smith, A. J., *The Metaphysics of Love* (Cambridge University Press, 1985), chapter 3

Stachniewski, John, 'John Donne: The Despair of the "Holy Sonnets"', *ELH* 48 (1981): 677–705

Stein, Arnold, *John Donne's Lyrics: The Eloquence of Action* (Minneapolis: University of Minnesota Press, 1962)

Summers, Claude J., and Pebworth, Ted-Larry (eds.), *The Eagle and the Dove: Reassessing John Donne* (Columbia: University of Missouri Press, 1986)

Young, R. V., 'Donne's Holy Sonnets and the Theology of Grace', in *'Bright Shootes of Everlastingnesse': The Seventeenth-Century Religious Lyric*, ed. Claude J. Summers and Ted-Larry Pebworth (Columbia: University of Missouri Press, 1987), pp. 20–39.

7

RICHARD HELGERSON

Ben Jonson

Ben Jonson wrote plays before he wrote poems and laid bricks before he did either. These activities – to which we should add his still later writing of court masques and entertainments – represent steps in a difficult but extraordinarily successful climb Jonson made up the steep face of fortune's hill, a climb that marked everything he wrote.

According to his own account, Jonson was born the posthumous son of an English clergyman, the grandson of 'a gentleman' who had served King Henry VIII. But this gentle lineage was obscured by his mother's marriage to a London bricklayer, whose craft Jonson was 'put to' at the age of sixteen: a humiliation he could, as he later said, 'not endure'.[1] Military service in the Low Countries offered a first escape from bricklaying; acting and writing plays provided a second. The rapid success Jonson achieved as a playwright did not, however, satisfy his ambition – nor could it. The audience for plays was predominantly common and unlearned; actors were mere artisans; playwrights were a rag-tag mix of would-be gentlemen and players. Writing poems and circulating them through the private network of manuscript transmission opened the way to more elevated company. Among Jonson's earliest datable poems are an epitaph on Margaret Radcliffe (a maid of honour to Queen Elizabeth), an ode to James, Earl of Desmond, a 'proludium' and 'epode' to Sir John Salusbury, an ode to Lucy, Countess of Bedford, and a verse epistle to Elizabeth, Countess of Rutland – all figures of considerable social distinction. But Jonson did not stop there. The production of masques and entertainments carried him still higher, to the royal summit of power and prestige. He wrote masques and entertainments directly for the king, who was their chief spectator; they were performed by the queen, the princes, and the leading aristocratic courtiers.

Complementing, but also complicating, the social ambition inscribed in this succession of trades and genres was a more properly literary ambition. Jonson aspired to be in the England of Queen Elizabeth and King James what Virgil and Horace had been in the Rome of Emperor Augustus: he aspired to be a laureate poet, a poet who would not only serve the ruler but would stand on a level with the ruler. *Solus rex aut poeta non quotannis nascitur*, he liked to say – 'only the king and the poet are not born each year' (8.637). As Jonson imagined it, the relation of the laureate and the king would be one of mutual support and mutual dependency. 'Learning', he wrote (and among the learned he clearly included poets), 'needs rest; sovereignty gives it. Sovereignty needs counsel; learning affords it. There is such a consociation of offices between the prince and whom his favour breeds that they may help to sustain his power, as he their knowledge' (8.565).

But a troubling asymmetry mars this proclaimed 'consociation of offices'. Though Jonson might enjoy thinking of the king and the poet as of equally rare birth, they are quite obviously not equal, nor does 'birth' function similarly in their elevation. Birth and due inheritance alone make the king a king; the laureate poet is 'bred' by the king's 'favour'. Whether moral or immoral, skilful or inept, the king remains king. The poet belongs to a different order, and his claim is of a different sort. 'For', as Jonson acknowledged, 'if men will impartially, and not asquint, look toward the offices and function of a poet, they will easily conclude to themselves the impossibility of any man's being the good poet without first being a good man' (5.17). For the kind of poet Jonson strove to be, social elevation could only ratify a pre-existing elevation based on merit, merit that was as much moral as aesthetic. The bricklayer's stepson wanted to join the company of aristocrats and kings, but he wanted to do it on his own terms, by virtue of an office as lofty as theirs.

Jonson and his poetry were caught between competing systems of value: a system of ascribed status and personal patronage belonging to the traditional feudal order, and a system of earned status belonging to the newer market economy and to the meritocratic state imagined by Renaissance humanism. As an aspiring laureate, he was obliged to translate one set of values into the other, to make a community of ascribed rank look like the kind of community of merit to which he and his work might properly belong. But such translation was not easy, for there was always a suspicion – as there would be still – that praise for the virtue of the rich and high-born might be no more than self-serving flattery, a suspicion that threatened to undermine the apparent flatterer's reputation for virtue. Instead of seeing merit recognize merit, we see (or suppose we see) sycophancy bow to power. As a result, the highest reach of the poet's social ambition can easily lead to the lowest estimate of his poetic accomplishment. Something of just that sort has happened to Jonson. The works posterity has most admired – comedies like *Volpone*, *The Alchemist*, or *Bartholomew Fair* – were initially presented to the basest audience and are least concerned with the social and political hierarchy of Jacobean England or with Jonson's relation to that hierarchy. The works posterity has least admired – the masques and entertainments – were presented to the king and the court and spend most of their energy extolling the hierarchical arrangement of privilege and power. If the masques have recently attracted considerable academic attention, so much so that they have come to seem *the* paradigmatic works of early-seventeenth-century English literature, it is less for their artistic merit than for the welcome frisson of revulsion their involvement in the machinations of power excites. Suspicious of all art, we are gratified to have our doubts so richly confirmed. But these are hardly the terms in which Jonson sought to be valued.

Jonson's non-dramatic poems are located at the point of maximum tension, just where the opposed hierarchies of social and literary status cross. In the great 1616 folio of his collected *Works*, Jonson put his poems in the middle, following his plays and preceding his masques – 'Halfway up the social ladder', he seems to be saying; 'Halfway down the literary', we are likely to respond. To regard Jonson's poems simply as a point of intersection is, however, to deny them any significant change over time, any real development of their own, and to deny them as well the formal affinities they owe to the successive collections into which Jonson and his literary executors have arranged them. It is nevertheless an understandable temptation, one to which some of the best and most illuminating accounts of this poetry have succumbed.[2] However one defines the opposed forces that pull at Jonson's poetry, those forces keep pulling all the way through his lengthy career. Though ambition and the changing literary scene made Jonson a man on the move, he often seems never to get anywhere, to be forever stuck with the same set of unresolved problems. But that impression can result as much from our interpretive strategies, from our desire to see poets whole, as from any real stasis in the poets themselves.

Still, Jonson does invite such misrepresentation in a way that others do not. He was obsessively concerned to remain true to himself, to 'live to that point', as he put it, 'for which I am a man, / And dwell as in my centre as I can' (*Underwood* 47), and that concern, which was a necessary part of his laureate undertaking, makes him unusually vulnerable to a static reading. But if his poems were meant to represent, as he liked to say, a 'gathered' self, he nevertheless gathered the poems themselves into distinct collections, collections that reveal progress, change and internal difference, and he left a significant number of scattered poems for later editors to gather. By attending to the various collections of Jonson's verse – the *Epigrams* and *The Forest* from the 1616 folio, *The Underwood* from the posthumous second folio of 1640, and the *Ungathered Verse* from modern editions – we can better see how the continuing and sometimes contradictory pressures of social and literary ambition expressed themselves in different orderings (and disorderings), in different genres, and at different times.

EPIGRAMS

In a dedicatory epistle to the Earl of Pembroke, Jonson called his *Epigrams* 'the ripest of my studies', and he insisted that 'in my theatre . . . Cato, if he lived, might enter without scandal' (8.25–6). By the time Jonson published his *Works* in 1616, epigrams had long ceased to be a novelty. Along with other satiric modes, the epigram had, on the contrary, been one of the most prominent signs of Jonson's literary generation, the generation that came of age in the 1590s. Thomas Bastard, John Weever, Sir John Davies, Everard Guilpin, Sir John Harington, and John Donne all wrote them. But no-one else made the claim for epigrams that Jonson did. No-one else called epigrams the product of serious study. More characteristic was Bastard, who termed his 'the accounts of my idleness'.[3] And no-one else thought such poems deserved the regard of a severe moralist like Cato. A generation earlier, Edmund Spenser had already drawn a line between pleasing poetry and profitable study and had put himself on the pleasing side, Cato on the profitable; and Sir Philip Sidney had reportedly ordered the destruction of his *Astrophil and Stella* and *Arcadia* out of fear that they could not be made to 'abide the censure of the most austere Cato'.[4] Where pastoral, sonnet, and romance had failed, there was no reason to think epigram would succeed. Even Martial, the ancient exemplar of the form, had ordered that 'no Cato enter my theatre'.[5] In reversing Martial's sentence, Jonson defied expectation.

A strong note of defiance runs through Jonson's *Epigrams*. These are pushy poems. They bully their subjects, and they bully their readers. If you don't like them, Jonson tells us, and if you don't take them at their own valuation, you're a fool. But he knows how wide the gap is between what we are likely to think and what he tells us to think. 'It will be looked for, book', he writes in the second epigram:

> when some but see
> Thy title, *Epigrams*, and named of me,
> Thou shouldst be bold, licentious, full of gall,
> Wormwood and sulphur, sharp and toothed withal;
> Become a petulant thing, hurl ink and wit
> As madmen stones, not caring whom they hit.

Not only the genre had a reputation for indiscriminate violence; Jonson himself – the man who had challenged an enemy to single combat in the Low Countries and killed him, who had killed another man in a duel in London, who had brawled with still others, who had quarrelled publicly with most of his theatrical rivals, who had been jailed for the moral and political impropriety of plays from the *Isle of Dogs* to *Eastward Ho*, who had represented himself on stage as the bitter Asper and biting Macilente – had just such a reputation. But he now intends to disprove all that. 'Deceive their malice', he tells his book:

> who could wish it so.
> And by thy wiser temper let men know
> Thou art not covetous of least self-fame
> Made from the hazard of another's shame;
> Much less with lewd, profane and beastly phrase,
> To catch the world's loose laughter or vain gaze.
> He that departs with his own honesty
> For vulgar praise, doth it too dearly buy.   (*Epigrams* 2)

But the questions remain – indeed, Jonson forces them on us: What price has he paid? And what has he bought? Is the deception demanded of his poems just a disappointment of the malicious, or is it a lie?

As we read through the collection, we find it increasingly difficult to give a clear answer to such questions. Many of the *Epigrams* do upset expectation, but many others do not. It would be hard to imagine a poem better calculated 'to catch the world's loose laughter' than the scurrilous mock-heroic 'Famous Voyage' with which the collection ends. *Lewd, profane,* and *beastly* may not be the right words for this shit-besmeared, 216-line account of a trip through the London sewer. *Epigram* isn't the right word either. But the 'Famous Voyage' is certainly among the filthiest, the most deliberately and insistently disgusting poems in the language. That Jonson should have included it in this collection and put it last cannot help but undermine his claim to 'honesty' and 'wiser temper'. Nor, despite its generic incongruity, is the 'Famous Voyage' wholly out of keeping with the rest of the *Epigrams*. Rather it stands as a metaphor for Jonson's caustic epigrammatic survey of the court worms and parrots, the fools and knaves, the usurers, whores, bawds and pimps, the plagiarists, playwrights and poet-apes, the lusty maids and willing pages, the catamite and bestial voluptuaries of Elizabethan and Jacobean London. As the wandering heroes of the 'Famous Voyage' brave the filth of Fleet Ditch, so Jonson braves the folly and corruption of court and city. But you can't splash around in the sewer without getting dirty. Basing your reputation for virtue on the witty display of vice is equally perilous, especially if you want not to be thought 'bold, licentious [and] full of gall'.

About half of Jonson's epigrams do fit the usual expectation. These are poems of satiric blame. If they do not share all the frothing, rabid violence of the most savage Elizabethan satires, they do inhabit much the same world and take a similarly perverse pleasure in its corruption. But another half of Jonson's epigrams are of a different sort altogether: poems of praise, addressed by name to many of the most prominent and powerful figures of the Jacobean court.

In *Timber, or Discoveries*, the commonplace book he kept for many years, Jonson wrote that 'our whole life is like a play wherein every man, forgetful of himself, is in travail with expression of another. Nay, we so insist on imitating others, as we cannot (when it is necessary) return to ourselves.' This obsessive mimicry, this theatrical abandonment of self, characterizes the objects of Jonson's satire. Against these, he sets what he calls 'good men':

> Good men are the stars, the planets of the ages wherein they live and illustrate the times ... These, sensual men thought mad, because they would not be partakers or practicers of their madness. But they, placed high on the top of all virtue, looked down on the stage of the world and contemned the play of fortune. For though the most be players, some must be spectators.   (8.597)

In his epigrams of praise, Jonson attempts to represent this elevated immobility of virtue and to identify both himself and his distinguished friends and patrons with it.

Consider, for example, *Epigrams* 98, 'To Sir Thomas Roe':

> Thou hast begun well, Roe, which stand well too,
>   And I know nothing more thou hast to do.
> He that is round within himself, and straight,
>   Need seek no other strength, no other height;
> Fortune upon him breaks herself, if ill,
>   And what would hurt his virtue makes it still.
> That thou at once, then, nobly mayst defend
>   With thine own course the judgement of thy friend,
> Be always to thy gathered self the same,
>   And study conscience more than thou wouldst fame.
> Though both be good, the latter yet is worst,
>   And ever is ill-got without the first.

Like many of Jonson's epigrams of praise, this achieves in little space a massive stillness. It seems meant to be carved in stone. Lapidary couplet follows lapidary couplet, and nearly every couplet, whether it takes the form of a statement or an injunction, resounds with the imperturbable solidity of self-evident truth. Indeed, so evident are these truths to good men like Jonson and Roe and so fully a part of their very nature, that the poem has hardly begun before it proclaims that it has nothing to say and its subject has nothing to do. Truth and goodness simply are. They need no elaboration, no augmentation.

Yet, for all its accomplishment and all its stillness, *Epigrams* 98 is as shot through with contradiction as are any of the epigrams of blame. Jonson denies change but talks of a beginning ('thou hast begun well') and a 'course'. He urges disinterest in fame but worries what we will think of his judgement. And he proclaims an identity between self-sufficiency and virtue but makes himself dependent on Roe. If Roe should not 'be always to [his] gathered self the same', if his end should not match his beginning, Jonson's poem would no longer testify to its author's judgement or his virtue. The problem is endemic to Jonson's moral and poetic enterprise. Immediately following two epigrams of lavish praise for Robert, Earl of Salisbury, he places a third, *Epigrams* 65, berating his muse for betraying him 'to a worthless lord' and making him write things 'smelling parasite', and he points out that such a slip can have material consequences: it has cost him both reputation and patronage. Dependence is the enabling condition of Jonson's poetry, its generating occasion. Jonson depends on his subjects' status, wealth, and power, as well as on their reputation for virtue. He is dependent in another way as well: the very lines in which he talks of self-sufficiency are translated almost verbatim from Horace. The mimicry Jonson condemns in *Timber* as the antithesis of virtue underlies everything he wrote. Such mimicry was, of course, recommended by Renaissance humanism. The only way to revive the culture of antiquity was to copy it. Jonson himself, elsewhere in *Timber*, says that the poet should 'make choice of one excellent man above the rest, and so ... follow him till he grow very he' (8.638). But what then becomes of the self to which he is always to be the same?

The contradictions that we find in *Epigrams* 98 and that are multiplied and amplified in the collection as a whole derive from the more general cultural contradiction between ascribed status and status based on accomplishment. The ideal of unchanging self-sufficiency, though informed by Senecan stoicism, belongs to a world of ascribed status, a world where position and power follow inherited wealth and all three create the presumption of merit. In *Epigrams* 98 Roe's self-sameness will '*nobly*' defend Jonson's judgement, and in *Epigrams* 102 the Earl of Pembroke's '*noblesse* keeps one stature still / And one true posture'. Jonson tries to assimilate the status of poets to this class-based model. In an epigram addressed to Sir Philip Sidney's daughter, the Countess of Rutland, he declares: 'That poets are far rarer births than kings / Your *noblest* father proved' (*Epigrams* 79). But Sidney was not only a poet, he was also the son of a lord deputy, grandson of a duke and nephew of two earls. His status had a quite different basis than Jonson's. Though both depended on patronage, Jonson's dependence was far more obvious. Sidney could pretend to be led astray by poetry and the passion that inspired it from the higher calling to which he was born. Whatever place Jonson had, he owed to poetry and the patronage it earned him.

Virtue has no story. It remains forever one and the same. In their refusal to narrate, Jonson's epigrams of praise are true to this principle. But the collection as a whole records an autobiographical action, Jonson's own movement from the contaminating company of knaves and fools into the elevating presence of the great and good. The *Epigrams* may contain about as many poems of blame as of praise, but the two sorts are not distributed evenly. Far more of the poems of blame come early in the sequence; far more of the poems of praise come toward the end. Furthermore, among the poems of blame, there is a slight but noticeable shift in emphasis from those that speak directly to the objects of their scorn and thus put the poet in their degrading company, to those that speak only about them and thus imagine an audience that shares the poet's values. The poet of the first half is still fighting his way free from base associations; he is angry and aggressive. The poet of the second half has made it. And where in the first half the scattered poems of praise commend mainly lower-ranking, private friends and relations, the far more numerous poems of praise in the second half concern many of the highest-ranking figures in England. As Jonson's recent biographer, David Riggs, remarks, 'Anyone perusing the 1616 folio would have immediately registered the aura of power and prestige that surrounded these [figures] and would have sensed that the poet's fortunes were on the rise.'[6]

At about the time of his earliest datable poems, Jonson wrote three plays, 'comical satires' he called them, that imagine for their central character a story like the one recorded in the *Epigrams*. In *Every Man Out of His Humour* (1599), the appearance of Queen Elizabeth cures Jonson-like Macilente of his biting humour; in *Cynthia's Revels* (1600), the patronage of noble Arete and the recognition of royal Cynthia removes Crites, another Jonson lookalike, from base and menacing company; and in *Poetaster* (1601), Maecenas and Augustus similarly rescue and grace Jonson's favourite alter ego, the poet Horace. Reprinted a decade and a half later in the folio *Works*, these plays are proved prophetic by the *Epigrams* that follow them. Both Jonson's social and his literary ambition are shown to have succeeded in much the way he hoped they might. And the vehicles of that success, the *Epigrams* themselves, not only provide sharply honed examples of the satiric wit that marked Jonson's literary generation, they move epigrammatic form into the less familiar territory of praise, adorning that territory with an impressive collection of celebratory monuments. But, as we have seen, questions much like those that haunted the comical satires continue to haunt the *Epigrams*. Why is virtuous self-sufficiency so dependent on wealth and power? How can virtue serve wealth and power except by flattery? Any why must virtue spend so much time in the company of vice? 'O, how despised and base a thing is man', Crites exclaims in one of Jonson's rare expressions of open self-doubt:

> When even his best and understanding part,
> The crown and strength of all his faculties,
> Floats, like a dead drowned body, on the stream
> Of vulgar humour, mixed with commonest dregs!   (4.62)

From the commonest dregs to the crown: these are the beginning and end of Jonson's imagined trajectory. But, as these lines suggest, the direction of travel could easily be reversed. In Jonson's *Epigrams*, it is reversed. After mounting from blame to praise, the collection slips back with the 'Famous Voyage' to float 'on the stream / Of vulgar humour, mixed with commonest dregs', and hard-earned self-congratulation is sickened with disgust.

THE FOREST

In the concluding lines of *Poetaster*, the Emperor Augustus advises Horace and Virgil not to let their 'high thoughts descend so low' as to notice the 'despised objects' of the play's satire. 'Be you yourselves,' Augustus continues, 'And as with our best favours you stand crowned, /So let your mutual loves be still renowned' (4.316). And in the 'Apologetical Dialogue' Jonson appended to the play, the 'Author' – Jonson himself – resolves to sing 'high and aloof, / Safe from the wolf's black jaw and the dull ass's hoof' (4.324). *The Forest*, the collection of poems that follows the *Epigrams* in the 1616 folio, shows Jonson obeying such promptings. The despised objects that populated the satiric epigrams are left safely out of sight as the poet effects a Horatian withdrawal from court and city.

The Forest is a much shorter collection than the *Epigrams* but formally more various. The title translates the Latin *sylva*, a term commonly used for a poetic miscellany 'in which', as Jonson defined it, 'there were works of diverse nature and matter congested' (8.126). His own sylva fits this definition. Its fifteen poems include an ode, a proludium and epode, three epistles, a country-house poem, four songs, two complaints, a brief introductory lyric and a penitential meditation. Yet despite its variety, *The Forest* has a clear order and serves a coherent self-presentational purpose. Its first and last poems, 'Why I Write Not of Love' and 'To Heaven', give the collection a firm beginning and ending. Within this outermost frame is another made up of five longer poems directed to specific members of the gentry or aristocracy: 'To Penhurst' (*Forest* 2), on the estate of Sir Robert Sidney; epistles to Sir Robert Wroth (*Forest* 3), Elizabeth, Countess of Rutland (*Forest* 12), and Katherine, Lady Aubigny (*Forest* 13); and a birthday ode to Sir William Sidney (*Forest* 14). In each of these, Jonson speaks in his own person, proclaims values to which he publicly subscribes, and defines the community to which he belongs. The next poem moving in from the start, 'To the World: A Farewell for a Gentlewoman, Virtuous and Noble' (*Forest* 4), represents a transition. Its moral concerns are similar to those of the preceding two poems, but they are more general and more conventional and the speaker is no longer Jonson. The 'Proludium' and 'Epode' (*Forest* 10 and 11), the next poems moving in from the end, represent a transition of another sort. Here Jonson's voice returns and with it returns a strong moral and self-presentational pressure, but the poem's noble subjects, the Phoenix and the Turtle, remain, like the virtuous gentlewoman of *Forest* 4, unnamed and indistinct, and its neo-Platonic preoccupations are not characteristically Jonsonian. The five central poems – two seduction songs from *Volpone* (*Forest* 5 and 6), a misogynistic 'Song: That Women Are but Men's Shadows' (*Forest* 7), a complaint 'To Sickness' (*Forest* 8), and the famous love song 'Drink to me only' (*Forest* 9) – stand at the furthest remove from Jonson's gathered self. They are poems by him and thus display his skill at graceful and learned 'making', but they are not of him: they do not emerge from his moral centre. In this way, the songs are consistent with the programmatic assertion they seem to contradict, the opening assertion that 'I' will 'not write of love'. The 'I' of that first poem is not the 'I' of the middle poems.

To retreat, as Jonson does in *Forest* 4 to 11, from himself, he must first retreat into himself. Such a retreat is the main action of *The Forest*, particularly as it relates to the works that surround it in the 1616 folio. The plays and *Epigrams* that precede and the royal entertainments that follow it are all deeply involved in the public world of city and court. *The Forest* withdraws from the world. Even the refusal to write of love, the favourite subject of most Elizabethan and Jacobean poets, removes Jonson from the company of his literary predecessors and contemporaries. He is not a mere 'courtly maker'. And 'To Heaven' announces a more radical removal. 'Laden with . . . sins', its speaker seeks to live in God. Between these poems, in the second frame, there is a repeated and powerful insistence on the physical and moral separation of Jonson and those he addresses from the world represented in his other works. 'Not . . . built to envious show', Penhurst stands apart from its ambitious neoclassical rivals with their 'touch or marble', their 'polished pillars' and their 'roof[s] of gold'. In his country retirement, Sir Robert Wroth lives similarly 'Free from proud porches or their gilded roofs', and he wins Jonson's special approval for not 'throng-[ing], when masquing is, to have a sight / Of the short bravery of the night'. In the epistle to the Countess of Rutland, poetry itself stands against 'those other glorious notes, / Inscribed in touch or marble', and in the epistle to Lady Aubigny, virtue resides 'Far from the maze of custom, error, strife' and turns its regard away from those 'spectacles and shows' that enchant the 'turning world'. Retirement distinguishes the subjects of all four of these poems, as it does the poet who commends them.

With the exception of the ode to Sir William Sidney, which reverses the usual Jonsonian valence of such key notions as 'dwelling' and 'standing still' and urges its youthful addressee out into the great world, the poems in this second frame all 'make [their] strengths', as Jonson has the noble and virtu-ous gentlewoman of *Forest* 4 say she will do, 'Here in my bosom, and at home'. These poems are, moreover, all Horatian in form and content. Horace's praise of the country life echoes through 'To Penshurst' and 'To Sir Robert Wroth'; his poems on poetry inform 'To Elizabeth, Countess of Rutland' and 'To Katherine, Lady Aubigny'; and his epistolary mode shapes all four. In *Poetaster*, Jonson had presented himself in the guise of Horace. Here he re-emerges as an English Horace, not now, as in the play, in a wishful fiction, but with the reality of well-known aristocratic patrons he can name and address and an actual country estate he can visit. In this sense, *The Forest* marks a further culmination of both Jonson's literary and his social ambition. King James is a welcome guest at Penshurst, and so is laur-eate Ben.

The exception, the birthday ode to Sir William Sidney, is nevertheless significant. Addressing the scapegrace son of Sir Robert Sidney, Jonson reveals the meritocratic basis of his own ascension. Even an offspring of the noble Sidneys must 'strive ... to outstrip [his] peers'; he

> must seek for new,
> And study more;
>   Not, weary, rest
>   On what's deceased.
>   For they that swell
>   With dust of ancestors, in graves but dwell.   (*Forest* 14)

He must, in short, win the right to stand still by moving energetically. This is what Jonson had himself been doing. Indeed, he is doing it in *The Forest*. He strives to outstrip his peers, he seeks for new, and he studies more. He even lays claim to Sir William Sidney's ancestors, as though lineage could be earned as well as inherited. Standing behind all four of the poems Jonson addresses to members of the Sidney family is the figure of Sir Philip Sidney, 'god-like Sidney', the great aristocrat-poet of the preceding generation, whose heir is no more his brother or his daughter or his niece and nephew, all of whom Jonson addresses, than it is Jonson himself. The 'high and noble matter' that once distinguished Sidney's poems now distinguishes his. If Jonson is an English Horace, he is also a modern Sidney.

For all his talk of dwelling in himself and at home, Jonson had gone a long way. Penshurst was far from the Charing Cross cottage where he grew up; Horace and the Sidneys, far from the bricklayer stepfather who raised him. In *The Forest*, Jonson does not so much retire into himself as move into a better neighbourhood and construct a better self to go with it. These actions represent, as I have said, a culmination of ambition, a social and literary triumph. But the triumph, though real enough, is tinged with melancholy and defeat. The collection begins with a humorous admission of failure, the aging poet's unsuccessful attempt to capture Cupid in his verse, and it ends with a more serious expression of guilt and world weariness. Between the two, we hear how Jonson has been 'forsook / Of fortune', how he sends verses for want of gold, how another poet (a mere 'verser' in his account) has been preferred to him, how the 'pains' and the 'wit' of his masques have been 'wasted' ('some not paid for yet'), how just getting enough to eat at a great man's table can be a humiliating struggle. And what the poems do not tell us, other sources do. The lord of Penshurst 'dwells' while other lords 'have built' not only because dwelling is more virtuous than building, but also because the owner of Penshurst, Sir Robert Sidney, was broke and could not afford to build. *The Forest*'s praise of Sidney's son-in-law, Sir Robert Wroth, is similarly shadowed. 'My lord Lisle's daughter, my Lady Wroth', Jonson later remarked, 'is unworthily married on a jealous husband' (1.142). Another of Jonson's conversational revelations clouds the epistle to the Countess of Rutland and its praise of her 'brave friend and mine': 'Ben one day being at table with my lady Rutland, her husband coming in, accused her that she kept table to poets; of which she wrote a letter to him, which he answered. My lord intercepted the letter, but never challenged him' (1.142). From this perspective, the easy self-sufficiency of Jonson's Horatian retirement seems rather a forced marginalization. The Sidneys were on the margin of the social and political life of the kingdom, and Jonson was on the precarious margin of that margin. His *Forest* could be a dangerous and uncomfortable place.

Both the retirement and the discomfort are marked by a shift in gender from the *Epigrams* to *The Forest*. The *Epigrams* are overwhelmingly masculine. A few are directed to (or at) women, but most concern men and the world of men's business. *The Forest* gives far more attention to women. Two of its three epistles are addressed to women; the third makes conspicuous mention of its addressee's wife; and 'To Penshurst' says more about the lady of the manor than about the lord. Even more striking, 'To the World' is spoken by a woman, and the romantic and platonic idealization of both 'Drink to me only' and the epode on the Phoenix and the Turtle concerns women. The same gender shift finds negative expression in four of the five less manifestly personal poems at the collection's centre: in the cynicism of the two songs from *Volpone*, the sexism of 'That Women Are but Men's Shadows', and the blatant misogynism of 'To Sickness'. That Jonson turns his attention to women in these ways, that he shows himself in their company and lets one of them speak through his verse, is a sign of the virtuous retirement enacted by *The Forest*. As Jonson presents them, women stand more easily for an unworldly adherence to indwelling, domestic virtue than do men. But women are also defeated and excluded by the world, passive objects of lustful desire, mere shadows of men, repositories of contagious illness. In a valuable essay on *The Forest*, Don E. Wayne has discerned marks of Jonson's status anxiety in both the positive and the negative portrayals of women. While the poems in praise of female aristocrats 'express an identification with the ruling patriarchy from which the poet is excluded on the basis of rank but not on the basis of gender', the aggressively negative poems 'provid[e] a release of the animus that issues from Jonson's sense of inequity concerning his own social position with respect to the male members of a ruling class … his poems must serve'.[7] When we remember scenes like the one Jonson described 'at table with my lady Rutland', the painful reality displaced by this double response to women reasserts itself. In the houses of the great, the poet can almost imagine himself the lordly proprietor: 'All is there', he says to Penshurst, 'As if thou then wert mine, or I reigned here' (*Forest* 2). But, clearly, all is not his, and he does not reign. Instead, the poet's position and the woman's are troublingly alike. His retirement enforces that resemblance, but his aggression toward women tries to erase it.

Being yourself, singing high and aloof, was a more arduous undertaking than *Poetaster* seemed to suggest, particularly when the appropriate self needed to be constructed out of sometimes ill-suited materials and the height was already occupied. In this undertaking, *The Forest* had nevertheless succeeded to a remarkable degree. 'To Penshurst', the epistles, and some of the songs have done much to establish the reputation Jonson continues to enjoy – and deserves to enjoy – for poetic integrity and moral rectitude. But they and the other poems in the collection also give evidence of that other Jonson, the Jonson who did not and could not know himself and who could never fully escape 'the wolf's black jaw and the dull ass's hoof' – could not escape them because, even in retirement, those violent instruments of satiric denigration were still his own. The tension between these two Jonsons provides a large part of the excitement of *The Forest* and helps give the collection its enduring value as both poetry and document.

THE UNDERWOOD

Before his death in 1637, Jonson began assembling material for a second volume of his collected 'works'. When the book finally appeared in 1640, it contained a large gathering of poems called *The Underwood* – a title chosen, Jonson tells us in a prefatory address 'to the reader', 'out of the analogy they hold to *The Forest* in my former book, and no otherwise' (8.126). Though *The Underwood* includes some of Jonson's best and most ambitious poems, it is marked by an often wry and self-mocking sense of the 'lesser' and 'later' mentioned in its preface and suggested by its title. By the time he wrote these poems, Jonson had both a royal pension and a recognized place at court. He was the 'king's poet'; he wrote with familiar ease to the greatest and most powerful figures in the land; and he received the homage of younger men suing 'to be sealed of the Tribe of Ben'. The extraordinary ambitions he had proclaimed in the 1590s had thus been largely fulfilled. But illness, age and poverty, a bloated body, and a weakened and unsympathetic king put those accomplishments in danger. In *The Underwood*, Jonson is more vulnerable and less in control than he had seemed to be in the earlier collections. He now admits his dependence, and he recognizes, as he had rarely done before, that his struggle for stable and pre-eminent selfhood was often a struggle against himself.

Dependence begins with the very existence of *The Underwood*. Though Jonson named the collection and began putting it together, it was completed by his friend, patron, and literary executor, Sir Kenelm Digby. No-one can say precisely how large a part Jonson had in the selection and ordering of the poems that appear in *The Underwood*, but the fact that subsequent editors have credited three of them to other writers and have thought another three of doubtful authorship suggests that Jonson's control was far from complete. Editors and critics have also seen Digby's hand in the placement of 'Eupheme', Jonson's fragmentary, ten-piece eulogy on Digby's late wife, Lady Venetia Digby, as the last of the original poems in the collection. But here the evidence is tellingly unclear. 'Eupheme' does draw heavily on Digby's own prose letter book 'In Praise of Venetia Digby' and it contributes importantly to Digby's defence of his wife's posthumous reputation, yet, as one of Jonson's last works and as a deliberate farewell to his life and art, it seems both well placed and significantly self-reflective. Furthermore, whether Jonson or Digby was responsible, 'Eupheme's' symmetrical relation to the collection's other ten-piece sequence, the 'Celebration of Charis', works much as the framing devices of *The Forest* had done, thus suggesting a similar authorial design. What we guess concerning *The Underwood*'s editorial provenance is characteristic of the collection as a whole. Dependence and independence, self-making and reliance on the material and moral support of others, play intriguingly against one another throughout.

Jonson had opened *The Forest* by explaining why he wrote not of love and declared in the 'Proludium' that he had no muse for his 'own true fire'. *The Underwood* reverses both positions. In 'A Celebration of Charis' and several other poems, Jonson is explicitly presented as a lover, and in 'Eupheme' he calls Venetia Digby his 'muse': the 'life of all I said, / The spirit that I wrote with, and conceived'.[8] Both reversals suggest a new dependence, particularly on women, and both portray Jonson in decline. The lover is a comic figure. Blinded and paralyzed by the sight of Charis:

> I stood a stone,
> Mocked of all, and called of one
> (Which with grief and wrath I heard)
> Cupid's statue with a beard,
> Or else one that played his ape
> In a Hercules his shape.

And the muse-bereft poet declares his own death: 'What's left a poet, when his muse is gone? / Sure, I am dead, and know it not!' Between the two are many passages revealing a grotesque, feeble, erring, and impoverished Jonson. 'Let me be what I am', he proclaims in one poem, 'As Virgil cold, / As Horace fat, or as Anacreon old'. The resonant ancient names recall his laureate ambition; the bare adjectives wryly qualify it. In another, he talks of his 'hundred of grey hairs', his 'mountain belly', and his 'rocky face', and in still another he presents himself as:

> a tardy, cold,
> Unprofitable chattel, fat and old,
> Laden with belly, [who] doth hardly approach
> His friends, but to break chairs or crack a coach.

Other poems describe him 'buried in ease and sloth', compare him to 'the tun at Heidelberg', confess that his fortune 'humble[s]' him 'to take / The smallest courtesies with thanks', proclaim him 'broke', admit that he cannot pay his bills, beg to be relieved of 'the poet's evil, poverty', lament the loss to fire of his books and papers, reveal that others judge 'parts of me … decayed', call him 'the old bard', 'a bed-rid wit', and take sore comfort that 'we last out, still unlaid'. In poems like these, the ground for Jonson's claim shifts. Instead of merit, he stresses need. With this change comes another. The hierarchy of birth and fortune that Jonson's imagined meritocracy had earlier pretended to subvert is effectively reinstated. No longer is the laureate the spiritual equal of the king. Royal birthday poems and versified New Year's gifts point rather toward the role Jonson assigns the poet in *Neptune's Triumph*, the role official poets laureate would find themselves playing for the next several centuries: 'the most unprofitable of [the king's] servants ... A kind of a Christmas engine, one that is used at least once a year for a trifling instrument of wit, or so' (7.682–3).

Seeking to realize in himself the ideal of the great public poet, Jonson had tested some of the deepest and most contradictory values of his culture. The *Epigrams* and *The Forest* are instruments of that test. They powerfully assert the moral order on which the poet's special eminence depends, define by acts of inclusion and exclusion the community to which he belongs, revive and domesticate the literary forms through which his greatness should speak itself. *The Underwood* presents the sometimes sorry results. Having gained an intimate acquaintance with the real interests and concerns of the court and the upper aristocracy, Jonson must acknowledge that his divine ambition was misplaced. Far from of aspiring to godhead, he now looks with envy even on brute beasts. 'I began', he says in an epigram to the Earl of Newcastle, 'to wish myself a horse' (*Underwood* 53). Horsemanship, like other aristocratic pastimes, matters more than poetry, 'For never saw I yet the muses dwell, / Nor any of their household, half so well' as the horses in Newcastle's stable. Jonson's ironic wish echoes the opening of the *Defence of Poesy*, where Sidney, the heroic champion of Jonson's earlier poetry, tells how the Italian riding master, John Pietro Pugliano, praised horsemanship with such eloquence 'that if I had not been a piece of a logician before I came to him, I think he would have persuaded me to have wished myself a horse'.[9] In Jacobean and Caroline England, Pugliano's values more nearly match reality than Sidney's, and Jonson finds himself forced to revise his sense of literary and political tradition: 'Away with the Caesarian bread! / At these immortal mangers Virgil fed'.

Many of the ninety poems in *The Underwood* share the disillusionment comically expressed by the Newcastle epigram. But many others don't. The most conspicuous of these exceptions are a half-dozen longer poems: the epistles to Sir Edward Sackville, to John Selden, to a 'friend' persuading 'him to the wars', and 'to one that asked to be sealed of the Tribe of Ben', 'A Speech according to Horace' and the famous Cary–Morison ode (*Underwood* 13, 14, 15, 44, 47, 70). All six draw obviously and heavily on classical precedent, and all but one are addressed to younger men whose admiration of Jonson is made clear. As it had been throughout his career, a double sense of community remained essential to the maintenance of Jonson's laureate identity. He had to be at one both with the ancients and with a circle of virtuous and supportive friends. Indeed, without the second he seemed unable fully to participate in the first. The meritocracy of great poets could only survive and renew itself as part of a meritocracy of like-minded contemporaries. The reverse was also true. The meritocracy of contemporaries could only know and express itself by appropriating the work of the Greek and Roman past. In the last decades of his life, Jonson's modern meritocracy seems to have been populated almost exclusively by those younger men who came collectively to be known as the 'Sons of Ben'. Their sense of what Jonson had been – of the role he had claimed for himself, of the society he had imagined and represented, of the ancient poetic means he had revived – made it possible not only for him to reappear in his full laureate guise but to invent through classical imitation a new and more challenging form for its assertion.

Though five of these poems are clearly Horatian and thus resemble poems in *The Forest*, the sixth is strikingly innovative. This poem, a consolatory address to Sir Lucius Cary on the death in 1629 of his friend Sir Henry Morison, is usually identified as the first Pindaric ode in English. But even with regard to his Greek original, Jonson innovates. He translates the Greek strophe, antistrophe, and epode in a way that suggests his own sense of a firmly centred virtue: 'turn', 'counterturn', and 'stand'. The abrupt and vigorous movement of his poem comes always to rest on an unchanging moral centre. It thus answers the question implied in its opening stanza by the 'brave infant of Saguntum', who took one look out of his mother's womb, saw the dreadful state of the world, and crawled back in: 'How summed a circle didst thou leave mankind / Of deepest lore, could we the centre find' (*Underwood* 70). That elusive centre is found in the dutiful behaviour of Henry Morison, in the perfect friendship of Morison and Cary, in the classical form of the Pindaric ode, and in the laureate presence of Jonson himself:

> Call, noble Lucius, then for wine,
> And let thy looks with gladness shine;
> Accept this garland, plant it on thy head;
> And think, nay know, thy Morison's not dead.
> He leaped the present age,
> Possessed with holy rage
> To see that bright eternal day,
> Of which we priests and poets say
> Such truths as we expect for happy men;
> And there he lives with memory, and Ben

> *The Stand*
> Jonson, who sung this of him, ere he went
> Himself to rest.

In what is certainly the boldest enjambment in the history of English poetry, Jonson not only couples lines and stanzas, he joins heaven and earth. 'Ben' lives in 'that bright eternal day' with memory and Morison, while 'Jonson' remains with Cary here below. Such poetic transcendence is far beyond the reach of the petrified Ben of the 'Celebration of Charis', 'Cupid's statue with a beard, / Or one who played his ape / In a Hercules his shape'. The Charis poems recall Jonson's heroic ambition only to turn it to ridicule. In the Cary–Morison ode, his ambition is triumphantly realized.

That *The Underwood* should contain both the ridicule and the triumph testifies to the extraordinary difficulty of Jonson's undertaking. Only with a small group of younger admirers could he maintain the pretence of his vatic role. Elsewhere, his very achievement, his recognized position as the king's poet, especially when coupled with want and physical infirmity, reduced his pretension to something more deserving the name of 'underwood' than 'forest'. But, curiously, the lesser 'shrubs' in which Jonson reveals his weakness are among his most attractive and engaging poems. The acknowledged vulnerability and dependence of this great man contribute more to our sense of his real greatness than do most of his strident assertions of moral self-sufficiency.

UNGATHERED VERSE

Though Jonson's *Ungathered Verse* did not become a collection in its own right until the twentieth century, it is as much a product of authorial intention as any of the other three. Some of its poems may have been forgotten or misplaced and thus excluded from the *Epigrams*, *The Forest*, and *The Underwood* by accident. But most must have been left out on purpose. And since half the poems in the *Ungathered Verse* belong to a single generic category only marginally represented in the other collections, this appears a categorical exclusion. What Jonson did not want to represent him in his folio *Works* were poems written to praise the books of other writers.

No English poet before Jonson had used the printed book quite so deliberately to make a claim for himself as Jonson did, especially in the 1616 folio. Jonson took plays and masques, the ephemeral entertainment of stage and court, and called them 'works'. In doing so, he transformed material from the performance culture in which he had participated as an actor, playwright, and masque-maker into the stuff of a newly emerging print culture, a culture of the printed book. But, curiously, when it came to deciding which poems he would include in his printed *Works*, he omitted those whose original occasions tied them most closely to print culture and chose instead those belonging to the culture of manuscript transmission and oral performance. With rare exceptions, the poems that found their way into the *Epigrams*, *The Forest*, and *The Underwood* imagine themselves not printed and read by an anonymous audience of bookbuyers, but rather spoken or written out by hand and presented to a small coterie of highly selected auditors and readers. Jonson's community of merit thus shares with the community of birth it pretends to replace an aristocratic aversion to print, and his great book is made to appear untainted by the new print culture to whose development it was making such a large contribution. As Jonson published plays against the play and masques against the masque, so he publishes a book against the printed book. His ambition was such that it could only be realized in opposition to the very conditions of its own expression.

Yet, for all Jonson's paradoxical avoidance of the socially demeaning stigma of print in his printed *Works*, the commendatory poems that have since been collected and reprinted as the largest part of his *Ungathered Verse* do much to legitimate the printed book and its culture. Perhaps most significant in this regard are the two poems Jonson contributed to the 1623 folio of William Shakespeare's *Comedies, Histories, and Tragedies*. Unlike Jonson, Shakespeare seems to have been genuinely uninterested in securing for his plays the stability and permanence of print. At the time of his death in 1616, only eighteen of the folio's thirty-six plays had been printed, and even those, unlike the quarto editions of Jonson's plays, gave little sign of authorial supervision. For years, Jonson had mocked Shakespeare as the chief of those theatrical hacks who, yielding to the 'concupiscence' of the popular stage, begat 'tales, tempests, and such-like drolleries' (6.16). Print was the place of reason and art; the stage, the place of absurdity and cheap entertainment. Jonson belonged to one; Shakespeare, to the other. But when, in obvious imitation of Jonson's own folio *Works*, Shakespeare's plays were gathered and printed in a handsome folio edition, Jonson was there to welcome the erstwhile hack into the palace of art. Once condemned for his subservience to the age, Shakespeare now stands forth 'not of an age, but for all time!' What has made the difference? Nothing but print. 'Thou art a monument without a tomb', Jonson proclaims, 'And art alive still while thy book doth live' (*Ungathered Verse* 26). And he concludes with a conceit that recalls his image of 'good men' as 'the stars, the planets of the ages wherein they live', who, 'placed high on the top of all virtue, looked down on the stage of the world and condemned the play of fortune':

> Shine forth, thou star of poets, and with rage
>   Or influence chide or cheer the drooping stage;
> Which, since thy flight from hence, hath mourned like night,
>   And despairs day, but for thy volume's light.

The fortune-ridden stage carries on its trivial business in moral darkness. Light radiates from the transcendent fixity of print.

A number of other commendatory poems from the *Ungathered Verse* exalt the published book as 'the master print' where one can see 'a mind attired in perfect strains' (*Ungathered Verse* 2). For the countervailing imperfection, the *Ungathered Verse* presents the masque and its designer, Inigo Jones. In the folio collections, blame had been directed at types or at unnamed individuals. The *Ungathered Verse* contains three poems aimed specifically at Inigo Jones and another at Alexander Gill. The quarrel with Jones seems to have arisen when Jonson, appropriating a masque on which they had collaborated, had *Love's Triumph Through Callipolis* printed with his name before Jones's on the title page. Jones objected, and Jonson responded by printing still another of their masques, this time under his name alone, and by writing the three satiric poems. Years earlier, in publishing *Hymenaei*, Jonson had opposed the 'body' of the masque to its 'soul', associating the body with the designer's 'show' and the soul with the poet's 'invention' (7.209). Now he must angrily admit that 'painting and carpentry are the soul of masque':

> O shows! Shows! Mighty shows!
> The eloquence of masques! What need of prose,
> Or verse, or sense to express immortal you?
> You are the spectacles of state!   (*Ungathered Verse* 34)

Jones had clearly won. The king and the court cared more for show than sense. If the poetic soul of the masque was to survive at all, it would have to be away from court in the socially stigmatized medium of print, the medium that had transformed Shakespeare from careless play-botcher into the 'soul of the age'.

Jonson's social and literary ambition had drawn him to court and into the company of the chief aristocratic courtiers, the company the *Epigrams*, *The Forest*, and *The Underwood* represent. But the very publication of those collections in two fat printed books pulled Jonson in another direction, one better suggested by the commendatory poems he left out of his folio volumes. As many early-sixteenth-century humanists had sensed, learning's place was to be in print shops and book stalls rather than at court or in the country houses of the titled elite. The choice of 'A Speech out of Lucan' as the last poem in the *Ungathered Verse* is thus particularly appropriate, for it provides a sharp retrospective judgement on Jonson's career-shaping hope of reviving a 'consociation of offices' between prince and poet, between power and virtue:

> He that will honest be may quit the court:
> Virtue and sovereignty, they not consort.
>
> (*Ungathered Verse* 50)

Jonson never voluntarily quit the court, but he did explore an alternative to the court in the commercial dissemination of print. The ideal of moral goodness that he associated with the great poet may have been no more available in one than the other, but the promotion of merit irrespective of birth did have greater scope in print. It is, in any case, on print that Jonson's various collections of poems, including his *Ungathered Verse*, depend for their coherence and stability and to print that they owe their fame. For a poet of Jonson's self-contradictory ambition, print and the marketplace had become the soul of verse.

NOTES

1 *Ben Jonson*, ed. C. H. Herford, Percy Simpson, and Evelyn Simpson, 11 vols., (Oxford: Clarendon Press, 1925–52), vol. 1, p. 139. Subsequent quotations from this edition, with the exception of quotations from Jonson's poems, are cited by volume and page number in the text. Poems are identified by the collection to which they belong – *Epigrams*, *The Forest*, *The Underwood*, or *Ungathered Verse* – and their number within the collection. Spelling and punctuation have been modernized in all quotations from Jonson and from others.

2 See, for example, Thomas M. Greene, 'Ben Jonson and the Centered Self', *SEL* 10 (1970): 325–48; Arthur F. Marotti, 'All About Jonson's Poetry', *ELH* 39 (1972): 208–37; Stanley Fish, 'Authors–Readers: Jonson's Community of the Same', *Representations* 7 (1984): 26–58.

3 Thomas Bastard, *Chrestoleros, Seven Bookes of Epigrames*, Spenser Society (1888; rpr. New York: B. Franklin, 1967, p. 4).

4 *The Works of Edmund Spenser: A Variorum Edition*, ed. Edwin Greenlaw et al. (Baltimore: John Hopkins University Press, 1932–57), vol. 10, p. 10, and Sidney in Thomas Moffett, *Nobilis, or a View of the Life and Death of a Sidney*, trans. and ed. Virgil B. Heltzel and Hoyt H. Hudson (San Marino, Calif.: Huntington Library, 1940), p. 74.

5 Quoted by Herford, Simpson, and Simpson, *Ben Jonson*, 11.1.

6 David Riggs, *Ben Jonson: A Life* (Cambridge, Mass.: Harvard University Press, 1989), pp. 229–30.

7 Don E. Wayne, 'Jonson's Sidney: Legacy and Legitimation in *The Forrest*', in M. J. B. Allen (ed.), *Sir Philip Sidney's Achievement* (New York: AMS Press, 1990), p. 243.

8 The poems mentioned or quoted in this paragraph are (in order of their appearance) *Underwood*, 84.9, 2.2, 84.9, 42, 9, 56, 23, 52, 13, 38, 17, 62, 43, 76, 68, 71, and 76.

9 Sir Philip Sidney, *A Defence of Poetry*, ed. J. A. Van Dorsten (1956; rpr. Oxford University Press, 1989), p. 17.

FURTHER READING

Editions

The standard edition of Jonson's work is the eleven-volume *Ben Jonson*, ed. C. H. Herford, Percy Simpson, and Evelyn Simpson (Oxford: Clarendon Press, 1925–52). Jonson's poems are found in vol. 8. William B. Hunter, Jr (Garden City, N.Y.: Anchor Books, 1963) and Ian Donaldson (Oxford University Press, 1975) have produced single-volume, annotated editions of the complete poetry, Hunter in old spelling, Donaldson in a modernized version.

Critical and biographical studies

David Riggs's informative and entertaining *Ben Jonson: A Life* (Cambridge, Mass.: Harvard University Press, 1989) supersedes all previous biographical accounts of Jonson. Earlier criticism has been ably described by Jonas A. Barish in the introduction to his *Ben Jonson: A Collection of Critical Essays* (Englewood Cliffs, N.J.: Prentice-Hall, 1963), which reprints important comments by T. S. Eliot, L. C. Knights, Harry Levin, and Edmund Wilson. Beginning with Wesley Trimpi's *Ben Jonson's Poems: A Study in the Plain Style* (Stanford University Press, 1962), Jonson's non-dramatic poetry has received much specific attention. Particularly influential have been three articles that deal with the full range of that poetry: Thomas M. Greene's 'Ben Jonson and the Centered Self', *Studies in English Literature* 10 (1970): 325–48; Arthur F. Marotti's 'All About Jonson's Poetry', *ELH* 39 (1972): 208–37; and Stanley Fish's 'Authors–Readers: Jonson's Community of the Same', *Representations* 7 (1984): 26–58. Among books devoted wholly or in large part to Jonson's poetry are J. G. Nichols's *The Poetry of Ben Jonson* (New York: Barnes and Noble, 1969); George Parfitt's *Ben Jonson: Public Poet and Private Man* (New York: Barnes and Noble, 1977); Richard S. Peterson's *Imitation and Praise in the Poems of Ben Jonson* (New Haven: Yale University Press, 1981); Sara J. van den Berg's *The Action of Ben Jonson's Poetry* (Newark: University of Delaware Press, 1987), Robert C. Evans's *Ben Jonson and the Poetics of Patronage* (Lewisburg, Pa.: Bucknell University Press, 1989); Jonsook Lee's *Ben Jonson's Poesis: A Literary Dialectic of Ideal and History* (Charlottesville: University Press of Virginia, 1989); and Michael McCanles's *Jonsonian Discriminations: The Humanist Poet and the Praise of True Nobility* (University of Toronto Press, 1992). The *Epigrams* have been discussed by Don E. Wayne in 'Poetry and Power in Ben Jonson's *Epigrammes*: The Naming of "Facts" or the Figuring of Social Relations?', *Renaissance and Modern Studies* 23 (1979): 70–103; by James A. Riddell in 'The Arrangement of Ben Jonson's *Epigrammes*', *SEL* 27 (1987): 53–70; and by Jack D. Winner, Jonathan Z. Kamholtz, and Jennifer Brady in separate essays in *SEL* 23 (1983): 61–112. Wayne has also written an important article on *The Forest*, 'Jonson's Sidney: Legacy and Legitimation in *The Forest*', in *Sir Philip Sidney's Achievements* ed. M. J. B. Allen (New York: AMS Press, 1990), pp. 227–50, and an exemplary book on *The Forest*'s most significant poem and the relation of that poem to the Sidney family estate which is its subject, *Penshurst: The Semiotics of Place and the Poetics of History* (Madison:

University of Wisconsin Press, 1984). In two closely related essays, Annabel Patterson suggests that the ordering of *The Underwood* is less accidental than it has sometimes appeared: 'Lyric and Society in Jonson's *Under-wood*', in *Lyric Poetry: Beyond New Criticism*, ed. Charviva Hosek and Patricia Parker (Ithaca, N.Y.: Cornell University Press, 1985), pp. 148–63; and 'Jonson, Marvell, and Miscellaneity?', in *Poems in Their Place*, ed. Neil Fraistat (Chapel Hill: University of North Carolina Press, 1986), pp. 95–118. G. W. Pigman III examines Jonson's elegiac poetry in 'Suppressed Grief in Jonson's Funeral Poetry', *English Literary Renaissance* 13 (1983): 203–20; Lawrence Venuti explores the meaning of Jonson's avoidance of the amatory in 'Why Jonson Wrote Not of Love', *Journal of Medieval and Renaissance Studies* 12 (1982): 195–220; and two critics take up the weighty topic of Jonson's 'mountain belly': Joseph Loewenstein in 'The Jonsonian Corpulence, or the Poet as Mouthpiece', *ELH* 53 (1986): 491–518, and Bruce Thomas Boehrer in 'Renaissance Overeating: The Sad Case of Ben Jonson', *PMLA* 105 (1990): 1071–82. Jonson's authorial self-presentation is the subject of Richard Newton's '"Ben. / Jonson": The Poet in the Poems', in *Two Renaissance Mythmakers: Christopher Marlowe and Ben Jonson*, ed. Alvin B. Kernan (Baltimore: Johns Hopkins University Press, 1977), pp. 165–95; John Lemley's 'Masks and Self-Portraits in Jonson's Late Poetry', *ELH* 44 (1977): 248–66, and the Jonson chapter of my *Self-Crowned Laureates: Spenser, Jonson, Milton and the Literary System* (Berkeley: University of California Press, 1983). Other useful essays on Jonson's poetry can be found in two volumes edited by Claude J. Summers and Ted-Larry Pebworth, *Classic and Cavalier: Essays on Jonson and the Sons of Ben* (University of Pittsburgh Press, 1982) and '*The Muses Common-Weale': Poetry and Politics in the Seventeenth Century* (Columbia: University of Missouri Press, 1988).

8

LEAH S. MARCUS

Robert Herrick

Robert Herrick (1591–1674) and his *Hesperides* have long been admired for their lyricism. After a century of relative neglect between the poet's death and the late eighteenth century, interest in Herrick was revived by John Nichols through the *Gentleman's Magazine*. Poems like 'To the Virgins, to make much of Time', 'Corinna's going a Maying', 'Delight in Disorder', 'To Live Merrily, and to Trust to Good Verses', 'How Roses came Red', and 'How Violets came Blue' made Herrick the darling of nineteenth-century anthologists; Algernon Charles Swinburne called him 'the greatest song-writer – as surely as Shakespeare is the greatest dramatist – ever born of English race'.[1] The copy of *Hesperides* now in the Newberry Library (Chicago, Illinois) was once owned by a Mr William Combes of Henley, an amiable gentleman book collector who was said to carry *Hesperides* in his right-hand coat pocket and Izaak Walton's *Complete Angler* in his left whenever 'with tapering rod and trembling float, he enjoys his favourite diversion of angling on the banks of the Thames'.[2] But the genteel songster of this pastoral vignette was not the only image of the poet to surface during the nineteenth century: at least one Herrick poem, 'To Daffodils', was appropriated by Chartist writers, who identified him as a poet 'for the People'.[3]

During the early twentieth century, Herrick continued to be frequently anthologized, but his association with lyric ease and country jollity did not help his reputation among critics who admired the 'strong lines' of Ben Jonson and John Donne. Ezra Pound owned and annotated a copy of his verses; other modernists read him, but often found him lacking. For F. R. Leavis he was 'trivially charming'; for T. S. Eliot, he was the paradigmatic 'minor poet'.[4] In the late 1960s and early 1970s, however, a revival of sorts began, not because the ideal of rural merriment with which Herrick was so strongly associated had come back into fashion, but because critics had become more interested in reading *Hesperides* as a whole than in admiring its anthologized parts. Taken all together, *Hesperides* is a huge, sprawling mass of 1,130 poems, not counting prefatory material – 1,402 poems if we include *His Noble Numbers*, the collection of 'Pious Pieces' published along with *Hesperides* in 1648 and integrally attached to the volume. Leafing through the 1648 edition itself, we receive a strong, immediate impression of extreme diversity in terms of the book's typography and the length, shape, and subject-matter of individual poems. There is the expected abundance of verses on rural life and festivity, as announced in 'The Argument of his Book':

> I sing of *Brooks, of Blossomes, Birds,* and *Bowers:*
> Of *April, May,* of *June,* and *July*-Flowers.
> I sing of *May-poles, Hock-carts, Wassails, Wakes,*
> Of *Bride-grooms, Brides,* and of their *Bridall-cakes.* (p. 5)

But crowding up against these poems are epigrams to various personages on a variety of subjects: some celebrate Herrick's membership in the Tribe of Ben; some, like 'Upon Shopter', about a widow with rheumy eyes, are little gems of physical disgust; some are formal panegyrics to Charles I and members of the royal family. These poems are given visual prominence in the collection through ceremonial titles in block capitals nearly a centimetre high. Yet the royal panegyric is sometimes highly equivocal, alluding to defeats as well as victories in the English Civil War which was to bring Charles I's reign to a violent end shortly after the publication of Herrick's book. 'To THE KING, To cure the Evil' celebrates Charles I and the sacramental magic of his touch for curing scrofula and other unspecified ills: Charles is the 'Tree of Life', the healing waters of Bethesda, and its Angel combined in a single sacred personage (p. 61); 'To THE KING, Upon his taking of Leicester' celebrates a royal victory in the Civil War; but 'To the King and Queene, upon their Unhappy Distances' records the royal pair's separation as a result of the exigencies of war. Alongside the poems of praise are very brief poems of advice on kingship, some of which undercut the seemingly adulatory royalism of the panegyrics. In 'Examples, or like Prince, like People', for instance, Herrick notes, 'Examples lead us, and wee likely see, / Such as the Prince is, will his People be' (p. 255) – scarcely a comforting message for a monarch whose subjects are in open rebellion. Other poems, like 'The Bad Season makes the Poet Sad', records the devastation that the war and pillaging were bringing to the populace and landscape celebrated in Herrick's seemingly carefree poems of country life. Yet another category of poem interspersed among the *Hesperides* is Herrick's many seduction poems and miscellaneous erotica addressed to various putative mistresses – especially Julia, but also Corinna, Perilla, Lucia, and others – or celebrating the poet's own virile member, as in 'The Vine'. Alongside those poems, we encounter exquisite epitaphs for the deaths of flowers and children. Read as a whole, *Hesperides* is broader and stronger than the sum of its parts, but also more bewildering: where earlier readers and editors would have culled out the flowers from Herrick's garden and left the rest, ignoring the politically topical poems and relegating the poems of physical disgust to appendices where they could fester unnoticed, more recent readers have become interested in searching out patterns of order within the collection's wild abundance.

The most obvious unifying feature of the collection is that on nearly every page we are made emphatically aware that it belongs to Herrick, the poet, its author. We are accustomed to coming at the seventeenth century from the perspective of the late twentieth, in which an author's possession of the work, his or her marking of it throughout with the stamp of authorial individuality, seems a self-evident feature of literary composition. That was by no means the case in Herrick's own era. His verses circulated widely in manuscript and were sometimes attributed to him in manuscript miscellanies, but many of the poems that would later be incorporated into *Hesperides* made their publishing debut in anonymous anthologies, in which any sense of his authorship was lost. Herrick's 'father' Ben Jonson had been one of the first English writers to behave more or less as we now expect authors to behave, planning an edition of his own collected *Works* (1616) and seeing it through the press, struggling to retain control over his writings after they left his hands. Herrick's *Hesperides*, although a smaller production than Jonson's, is also subtitled *Works* in the 1648 edition – *The Works both Humane & Divine of Robert Herrick Esq*. Unlike Jonson's, Herrick's *Works* features a frontispiece portrait presumably of the author himself, resplendent with curls and Roman nose. His bust is poised upon a classical-looking monument and surrounded by nymphs, garlands, and other accoutrements of the poet. The bust is in profile: the author appears to gaze beneficently at his own facing title page, a demigod approving of his creation.

Within the volume, Herrick entitles numerous poems 'His', beginning with the very first, 'The Argument of his Book', and continuing through 'To his Muse', several poems 'To his Book', 'When he would have his Verses Read', 'His Poetry his Pillar', 'To Music to becalm his Fever', 'Upon the Death of his Sparrow: An Elegy', and so forth throughout the collection. Numerous poems from *Hesperides* are at least quasi-autobiographical, recording his discontents in Devonshire, where he held an ecclesiastical living until he was ousted by Puritan forces in 1647, and his joyous return to the London of his birth. These poems interfuse his creation with a sense of personal possession, the felt presence of his life. The 'divine' poems at the end are similarly marked by his ownership – they are *His Noble Numbers:*

or, His Pious Pieces, Wherein (amongst other things) he sings the Birth of his Christ: and sighes for his Saviours suffering on the Crosse. Even the volume's errata list is marked, in a way that is uncommon for the first half of the seventeenth century, by the poet's insistence on surveillance over the book and the image of him it communicates: he protests, in a rueful ditty prefacing the list of faults escaped, that he gave the printer '*good Grain*'; if that careless individual sowed '*Tares*' throughout the volume, then they must be fastidiously sought out and eradicated (p. 4).

Another feature of authorship (as we understand the term) that can be observed through comparison of the first and second printed states of *Hesperides* is Herrick's willingness, also fairly rare for the time, to fine tune his text even during the process of printing. In 'To his maid Prew', for example, the poet praises his servant for her steadfastness toward him in summer and winter alike. The last line of the cancelled version of the poem reads 'Not one, but all the seasons of the yeare', which he made more consistent with the rest of the poem in the new version, 'Not two, but all the seasons of the yeare' (p. 151). Similarly, in 'To Deanbourn, a rude River in Devon, by which sometimes he lived', he bids a cheerful farewell to the river and the uncivil inhabitants of its banks, but while at least one copy of the cancelled version terms them 'rude as rudest Salvages', the verdict is softened in the revision, 'rude (almost) as rudest Salvages' (p. 29). In *Hesperides*, we encounter not only authorship, but a hypercathexis of authorship: for all its squibs of frivolity and its interpolation of seemingly heterogeneous materials, *Hesperides* is unified by the poet's pathbreaking insistence on its intimate relationship to himself.

If the volume is Herrick's in terms of composition, however, it also belongs to Prince Charles (the future Charles II), to whom it is dedicated, and who has authored it in a more metaphoric sense. One of the ways in which recent critics have rescued *Hesperides* from the modernist charge of triviality is by foregrounding the political and cultural agenda that runs through the collection. The dedicatory epistle to Prince Charles links the 'little stars' of *Hesperides* to the prince's great '*Light*' – not only the mythical gardens of Hesperus, but also the planet Hesperus with which Prince Charles had been associated since his birth, when it suddenly and miraculously appeared in the midday sky.[5] The volume belongs to the prince in the sense that he has inspired it as 'my Works *Creator*, and alone / The *Flame* of it, and the *Expansion*' (p. 3). Similarly, 'To THE KING' and 'To THE QUEEN' invite Charles I and Henrietta Maria to repose in Herrick's garden as their own. The royal family's metaphoric light is shed typographically throughout the 1648 volume. The large block capitals used as ceremonial markings for the titles of poems to the royals (and only for those titles) also appear as the decorative enlarged initial letter of every single poem in the collection, so that, if read in the 1648 edition, *Hesperides'* myriad verses, its 'little stars', are typographically linked with a greater source in Hesperus, the prince, and other members of the royal family, at least for those portions of the collection in the immediate vicinity of the large block titles themselves. The effect is lost in modern reprints, but quite striking in the 1648 volume.

If we read Herrick's book within the strongly pro-Stuart framework that the dedication and ceremonial poems seem to construct, then many features of *Hesperides* that may on the surface seem little more than a delight in trivia suddenly carry a distinct ideological agenda. In the decades before the Civil War, the Stuart kings were strongly committed to protecting traditional English holiday pastimes from local Puritan and judicial attempts to suppress them. Through the *Book of Sports* issued by James I in 1618 and reissued by Charles I in 1633, the crown sought to encourage the old customs as a bulwark of the established church and the established social order. It specified:

> And as for Our good peoples lawfull Recreation, Our pleasure likewise is, That after the end of Diuine Seruice, Our good people be not disturbed, letted, or discouraged from any lawfull Recreation; Such as dauncing, either men or women, Archery for men, leaping, vaulting, or any other such harmelesse Recreation, nor from hauing of May-Games, Whitson Ales, and Morris-dances, and the setting vp of Maypoles and other sports therewith vsed, so as the same be had in due and conuenient time, without impediment or neglect of diuine Seruice.[6]

Throughout the 1620s and 1630s, there were localized skirmishes between advocates of the old pastimes and those who wanted them suppressed. Even the Anglican clergy became involved, with some 'merry' priests going out of their way to encourage May games and kindred sports among their parishioners. Read in the context of the controversy over the *Book of Sports*, Herrick's *Hesperides*, with its repeated invitation to the delights of 'May-poles, Hock-carts, Wassails, Wakes' as enumerated in 'The Argument of his Book', can easily be read as a contribution to the Stuart cause. Indeed, 'Corinna's going a Maying', can be interpreted as making direct reference to the *Book of Sports*. Herrick urges Corinna not to stay abed, but to follow the troop of village merrymakers into the countryside to gather the traditional flowers and boughs of whitethorn:

> Come, we'll abroad; and let's obay
> The Proclamation made for May:
> And sin no more, as we have done, by staying;
> But my *Corinna*, come, let's goe a Maying.   (p. 68)

The lines set two moral systems at odds: for Puritan controversialists of the period, May Day rituals were 'sin'. But if Corinna refuses to participate, she will sin more powerfully against the royal *Book of Sports*, the 'Proclamation made for May', and against the Stuart advocacy of traditional pastimes. As the poem progresses it widens out to form an ever more inclusive landscape of festivity and rural harmony. The sexual licence strongly associated with the holiday is not glossed over, but assimilated into marriage: while Corinna drowses at home, young couples have 'wept, and woo'd, and plighted Troth, / And chose their Priest' (p. 69). The final stanza of the poem, with its argument of *carpe diem* in the face of death and decay, may appear abruptly to extinguish the celebratory tone of the earlier stanzas, but it echoes not only folk carols for the maying season, but even the Anglican liturgy for May Day, the feast of Philip and James the Less.[7]

Other poems of *Hesperides* similarly commemorate threatened holiday pastimes: a group of Candlemas poems (pp. 285, 304); numerous 'ceremonies' and 'carols' for Christmas, some specified for performance before the king; 'The Maypole', several poems offered as New Year's gifts, 'Twelfth night, or King and Queen', 'The Wake', and 'The Wassail'. 'The Hock-cart, or Harvest Home' is particularly noteworthy for its linking of the harvest festival to the preservation of a feudal or immediately post-feudal agrarianism. Herrick's subtitle dedicates the poem 'To the Right Honourable, Mildmay, Earl of Westmorland', but the verses themselves are addressed partly to the lord and partly to his labourers, the 'Sons of Summer, by whose toile, / We are the Lords of Wine and Oile' (p. 101). In this poem, as frequently in *Hesperides*, the observance of a traditional custom has almost magical efficacy in preserving a traditional pattern of mutual obligations: the Earl of Westmoreland feeds the labourers, and they in turn, sustain him through their 'toile'. The poem is remarkably frank about the costs of this support: although today they feast on mutton, veal, bacon, and 'Fat Beefe', on the morrow they will be expected to return to their labours: 'this pleasure is like raine, / Not sent ye for to drowne your paine, / But for to make it spring againe' (p. 102). By laying bare the 'paine' upon which the system is built, 'The Hock-cart' demystifies the reciprocity between lord and labourers even while arguing for its continuance. Herrick's poems of holiday festivity, appearing as they do amidst a highly varied body of verse that laments the faltering royal cause and even makes indirect reference to royal defeats,[8] take on a strongly elegiac quality – more a lament for a Stuart 'Merry England' past than a defence of festival as a bulwark of traditional order in the volume's strife-torn present. Even as Herrick asserts the value of Stuart ceremony, he records its passing, along with every other human institution, as a result of 'Times trans-shifting' (p. 5).

To assert such a political impetus behind the whole of *Hesperides*, however, is to miss much of the strange heterogeneity of the collection. Critics who have argued strongly for the royalist and conservative Anglican nature of Herrick's book have generally based themselves on a strongly dualistic and agonistic model of seventeenth-century history, by which the ideological conflict between the established church and its Puritan opponents in the early decades of the century is seen as both prelude and cause of the English Civil War. More recently, revisionist historians have argued for a less rigidly polarized configuration of the political and ecclesiastical allegiances of the period. Their work has enabled recent critics like Ann Baynes Coiro to see nuances and complexities in Herrick's system of allegiances that qualify the characterization of *Hesperides* as a document in Stuart panegyric. Coiro prefers to think of *Hesperides* in terms of the epigram-book tradition, a tradition that, beginning at least as far back as Martial, offers a caustic mix of political and personal approbation and criticism. Like Martial, whose poems were dedicated to the Emperor Domitian but played dangerous and interesting games with critique of the tyrant, and like several earlier English epigrammatists, among them Ben Jonson, Herrick's royalism is part of a complex dynamic of praise and blame of the monarch and of other figures, public and private. As Coiro and others have pointed out, at least a few of the personages praised in *Hesperides* were opponents of the royal cause, rather than adherents: Herrick's epigram 'To his Kinsman, Sir Tho. Soame' praises a prominent Londoner (Herrick's first cousin) with numerous Puritan and Parliamentary connections; another epigram, 'To the most accomplished Gentleman Master Michael Oulsworth', commemorates a *'Brave Man'* who sat on both the Short and Long Parliaments (p. 329).[9] Some recent critics have carried the hunt for political dissidence in Herrick too far: one article centres on 'A Carol presented to Dr Williams B[isho]p of Lincoln as a New Year's gift' as the centrepiece for an argument about 'resistance literature' in *Hesperides*, unfortunately failing to note that the poem was excluded by the poet from *Hesperides*, and was not, in fact, published at all until modern editions.[10] Nevertheless, despite the pro-Caroline frame of the collection, Herrick's verses construct a varied gallery of luminaries that cut across the broad ideological divisions of the pre-war period. Although *Hesperides* belongs to Prince Charles, its dedicatee and metaphoric creator, it also belongs to the poet Herrick himself, his kin, friends, and neighbours, and the two systems of ownership are not always in accord.

Above all, readers have responded to the playfulness and eroticism of Herrick's poetry – yet another feature of the collection that coexists uneasily with the praise of the royal family. Like several other poets of the pre-war and Civil War period who are often grouped together as 'the Cavaliers', Herrick declares his independence of the chaste Platonic love promoted in the court of King Charles and Queen Henrietta Maria through numerous poems of sexual liberty that revel in amatory solipsism. Some readers have found Herrick's sexuality curiously, even disturbingly, infantile: rather than celebrating sexual consummation, as Thomas Carew, for example, does in 'The Rapture', Herrick focusses on his mistresses' feet ('The Night-Piece, to Julia'), or their nipples and the 'Via Lactea' between them ('Upon Julia's Breasts', p. 96), or the flowers, dainties, and little ceremonies with which they surround themselves and him. 'Julia's Petticoat' displaces onto her glittering garment the heaving, panting 'transgression' of a willing mistress (p. 66). 'Delight in Disorder' is modelled upon Jonson's 'Still to Be Neat', but kindles that poem's moral distrust of overprecision in dress into a kinetic vision of female sartorial 'wantonnesse': lawn thrown into 'fine distraction', 'erring Lace', 'Ribbands' that 'flow confusedly', 'carelesse' shoestrings, and, above all, the 'tempestuous petticote' (p. 28). However we interpret the sexuality of these poems of bewitching 'wilde civility', they create a charge of playful and highly personalized eroticism that surges seemingly unchecked through the garden of *Hesperides*, although it wanes somewhat in the volume's second half.

By interpreting the 1,130 poems of *Hesperides* as an epigram book and dividing it into hypothetical centuries of poems (like Martial's), Coiro has created a rough system of classification that allows us to recognize striking differences between disparate parts of the collection. In such a large body of verses, the immediate context of a given group of lyrics may play a determining role in the reader's perception of them. In *Hesperides*, Coiro suggests, we can identify a pattern of increasing alienation from the ideals of early centuries as the collection winds on, with the late centuries, like a 'masque turned upside down', expressing a spirit of 'mockery, disorder, and warning' quite alien from the charming 'Merry England' materials and the sexual titillation of the first half of the volume.[11] That is not to say that there are no evocations of war and dissolution early on: among the first hundred poems of the volume are 'All things decay and die', 'To THE KING, upon his comming with his Army into the West', and 'To the King and Queen, upon their Unhappy Distances'. Nevertheless, Coiro may be right that reading through *Hesperides seriatem* rather than browsing here and there, we receive an impression of increasing fragmentation and dejection, with sententious poems gradually replacing the more joyous ceremonial verses of earlier parts of the collection. As the idealized image of the monarchy and the myth of Merry England are gradually hedged about by poems that undercut them, their lustre is inevitably darkened.

Such, at least, is the impression of *Hesperides* we are likely to receive if we leave out the last 270 or so poems, those comprising *Noble Numbers*. In modern editions of Herrick, the editors regularly take care to separate Herrick's 'Pious Pieces' from *Hesperides* proper: in L. C. Martin's edition, there is a page and a half of white space between the end of *Hesperides* proper and the beginning of *Noble Numbers*; in J. Max Patrick's edition, still more strikingly, almost two leaves intervene, with the second bearing a half title of the kind one would expect at the beginning of a separate work. Modern editors have worked to distance *Noble Numbers* from *Hesperides* in large part because they find the 'Pious Pieces' a woeful falling off from the aesthetic standards of Herrick's secular verse. As some editors have speculated, *Noble Numbers* may at one point have been intended by the poet as a separate publication, but if we peruse the 1648 *Hesperides*, the two parts of the collection appear inextricably linked. The title page for the *Hesperides* announces that it is to include 'The Works Both Humane & Divine' of its author, so that the name *Hesperides* encompasses both; 'The Argument of his Book' ends, 'I write of *Hell*; I sing (and ever shall) / Of *Heaven* and hope to have it after all' (p. 5), placing the divine subjects at the end of his introductory poem, just as *Noble Numbers* appears at the end of the volume. *Noble Numbers* is given a separate title page in the 1648 edition, but one lacking the full publication information offered on the title page for the volume as a whole in the four copies I have consulted. Moreover, its numbering begins with sig. Aa, not sig. A, as we would expect if it were being offered as a separate work. The list of errata at the beginning of *Hesperides* includes faults escaped from *Noble Numbers*. Beyond that, the last two pages of *Hesperides* proper feature a number of poems that mark the closing of the first part of the collection, but also advise the reader that the voyage is far from over – more verses are to come. At the bottom of page 297 (Cc7r), a poem entitled 'The End of his Work' appears to be moving toward closure, but its text promises that the closure is temporary, not final: 'Part of the worke remaines; one part is past: And here my ship rides having anchor cast.' If we turn the leaf, we encounter the last poems of *Hesperides* proper on the left and, without any blank space whatsoever, the title page of *Noble Numbers* on the right. The poet may have reached a *terminus* and set anchor temporarily, but he is poised to re-embark, to offer the other 'part of the worke'.

If we take *Noble Numbers* to be an integral part of the whole of *Hesperides* rather than a completely separate work, we are forced to rethink the pattern of gradual decline and disillusionment that appears to be traced in the first 1,130 poems. In *Noble Numbers*, the king and court shine once more in a series of poems announced as having been sung in the royal presence at Whitehall: 'To God: An Anthem, sung in the Chapel at Whitehall, before the King', 'The Star-Song: A Carol to the King; sung at Whitehall', and several others. Appearing as they do after the apparent demise of order in the secular part of *Hesperides*, these poems serve to constitute almost a 'real presence' of the monarch and courtly ceremony amidst the devastation of war. Most of the poems of *Noble Numbers* are much simpler than their counterparts among the secular lyrics, and several, like 'To his Saviour, a Child: A Present, by a Child' and 'Graces for Children', are explicitly designed for children. Indeed, in *Noble Numbers*, the poet himself assumes the persona of a dutiful child of the church: the poems announced as '*His*' are strikingly similar in tone and language to the poems expressly for children. Herrick appears to have shared at least some of these poems with his parishioners at Dean Prior: a visitor to the village in 1809 found that several of his *Noble Numbers* were still being used as prayers by local people.[12] Perhaps the Chartists were not far wrong in identifying Herrick as a poet 'For the People'. Despite the obvious elitism of many features of *Hesperides*, he was capable of writing in a popular vein: *Noble Numbers*, with its markedly humbler and more uniform lyrics than earlier parts of the collection, can be regarded as a retreat into simplicity and a resuscitated Anglican community amidst the uncertainties of war – as the poet's final resort against the ravages of 'Times trans-shifting'.

Arguably, what recent readers have responded to most warmly in *Hesperides* is its 'Delight in Disorder' – a phrase that describes the pleasant disarray of secular lyrics as a whole as well as the poem bearing the name. But the poet creates a clear line of demarcation between the playful eroticism of the first part of the volume and the more constricted piety of the second through the couplet that immediately precedes the 'Pious Pieces': 'To his Book's end this last line he'd have plac't, / *Jocund his Muse was; but his Life was chast*' (p. 335). After this Ovidian palinode, *Noble Numbers* offers simplicity and bedrock sincerity – a pared-down verse in stark contrast with the curious and pleasant vagaries of the secular part of the book. *Hesperides* considered as a whole is bounded by a fanfare of royal allegiance at its beginning and a retreat to communal Anglican piety at its end, but in between it offers a seductively sweet, strangely tumultuous exploration of love, war, friendship, festivity, and loss.

NOTES

1 Algernon Charles Swinburne, Preface, *The Hesperides and Noble Numbers*, ed. Alfred Pollard, 2 vols. (1891; rev. edn, New York: E. P. Dutton; London: George Routledge and Sons, (1920)), vol. 1, p. xi. Here and throughout titles and quotations from Herrick's poetry are from *The Poetical Works of Robert Herrick*, ed. L. C. Martin (Oxford: Clarendon Press, 1956).

2 T. F. Dibdin, *The Library Companion: Or, The Young Man's Guide and the Old Man's Comfort, in the Choice of a Library* (London, 1824), p. 703n.

3 Crys Armbrust, 'Robert Herrick and Nineteenth-Century Periodical Publication: *The Gentleman's Magazine* and *The National: A Library for the People*', in Ann Baynes Coiro (ed.), *Robert Herrick*, a special double issue of the *George Herbert Journal* 14.1–2 (Autumn 1990, Spring 1991): 113–126.

4 F. R. Leavis, *Revaluation: Tradition and Development in English Poetry* (London: Chatto and Windus, 1936), p. 36; T. S. Eliot, 'What Is Minor Poetry?', *Sewanee Review* 54 (1946): 1–18. Here and through much of the present essay, I am indebted to Ann Baynes Coiro, *Robert Herrick's 'Hesperides' and the Epigram Book Tradition* (Baltimore: Johns Hopkins University Press, 1988).

5 See the explication of the poem in J. Max Patrick (ed.), *The Complete Poetry of Robert Herrick* (1963; repr. New York: W. W. Norton & Co., 1968).

6 *The King's Maiesties Declaration to His Subjects, concerning lawfull Sports to be vsed* (London, 1618), pp. 6–7.

7 For fuller discussion of the poem and of the *Book of Sports* controversy more generally, see, among numerous other studies, Leah S. Marcus's *The Politics of Mirth: Jonson, Herrick, Milton, Marvell, and the Defense of Old Holiday Pastimes* (University of Chicago Press, 1986), pp. 140–68; Peter Stallybrass, '"We Feaste in our Defense": Patrician Carnival in Early Modern England and Robert Herrick's "Hesperides"', *ELR* 16 (1986): 234–52; Christopher Hill, *Society and Puritanism in Pre-Revolutionary England*, 2nd edn (New York: Schocken, 1967); and David Underdown, *Revel, Riot, and Rebellion: Popular Politics and Culture in England 1603–1660* (Oxford: Clarendon Press, 1985).

8 See Claude J. Summers, 'Herrick's Political Counterplots', *SEL* 25 (1985): 165–82.

9 Patrick (ed.), *Complete Poetry*, pp. 236, 434; Coiro, *Robert Herrick's 'Hesperides'*, pp. 141–3.

10 Janie Caves McCauley, 'On the "Childhood of the Yeare": Herrick's *Hesperides* New Year's Poems', in Coiro (ed.), *Robert Herrick*, pp. 72–96. Since Williams died in 1649, it is unlikely that Herrick wrote the poem after the completion of *Hesperides*, which leaves us with the strong probability that he deliberately omitted it.

11 Coiro, *Robert Herrick's 'Hesperides'*, p. 24.

12 *The Quarterly Review* 4 (August 1810), article 11, p. 172. See also the more elaborate discussion in Leah S. Marcus, *Childhood and Cultural Despair: A Theme and Variations in Seventeenth-Century Literature* (University of Pittsburgh Press, 1978).

FURTHER READING

Chute, Marchette, *Two Gentle Men: The Lives of George Herbert and Robert Herrick* (New York: Dutton, 1959)

Coiro, Ann Baynes, *Robert Herrick's 'Hesperides' and the Epigram Book Tradition* (Baltimore: Johns Hopkins University Press, 1988)

Coiro, Ann Baynes (ed.), *Robert Herrick*, special issue of the *George Herbert Journal* 14.1–2 (Autumn 1990–Spring 1991)

Corns, Thomas, *Uncloistered Virtue: English Political Literature 1640–1660* (Oxford: Clarendon Press, 1992)

Deming, Robert H., *Ceremony and Art: Robert Herrick's Poetry* (The Hague and Paris: Mouton, 1974)

Deneef, A. Leigh, *'This Poetick Liturgie': Robert Herrick's Ceremonial Mode* Durham, N.C.: Duke University Press, 1974)

Hageman, Elizabeth H., *Robert Herrick: A Reference Guide* (Boston, Mass.: G. K. Hall & Co., 1983)

Hammond, Gerald, *Fleeting Things: English Poets and Poems 1616–1660* (Cambridge, Mass.: Harvard University Press, 1990)

Marcus, Leah S., *The Politics of Mirth: Jonson, Herrick, Milton, Marvell, and the Defense of Old Holiday Pastimes* (University of Chicago Press, 1986)

Miner, Earl, *The Cavalier Mode from Jonson to Cotton* (Princeton University Press, 1971)

Rollin, Roger B., *Robert Herrick*, rev. edn, Twayne's English Authors Series (New York: Twayne Publishers; Toronto: Maxwell Macmillan Canada; Oxford, Singapore, Sydney: Maxwell Macmillan International, 1992)

Rollin, Roger B., and J. Max Patrick (eds.), *Trust to Good Verses: Herrick Tercentenary Essays* (University of Pittsburgh Press, 1977)

9

HELEN WILCOX

George Herbert

The posthumous publication in 1633 of a small volume entitled *The Temple: Sacred Poems and Private Ejaculations, By Mr George Herbert* was one of the most notable events in the history of seventeenth-century English poetry and devotion. Within seven years the book was into its sixth edition, and five subsequent editions appeared before the century was out. It was read by members of a whole spectrum of religious and political groups in that most sectarian of periods in English history; Cromwell's personal chaplain recommended *The Temple* to his own son, and Charles I read it in captivity before his execution. Herbert became known as the 'sweet singer of the Temple', inviting comparisons with the Psalmist; he alone in his age was said to be one who 'rightly knew to touch Davids Harpe'.[1] The poems were widely imitated by seventeenth-century writers, and cited by other admiring early readers in texts of piety and education. The foundations were laid for an appreciation of possibly the greatest devotional poet in the English language.

However, Herbert's more modern readers may find themselves less certain about ways of responding to, and assimilating, his poetry. Does one have to be knowledgeable in the mysteries of theology and church history to appreciate *The Temple* fully? Are the poems closer to prayer than art, and therefore best read by Herbert's fellow believers and not by students of literature? If approached directly as literary texts, do the poems display worrying elements of naivety or poetical quaintness? There are, of course, no simple answers to these often perplexing questions, but this essay attempts to open up ways of understanding the artistry of Herbert's poetry for those reading it four hundred years after the poet's birth. Five major aspects of the artistry of *The Temple* are explored here – frameworks, metaphors, clarity, invention, endings – and each is tested and illustrated with reference to one lyric in some detail. This highlighting of five poems to examine five key elements of Herbert's art will, it is hoped, enable readers to go on and read more widely in *The Temple* for themselves, with insight and 'delight'.[2]

The first framework within which Herbert's *Temple* was constructed and may be understood is, of course, the idea of the temple itself. The short lyric poems for which Herbert is famous were not designed to be read in isolation; they come from the extended middle section of a three-part poetic structure, 'The Church-porch', 'The Church' and 'The Church Militant', which were published under the overall title of *The Temple*. Together the poems make an architectural structure, a metaphorical temple building which the reader enters and within which God is 'praised' and the conflicts of devotion and rebellion are 'bewailed'.[3] Typically, Herbert took a tradition or framework – in this case the Old Testament, and classical, idea of a temple – and redefined it to serve the cause of the Christian church. In addition to being new psalms sung within an old temple, Herbert's poems and their collective title are an evocation of the New Testament image of the human soul as a temple of the Holy Spirit. As Herbert wrote in his poem 'Sion', the temple which primarily concerns him is the individual human breast, expressive of a new divine architecture whose 'frame and fabric is within'. Thus each of the one hundred and fifty or so lyrics of the central part of *The Temple* asks to be read both in the context of an Old Testament temple – 'Solomons sea of brasse and world of stone' – and as part of the fluctuating narrative of the individual's New Testament-style relationship with God. It is in this lively inner temple, where God finds himself 'struggling with a peevish heart', that we find the combined experience of love and affliction for which Herbert's poems are remembered.

Herbert's sequence of lyrics, though akin to the principle of a sonnet sequence in its ups and downs of a spiritual lover's joys and sorrows, does not tell a straightforwardly chronological story of the poet's dealings with God. However, there is some overt structuring in the order of the poems: a short sequence about the death and resurrection of Christ, for example, placed at the beginning of *The Temple*, and a cluster of lyrics on death and heavenly matters at the end. Undoubtedly the context of each poem enriches its possible meanings by expressive juxtapositions, and the repetition and development of recurring ideas and issues are a hallmark of Herbert's style. As he wrote in the second of his two sonnets on 'The H[oly] Scriptures', each verse of the Bible benefits from echoes and cross-references, and the same may be said of *The Temple*:

> Oh that I knew how all thy lights combine,
> And the configurations of their glorie!
> Seeing not only how each verse doth shine,
> But all the constellations of the storie.

The Temple, like the Bible here, may be seen as a 'book of starres' whose total impact as a 'constellation' is greater than the sum of its verses.

Within this collective framework of the temple in its many senses, the poet-builder requires materials. What were Herbert's? It is clear already that the resources of the Bible were richly drawn upon in *The Temple*, but there were many other influences which framed Herbert's poetic creativity. Several of these may be discerned in a reading of 'Easter', one of the poems of the Passion and resurrection which precede, symbolically and actually, all the other lyrics in 'The Church':

> Rise heart; thy Lord is risen. Sing his praise
> > Without delayes,
> Who takes thee by the hand, that thou likewise
> > With him mayst rise:
> That, as his death calcined thee to dust,
> His life may make thee gold, and much more just.
>
> Awake, my lute, and struggle for thy part
> > With all thy art.
> The crosse taught all wood to resound his name,
> > Who bore the same.
> His stretched sinews taught all strings, what key
> Is best to celebrate this most high day.
>
> Consort both heart and lute, and twist a song
> > Pleasant and long:
> Or since all musick is but three parts vied
> > And multiplied;
> O let thy blessed spirit bear a part,
> And make up our defects with his sweet art.
>
> I got me flowers to straw thy way;
> I got me boughs off many a tree:
> But thou wast up by break of day,
> And brought'st thy sweets along with thee.
>
> The Sunne arising in the East,
> Though he give light, and th'East perfume;
> If they should offer to contest
> With thy arising, they presume.
>
> Can there be any day but this,
> Though many sunnes to shine endeavour?
> We count three hundred, but we misse:
> There is but one, and that one ever.

Perhaps the most striking feature of this poem is the variety of poetic and related traditions from which it draws to build its own, ultimately distinctive, qualities. The two sections of the poem clearly delineate two rhetorical traditions which 'vie' in Herbert's work: the high and complex 'art' of the first three stanzas, a rich poetic resource familiar to Herbert as former rhetorician and public orator for the University of Cambridge,[4] and the simpler lyric tradition of the last three stanzas. It is typical of Herbert that the poem should begin with the high art – it is, after all, a celebration of 'rising' and an attempt to honour with 'heart and lute' this 'most high day' – and equally representative of Herbert's achievements that it should then find its resolution in the plainness of common metre and the triumphant clarity of a song proclaiming the one eternal day.

Linking the high and low styles of 'Easter' are a number of traditions central to Herbert's aesthetic. First among these is the framework of the liturgy of the English church, an established pattern of time, texts and ritual which underpins much of Herbert's writing. The poem celebrates the major feast day in the church's year, and represents a conscious act of loyalty to the established church and its liturgical cycle, in defiance of contemporary Puritan disapproval of such festivity in religion.[5] The poem's opening lines demonstrate the influence of the liturgy on the detail of Herbert's art, wittily echoing Psalm 47, which was prescribed to be sung in church every Easter Sunday. But the relationship with the liturgy is never a derivative or passive one. The intense and 'twisting' rituals of the first part of the poem, closely associated with church worship, give way to a simple love song, and then the climax of even this apparently naive song challenges the neat pattern of the church calendar and the 'three hundred' days of an earthly year. The speaker's dependence on the prescribed readings for church services is also gently mocked in the use of the word 'straw' in the first line of the song, an unusual verb found in the gospel reading for Palm Sunday, the week before Easter. The speaker goes on to realize that he was too late to meet Christ, who was already risen from the dead, 'up', like the sun, 'by break of day', always one step ahead of human wishes and needs. The liturgical echo, from the readings of the *previous* Sunday, is an ironic reinforcing of the point.

In addition to the liturgical and biblical materials so inventively used by Herbert, the profound influence of music on his verse is evident in 'Easter'. The very idea of the poem is conceived in musical terms: to praise is to 'sing', and to sing is to write. The principle of the musical triad, emblematic of the trinity – 'all musick is but three parts vied / And multiplied' – is made the basis of the counterpoint of the poem, in which 'heart', 'lute' and Holy Spirit (emotion, art and inspiration) combine in harmony. The central conceit, focal point of the wit of the poem, is musical, too: the startlingly evocative conception of Christ on the cross as a musical instrument, the divine example of sinews stretched across wood in order to 'resound'. This conceit was not original to Herbert, and its link with the tradition of visual emblems reminds us of another of Herbert's resources;[6] but the imaginative use of the crucifixion 'struggle' as a source of the joyful music of the resurrection is distinctively Herbertian. Music is thus the metaphysical idea underlying the poem, the source of its most powerful metaphor and, of course, the embodiment of the poem's aim – to 'twist a song / Pleasant and long'. The overall structure of 'Easter', progressing successfully to its song, is in itself the poet's evidence of the intervention of the Holy Spirit to 'make up our defects' – musical, poetic and spiritual – 'with his sweet art'.

The poet-builder, then, used a range of materials for his poetic temple: rhetorical, homely, liturgical, biblical, musical, and emblematic, to name a few. Drawing on this variety of traditions in combination, and writing with a clear purpose to 'wash' the inherited 'sweet phrases, lovely metaphors' and bring them 'to Church well drest and clad' ('The Forerunners'), Herbert rendered them new, refreshed and distinctive. In particular, he achieved a rare equilibrium between given poetical materials and a created personal voice, epitomized in the movement during 'Easter' from the objectified self in 'heart' and 'lute' to the simple active 'I'. He worked within frameworks of idea and tradition, but was always ready to transcend and break out from them, as at the end of the 'Easter' song when conventional modes of thought are shown to 'miss' and are therefore briskly abandoned in favour of an eternal and radically unframed perspective.

One vitally important item among Herbert's basic poetic materials is the metaphors he chose to use as a means of mediation between the earthiness of this 'merrie world' ('The Quip') and the spiritual dimension 'hid' within it ('Colossians 3.3'). 'Materials' is a peculiarly apt term here, since Herbert's metaphorical inspiration often came from remarkably tangible items: money, musical instruments, the natural world, food, and 'household-stuffe' ('Affliction (I)') from knives to handkerchieves. Many of these physical analogies for metaphysical experiences derive from the Bible, particularly the Psalms and the parables, and the remainder stem from a similar principle to that of the scriptures, namely, asserting the potential holiness of everyday things. As Herbert wrote in his handbook for a Country Parson, 'things of ordinary use are not only to serve in the way of drudgery, but to be washed, and cleansed, and serve for lights even of Heavenly Truths'.[7] But the distinctive quality of Herbert's metaphors lies not only in their accessibility, but also in an apparent contradiction within his poetry: that he was metaphoric by instinct but at the same time doubted the capacity of such descriptive language ever to capture spiritual experience.

This paradoxical poetics, in which imaginative scope is celebrated even as it confronts the limits of the expressible, is nowhere more evident than in the first of Herbert's two poems entitled 'Prayer'. This sonnet, known as an 'epithet sonnet' because of its almost obsessive fascination with ways of describing prayer, also shows Herbert's skills with metaphor at their richest:

> Prayer the Churches banquet, Angels age,
>   Gods breath in man returning to his birth,
>   The soul in paraphrase, heart in pilgrimage,
>   The Christian plummet sounding heav'n and earth;
>
> Engine against th' Almightie, sinners towre,
>   Reversed thunder, Christ-side-piercing spear,
>   The six-daies world-transposing in an houre,
>   A kind of tune, which all things heare and feare;
>
> Softnesse, and peace, and joy, and love, and blisse,
>   Exalted Manna, gladnesse of the best,
>   Heaven in ordinarie, man well drest,
>   The milkie way, the bird of Paradise,
>
>   Church-bels beyond the starres heard, the souls bloud,
>   The land of spices; something understood.

In this entire sonnet there is no main verb and no plain statement; it is even unclear whether the avalanche of description is an address to 'Prayer' itself (an outpouring of praise for the means of praise), or an account of the phenomenon, with an implied 'prayer is . . . ' All is metaphoric, without even the breathing space which an occasional simile would offer; every epithet requires interpretation, and cumulatively the poem becomes an exhaustive survey of kinds and aspects of prayer. This activity of conversation with God – so fundamental to Herbert's concept of the devotional lyric – is shown to be communal ('the Churches banquet'), reciprocal ('heaven in ordinarie, man well drest'), powerful ('Engine against th' Almightie'), and paradisal ('The land of spices').

The sources of Herbert's metaphors are the traditions which were identified in the previous section as fundamental to 'Easter': liturgical, biblical, bodily, and musical. These categories often overlap, as in the vivid penultimate line, 'Church-bels beyond the starres heard'. The juxtaposition of the familiar local church bells calling parishioners to worship, and the mysterious realm 'beyond the starres' (uniting the earlier references to the 'milkie way' and a paradisal state) is descriptive enough in its own right. However, recalling the many instances of inversions among the phrases encapsulating prayer – breath being sent back in speech to its originator, thunder reversed, heaven lowering itself, and the human supplicant dressing up – it becomes possible to interpret the church bells from two different perspectives. 'Beyond the starres' can be treated either as an adverbial phrase (specifying the place where the bells are 'heard') or an adjectival phrase (locating the 'bells' themselves). These may be heavenly bells, heard from the earth, recognizably homely yet giving a hint of the mystery of 'Paradise'; but prayer is a two-way process, and the heavenly perspective is also envisaged, from which prayer is signalled by distant bells on earth, emblematic of the transition from everyday affairs to a moment of spiritual refreshment.

There is scope here for interpretation from at least two angles, and this is true of the language of much of the sonnet, as in 'sinners towre' which is both the audacious Tower of Babel and a practical lookout tower from which to catch a glimpse of heaven. The poet appears to try everything in an effort to define and describe prayer, from the disturbing ('Christ-side-piercing spear') to the comforting ('Softnesse, and peace, and joy'). But to what does this lead? After thirteen and a half lines of amazingly inventive descriptive language, the poem suddenly and conclusively changes direction with its closing phrase, 'something understood'. Metaphoric language has been abandoned; prayer is no longer to be visualized or felt, but undertaken and experienced. Has the attempt to describe prayer failed? Is the ending a rejection of all our attempts to define and express the potentially inexpressible in language, particularly language based on a system of relationships and parallels? Or is 'something understood', even with its plainness which challenges the richness of the preceding lines, a kind of triumphant assertion that the metaphoric instinct will lead eventually to a plane of understanding?

The perplexing possibilities in this intriguing final phrase are further complicated by the uncertainty over what exactly is 'understood' – God's love, the human being doing the praying, or prayer itself? Whereas the metaphoric language, however vivid, kept the speaker and reader outside prayer in the activity of speaking about it, the activity of puzzling over the last phrase becomes, perhaps, a drawing in, almost an enticing, into the beginning of prayer itself. Many of Herbert's lyrics enact this movement from description, or narrative, to the puzzle of real knowledge; and, here in 'Prayer (I)' as in 'Affliction (I)' and 'Jordan (II)', that concluding uncertainty is expressed in a riddle. 'Prayer (I)' is, therefore, a compressed and intense version of the implied debate in Herbert's writing over the relationship between words and truth, describing and knowing. For much of the time, Herbert was committed to the power of creativity in poetic language and form; but the endings of his poems frequently undermine this principle and call into question any words other than God's, and any knowledge other than that of experience.

The readings of 'Easter' and 'Prayer (I)' have introduced the work of a complex writer who synthesized many rich aesthetic traditions but was sharply aware that the devotional poet needs to go beyond even their capacity for evocation. However, it is important to reassure readers that Herbert's poetry is simultaneously difficult and transparent; it manages to hold in tension a fascinating complexity and a startling clarity. What could be simpler than this lyric, entitled 'Virtue'?

> Sweet day, so cool, so calm, so bright,
> The bridall of the earth and skie:
> The dew shall weep thy fall to night;
>   For thou must die.
>
> Sweet rose, whose hue angry and brave
> Bids the rash gazer wipe his eye:
> Thy root is ever in its grave,
>   And thou must die.
>
> Sweet spring, full of sweet dayes and roses,
> A box where sweets compacted lie;
> My musick shows ye have your closes,
>   And all must die.
>
> Onely a sweet and vertuous soul,
> Like season'd timber, never gives;
> But though the whole world turn to coal,
>   Then chiefly lives.

The lyric appears to be clear and unassuming. It functions within a familiar poetic framework, whether we describe that as a repeated pattern overturned by the final stanza, or label it more precisely as a version of the *carpe diem* tradition popular in the seventeenth century. The structure of the poem is uncomplicated and its stanza form modest; the vocabulary employed is straightforward and repetitive, and there is little metaphoric activity. The restraint in its tone strangely intensifies the simple beauty of the lyric.

There has to be, of course, another side to the story – not denying any of the above statements but amplifying the account of the poem. First of all, the *carpe diem* tradition is a secular mode which Herbert transforms by making it the framework for a sacred argument; the final stanza contains the double surprise of a change of direction from death to life, and from natural to spiritual 'sweetness'. The stanza form chosen by Herbert underlines this development, with its shortened refrain line emblematic of mortality and encapsulating the poem's argument in its subtle shifts: 'For thou must die' becomes the more inclusive 'And thou ... ' and the all-encompassing 'And all ... ' before the utter conversion into 'Then chiefly lives'. The poem's language is indeed repetitive, but with an enriching of meaning at each new usage (as the refrain demonstrates) and a deliberate recurrence of particularly significant words which echo between poems in *The Temple* as well as within the individual lyric. 'Sweet', for example, is one of Herbert's favourite adjectives for the experience of redemption, and as he uses it in 'Virtue' it seems to be itself a 'box where sweets compacted lie', a word packed with potential meanings and resonances which the poet releases. The sweetness of the new day is a kind of purity, a virginal innocence as on the 'bridall' day, and its passing is not only 'nightfall'; it epitomizes all 'falls' into sin and morality. The sweetness of the rose is beauty, the sensual attraction of the defiant red flower which, like all physical pleasure, renders the 'rash gazer' vulnerable to its thorns. The sweetness of spring encompasses these other sweetnesses but is also the delicious anticipation of them, the sweetness of potential. All these meanings are present to the reader when the adjective 'sweet' is transferred to the 'vertuous soul', and it is only at this point in the poem that the relevance of the title becomes clear: 'vertue' is all these qualities, and more.

The lyric is thus both plain and intense, clear on a first reading and yet densely packed with layers of meaning. The compactness of the line 'Thy root is ever in its grave' is typical; in simple vocabulary and syntax it manages nevertheless to suggest the archetypal transitoriness of all living things, the circularity of being rooted in, and gaining life from, the very element in which we will subsequently be buried (recalling the liturgical phrase 'dust to dust'), and the incapacity of even the 'brave' to uproot themselves from inherent mortality. Perhaps the line 'My musick shows ye have your closes' is a little less ambitious, but it too resonates with meaning. A 'close' is a musical cadence, and the argument is that even something as lovely as music has to reach its final chord; in fact, there is an anticipation here of the shift of mood in the final stanza, since harmony only finds its resolution or fulfilment in the cadence which returns it to its home key – like the soul to heaven. The 'musick' referred to must also be understood as the poet's own song, whose short refrain lines do indeed 'close' each stanza with a reminder of 'closure' in a more metaphysical sense. And finally, what of 'season'd timber'? The simile is a slightly disappointing choice after the sweet freshness of springtime and roses; why should the soul be likened to wood which has been left out in all weathers? There is clearly a practicality here – this timber has been toughened by harsh experience, and according to the other lyrics in *The Temple* the struggle for Christian virtue involves much 'affliction' (Herbert no doubt being conscious of the Latin root of 'vertue', meaning strength). This is also a kind of wood which will not burn up, metaphorically or physically, on Judgement Day when the 'whole world' will 'turn to coal'. But more important than these contrasts between the virtuous soul and the rest of creation is the similarity, evoked by the 'timber', to the cross of Christ; the soul can only 'chiefly live' because of the crucifixion and resurrection of Christ.

'Virtue' is just one instance of the paradoxically complex plainness of Herbert's lyrics, which is one of the most widely recognized features of his artistry. The terms 'art' or 'artistry' are appropriate, for this does not come about by accident; it is an intensely skilful aesthetic, which we might call a rhetoric of clarity. The poems embody an achieved simplicity, related to an ideal of plainness – the 'beauty' which resides in 'truth' ('Jordan (I)') – but enacted through cross-reference, creative repetition, and deference to the depths of meaning which reside in language as in any other part of the creation.

The reference in 'Virtue' to 'my musick' draws attention not only to Herbert's sense of his verse as song, but to his recurring self-consciousness of the process of writing. This stems partly from the fact that writing was to Herbert synonymous with living; as he says in 'The Flower',

> And now in age I bud again,
> After so many deaths I live and write;
> I once more smell the dew and rain,
> And relish versing.

But Herbert's awareness of himself as a poet went further even than this fundamental 'relishing' of natural and verbal life. For him 'versing' epitomized the clash between vocation and fallenness; the need to love God, but the impossibility of fully doing so, was vividly expressed in the devotional poet's urge to write, and simultaneous knowledge that his poems could never adequately celebrate their divine subject. He was constantly aware of human weakness, summing up 'man' as 'a brittle crazie glass' ('The Windows') and a fine instrument so easily 'untun'd, unstrung' ('Denial'). So it is not surprising that, as one who naturally turned to verse as a means of devotion, Herbert found that the problem of writing appropriately became one of his recurring concerns. The fullest account of his dilemma is to be found in 'Jordan (II)':

> When first my lines of heav'nly joyes made mention,
> Such was their lustre, they did so excell,
> That I sought out quaint words, and trim invention;
> My thoughts began to burnish, sprout, and swell,
> Curling with metaphors a plain intention,
> Decking the sense, as if it were to sell.

Thousands of notions in my brain did runne,
Off'ring their service, if I were not sped:
I often blotted what I had begunne;
This was not quick enough, and that was dead.
Nothing could seem too rich to clothe the sunne,
Much lesse those joyes which trample on his head.

As flames do work and winde, when they ascend,
So did I weave my self into the sense.
But while I bustled, I might heare a friend
Whisper, *How wide is all this long pretence!*
There is in love a sweetnesse readie penn'd:
Copie out onely that, and save expense.

The excitement of writing about God is conveyed in the creative energies of the first two stanzas, in which the resources of language are ransacked, more and more uneasily, in order to weave a fabric 'rich' enough to 'clothe the sunne'. But this punning phrase immediately also draws attention to the doomed nature of the enterprise. To praise God the 'son' requires the richest possible poetry, but to attempt to clothe the 'sun' is a foolhardy exercise which will shut off the source of light and life. Christ is both 'son' and 'sun', and thus the desire to honour him in verse of one's own making is shown to be self-defeating; the process of poetic praise obscures the very object of that praise.

Read with this in mind, 'Jordan (II)' is a poem about words getting out of hand. The opening sets the poet's own 'lines' alongside 'heav'nly joys', and already by the second line it is not entirely clear whether the 'lustre' and 'excelling' belong to the 'joyes' or to the 'lines' themselves, which already threaten to displace heaven as the poem's focus. The metaphors of growth in the fourth line – 'burnish, sprout, and swell' – suggest not only exuberant energy but also the potential for intrusive conceit, just as 'swelling' is identified with pride at the end of 'The Flower'. The words, and the poet in whom they 'runne', are 'blotting' the task they have 'begunne'; the plain simplicity of the poet's project, to praise God, becomes 'curled' with complexity. This 'curling' motion, originating in the plant metaphors of the first stanza, also anticipates the 'working', 'winding' and 'weaving' action of the third, when the 'bustling' activity of the poet comes to a head. It is then that the speaker's failure is made clear; he began with an attempt to focus on 'heav'nly joyes' but ended with a disordered and distressed poem about his own 'self'.

How, then, can the dilemma of the poem be resolved? As in many of Herbert's lyrics, the intervention of another voice – a 'whispering' friend whose presence is like that of the biblical 'still, small voice' of God (1 Kings

19:12) – gives the poem its conclusion and the first speaker an honourable way out.[8] In a sacred rewriting of the end of Philip Sidney's first *Astrophil and Stella* sonnet, where the poet is advised by the muse to look into his own heart to find inspiration, Herbert's speaker is told gently to 'copie' from the source of love and 'save expense'. The splendid irony of this final phrase is that the Christ-like voice echoes the troublingly mercantile vocabulary of the end of the first stanza. There the poet reported 'decking the sense' – that is, enriching the poem's meaning but at the same time appealing to the 'senses' and obscuring the real 'sense' – as if the poem were destined for the marketplace. The 'friend' sees that all this furious poetic activity is wasteful and that it in fact represents expenditure on the part of the speaker; he advises instead a kind of poetic and spiritual thrift. The poet is to make use of existing materials; the longed-for 'sweetnesse' of his verse (so vital to its vision, as 'Virtue' makes clear) is to be found 'readie penn'd' in love itself.

This is no easy conclusion; it came out of one poetic crisis, but in many ways begins another. What is this 'love' which must be copied? If it is Christ himself, then this is a recipe for living the Christian life, not for writing successful devotional poetry. If it is the life of Christ as recorded in the Bible, then the poet's task is simply to echo it – but then this is no poem, unless, as in 'Jordan (I)' and a number of other poems, Herbert writes an entire poem about paring his poetry down to a plain biblical phrase ... and we are back to the dilemma of 'Jordan (II)'. If 'love' refers also to human affection, then the advice is a reminder to the poet to use the established framework of the secular love lyric and transpose it to the higher pitch of divine praise – again, the activity we have witnessed in 'Easter', 'Virtue' and 'Jordan (II)'. The message of the 'friend' is thus by no means a simple resolution but, like most of Herbert's endings, takes the problem to another plane and triggers off a puzzling and rethinking on the part of the reader. We find ourselves reading the poem for a second time, and realizing that the title, though not referred to directly in the text, may, as is typical of Herbert's short but tightly packed titles, stand as an emblem of the poem's significance. The river Jordan signified for the Jews a boundary to be crossed in order to reach the Promised Land; the poem attempts to find a way into the enticing territory of devotional verse, where the basic poetic materials, like the Jews themselves, remain the same, but the perspective, and 'sweetnesse', are radically new. The title's other significance is from New Testament and Christian practice, in which the Jordan is associated with baptism, the sort of spiritual cleansing and renewal which the poet seeks for his 'lines'.

But in its early draft the poem had another title – 'Invention' – and this, too, helps us to understand the aesthetic of devotional writing suggested by 'Jordan (II)'. 'Invention' can so easily be taken to mean poetic ingenuity, those very 'trim' ideas referred to in the first stanza, but the original meaning of *inventio* in rhetoric was discovery; the poet's invention was not to originate but to uncover or reveal meanings. This shifting of the centre of poetic skill from witty novelty to revelation is, of course, the progress of 'Jordan (II)' itself, and is the foundation of Herbert's entire aesthetic. As he wrote in one of his earliest poems, 'Lord, in thee / The *beauty* lies, in the *discovery*'.[9] The process of all the lyrics of *The Temple* is (re)discovery: of perceptions beyond ordinary description, of the mystery of affliction, of the simplicity to be wrung from the most perplexing narrative corners and, above all, of the discovery of God's love in the most surprising places (as amidst the 'ragged noise and mirth / Of theeves and murderers' at the end of 'Redemption'). These are the stories and revelations of Herbert's poems; but discovery is enacted in their forms, too, which are tailor-made for virtually each individual lyric. Their visually expressive shapes (as in 'Easter Wings' and 'The Altar') are far from naive; they point to a sense of the innate power of the 'word', in all its dimensions, which poetic form can reveal. The 'mending' of the poet's 'ryme' in 'Denial' also acts as a sign that spiritual meaning can reside in sounds, echoes and patterns, all of which are exploited to the full in *The Temple*. The poems assert the belief that 'Thy word is all, if we could spell' ('The Flower'), and their aesthetic principle may be described as a 'spelling' of the 'word' in its multiple forms as the Bible, Christ himself, and the potential of language. 'Spelling' is learning to read, or discover, the word in the everyday, as in 'Colossians 3.3' where the poem progressively reveals a biblical quotation embedded as a diagonal text 'hid' within the horizontal lines. The act of 'spelling' is also a breaking down of a word into its individual letters, as in the small poem 'Jesu' where the broken-hearted speaker finds that the name Jesu has broken down, in response, into 'I ease you'. This may be invention in the familiar sense of wit or ingenuity, but it enacts the other kind of 'invention' – the almost sacra-mental showing forth of the gains to be made from a word, especially 'the Word', when it is poetically fragmented as well as discovered whole.

It is not surprising that Herbert, as a poet of 'discovery', was an artist whose greatest skill is shown in his poetic endings. The last lines of Herbert's lyrics, simultaneously, can surprise both reader and speaker, com-plete the movement of the poem and disrupt us into new readings – new discoveries – as has been seen in 'Prayer (I)', 'Virtue' and 'Jordan (II)'. The last poem of 'The Church' (the main section of *The Temple*) is an example of Herbert's endings on a larger scale – closing the lyric sequence – as well as a fine instance of a moment of revelation saved for the very last line of a lyric. This final poem is 'Love (III)', and it is indeed in keeping with the doctrinal and emotional mood of the collection that it should end with love. The poem is a triumphant, but also intimate and homely, portrayal of the heavenly banquet:

> Love bade me welcome, yet my soul drew back,
> > Guiltie of dust and sinne.
> But quick-ey'd Love, observing me grow slack
> > From my first entrance in,
> Drew nearer to me, sweetly questioning,
> > If I lack'd any thing.
>
> A guest, I answer'd, worthy to be here:
> > Love said, You shall be he.
> I the unkinde, ungratefull? Ah my deare,
> > I cannot look on thee.
> Love took my hand, and smiling did reply,
> > Who made the eyes but I?
>
> Truth Lord, but I have marr'd them: let my shame
> > Go where it doth deserve.
> And know you not, sayes Love, who bore the blame?
> > My deare, then I will serve.
> You must sit down, sayes Love, and taste my meat:
> > So I did sit and eat.

The sequence thus closes with one of Herbert's favourite metaphors for redemption – tasting, eating, being nourished by love. The scene in which it occurs is a mixture of the communion service, encountered regularly on earth, and the heavenly meal which the sacrament prefigures. The presence of Christ is given double significance as both the host who 'welcomes' the guests to the supper he serves and the 'host' which is Christ's own body in the communion – 'my meat'. In its understated way the poem celebrates both the generosity and the self-sacrifice of God's love for the 'marr'd' human individual.

The tension of the poem lies in the speaker's unwillingness to accept that this heavenly love is freely offered, regardless of mortal 'dustiness' or human 'sinne'. His soul 'drew back' from the approaches of Love, and the lyric recounts his struggles to find something to do to appease his 'guilt' – he looks away, he wants to leave the banquet or, at the very least, to 'serve' the other guests. But, as in 'The Holdfast', he has to learn to give in gracefully and accept that even these apparently humble gestures are a kind of pride, an inability to let go: for 'to have nought is ours, not to confesse / That we have nought'. In the central paradox of Christianity, such an emptying enables the fulfilling of redemption: as Christ enquires in 'Love (III)' with implicit reference to the crucifixion, 'And know you not ... who bore the blame?'

The reluctant guest is persuaded to receive the gifts of love by the kindly but probing questions of the divine host – a reminder of the enquiring dialogues which play an important role throughout *The Temple*. The voice of the Christ figure is a teasing one, not above a pun on 'eye'/'I' to highlight the fundamental truth that God's being, his 'I', is present in all the creation. Christ's constructed presence in the poem here is 'quick-ey'd' and playful, but also sensual, 'sweet' and 'near', taking the speaker's hand in the same way as in 'Easter' and the 'Clasping of Hands'. Again we are reminded of the closeness of Herbert's devotional poems to the secular love lyrics of his day and to the inherited language of desire as animated by Sidney in the sonnets of *Astrophil and Stella*. So much is interwoven in this lyric: the physical and the spiritual, lyric patterning and the naturalness of dialogue, generosity and unease, and elegance with ultimate plainness. After the tactful rejection of all his excuses, the speaker finally accepts that there is nothing to be done but to accept – and the power of the last line lies in its monosyllabic simplicity, the resonant plainness of a commonplace narrative statement, 'So I did sit and eat.' As in the conclusion of 'The Collar', debate and metaphor give way to union and directness.

However, the impact of such endings is far from simple, as the situation of 'Love (III)' demonstrates. The poetic sequence has closed with the reluctant speaker seated at last in the heavenly banquet, an emblem of finality, it would seem. But the meal is also the communion, and meals, whether homely or spiritual, are generally eaten in order to live; the end is not death but nourishment and new life, not a closure but a new beginning. This is true of Herbert's best poetic endings, which return us to the dilemmas and experiences with which the text began; it is also true of the sequence as a whole, when the final 'sit and eat' places us where 'The Church' began, at 'The Altar'.

It is always appropriate to end with thoughts about endings – especially if, as in *The Temple*, they take you back to a new starting-point. Reading Herbert's verse is helped, it seems, by an awareness of paradoxes. The five poems on which we have concentrated highlight five major paradoxes in Herbert's artistry. The lyrics are framed by traditions, yet are entirely fresh; they use richly evocative language, yet are more interested in the process of knowing than describing. The poems are rightly described as clear and transparent, even though they contain rhetorical surprise and complexity; as Herbert wrote in 'Praise (II)', the poet uses 'utmost art' to express ordinary human experience of God's (extraordinary) love. These are lyrics which make things inventively new, but are committed to an aesthetic of discovery and 'copying'. Finally, Herbert's poems are, like his spirituality, end-focussed; the lyrics lead to dynamic endings which startle and yet confirm, reopen and yet resolve. So the process of reading Herbert involves being open to simultaneous pleasure and puzzlement; as he wrote in 'The H[oly] Scriptures (I)' of the Bible, 'thou art a masse / Of strange delights, where we may wish and take'. Though we may read *The Temple* and appreciate its artistry in ways very different from its original seventeenth-century admirers, our common ground may perhaps be discerned in the comment of Herbert's older contemporary, Francis Bacon, on the poet's skills: 'in respect of Divinitie, and Poesie, met', he felt that he 'could not make better choice'.[10]

NOTES

1 Barnabus Oley, 'A Prefatory View of the Life and Vertues of the Authour', *Herbert's Remains* (1652), p. 119; Ralph Knevet, *Shorter Poems*, ed. Amy Charles (Columbus: Ohio State University Press, 1966), p. 281.

2 See 'The Church-porch', lines 5–6: 'A verse may finde him, who a sermon flies, / And turn delight into a sacrifice', in *The English Poems of George Herbert*, ed. C. A. Patrides (London: Dent, 1974), p. 33. For some student readers of Herbert, it may be appropriate to reverse the poet's original formula and hope to turn 'sacrifice' into a 'delight'.

3 'Bitter-sweet', in *The English Poems*, p. 177. All further quotations of Herbert's lyrics are taken from this edition but are cited in the text by poem title rather than page number, to simplify matters for readers using other editions.

4 For details of Herbert's biography, see Amy M. Charles, *A Life of George Herbert* (Ithaca: Cornell University Press, 1977).

5 Herbert's writing has often been characterized as private and withdrawn from controversy. It is true that *The Temple* is less overtly polemical than some contemporary poetry, and indeed than his own lyrics in their earlier drafts, but Herbert's relationship to the liturgy represents a firm political position and was interpreted as such by his first readers. The earliest extant poem in praise of *The Temple*, by one John Polwhele (Bod. MS Eng. poet f. 16, f. 11r), describes Herbert's temple building as showing most 'Catholique Conformitie', with no characteristically Puritan features 'spoylinge' the 'harmonie'.

6 The idea may be found in medieval devotional texts and seventeenth-century emblem books; see Rosemund Tuve, *A Reading of George Herbert* (University of Chicago Press, 1952), pp. 144–6; and Barbara Kiefer Lewalski, *Protestant Poetics and the Seventeenth-Century Religious Lyric* (Princeton University Press, 1979), pp. 204–5.

7 *A Priest to the Temple, or, The Countrey Parson his Character and Rule of Holy Life*, chapter 21. In *The Works of George Herbert*, ed. F. E. Hutchinson (Oxford: Clarendon, 1941), p. 257.

8 For similar scenarios in which a 'bustling', self-important speaker learns a lesson through the calling of a divine voice, see 'Redemption' and 'The Collar'.

9 The ending of the second of two sonnets written by Herbert to his mother in 1610

and printed in Walton's *Life of Mr George Herbert*, 1670; see *The English Poems*, pp. 205–6.

10 Francis Bacon, *Translation of Certaine Psalmes into English Verse* (1625), A3v. Bacon dedicated this translation to Herbert and the description of his skills makes it clear that Herbert's reputation as a poet was becoming established even before the publication of *The Temple* in 1633.

FURTHER READING

Benet, Diana, *Secretary of Praise: The Poetic Vocation of George Herbert* (Columbia: University of Missouri Press, 1984)

Bloch, Chana, *Spelling the Word: George Herbert and the Bible* (Berkeley: University of California Press, 1985)

Charles, Amy M., *A Life of George Herbert* (Ithaca: Cornell University Press, 1977)

Fish, Stanley, *The Living Temple: George Herbert and Catechizing* (Berkeley: University of California Press, 1978)

Harman, Barbara Leah, *Costly Monuments: Representations of the Self in George Herbert's Poetry* (Cambridge, Mass.: Harvard University Press, 1982)

Miller, Edmund, and DiYanni, Robert (eds.), *Like Season'd Timber: New Essays on George Herbert* (New York: Peter Lang, 1987)

Patrides, C. A. (ed.), *George Herbert: The Critical Heritage* (London: Routledge and Kegan Paul, 1983)

Roberts, John R., *George Herbert: An Annotated Bibliography of Modern Criticism*, (rev. edn, 1905–84) (Columbia: University of Missouri Press, 1988)

Sherwood, Terry G., *Herbert's Prayerful Art* (University of Toronto Press, 1989)

Stewart, Stanley, *George Herbert* (Boston, Mass.: G. K. Hall, 1986)

Strier, Richard, *Love Known: Theology and Experience in George Herbert's Poetry* (University of Chicago Press, 1983)

Summers, Claude J., and Pebworth, Ted-Larry (eds.), *'Too Rich to Clothe the Sunne': Essays on George Herbert* (University of Pittsburgh Press, 1980)

Summers, Joseph H., *George Herbert: His Religion and Art* (London: Chatto and Windus, 1954)

Vendler, Helen, *The Poetry of George Herbert* (Cambridge, Mass.: Harvard University Press, 1975)

10

THOMAS N. CORNS

Thomas Carew, Sir John Suckling, and Richard Lovelace

Thomas Carew, Sir John Suckling, and Richard Lovelace, together with Robert Herrick, the subject of a separate essay, frequently have been seen by the critical tradition to constitute a group, often termed 'Cavalier' poets. The configuration is of considerable antiquity, and some points of association between some of them were sometimes recognized in the mid seventeenth century, shortly after the death of Carew (in 1640?) and Suckling (in 1641?). The perception that they are in some senses a group persists, reinforced by modern anthologists as well as critics. The agenda of this essay is to explain and thus dismantle the origins of that critical orthodoxy and to distinguish the characteristics not only of individual poets but also of the Caroline court culture before and after the inception of the Civil War, though paradoxically the mere title works to confirm that which I would set aside.

Carew (born c.1594) and Herrick (born 1591) reached creative maturity in the 1620s and early 1630s and Suckling (born 1609) flourished throughout the 1630s, yet very little of their poetry appeared in print before 1640. Their poems lived, rather, in the song settings of court musicians and in manuscript circulation, at first, no doubt, within the court coterie and among friends, and later in a widening circle of manuscript anthologies. When their pre-1640 works were delivered into print it was into a radically changed political and cultural world from that in which they were conceived. Lovelace and Herrick, publishing their major collections in 1648 and 1649, had the opportunity to revise and organize their works in the light of the dispersal of the Caroline court and the eclipse of the royalist cause, and they could and did write works in the 1640s which engaged both their personal catastrophes and those of the cause they espoused. For Carew and Suckling, their work was absorbed into that process of royalist lamentation as if through a process of retrospective revision. The title page of Suckling's collected works (1646) indicated well the tendency: *Fragmenta Aurea. A Collection of all the Incomparable Peeces, Written by Sir John Suckling. And published by a Friend to perpetuate His Memory. Printed by his owne Copies.* Fittingly, the bookseller responsible was the royalist Humphrey Moseley, who, besides publishing Milton's early verse in 1645, published much of the best poetry and drama vouchsafed to print in the 1640s and 1650s, including much of the work of the poets and dramatists of the dispersed court of Charles I.[1] *Fragmenta Aurea* – that is, *Golden Pieces*, the broken remains of a writer and a culture both now perceived to have been destroyed by the political turmoil occasioned by the Puritan and Parliamentary opposition to the king. *'Published by a Friend'* rehearses a recurrent motif of royalist writing in the 1640s, the friendship and the generosity which were perceived as keeping the old ideologies and loyalties alive. That it is printed from his own copies is a reasonable point for Moseley to foreground, indicative of his own bibliographical probity; but it points, too, to the fact that the text emerges from a source within the coterie in which Suckling functioned. Moseley's 'third edition' of Carew (1651) has a similarly plangent title page: *Poems. With a Maske, by Thomas Carew Esq; One of the Gent. of the privie-Chamber, and Sewer in Ordinary to His late Majesty. The Songs were set in Musick by Mr. Henry Lawes Gent: of the Kings Chappell, and one of his late Majesties Private Musick.* It reads like the obituary for a way of life. The dead king is twice recalled. So, too, is the defunct court genre of the masque – a late and splendid example of which, *Coelum Britannicum* (1633), had been written by Carew. Though Henry Lawes is perhaps best remembered now for collaborating with the young Milton on *Comus* (the masque presented at Ludlow Castle to celebrate the elevation of the Earl of Bridgewater to presidency of the Council of Wales) in his own age his reputation as composer to the king's court was very considerable. He was, moreover, something of a royal martyr in that his brother William, another prominent composer, had been killed at the siege of Chester in 1645 while in arms for the king; Henry himself had been displaced from his court appointments during the 1640s. Herrick in his collection of 1648 had similarly memorialized the superseded golden age of the court of Charles I.[2]

The poetry of Carew and Suckling received then a new ideological value in the 1640s; what had celebrated, untendentiously, the life and the values of the personal rule of Charles I carried a new freight of political significance as a sort of reservoir of a culture that was (royalists hoped temporarily) suspended or superseded. Performance poetry and manuscript coterie poetry appear displaced into the stabler and more portable medium of print, more serviceable to the courtly diaspora of the 1640s.

Suckling and Carew were courtiers, gentlemen of the royal privy chamber; they become metamorphosed into cavaliers. The transformation had begun in the final years of their lives. Most of their writing dates from the period when Charles I continued the scrupulously irenic policies by which his father had kept England from active involvement in the Thirty Years War which plagued Europe (and in so doing obviated the need for recourse to calling parliaments). However, in 1639 and 1640 conflict with his Scottish subjects caused Charles to mobilize forces which included Suckling and Carew, as well as Lovelace, though the two abortive campaigns, the First and Second Bishops' Wars, produced little that could honestly be regarded as engagement with the enemy. Carew died shortly afterwards, perhaps of syphilis. Suckling, however, played a prominent part in the so-called First Army Plot of 1641, a wholly abortive military coup to overthrow the Long Parliament, which had finally convened in 1640, and an exploit which precipitated Suckling's flight into exile, where he died in uncertain circumstances.[3]

Suckling's reputation epitomizes the transformations of the word 'cavalier' in the early 1640s. Two alternative stereotypes leapt up fully armed from the pages of the political press, one wholly hostile, the other wholly positive. To Parliamentary apologists, the armed supporters of the king were whoremongering and raping roisterers, their mouths full of the foulest blasphemies, their bellies swilled with alcohol, their bodies wracked by venereal disease, their attire manifesting the wildest excesses of continental fashion, and they fought primarily to repair their blighted fortunes by plundering the godly.[4] Milton, late in the decade dismissed the 'gentlemen' with whom Charles surrounded himself in his abortive attempt in 1642 to arrest leading parliamentarians with 'Gentlemen indeed; the ragged Infantrie of Stewes and Brothels; the spawn and shipwrack of Taverns and Dicing Houses'.[5] Suckling, whose own plot was precursor to that bid, appears persistently, depicted in such terms, in pro-Parliamentary publications of the early 1640s.

Yet to his political confrères he was represented as the gilded youth martyred to a cause he served beyond the call of commonplace loyalty. As Moseley, a writer in my view of some unacknowledged eloquence, put it in his epistle to the reader:

> Among the highest and most refined Wits of the Nation, this Gentile and Princely Poet took his generous rise from the Court; where having flourish'd with splendor and reputation, he liv'd only long enough to see the Sun-set of that Majesty from whose auspicious beams he derived his lustre, and with whose declining state his own loyal Fortunes were obscured.[6]

But the positive image of the cavalier came to incorporate other elements besides a capacity for self-sacrifice. The most eloquent explicit exposition of the construct is perhaps Herrick's poem entitled 'His Cavalier':

> Give me that man, that dares bestride
> The active Sea-horse, & with pride,
> Through that huge field of waters ride:
> Who, with his looks too, can appease
> The ruffling winds and raging seas,
> In mid'st of all their outrages.
> This, this a virtuous man can doe,
> Saile against Rocks, and split them too;
> I! and a world of Pikes passe through.[7]

Note the way in which reckless equestrianism, wedded to purity of heart, ultimately achieves improbable success. As we shall see, Lovelace will negotiate ingeniously a creative relationship with this species of active virtue (and even, defiantly, with the negative image of cavalierism). Moreover, we should recognize both versions for what they were, ideologically potent contructs which touched but lightly real social characteristics differentiating the officer cadres of Parliament and the king.[8] My immediate concern, however, is that we should factor out these stereotypical assumptions of the 1640s from our reading of the poetry which Carew and Suckling wrote in the 1630s and (particularly in Carew's case) the 1620s. The making of the cavalier occasioned a remaking of the culture of the Caroline court. The next task is to reposition that literary achievement in its pre-war setting.

Two elements central to the character of that court profoundly shape Carew's poetry, the one a continuity of Jacobean policy, the other a sharp distinction between the ethos of the court of Charles I and that of his father.[9] Charles I perceived the advantages James had enjoyed through an irenic stance that kept England out of the widespread European war. However, the court of James had been quite scandalous to those of a godly inclination, its moral tone, in Parry's phrase, 'often seedy'. James had indelicately pursued his favourites; his love affair with the Duke of Buckingham, his most powerful minister, was 'carried on in public'.[10] In sharp contrast, Charles excluded the openly scandalous from his court, and his personal morality reflected a respectful and monogamous regard for his wife, Henrietta Maria, which found expression in the encouragement of a cult of idealized Platonic love and in the celebration of their reign as an equal partnership. Charles's personal style 'was strict and serious ... chaste and even prudish'.[11] In the visual arts, his affections manifested themselves in the celebration of the royal pair in double portraits depicting them together (something of an innovation). The happiness and the mutuality of the couple was a recurrent motif of the court masque.

These emphases, on pacifism and on respectability, are eloquently celebrated in Carew's poem 'In Answer of an Elegiacal Letter upon the Death of the King of Sweden from Aurelian Townsend, Inviting me to Write on that Subject'.[12] Townsend, court poet and masque-writer, had sent to Carew a poem 'upon the death of the King of Sweden',[13] the occasion for which was the request that the latter, an accomplished elegist as we shall see, should apply his talents to commemorate the late Gustavus Adolphus, who had played a signal role on the predominantly Protestant side in the current war until his death at the battle of Lutzen. Townsend's deeper argument seems to suggest that his demise leaves a vacuum in the Protestant leadership of Europe, hinting perhaps at the notion that Charles I should fill it: 'His gloryus gauntletts shall unquestioned lye, / Till handes are found fitt for a monarchie' (lines 35–6).

Carew's reply builds a striking schema of Caroline transcendence. He offers a roll-call of Swedish victories and beaten adversaries:

> *Frankfort, Leipsigh, Worsburgh*, of the *Rhyne*;
> The *Leck*, the *Danube, Tilly, Wallestein*,
> *Bavaria, Papenheim, Lutzenfield* where hee
> Gain'd after death a posthume Victorie.   (lines 19–22)

The un-Englishness of the proper names he lists suggests the outlandishness of a conflict alien to English interests and inappropriate for English involvement, and it ushers in the paradox of the posthumous victory; evidently, such paths of glory lead but to the grave. Carew culminates his reduction of the achievement of the Protestant warrior with a stunning image of the charnel house continental Europe has become:

> And (since 'twas but his Church-yard) let him have
> For his owne ashes now no narrower Grave
> Then the whole *German* Continents vast wombe,
> Whilst all her Cities doe but make his Tombe.   (lines 31–4)

In this distinctly Donneish image, Carew's well-informed contemporaries would recall at once the carnage of the Thirty Years War, the devastation of cities like Magdeburg, sacked in 1631 with the estimated slaughter of 40,000 Protestant co-religionaries. If you seek a monument to Gustavus Adolphus and the martial impulse, look around Germany. The reader's gaze turns homeward with relief:

> But let us that in myrtle bowers sit
> Under secure shades, use the benefit
> Of peace and plenty, which the blessed hand
> Of our good King gives this obdurate Land.   (lines 45–8)

'Obdurate', presumably, in that some still resist the arguments against participating in the war. In place of devastation Charles brings the arts of peace, pre-eminently (and appropriately since Townsend wrote in this genre) the art of the masque. The focus of Carew's poem switches to the English court and, at its centre, the relationship of Charles and Henrietta Maria. He recalls the 'glorious night' when:

> in their Angel-shapes
> A troope of Deities came downe to guide
> Our steereless Barkes in passions swelling tide
> By vertues Carde [probably a compass, though possibly a map], and
>   brought us from above
> A patterne of their owne celestiall love. (lines 60–4)

Townsend and the court circle would recognize that the terms in which Carew chooses to praise the virtue of the royal couple, and particularly the queen, are invoked from Townsend's masque, *Tempe Restored*, performed on Shrove Tuesday, 1632. The argument of the entertainment is that 'Divine Beauty', embodied by the queen, displaces the reign of Circe, under which men had been turned into 'voluntary beasts'.[14] After 'The Queen and the ladies dance their entry', the Chorus sings:

> But we most happy that behold
> Two [i.e., Charles and Henrietta Maria] that have turned this age to gold,
> Making old Saturn's reign
> In theirs come back again. (lines 250–3)

For the courtiers who had attended, that masque had constituted the highest realization of the Caroline vision, a court blessed with peace in a Europe dominated by war, a court presided over by a royal couple who proclaimed and embodied the cult of virtuous and mutual love.

Charles had been delighted: as the watching Venetian ambassadors had reported home, 'The king himself by gaily taking part in the dancing proved the pleasure which he took in it.'[15] Ten years on, of course, England was at civil war; seventeen years on, Charles was led from the windows of the Whitehall Banqueting House where the masque had been staged to be decapitated by the executioners of the English Republic. Summers's comment on the Gustavus Adolphus poem, that it shows 'a smugly insular assumption of prosperity and an eternal party, like dancing on a volcano',[16] manifests a smugness of its own. But to the courtiers of the royalist diaspora, reading later editions of Carew, the poignancy of retrospection would have been acute enough. But retrospection is only one perspective; contextualized in the period of its composition, the poem celebrates the high summer of the Caroline court.

Alluding to Townsend's masque and borrowing his mode of compliment have a singular felicity in a poem that in some sense aims to answer him. But it is indicative, too, of another important characteristic of Carew's poetry. In his influential study of poetry in the Caroline period Earl Miner has argued, 'The social mode is as much a radical feature of Cavalier poetry as is the private of the Metaphysicals or the public of Milton, Dryden, and Pope.'[17] Whatever uncertainties one may feel about his larger categories, 'social mode' defines exactly a quality at the core of Carew's aesthetic. For these are poems about named, historical people, addressed to such people, on occasions and in circumstances that are sometimes explicitly defined. No doubt they have a larger resonance, and they rapidly acquired a currency outside the immediate context and the tight coterie, in manuscript and relatively soon in print. Yet the specific social context is persistently foregrounded.

Much of the best of Carew's verse takes the form of funeral elegy commemorating the recently dead. Sometimes, as in the case of the poem entitled in the early printed versions 'Maria Wentworth, Thomae Comitis Cleveland, filia praemortua prima Virgineam animam exhalauit An. Dom. 1632 Aet. suae 18', versions of the text were incorporated into funerary monuments. The poem itself begins with an exploration of the problems of premature death in terms which offer immediate comfort:

> And here the precious dust is layd,
> Whose purely-tempered Clay was made
> So fine, that it the guest betray'd.
>
> Else the soule grew so fast within,
> It broke the outward shell of sinne,
> And so was hatchd a Cherubin.   (p. 56, lines 1–6)

That initial coordinating conjunction offers a momentary point of enigma which is set aside but not resolved. What earlier speech act is implied by it? That the poet speaks as if to someone who views, serially, several tombs, 'and here the tomb of Maria Wentworth'? The two stanzas offer two quite striking images, each suggestive of a radically different way of perceiving the relationship of body and soul. In the first the dust, the 'Clay' of her perfect body, is conceptualized as not crude enough to restrain the soul within it. In the second, the body becomes a 'shell' (something of a commonplace), but a shell that cracks open to liberate the fledgeling cherub, in an elegant metamorphosis.[18] Both offer to the reader/viewer a sense that we witness another version of the empty tomb; what mattered most about Maria Wentworth is no longer here. Thereafter the poem works with a restrained eloquence through a rehearsal of the dead young woman's perceived virtues:

> Good to the Poore, to kindred deare,
> To servants kind, to friendship cleare,
> To nothing but her selfe, severe.   (lines 13–15)

In a sense, the modesty of Carew's claims for her both confirms her own modesty and fixes honestly the limited and limiting social role of the young dead aristocrat; hers was a world bounded by family, friends, and servants; her virtues the parochial ones of kindness and charity. The penultimate stanza rehearses a paradox perhaps of Carew's making, that she is 'though a Virgin, yet a Bride' in that she married 'every Grace' in a 'chaste Poligamie' (lines 16–18); behind it, the reader perceives the older, profounder paradox of the apocalyptic vision of the virginal brides of Christ. The poem ends in an admonition to the reader who stands before the tomb:

> Learne from hence (Reader) what small trust
> We owe this world, where vertue must
> Fraile as our flesh, crumble to dust.   (lines 19–21)

Curiously, the version actually inscribed on Maria Wentworth's tomb omitted this last stanza,[19] thus making the poem more enclosed within the social grouping of her family and friends, rather than public and sermonic to the larger community.

Carew's most famous elegy, 'Upon the death of the Dean of Paul's Dr John Donne' (pp. 71–4), discloses the next aspect of his work I want to consider. Probably more than any poet of the Caroline period Carew had a precise and sensitive familiarity with his immediate precursors, pre-eminently Donne himself and Ben Jonson, together with a thoughtful awareness of his own relationship to their achievements. That elegy reveals him to be a critic of extraordinary shrewdness, remarking, among other telling points, on the erotic quality of Donne's divine verse ('thy brave Soule . . . / Committed holy Rapes upon our Will', lines 15–17) and on his purging of the English love poetry tradition of 'Pedantique weedes' and the 'traine / Of gods and goddesses' (lines 25, 63–4). Though he plainly senses that a remarkable age of poetry has passed with Donne, in his own poetic practice Carew preserves and synthesizes important elements of Donne's and Jonson's characteristics, while eliminating those elements perhaps less acceptable to the narrower decorum of Caroline taste and to the courtierly cult of *sprezzatura* or studied carelessness. Carew's poems never set prosodic conundrums in the manner of Jonson's Cary–Morison ode. Nor is there the invocation of recondite knowledge and the demanding argumentation of Donne's 'Air and Angels', for example. But the elegy for Maria Wentworth indicates well what he preserves from his greater precursors in that neatly turned image (from Donne) of the body-as-shell and soul-as-fledgeling; and in the spare and (here literally) lapidary eloquence of the central stanzas, which owes much to Jonson. What he adds to this synthesis is something of the rather Baroque sensibility of the Caroline court, though the point is intractable to brief exposition.

His most protracted *homage* to Jonson comes not in elegy nor in verse epistle but in his two accomplished attempts at the country-house poem, 'To Saxham' (pp. 27–9) and 'To my friend G. N. from Wrest (pp. 86–9); especially the former relates intricately to 'To Penshurst', Jonson's seminal work in this genre. Jonson's poem is almost twice as long as Carew's, and, though the argument of each is broadly the same (each unostentatious house manifests the virtues of its inhabitants, not least in their charity and generosity), the most significant silence in Carew's poem is the social edginess which pervades Jonson's. The point is primarily a class one. Jonson, the bricklayer's stepson, needs to work hard to argue that he is entertained on equal terms by Lord Lisle, the future Earl of Leicester. Thomas Carew, younger son of Sir Matthew Carew, was a friend and contemporary of a younger son of Sir John Crofts, owner of Saxham. It would simply be bad form for him to protest, as Jonson had, 'the same beere, and bread, and self-same wine, / That is his Lordships shall be also mine'.[20] Behind both Jonson's poem and Carew's stands the classical model of a poem by Martial, on 'The Baian villa . . . of our friend Faustinus'.[21] Interestingly, the easy assumption of social equality is shared by Carew and Martial; the element of fragile self-assertion is Jonson's addition.

Besides the ideological points there is a strictly literary one. Carew, delicately, teases the controlled idiom of Jonson into more Donneish directions. Jonson had written of gamebirds and the fish from the rivers and ponds of the estate giving up themselves to the dinner table (lines 28–38). Carew, taking a hint from this and perhaps from 'The Bait' in Donne's *Songs and Sonets*, produces a more consolidated fancy, in which the country house in winter becomes an ark:

> the birds, fearing the snow
> Might to another deluge grow:
> The Pheasant, Partiridge, and the Larke,
> Flew to thy house, as to the Arke.
> The willing Oxe, of himselfe came
> Home to the slaughter, with the Lambe,
> And every beast did thither bring
> Himselfe, to be an offering.
> The scalie herd, more pleasure tooke,
> Bath'd in thy dish, then in the brooke.   (lines 19–28)

That image of the fish bathing in the fish-kettle more readily than the brook, arresting and neatly turned though it is, is a little disconcerting, and the scrupulous may observe that the animals entered the original ark to survive, not to be slaughtered. Yet it gives the poem a shape and a dimension missing from Jonson's. The house appears as a place of refuge in a winter landscape. Like Martial (and unlike Jonson), Carew fixes his visit in a specific season. He may not review the whole estate since 'frost, and snow, lockt from mine eyes / That beautie which without dore lyes' (lines 1–2). Whatever the fate of other species, to the Crofts' poorer neighbours the house indeed functions as an ark for their survival: 'The cold and frozen ayre had sterv'd / Much poore, if not by thee preserv'd' (lines 11–12). The seasonal reference lends a cogency to the topos of generosity.

But there is another aspect of Carew's *œuvre* to be considered. Earlier I related his writing to the cult of Platonic love fostered and exemplified by Charles and Henrietta Maria. Yet he is known, too, as a libertine poet, indeed, a rather scandalous writer.[22] How may these notions be reconciled?

Certainly, much of his love poetry is wholly unobjectionable to the chaste sensibilities of the royal couple. Indeed, some poems could be conceived of as the antithesis of the seduction poem, such as 'Good counsel to a Young Maid' (p. 25), which counsels the preservation of virginity as an alternative to the lover's scorn: 'So shalt thou be despis'd, faire Maid, / When by the sated lover tasted' (lines 13–14). The more profoundly erotic impulse is characteristically socialized and rendered acceptable to the prevailing culture of the court in his marriage poems, as in 'On the Marriage of T. K. and C. C. the Morning Stormy' (pp. 79–80). The specificity and the circumstantiality are wholly typical of the social mode – T. K. is Thomas Killigrew, a friend and peer with whom (according to a traditional identification) Carew appears in a double portrait by Van Dyck; C. C., Cecilia Crofts, was the daughter of Sir John Crofts of Saxham.[23] This is a poem from deep within a coterie of the Caroline court, but it resonates with a sustained, masculinist sexuality in which the Platonism of the courtly ideal is overwhelmed by simpler rites:

> Thinke on the mercy freed thee, thinke upon
> Her vertues, graces, beauties, one by one,
> So shalt thou relish all, enjoy the whole
> Delights of her faire body, and pure soule.
> Then boldly to the fight of Love proceed,
> 'Tis mercy not to pitty though she bleed,
> Wee'le strew no nuts, but change that ancient forme,
> For till to morrow wee'le prorogue this storme,
> Which shall confound with its loude whistling noyse
> Her pleasing shreekes, and fan thy panting joys.   (lines 27–36)

The consummation in the storm perhaps provokes recollection of a Virgilian analogue, the consummation of the relationship of Dido and Aeneas

(*Aeneid* 4.160–72); but the event is detached from the mythic plane by its clear situation in the bridal chamber of upper-gentry-class friends.

Though this uneven 'fight of Love' suggests a sadistic edge to Carew's eroticism, his poems of erotic compliment sometimes appear passionlessly remote from any human experience. Thus, 'Upon a Mole in Celia's Bosom' (pp. 113–14) ponders improbably the origins of the mistress's birthmark in a way that removes any sense of the woman or the relationship. Among such poems of compliment a libertine strain, familiar from the secular lyrics of Donne, occasionally intrudes, as in 'The Complement' (pp. 99–101). But it is his two 'raptures', and especially the first (pp. 49–53), which supported his early reputation as a libertine poet and which most contradict the prevailing sexual ethics of the Caroline court; indeed, there is reason to think it dates from the late Jacobean period, though it was much copied and widely circulated in the Caroline period.[24]

The title itself, 'A Rapture', merits some consideration. Though its primary meaning here is 'a transport of ecstatic delight' it could also, contemporaneously, mean sexual violation. Once more, male threat is at the heart of Carew's vision. Part of the poem, which is set in 'Loves Elizium' (line 2), a realm where the social constraint of honour does not obtain, envisages rape-victims Lucrece and Daphne (as well as Ulysses' celibate Penelope and Petrarch's Laura) acceding avidly to ravishment:

> To quench the burning Ravisher, she [Lucrece] hurles
> Her limbs into a thousand winding curles,
> And studies artfull postures.   (lines 119–21)

A sordid reverie, but at least explicitly remote from the world as Carew expects his readers to know it. Within this realm, Celia, the mistress so often named in Carew's poems of compliment, responds passionately; the implication, clearly, is that such behaviour 'occurs', if that is quite the word, within fantasy. '*Now* in more subtile wreathes I will entwine / My sinowie thighes, my legs and armes with thine' (lines 79–80, emphasis mine) suggests that, outside the reverie, there is no such entwining. The sexual act is described in deeply suggestive (if occasionally anatomically dubious) imagery; penetration is like the docking of a ship:

> Yet my tall Pine, shall in the *Cyprian* straight
> Ride safe at Anchor, and unlade her fraight:
> My Rudder, with thy bold hand, like a tryde,
> And skilfull Pilot, thou shalt steere, and guide
> My Bark into Loves channell, where it shall
> Dance, as the bounding waves doe rise and fall. (lines 85–90)

The grandiloquence and the inappropriately high register subvert the phallic celebration; 'tall Pine', 'Rudder' – the images shift into mock-heroic, as if to say that this is of course merely a male fantasy, and, consciously, a rather silly one.

The poem functions on the border of Caroline court life, rehearsing the sexual desire that Charles and Maria have repressed and have purged from the public gaze. Like a licensed fool, the speaker articulates what others perhaps want to say but may not. But by proclaiming its status as fantasy the poem admits the primacy of the sexual ideology within which Carew, for the most part, positioned his erotic verse.

'To my friend G. N. from Wrest' (pp. 86–9) is probably Carew's last poem. In its specific social setting (a country house belonging to the Earl of Kent) and in its specificity of time (just after the Bishops' War of 1639) and object of address (though the precise identity of 'G. N.' is subject to some dispute[25]), it is fittingly typical of his work. Its concluding sentiment, which contrasts the joys of peace with the activity of hunting, itself a re-creation of the experience of war, could function as an envoi to an age:

> Thus I enjoy my self, and taste the fruit
> Of this blest Peace, whilst toyl'd in the pursuit
> Of Bucks, and Stags, th'embleme of warre, you strive
> To keepe the memory of our Armes alive.   (lines 107–10)

The social and irenic life remains only tenuously within his grasp.

Of the three poets this chapter treats, Suckling was probably, in the seventeenth century, the most widely read, certainly from the 1650s onwards; today that position is reversed. For example, he scarcely figures in a recent major anthology of verse of the period.[26] The reasons for the revaluation are perhaps not difficult to find. His poetic reputation was advanced by his sensational political manoeuvres of the early 1640s and by his status as royalist martyr. Further, his clearest contributions to the English literary tradition, which rest in the production of a strong and rather loutishly masculinist self-image and in the development of a robust conversational poetic mode, while they recommended his work to contemporary readers and to the consciously rakish style of the court of Charles II, seem often charmless now.

Carew is in some ways a curiously anonymous writer, taking on and expressing the values of the court in which he moved, functioning socially to celebrate the rites of passage of his class and his age, for the most part figuring in his poems only as a celebrant (or licensed critic) of those values. Suckling's poems are a star-vehicle for himself, or rather for an agreeable construct of himself.

Consider, for example, the poem known as 'The Wits' or 'A Sessions of

the Poets'.[27] The poem describes a meeting of contemporary poets and associated intelligentsia, convened to determine who should 'receive the bays'
from Apollo. It is the vehicle for coterie jokes about friends and rivals. The
most interesting sections deal with the devaluation of Carew and the representation of Suckling himself. The former is excluded from the role of laureate because 'His Muse was hard bound, and th'issue of's brain / Was
seldom brought forth but with trouble and pain' (lines 35–6). 'Hard bound'
– that is, constipated – makes a flippant connection between writing and
excreting, with the suggestion that, among the healthy, both are done with
facility. Most significantly, it values ease in composition, the poetry of non-
chalance. When he comes to represent himself directly, the whole undertaking is revalued:

> *Suckling* next was call'd but did not appear,
> And strait one whisperd *Apollo* in's ear,
> That of all men living he cared not for't,
> He loved not the Muses so well as his sport;
> And
> Prized black eyes, or a lucky hit
> At bowls, above all the Trophies of wit.   (lines 73–8)

Though Carew and Suckling were for long perceived by the critical tradition
to be in some sense friends, it has been observed that Carew never mentions
him; indeed, as Parker has observed, 'the artistic similarities between their
works are actually slight' and 'the differences are not accidental'.[28] Both in
the 'The Wits' and in the poems which address or represent conversation
with Carew the tone is insulting, reductive, or critical. Thus, his 'Upon
T. C. having the P.', a poem about Carew's venereal disease,[29] with its witty
sally about how difficult and painful 'Tom' now finds urinating, may well
not have been much to Carew's taste; it also rather smartly associates this
Caroline celebrant of married eroticism and Platonic love with a sexually
communicated disease in a way which may well carry a critical or reductive
force. Another poem, 'Upon my Lady Carlisle's Walking in Hampton Court
Garden' (pp. 30–2), simulates a 'dialogue' between Carew and Suckling, in
which quite delicately turned compliments from the former are capped by
earthier responses. For example, Carew is represented as praising her frag-
rance ('She threw rare perfumes all about', line 7); Suckling as dismissing
this ('I must confesse those perfumes (*Tom*) / I did not smell', lines 10–11).
Thus, the Countess of Carlisle, 'much admired for her beauty and wit by the
courtiers of Charles I',[30] though she is represented as constituting an object
of adoration by Carew, emerges in Suckling's responses as a reasonable and
accessible sexual target, already enjoyed by many (lines 43–9). The poem

simultaneously attacks a kind of sexual ideal and the poetic language associated with it.

That process of redefining Carew's perspective on love pervades Suckling's love lyrics. Sex is much overrated; the workers can produce enough
children for the economy to be kept up:

> Children then must be;
> So must bread too; but since there are enough
> Born to the drudgery, what need we plough?
> ('Against Fruition (I)', p. 37, lines 161–18)

As Low observes, the old sexual metaphor of ploughing receives an
additional charge from the 'scorn for the laborer' that Suckling implies.[31]
The reduction in effect offers a critique of the court's cult of love, and it
accords with the self-image of the young, rich tough which Suckling assidu-
ously projects. 'Proffered Love Rejected' (pp. 54–5; its French source
appears on p. 210) relates the passage of a relationship which begins 'not
four years ago' when he offered 'Forty crowns / To lie with her a night or
so' (lines 1–3), an offer which 'She' (she is never named) rejected; it ends in
the poet rejecting her when

> This present morning early she
> Forsooth came to my bed,
> And *gratis* there she offered me
> Her high-priz'd maidenhead.   (lines 21–4)

Other poems, original works, take a similar jaundiced or jaunty view; this,
after all, is a poet who enjoys women as much as a good game of bowls.

Richard Lovelace's published poems appeared in two volumes, *Lucasta*
(1649) and *Lucasta: Posthume Poems* (1659). Though in his own age his
verse was markedly less popular than Carew's or Suckling's – no further
edition appeared for over 150 years[32] – he conforms more closely than either
to the notion of the poet-in-arms. His reputation, rightly in my view, is now
on the ascendant.[33] His first book appeared in the summer after the execution of Charles I. It offers a stoutly partisan rehearsal of the values of the
Caroline court at war, together with a convincingly unified self-image of the
poet as warrior and lover. Lovelace's biographical credentials are not
perfect in that he seems not to have participated in the Civil War. By the
time of publication he had twice been incarcerated by Parliament, in 1642,
before the outbreak of hostilities, when in rather minatory fashion he had
presented a royalist petition on behalf of Kent, his county of residence, and
again in 1648, probably as a measure to tighten control of royalists then
living in London in preparation for the prosecution of the king. But all his

military service in the 1640s would seem to have been abroad, more or less in exile, though it is possible that this may reflect merely the terms on which he had been released from his first period of imprisonment. He had participated in the forces levied for the Bishops' Wars,[34] and his brother Francis had commanded the royalist forces in the abortive defence of Carmarthen in 1645, where a younger brother had been killed. The circumstances in which Lovelace died have been variously reported and interpreted, but he would certainly seem to have seriously damaged his (fairly limited) personal fortunes in the royalist interest.

The first *Lucasta* offers a coherent and attractive image of the warrior-lover. Two poems, 'To Lucasta, Going to the Wars' (p. 18) and 'To Althea, From Prison' (pp. 78–9), define the role perfectly. The former offers a timely military variant on the familiar valediction topos, ending with the classic cavalier sentiment 'I could not love thee (Deare) so much, / Lov'd I not Honour more'. The erotic relationship, premissed on a boundless commitment far beyond reason and calculated self-interest, parallels the diehard loyalist's devotion to his king. The second stanza shows how the very unpleasant nature of the military conflict is accommodated and, in some ways, set aside by Lovelace:

> True; a new Mistresse now I chase,
> The first Foe in the Field;
> And with a stronger Faith imbrace
> A Sword, a Horse, a Shield.

Carew at the end of 'To my friend G. N. from Wrest', as we have seen, invoked the familiar notion of hunting as 'th'embleme of warre'; Lovelace treats war as an emblem for hunting. 'Chase' implies the hunt, and it also implies that the enemy will be running away. Again, note the suggestion that this conflict is a single combat, and that it is conducted by knights on horseback. 'Shield' connotes the world of chivalry; the English cavalry of the Civil War period generally did not use them. Its retention here invokes an early feudal ethos, with its implications of a structured loyalty to one's lord or king. It effects, too, a distancing of the real horrors of battles like Marston Moor and Naseby. In place of the shattered limbs, the gaping gashes, the festering bullet-wounds, pillaging of the dead, and communal graves Lovelace offers a version of war as tourney.

'To Althea, From Prison' works to establish a memorable juxtaposition of sex and politics, expressed in something more closely resembling a paradox:

> Stone Walls doe not a Prison make,
> Nor I'ron bars a Cage;
> Mindes innocent and quiet take

> That for an Hermitage;
> If I have freedome in my Love,
> And in my soule am free;
> Angels alone that sore above,
> Injoy such Liberty.

The process by which defeated royalists of the property-owning classes came to terms with Parliament was called 'compounding'. It involved the payment of sometimes large proportions of one's property (one-tenth, one-third, or in the case of the worst 'malignants' the denial of any settlement short of total confiscation) and the giving of an undertaking not to bear arms again. Compounders were obliged to admit they were in the wrong.[35] Resistance to that project underlies Lovelace's poem. Though he is in prison, he still has the intellectual freedom of the undefeated, the freedom to believe uncompromised in his cause. It has, too, its compensations. The incarcerated royalists may, with 'flowing Cups', sing 'The sweetnes, Mercy, Majesty, / And glories of my KING'. Moreover, he is visited by his Althea; because he is spiritually undefeated he may still command her loyalty. In a poignant and attractive image he plays with her hair through the bars of his cell: when she comes 'To Whisper at the Grates', he lies 'tangled in her haire'. Unbraided hair had long in western erotic iconography functioned as the emblem of female unrestraint, a notion Lovelace rehearses himself in 'To Amarantha, that she would Dishevel her Hair' (pp. 20–1) ('Let it flye as unconfin'd / As its calme Ravisher, the winde').[36] Here it defines the piquant role of the cavalier warrior-lover.

The poem 'The Grass-hopper: To my Noble Friend, Mr Charles Cotton' (pp. 38–40) has stimulated more interest than the rest of his *œuvre*.[37] The precise and felicitous natural description of the insect is moralized into a reflection on its failure to secure itself against 'the Sickle' and 'Sharpe frosty fingers', which leads to a reflection on how we cavaliers can survive the eclipse of the royalist cause:

> Poore verdant foole! and now green Ice! thy Joys
> Large and as lasting, as thy Peirch of Grasse,
> Bid us lay in 'gainst Winter, Raine, and poize
> Their flouds, with an o'reflowing glasse.

The first five stanzas describe the grasshopper; the second five praise 'my Noble Friend' and celebrate the contemplative and withdrawn friendship which, fortified with Greek verse, a warm hearth and good wine, will let them 'create / A Genuine Summer in each others breast'. As 'To Althea, From Prison' ends in the definition of true freedom, so 'The Grass-hopper' ends by defining true riches: 'he / That wants himselfe, is poore indeed'.

Poems on animals are a striking feature of *Lucasta: Posthume Poems*, and they generally imply some larger political significance, albeit for the most part of a fairly vague or enigmatic kind. Collectively, they imply a movement from the optimistic voice of the poem on the grasshopper to something altogether gloomier. Thus, the two poems on snails (pp. 136–8) praised the lowest of creatures for its politic self-containment:

> But banisht, I admire his fate
> Since neither Ostracisme of State,
> Nor a perpetual exile,
> Can force this Virtue change his Soyl;
> For wheresoever he doth go,
> He wanders with his Country too.

The fate of the insect in 'A Fly caught in a Cobweb' (pp. 155–6) dismally reflects that of royalist survivors who, rather than finding a glorious end, are sucked dry by the compounding process, forced to yield up funds that will be used by the republicans in actions against other royalists. The fly could have died in the 'Majestick Ray', singed to death by coming too close to 'the noble Flame'; instead, it is 'become / Slave to the spawn of Mud and Lome'; it dies 'by degrees'; and 'now devour'd [is] like to be / A Net spun for [its] Familie'. The melancholy shift is easily explained. The jaunty defiance of the first *Lucasta* may well have been tenable while royalists could feed their hopes on the military campaigns of the late 1640s and early 1650s. After the battle of Worcester (1651), the defeat of successive royalist plots, and the establishment of Cromwell as Lord Protector, the royalist cause lost many of its hitherto diehard supporters; that Lovelace's defiance seems desperate or jaundiced or threadbare is scarcely surprising.

In the first *Lucasta* a libertine dimension had asserted the maintenance of the spirit of Suckling in an age of Puritan sexual asceticism which far surpassed the modesty of the Caroline court. Such asceticism found its ultimate expression in the Adultery Act of 1650. Among other measures this introduced the death penalty for adultery and three months in gaol for fornication (though sentences of such severity were rarely exacted).[38] Thus 'The Fair Beggar' (pp. 98–9), in which the poet offers alms in return for sexual favours ('I'll cover thee with mine owne selfe'), observes the same dubious ethic of Suckling's 'Proffered Love Rejected';[39] the fevered eroticism of 'To Amarantha, that she would Dishevel her Hair' has its parallels in Carew's 'Rapture'. But in the erotic poems of *Lucasta: Posthume Poems* the voice of the libertine becomes less secure and it is marked by a fragile sleaziness which sharply devalues sexual relationships as a compensation in times of war. 'Love Made in the First Age: To Chloris' (pp. 146–8), like 'A Rapture', is explicitly a fantasy, though one set, not in 'Elizium', but in some former golden age when 'Lads, indifferently did crop / A Flower, and a Maiden-head' and 'each did Tipple / Wine from the Bunch, Milk from the Nipple'. But Carew's poem ends with a sober ethical point, about the contradictory obligations of honour in Caroline society. Lovelace ends by admitting that his fantasy is a masturbatory reverie and that onanism offers more reliable comforts than an uncertain relationship with Chloris:

> Now, *CHLORIS*! miserably crave,
> The offer'd blisse you would not have;
>   Which evermore I must deny,
> Whilst ravish'd with these Noble Dreams,
> And crowned with mine own soft Beams,
>   Injoying of my self I lye.

So much for the cult of love. 'Elinda's Glove' (pp. 58–9) in the first *Lucasta* has the lover bestowing kisses on the apostrophized glove of his absent mistress. A corresponding poem, 'Her Muff' (pp. 128–9), in *Lucasta: Posthume Poems* begins with a rather sensuous contemplation of Lucasta's 'polish'd hands' in the 'shagg'd fur' of her muff; but it ends by asserting that, while such compliments have a place, he would prefer to contemplate her pudendum:[40]

> This for Lay-Lovers, that must stand at dore,
> Salute the threshold, and admire no more:
>   But I, in my Invention tough,
>   Rate not this outward bliss enough,
> But still contemplate must the hidden Muffe.

'Lay-Lovers' recalls the religion of love: Lovelace is love's priest, devoted utterly to the service of his mistress. The illusion lasts less than three lines.

Such poems mark the end of the great tradition of the English love lyric. The tough invention of the later Lovelace does not tolerate the delicate compliments and the received role of the selfless lover. A new depth of cynicism about interpersonal relationships displaces the cavalier abandon of Lovelace's first collection. We are close to the spirit of the Restoration verse of John Wilmot, Earl of Rochester, with its unflinching gaze at the grosser follies of the human animal.

NOTES

1 On Humphrey Moseley, see J. C. Reed, 'Humphrey Moseley, Publisher', *Oxford Bibliographical Society Proceedings and Papers* 2 (1927–30); Lois Potter, *Secret Rites and Secret Writing: Royalist Literature, 1641–1660* (Cambridge University

Press, 1989), pp. 20–2; and Thomas N. Corns, *Uncloistered Virtue: English Political Literature, 1640–1660* (Oxford: Clarendon Press, 1992), p. 61.

2 See, for example, Robert Herrick, 'A Pastoral upon the birth of Prince Charles [i.e., the future Charles II], Presented to the King, and Set by Mr Nic: Laniere', *Hesperides* (1648), p. 95.

3 Thomas Clayton (ed.), *The Works of Sir John Suckling: The Non-Dramatic Works* (Oxford: Clarendon Press, 1971), pp. xlvii–lxi.

4 Corns, *Uncloistered Virtue*, pp. 3–8.

5 John Milton, *Complete Prose Works*, ed. Don M. Wolfe et al. (New Haven: Yale University Press, 1953–82), vol. 3, pp. 380–1.

6 *Non-Dramatic Works*, p. 6. All quotations are from this edition.

7 *Hesperides*, p. 31.

8 Corns, *Uncloistered Virtue*, pp. 5–7.

9 On the ethos of the Caroline court, see Graham Parry, *The Seventeenth Century: The Intellectual and Cultural Context of English Literature* (London: Longman, 1989), especially chapters 1 and 2; and Kevin Sharpe, *Criticism and Compliment: The Politics of Literature in the England of Charles I* (Cambridge University Press, 1987), especially chapter 1.

10 Parry, *Seventeenth Century*, p. 10.

11 Sharpe, *Criticism and Compliment*, p. 13.

12 *The Poems of Thomas Carew with his Masque 'Coelum Britannicum*, ed. Rhodes Dunlap (1949; Oxford: Clarendon Press, 1964), pp. 74–7; all references are to this edition.

13 The poem is printed in *Poems of Carew*, pp. 207–8.

14 Stephen Orgel and Roy Strong, *Inigo Jones: The Theatre of the Stuart Court* (Berkeley and Los Angeles: Sotheby Parke Bernet and University of California Press: London, 1973), vol. 1, p. 480 (the masque appears on pp. 480–3; all references are to this edition).

15 Quoted by Orgel and Strong, *Inigo Jones* 2.479.

16 Joseph H. Summers, *The Heirs of Donne and Jonson* (London: Chatto and Windus, 1970), p. 73.

17 Earl Miner, *The Cavalier Mode from Jonson to Cotton* (Princeton University Press, 1971), p. 3.

18 Carew adapts the notion from Donne, as Dunlap notes (*Poems of Carew*, p. 244).

19 *Ibid.*, p. 242.

20 'To Penshurst', lines 62–3, *Ben Jonson*, ed. C. H. Herford, Percy Simpson, and Evelyn Simpson (Oxford: Clarendon Press, 1947), vol. 7, p. 95.

21 Martial, *Epigrams* 3.58.1, Loeb edition (London: Heinemann, 1925), 1.197.

22 On his early reputation, see Dunlap's account, *Poems of Carew*, pp. xlvi–xlix.

23 *Ibid.*, pp. 253–4, xliv–xlv, and illustration facing title page; poignantly, Cecilia died within two years.

24 See *ibid.*, pp. 236–7.

25 *Ibid.*, p. 256.

26 See *The Penguin Book of Renaissance Verse 1509–1659*, selected and intro. David Norbrook, ed. H. R. Woudhuysen (London: Allen Lane, 1992), where he is represented only by a sixteen-line love lyric; he fares better in *The New Oxford Book of Seventeenth-Century Verse*, ed. Alastair Fowler (Oxford University Press, 1991), where quite a few of his songs appear.

27 *Non-Dramatic Works*, pp. 71–6.
28 Michael P. Parker, '"All are not born (Sir) to the Bay": "Jack" Suckling, "Tom" Carew, and the Making of a Poet', *English Literary Renaissance* 12 (1982): 341–68; p. 368.
29 The term 'pox' was used contemporaneously of any sexually transmitted disease; though the symptoms described by Suckling more closely resemble those of gonorrhoea, Carew is usually represented as dying of or coming close to death through the final stages of syphilis. The diseases were not well distinguished in his own age, and of course he could well have contracted both.
30 *Non-Dramatic Works*, p. 238.
31 Anthony Low, *The Georgic Revolution* (Princeton University Press, 1985), p. 255.
32 On the textual history of his work, see *The Poems of Richard Lovelace*, ed. C. H. Wilkinson (Oxford: Clarendon Press, 1930), p. lxxii; all references are to this edition.
33 Norbrook (*Renaissance Verse*) and Fowler (*Seventeenth-Century Verse*) select marginally more poems from Lovelace than Carew.
34 See *Poems of Lovelace*, pp. xiii–lxxi, for an attempt to make sense of the rather incomplete life records; for a rather different view of his biography and its implication for criticism, see Gerald Hammond, 'Richard Lovelace and the Uses of Obscurity', Chatterton Lecture on Poetry, 1985, *Proceedings of the British Academy* 71 (1985): 203–34.
35 For an account of compounding and sequestration, see Paul H. Hardacre, *The Royalists during the English Revolution* (The Hague: Martinus Nijhoff, 1956), pp. 19–23; on its ideological implications, see Corns, *Uncloistered Virtue*, pp. 64–6.
36 For some pertinent remarks, see Gerald Hammond, *Fleeting Things: English Poets and Poems, 1616–1660* (Cambridge, Mass.: Harvard University Press, 1990), pp. 341–4.
37 See, for example, Achsah Guibbory, *The Map of Time: Seventeenth-Century English Literature and Ideas of Pattern in History* (Urbana: University of Illinois Press, 1986), pp. 273–4; Low, *Georgic Revolution*, pp. 250–1; Raymond A. Anselment, *Loyalist Resolve: Patient Fortitude in the English Civil War* (Newark, London, and Toronto: University of Delaware Press and Associated University Presses, 1988), pp. 107–8.
38 On this legislation and its cultural implications, see Keith Thomas, 'The Puritans and Adultery: The Act of 1650 Reconsidered', in *Puritans and Revolutionaries*, ed. Donald Pennington and Keith Thomas (Oxford: Clarendon Press, 1978), pp. 257–82.
39 Hammond sees interesting connections between 'Profer'd Love Rejected' and 'Love Made in the First Age', *Fleeting Things*, pp. 317–18.
40 Hammond, *Fleeting Things*, pp. 308–9, links these poems in a rather different interpretation, which regards 'Elinda's Glove' as erotic *double entendre*, if I understand him correctly. He also argues that 'muff' in Lovelace's poem is an early example of the use of the word in the slang sense of 'female genitalia', a meaning it certainly had by the end of the century ('Lovelace', pp. 228–9). This reading I elsewhere dispute (*Uncloistered Virtue*, pp. 247–8); clearly, the word is used metaphorically.

FURTHER READING

Anselment, Raymond A., *Loyalist Resolve: Patient Fortitude in the English Civil War* (Newark, London and Toronto: University of Delaware Press and Associated University Presses, 1988)

Benet, Diana, 'Carew's Monarchy of Wit', in *'The Muses Common-weale': Poetry and Politics in the Seventeenth Century*, ed. Claude J. Summers and Ted-Larry Pebworth (Columbia: University of Missouri Press, 1980), pp. 80–91

Clayton, Thomas (ed.), *Cavalier Poets: Selected Poems* (Oxford University Press, 1978)

The Works of Sir John Suckling: The Non-Dramatic Works (Oxford: Clarendon Press, 1971)

Guibbory, Achsah, *The Map of Time: Seventeenth-Century English Literature and Ideas of Pattern in History* (Urbana and Chicago: University of Illinois Press, 1986)

Hammond, Gerald, *Fleeting Things: English Poets and Poems 1616–1660* (Cambridge, Mass.: Harvard University Press, 1990)

Low, Anthony, *The Georgic Revolution* (Princeton University Press, 1985)

Miner, Earl, *The Cavalier Mode from Jonson to Cotton* (Princeton University Press, 1971)

Parker, Michael P., ' "All are not born (Sir) to the Bay"; "Jack" Suckling, "Tom" Carew, and the Making of a Poet', *English Literary Renaissance* 12 (1982): 341–68

Parry, Graham, *The Seventeenth Century: The Intellectual and Cultural Context of English Literature, 1603–1700* (London: Longman, 1989)

Sharpe, Kevin, *Criticism and Compliment: The Politics of Literature in the England of Charles I* (Cambridge University Press, 1987)

Summers, Joseph H., *The Heirs of Donne and Jonson* (London: Chatto and Windus, 1970)

II

MICHAEL WILDING

John Milton: the early works

It would be difficult and indeed absurd to approach Milton's poetry without an awareness of his revolutionary commitment. One of the foremost polemicists against the bishops, the monarchy, and the rest of the baggage of the old order, he became Latin secretary to the republican Council of State and official propagandist of the new regime with his great Defences of the English people. After the Restoration his life was in danger, he was imprisoned and some of the books that he wrote were burned.[1]

Yet when we turn to his first book of *Poems*, the political, the revolutionary are not the immediate impression we receive.[2] Certainly the volume includes early work dating from before the revolutionary years. Yet the collection was published in 1645, after the conclusion of the first phase of the Civil War and at a point when Milton had already published polemical and increasingly radical prose tracts – *Of Reformation in England* (1641), *Of Prelatical Episcopacy* (1641), *The Doctrine and Discipline of Divorce* (1643), *Areopagitica* (1644).[3]

It is possible to extract revolutionary sentiments from the poems. But the dominant concern is poetry itself and the pursuit of the proper subject of poetry. What is poetry about, what are its concerns, what are its themes, what are its possibilities and limitations?

Throughout Milton's early poems the subjects of poetry, music, and song are recurrent. They are there in the topics – 'At a Solemn Music' – in the types of poet – Shakespeare, Lycidas, Orpheus – and in the images of the sirens and the music of the spheres. Arthur Barker remarked of the recurrence of the music of the spheres in Milton's poetry that 'the force with which this idea struck Milton's imagination is indicated by the fact that from the "Ode [on the Morning of Christ's Nativity]" to "Lycidas" he was almost incapable of writing on a serious subject without introducing the music'.[4] The seven spheres of the creation rotated around each other: mounted on each was a siren who sang and the interwoven notes of the sphere inhabiting sirens created this ideal music that, since the Fall, is no longer audible to humanity. Importantly, the music of the spheres is anthro-pomorphized: for Milton it is not a mechanical music produced by the spheres' rotation. The sirens actively sing it. And their singing it involves words, not only music. The music of the spheres is presented as ideal, tran-scendent song; but this ideal music has a verbal content. The verbal com-ponent is important for Milton as it allows for a parallel with poetry; it is not wordless music. 'On the Morning of Christ's Nativity' presents us with the shepherds 'Simply chatting in a rustic row':

> When such music sweet
> Their hearts and ears did greet,
> As never was by mortal finger struck,
> Divinely-warbled voice
> Answering the stringed noise,
> As all their souls in blissful rapture took.   (lines 93–8)[5]

The voice answers the strings. There is a duality, which we find again in 'At a Solemn Music':

> Blest pair of *Sirens*, pledges of Heav'n's joy,
> Sphere-born harmonious Sisters, Voice and Verse,
> Wed your divine sounds, and mixt power employ.   (lines 1–3)

The two sirens here represent voice and verse: that is, they represent music and words, song and substance. Milton is not celebrating a transcendental condition of musical abstraction, but stressing the duality of music and words, beauty and substance, form and content. The solemn music contains a message:

> the Cherubic host in thousand choirs
> Touch their immortal Harps of golden wires,
> With those just Spirits that wear victorious Palms,
> Hymns devout and holy Psalms
> Singing everlastingly.   (lines 12–16)

Milton's concept of this perfection is of a musical experience that is also a verbal experience. The beauty of the musical is wed to the meaning of the words.[6] These are hymns, psalms, songs. The collection of these early poems contains translations of two psalms which serve as adducible evi-dence so there can be no doubt. The psalms are content laden. They are about something.

Not only is this ideal model of earthly poetry content laden, it is also actively consciousness changing. Divine poetry is a practical poetry, con-cerned with changing the human condition:

> Ring out ye Crystal spheres
> Once bless our human ears,   (lines 125–6)

the poet implores in 'On the Morning of Christ's Nativity':

> For if such holy Song
> Enwrap our fancy long,
>   Time will run back, and fetch the age of gold,
> And speckl'd vanity
> Will sicken soon and die,
>   And leprous sin will melt from earthly mold,
> And Hell itself will pass away,
> And leave her dolorous mansions to the peering day.
>
> Yea, Truth and Justice then
> Will down return to men.   (lines 133–42)

Milton's Sirens, it can be seen, are very different from the sirens of Tzvetan Todorov:

> The Sirens have the most beautiful voices in the world, and their song is the most beautiful – without being very different from the bard's ... one cannot leave the bard so long as he sings; the Sirens are like a bard who never stops singing. The song of the Sirens, then, is a higher degree of poetry, of the poet's art. Here we must note especially Odysseus' description of it. What is this irresistible song about, which unfailingly makes those who hear it die, so great is its allure? It is a song about itself. The Sirens say only one thing: that they are singing.[7]

This is the anti-type of the Miltonic sirens and Miltonic poetry.

But this is, of course, all highly conceptual. Milton cannot hear the music of the spheres any more than we can; it is inaudible to fallen humanity. He can only describe the idea of it, not even paraphrase it. The existence of the music of the spheres is affirmed in 'On the Morning of Christ's Nativity' and is the sustained subject of seven stanzas. But what it is can only be gestured at. It has a message, it alters consciousness, it is not a song about itself. But the problem remains for the poet who wishes to approach it of what the proper message is. The poet experiences the poetic impulse, but to what should it be applied? What is poetry for, what is poetry about, what is the proper subject of poetry? This is the concern that runs through Milton's first volume. There is no doubt that the divine music be wed to words: that is never in dispute. But the recurrent anxiety is the search for the suitable theme.

It is remarkable how many of the poems in this first collection were written for specific occasions, written in response to invitations, commis-

sions, opportunities.[8] Whether Milton was invited to contribute 'On Shakespeare' to the Second Folio of Shakespeare's plays, or saw and seized an
opportunity is unknown: but it is certainly a poem that appeared alongside
other tributes, as did 'Lycidas'. The epitaphs on the Marchioness of Winchester and on the Cambridge carrier Hobson are likewise occasional
pieces. The poems on Christ's nativity, the passion, and the circumcision
may not be occasional in the sense of having been commissioned, but they
mark occasions in the Christian year. They are self-commissioned by a poet
who saw his art as something to be applied to a fit subject.

Not everything in the collection is occasional, of course; but this occasional note is dominant. This is clear if we contrast it with the alternative
model of 'sweetest *Shakespeare*, fancy's child', whom we see in 'L'Allegro'
'warble his native Wood-notes wild' (lines 133–4). This may not be a wholly
accurate characterization of Shakespeare's procedure, but it certainly
presents an anti-type to Milton's own practice. His 1645 volume is not one
that offers a spontaneous expression of powerful emotion. These are not
lyric outpourings. Even the sonnets are frequently responses to events and
occasions – the approaching army, a birthday. The poems arise when an
occasion or opportunity presents itself, when there is a function for the poet.

It is necessary to stress this concern with the proper subject and occasion of
poetry that Milton shows before discussing that recurrent concern of his
poetry: the concern with poetry itself. These are consistently poems about
poetry. Poetry and the figure of the poet recur time and time again. But this is
not that simple preoccupation beloved of theorists of postmodernism, poetic
self-referentialism. There is a strong self-referentialism, but this is only one of
the dialectical poles of Milton's art: against it stands the search for the proper
subject. Poetry's concern with itself is an endemic feature of poetry, and something that the poet has to keep in place: this self-concern with the art has to be
wed to a concern with content – with the world and the divine.

The opening poem of the collection, 'On the Morning of Christ's Nativity', opens with the poet's concern with his poetic art:

> Say Heav'nly Muse, shall not thy sacred vein
> Afford a present to the Infant God?
> Hast thou no verse, no hymn, or solemn strain,
> To welcome him to this his new abode ...   (lines 15–18)

These are not the very first lines. The poet is not that narcissistically self-
preoccupied. The first lines establish the time in the Christian year:

> This is the Month, and this the happy morn
> Wherein the Son of Heav'n's eternal King,
> Of wedded Maid, and Virgin Mother born ...   (lines 1–3)

Nonetheless, the poet's concern with poetry is rapidly introduced. The poet questions the muse, discussing the possibility of writing an appropriate poem for the occasion. The setting is of the poet meditating on his art. He sees:

> The Star-led Wizards haste with odours sweet:
> O run, prevent them with thy humble ode,
> And lay it lowly at his blessed feet;
> Have thou the honor first, thy Lord to greet,
> And join thy voice unto the Angel Choir.   (lines 23–7)

And then we are offered 'The Hymn'.

'On the Morning of Christ's Nativity' is not properly characterized by its usual short title, 'The Nativity Ode'. The poem is twofold: the four stanzas of invocation and poetic self-consciousness, followed by the twenty-seven stanzas of 'the hymn', the 'humble ode' (line 24). The 'ode' is prefaced by the poet's concern with his poetic art, which is also a part of the poem. The 'humble ode' is offered as an example of the poetic concern, a tentative, 'humble' possibility. There is a similar twofold structure in 'Lycidas', the poem which closes the English, non-dramatic section of the collection, where a concluding octave places the 'monody':

> Thus sang the uncouth Swain to th'Oaks and rills,
> While the still morn went out with Sandals gray;
> He touch't the tender stops of various Quills,
> With eager thought warbling his *Doric* lay.   (lines 186–9)

The 'doric lay' of lament is followed by the placing, self-referential lines of the full poem in which the nature of the lay is announced and distanced. We are offered in these opening and closing items not innocent poems, self-contained, unselfconscious effusions, but two works concerned to indicate and place their own nature and strategies. The 'humble ode' and 'doric lay' are framed by the poet's highly self-conscious dramatization of their situation. These are poems within poems. But they are not self-referential poems concerned only with themselves and their art. That self-concern is there; but the ode and lay have their own subjects – Christ's nativity, Lycidas' death.

With 'The Passion' we have a variant on this procedure. Here there is no framed ode or lay. All we have is the statement of intention:

> For now to sorrow must I tune my song,
> And set my Harp to notes of saddest woe.   (lines 8–9)

But the announced song is never delivered. A concluding note tells us 'This Subject the Author finding to be above the years he had, when he wrote it, and nothing satisfied with what was begun, left it unfinisht.'

It may well be that at some level the author was 'nothing satisfied with what was begun,' but at another level the failure is a mark of the poem's success. How could a mortal poet ever replicate Christ's passion? The enormity of the theme is such that it transcends human poetic ability, however many years the poet might have. There is an appropriate inevitability about the way the poet breaks off. It is a large-scale version of that device of classical rhetoric, *anacolouthon*, that Milton exploits in the first speech in *Paradise Lost* when Beelzebub first addresses Satan: 'If thou beest he; But O how fall'n !' (1.84) Beelzebub breaks off, the opening sentence uncompleted; it is a traditional device for expressing passion.

Is 'The Passion' incomplete? Or was it conceived as a broken fragment? The poem is even more than 'On the Morning of Christ's Nativity' and 'Lycidas' preoccupied with the problem of writing a poem. Its theme is the difficulty of poetically comprehending the passion rather than the passion itself. It opens with a remembrance of the earlier poem on the nativity:

> Erewhile of Music and Ethereal mirth,
> Wherewith the stage of Air and Earth did ring,
> And joyous news of heav'nly Infant's birth,
> My muse with Angels did divide to sing;
> But headlong joy is ever on the wing,
>   In Wintry solstice like the short'n'd light
> Soon swallow'd up in dark and long outliving night. (lines 1–7)

This first stanza sums up the poem's procedure: a reference to previous achievement, and then joy 'swallow'd up in dark and long outliving night', the darkness that takes over from the poetic impulse and engulfs the attempt. This is the poem in miniature.

The second stanza announces intention – 'For now to sorrow must I tune my song' (line 8) – and again concludes in incompletion, failure: 'labors huge and hard, too hard for human wight' (line 14). Christ's labours are implicitly paralleled with the poetic labour on the theme of Christ's labours – 'too hard for human wight'. There is an appropriate poetic self-reference, a symmetry of proclaimed theme and poetic methodology. The inadequacy of poet and poetry is the foregrounded theme:

> These latter scenes confine my roving verse,
> To this Horizon is my *Phoebus* bound.   (lines 22–3)

> My sorrows are too dark for day to know:
>   The leaves should all be black whereon I write,
> And letters where my tears have washt, a wannish white.
>
>   (lines 33–5)

The verbal tenses become conditional, hypothetical:

> Yet on the soft'ned Quarry would I score
> My plaining verse as lively as before;
>   For sure so well instructed are my tears,
> That they would fitly fall in order'd Characters.
>
> Or should I thence hurried on viewless wing,
> Take up a weeping on the Mountains wild.   (lines 46–51)

This is not like the achieved poem on the nativity that he can confidently look back to. Nor is it the stumbling approach to the passion with which he began. Now the concern is what I *would* write (if I could), what I *should* do to write (if it were possible).

Significantly, whereas in 'On the Morning of Christ's Nativity' and 'Lycidas' Milton invoked the muse for help, he does not do so here. He writes of having had the assistance of the muses in stanza 1, but makes no attempt to invoke them here. It is as if from the beginning he is committed to failure; or committed to demonstrating that the merely mortal poetic skills must fail on such a theme, just as mere mankind would fail in such a situation as the passion. So we have the mortal song, like the prefatory stanzas to the 'humble ode' on Christ's nativity, or the concluding octave to 'Lycidas'. But the divine song remains an absence, the inexpressible. It is a theme 'too hard for human wight'.

This thematic absence is given confirmation by the poem that follows in the 1645 edition, 'On Time'. The subject again is absence, what is lost and erased by time: 'glut thyself with what thy womb devours' (line 4). But here absence is turned back on itself. Time's capacity for destruction provides the triumphant conclusion in which time will destroy itself and erase its own destructive powers:

> When once our heav'nly-guided soul shall climb,
> Then all this Earthy grossness quit,
> Attir'd with Stars, we shall for ever sit,
>   Triumphing over Death, and Chance, and thee
> O Time.   (lines 19–23)

The poem concludes with that affirmation of resurrection and eternal life that 'The Passion' 'should have' reached, that is the ultimate purpose and meaning of Christ's passion.

The music of the spheres is a recurrent image in Milton's early poems. But it is not an accessible model for the mortal poet. As a touchstone of an ideal, or as a model of what might apocalyptically be regained, it has its practical function. But for an immediate model of poetic practice. Milton had to turn to other concepts. The poet-prophet is one that particularly appealed.[9] The seven stanzas dealing with the music of the spheres and the divine song of the heavenly choir in 'On the Morning of Christ's Nativity' are succeeded by seven stanzas (19–25) on the prophetic mode.[10] Again they are in the context of negation. Just as 'wisest Fate says no, / This must not yet be so' (lines 149–50), to the restorative effect of the music of the spheres, so the oracles are denied their oracular powers: 'The Oracles are dumb' (line 173). These are the classical oracles, superseded by the new testament of Christ. To devote seven stanzas to the silencing of the oracles, to the failure of oracular power, is consciously paradoxical. But this emphasis on loss, this powerful negation, nonetheless firmly establishes the idea of the prophetic as a one-time human possibility. The new prophets, the new prophet-poets, will draw their inspiration from Christian divinity, not from Apollo at Delphos:

> *Apollo* from his shrine
> Can no more divine,
>   With hollow shriek the steep of *Delphos* leaving.
> No nightly trance, or breathed spell,
> Inspires the pale-ey'd Priest from the prophetic cell.
>
> (lines 176–80)

It is a beautiful, haunting picture of loss. The failure of inspiration, the loss of poetic powers through death, the failure of achievement in the passing of time, were themes that powerfully engaged Milton. The anxiety of non-performance inspired his most memorable early performances – here, in 'Lycidas', in 'On Time', and in Sonnet 7, 'How soon hath Time, the subtle thief of youth'. There is a paradox here, a paradox that in the Christian context is, of course, no paradox. Classical inspiration may now be lost forever: but the death of the classical gods, or at least their defeat, is at the same time the moment of the triumph of the Christian. It is a type of the central Christian mystery, the resurrection. The Christian poet will be a better prophet than any of those who went before.

And so, with a more than witty self-referentialism, at the moment of writing about prophetic powers, Milton achieves prophecy. The parade of the defeated, superseded gods and priests is the parade of the defeated Catholics, extirpated by the Reformation, and of the Anglican bishops, disestablished by the English Revolution, and the ejected corrupted clergy:

> In vain with timbrel'd Anthems dark
> The sable-stoled Sorcerers bear his worship Ark.
>
> (lines 219–20)

Priests, anthems, sable stoles: these apply not only to the classical world but to the immediate context. But the Anglican bishops were not removed until 1642, and Milton wrote these lines – as is pointedly noted after the title of the poem, in 1629. The inclusion of the date of composition in the title is important; it demonstrates that he had achieved the power of prophecy. In the act of writing about the superseded classical prophetic oracles, he attained a divine pre-vision of the defeat of the corrupted clergy that was to come. It is a self-referentialism that transcends the limitations of the self-referential and reaches outward to society. In the poem within the poem he writes about types of the poet; and in writing of the prophetic type he attains prophetic powers himself.

These same powers are achieved in 'Lycidas', as he spells out in the head-note to the poem: it 'by occasion foretells the ruin of our corrupted Clergy then in their height'.

> 'How well could I have spar'd for thee, young swain,
> Enough of such as for their bellies' sake,
> Creep and intrude and climb into the fold?
> Of other care they little reck'ning make,
> Than how to scramble at the shearers' feast,
> And shove away the worthy bidden guest;
> Blind mouths! that scarce themselves know how to hold
> A Sheep-hook, or have learn'd aught else the least
> That to the faithful Herdman's art belongs!
> What recks it them? What need they? They are sped'.
>
> (lines 113–22)

It is one of the great impassioned political tirades in English poetry, 'an expression of the same spirit which had been long making itself heard in the Puritan pulpit and which was at the moment clamoring in the reckless pamphlets of Prynne and Lilburne', as William Haller put it.[11] And the prophecy is there in the retribution threatened, that was meted out in the revolution with the abolition of the bishops and the ejection of clergy:

> 'But that two-handed engine at the door
> Stands ready to smite once, and smite no more.'   (lines 130–1)

It is not an isolated digression in its preoccupations. The political note is there from the very beginning of 'Lycidas', the opening phrase 'Yet once more' bringing an apocalyptic threat from the Epistle to the Hebrews 12:25–7, 'now he hath promised, saying, Yet once more I shake not the earth only, but also heaven. And this word, Yet once more, signifieth the removing of those things that are shaken, as of things that are made, that those things which cannot be shaken may remain.'[12] Imminent social upheaval, the world turned upside down, is proclaimed immediately. The later request

'Look homeward Angel now' (line 163) carries a further radical implication: St Michael is implored to turn away from facing Spain, the traditional Catholic enemy whose armada had been defeated fifty years earlier, and to 'look homeward' at the reactionary enemy within – the Laudian church and the Stuart attempt at absolutist rule.[13] 'Lycidas' ends with an allusion to Revelation 7:17, 'wipe away all tears from their eyes', an implication of apocalyptic change shortly to come in the society at large, an implication reinforced in the poem's final line, 'tomorrow to fresh Woods, and Pastures new' (line 193). It is a vision of social hope, a determinedly positive ending.

As well as the 'corrupted Clergy', the speech denounces those other figures categorizable as bad shepherds. Bad academics are surely included: academics necessarily took holy orders, and the context of Cambridge with the shared studies of Lycidas and 'the uncouth Swain', and Camus's speech, firmly indicate such a context. At the same time, bad poets are indicted.

> 'And when they list, their lean and flashy songs
> Grate on their scrannel Pipes of wretched straw.' (lines 123–4)

Although the revolutionary indictment of the 'corrupted Clergy' is the fore-grounded reading, thanks to Milton's headnote, the political does not exclude the poetic.[14] Indeed, the poetic and political are inseparable. The poets are bad poets for the same reason the clergy are bad clergy and the academics are bad academics – their words lack substance. They deliver not religious or political truths, but empty wind that inflates and sickens their listeners:

> 'The hungry Sheep look up, and are not fed,
> But swoln with wind, and the rank mist they draw,
> Rot inwardly, and foul contagion spread.'   (lines 125–7)

'L'Allegro' and 'Il Penseroso' of all the poems in the 1645 volume are the closest to the lyric expression of mood and emotion. They have always been curiously resistant to interpretation.[15] After we have pointed to their contrasting moods, what else can be said of them? Indeed, even to characterize their 'moods' is difficult: what English words translate their titles?

They share with the other poems of the volume, however, the preoccu-pation with poetry and the subject of poetry. This component gradually reveals itself. Just before the mid-point of 'L'Allegro' 'the Milkmaid singeth blithe' (line 65),

> And every Shepherd tells his tale
> Under the Hawthorn in the dale.   (lines 67–8)

As evening comes on folk tales are told:

> Then to the Spicy Nut-brown Ale,
> With stories told of many a feat,
> How *Faery Mab* the junkets eat;
> She was pincht and pull'd, she said,
> And he, by Friar's Lantern led,
> Tells how the drudging *Goblin* sweat
> To earn his Cream-bowl duly set.   (lines 100–6)

When these tales are done, we move to more literary creations:

> Such sights as youthful Poets dream
> On Summer eves by haunted stream.
> Then to the well-trod stage anon,
> If *Jonson's* learned Sock be on,
> Or sweetest *Shakespeare*, fancy's child,
> Warble his native Wood-notes wild.
> And ever against eating Cares,
> Lap me in soft *Lydian* Airs,
> Married to immortal verse.   (lines 129–37)

The poem ends with a figure recurrent in the Miltonic pantheon, that type of the poet, Orpheus:

> Untwisting all the chains that tie
> The hidden soul of harmony;
> That Orpheus' self may heave his head
> From golden slumber on a bed
> Of heapt *Elysian* flow'rs, and hear
> Such strains as would have won the ear
> Of *Pluto*, to have quite set free
> His half-regain'd *Eurydice*.
> These delights if thou canst give,
> Mirth, with thee I mean to live.   (lines 143–52)

'These delights' have by the poem's end become quite clearly defined as the delights of poetry itself.

'Il Penseroso' likewise reveals a preoccupation with the poetic arts:

> And join with thee calm Peace and Quiet,
> Spare Fast, that oft with gods doth diet,
> And hears the Muses in a ring
> Aye round about *Jove's* Altar sing.   (lines 45–8)

The absent song of the nightingale is invoked, and though it remains absent it is nonetheless evoked into hypothetical being, into literary being. Again it is a play of absence, the bird unheard, the poet unseen:

> Sweet Bird that shunn'st the noise of folly,
> Most musical, most melancholy!
> Thee Chantress oft the Woods among,
> I woo to hear thy Even-Song;
> And missing thee, I walk unseen
> On the dry smooth-shaven Green.   (lines 61–6)

At the centre of 'Il Penseroso' is the poetic tower, site of mystical communion and poetic creation, and a creation linked with mystical divinatory understanding, prophetic powers:

> Or let my Lamp at midnight hour,
> Be seen in some high lonely Tow'r,
> Where I may oft outwatch the *Bear*,
> With thrice great *Hermes*, or unsphere
> The spirit of *Plato* to unfold
> What Worlds, or what vast Regions hold
> The immortal mind that hath forsook
> Her mansion in this fleshly nook.   (lines 85–92)

Rapidly we move on to 'Gorgeous Tragedy' (line 97), 'the tale of *Troy* divine' (line 100) and, yet once more, Orpheus:

> Or bid the soul of *Orpheus* sing
> Such notes as, warbled to the string,
> Drew Iron tears down *Pluto's* cheek,
> And made Hell grant what Love did seek.   (lines 105–8)

It is, notice, once again an affective, effective poetry. Orpheus's song achieves something.[16]

The survey of poetic possibility is extensive and comprehensive. There are the 'great Bards' (line 116), 'Anthems clear' (lines 163) and finally as the poem's conclusion, the poet-prophet:

> Where I may sit and rightly spell
> Of every Star that Heav'n doth shew,
> And every Herb that sips the dew;
> Till old experience do attain
> To something like Prophetic strain.
> These pleasures *Melancholy* give,
> And I with thee will choose to live.   (lines 170–6)

The presence of Hermes and Plato at the centre of 'Il Penseroso' is emphatic and serious. There is no lack of conventionally literary reference in these twin poems. But for Milton the true literary needs more than the literary. The poet must know the literary, and his work is steeped in allusion and reference. The mention of the bards reminds us that the training for the bards was a committal to memory of the entire bardic tradition. But as well as the literary, the poet must also have knowledge, divine knowledge.[17] There is no point in being a poet unless you have something to say, unless the literary skills are married to content. Technique is essential but not an end in itself. Plato might seem an odd inclusion for those whose immediate association is of Plato's excluding poets from the Republic. But the Plato the seventeenth century loved was the Plato of the *Phaedrus*, not the political but the spiritual philosopher. Plato and Hermes Trismegistus are here as sources of spiritual wisdom. More than that: they are guides for access to spiritual insight by meditation and spiritual communion:

> And of those *Daemons* that are found
> In fire, air, flood, or underground,
> Whose power hath a true consent
> With Planet, or with element.   (lines 93–6)

For all the knowledge of authorities and tradition, finally the poet needs inspiration, the cooperation of the muses. It is a traditional belief, of course. But this commitment to spiritual inspiration is absolutely subversive of traditional authority. To draw inspiration from the muse rather than from the library and the rulebook is to reject authority and the rules. Inspiration became the ideology of the radicals during the revolutionary period. A commitment to being moved by spirit was a mark of the radically subversive. After the Restoration the poets of the new order like Dryden, Davenant, and Butler were concerned to mock, discredit, and dismiss the idea of the muses. Milton's commitment to meditative insight here, and to the muses and divine inspiration throughout his poetic production, can too readily be misread as part of the traditional baggage of ancient poetry, unthought, conventional. It is a tradition, certainly, but it is a tradition consciously thought through and chosen, and in firm opposition to official authority and convention.[18]

The recurrence of 'L'Allegro' and 'Il Penseroso' of the bardic, the dramatic, the epic, the folk tale, the folk song, and high anthem identifies the theme of these twin poems as the poetic itself, the 'poetic' standing as shorthand for the range of oral and literary arts. The contrasting moods are the contrasting moods of inspiration, the sources of creativity – bubbling-over creative joy, simmering, brooding, creative melancholy. What is rehearsed is a list of possible topics for poetic treatment. Milton's manuscript lists of possible subjects for verse have survived. These two poems are no less lists, résumés of potential themes, catalogues of possibility. But characteristically this centralizing of the concern of poetry is outward reaching: the themes of poetry are the themes of life. The catalogue of subjects is in itself an inventory of existence.

The scenes of 'Merry England' – and the poems have become touchstones of the literary treatment of the idyllically English – are scenes for poetry, and the poetic, as always with Milton, leads into the political. The celebration of human activity, honest labour, is as present as the celebration of the possible poetic. This is a portrait of English rural activity that recognizes people at work – shepherd, ploughman, milkmaid, mower.[19] It is the pastoral of productive labour, not of literary evasion. But the absent song of the nightingale should alert us to significant absences. In this catalogue of poetic themes, certain themes are excluded. This rural England contains no maypoles, morris dancing, church wakes, there is none of the Stuart programme of social control that was enshrined in the *Book of Sports*.[20] There are no feasts, markets, wassails, skimmingtons, bear-baitings, mince pies, or plum porridge. Yet in no way is it bleakly, dourly 'puritan' in that joyless, repressive connotation of the term. There is song, dance, music, theatre, poetry, leisure. 'Lycidas' makes its political statement by the denunciation of the corrupted clergy. 'L'Allegro' and 'Il Penseroso' make their political statements by presenting a beautiful and idyllic rural life in which the Stuart social controls are splendidly absent. It is a vision of freedom in that regard. 'Sweet Liberty' is invoked in 'L'Allegro' alongside 'Mirth' (lines 35–7).

The absent nightingale is similarly significant. We are not offered songs of tragic love, sado-masochistic fables from Marie de France, courtly amours, adventures, adulteries, and retributions. The pastoral presented is not an eroticized pastoral. The milkmaids are not represented in sexual dalliance. The dawn is not an occasion for the aubade of the lovers' parting. The whole tradition of erotic poetry, so recently reasserted for Milton's contemporaries by the publication of John Donne's *Poems* (1633) is absent here.

It is a significant absence, and it is reintroduced as an absence again when the poet considers other poetic possibilities in 'Lycidas':

> Alas! What boots it with uncessant care
> To tend the homely slighted Shepherd's trade,
> And strictly meditate the thankless Muse?
> Were it not better done as others use,
> To sport with *Amaryllis* in the shade,
> Or with the tangles of *Neaera's* hair?   (lines 64–9)

There is a typical Miltonic ambiguity or duality here. Writing serious poetry is put up as an opposition to engaging in sexual adventures. But there is also another opposition. 'To sport with *Amaryllis* in the shade, / Or with the tangles of *Neaera's* hair' suggests, as well as adventures, the practice of the literary erotic. The complexities and subtleties of verse production, the games playing of shaded meaning to be decoded, the ambiguities and innuendoes to be disentangled are all implied here. The temptation is not only the simple temptation of lived sexuality, but the intertwined temptation of writing erotic poetry, in contrast with 'the homely slighted Shepherd's trade' which can be read as a metaphor for unpornographic pastoral and religious poetry. The rejection of eroticized pastoral, the rejection of the celebration of sexual adventure in verse is consistent in the practice of this first volume of Milton's poems; and it is spelled out in the contemptuous dismissal of the 'serenate, which the starv'd lover sings / To his proud fair, best quitted with disdain' in *Paradise Lost* (4.769–70).

Rejecting the erotic, Milton moves directly to the traditional motivation for poetry, Fame:

> *Fame* is the spur that the clear spirit doth raise
> (That last infirmity of Noble mind)
> To scorn delights, and live laborious days;
> But the fair Guerdon when we hope to find,
> And think to burst out into sudden blaze,
> Comes the blind *Fury* with th'abhorred shears,
> And slits the thin-spun life.   (lines 70–6)

But the fame topos is given a striking shift. Instead of the poet conferring fame on the subject – as in Sonnet 7 – here fame becomes the poet's motivation for writing the poem. It is presented as an 'infirmity', the disabling egotistic self-preoccupation of the poet, concerned with the reader's response to the poem and not with the proper subject and motivation.

Self-referentialism is applied here in a positive way, as self-inquisition. The poet's concern with writing a poem to secure fame for the poet is sardonically interrogated. Is this the proper motive? Is this a good motive? The fate of the poet Lycidas cut short in youth provokes the poet to question the value of writing for fame: what is the point when you won't be around to revel in it?

The answer is rapidly presented:

> '*Fame* is no plant that grows on mortal soil,
> Nor in the glistering foil
> Set off to th'world, nor in broad rumor lies,
> But lives and spreads aloft by those pure eyes
> And perfect witness of all-judging *Jove*;
> As he pronounces lastly on each deed,
> Of so much fame in Heav'n expect thy meed.' (lines 78–84)

Poetry is written for divine judgement. The apocalyptic note recurrent throughout 'Lycidas' is here brought into relationship with the recurrent concern with poetry. The final judgement will be applied to everyone. Just as corrupt rulers and corrupt clergy will be on trial when the divine 'pronounces lastly' (line 83), so will corrupt poets. The proper subject of poetry is a subject that will be acceptable to the divine. That is why the problem of the subject of poetry is so important, why poetry is ceaselessly interrogated in Milton's poetry. It is of a piece with the concern of Sonnet 7 and of that later great sonnet 'On his Blindness'; correct self-analysis is not the simple egotistical preoccupation with achieving fame, but with interrogating life and poetry in the expectation of judgement in 'my great task Master's eye' (Sonnet 7, line 14).

Poetic possibility is a dominant concern of 'Lycidas', appropriately enough since the subject of the elegy, Edward King, had written poetry:[21]

> Who would not sing for *Lycidas*? he knew
> Himself to sing, and build the lofty rhyme.   (lines 10–11)

The image of Orpheus is appropriately present yet again:

> What could the Muse herself that *Orpheus* bore,
> The Muse herself, for her enchanting son
> Whom Universal nature did lament,
> When by the rout that made the hideous roar,
> His goary visage down the stream was sent,
> Down the swift *Hebrus* to the *Lesbian* shore?   (lines 58–63)

Orpheus is the touchstone reference for the poet, and also of the poet's fate.[22] This is what happens to true poets. True poetry has the power of prophecy, both telling the future and denouncing the corruptions of the present, and it is not welcome. Milton was lucky not to share a comparable fate at the Restoration: probably only his blindness saved him from having his own severed head displayed on a pike.

'Lycidas' is another of the occasional poems. But the poet-prophet properly seizes the occasion to transcend the occasion. The political denunciation delivered has its literary precedents of course – notably Dante in the *Paradiso* (29.106–7). But how many poets in English had availed themselves of the tradition? To follow this tradition is to be at the same time untraditional.

The poem proceeds by a series of tonal contrasts and clashes. 'Begin, and somewhat loudly sweep the string' (line 17). With the denunciation Milton reaches out for the extreme note, for an excess of force and content that 'shrunk' the streams of Alpheus. In marked contrast to the speech of 'the pilot of the *Galilean* lake' (line 109) is the immediately preceding speech of Camus: '"Ah! Who hath reft" (quoth he) "my dearest pledge?"' (line 107). It is a nice dismissal of the useless university, unable to speak out, unable to say anything much at all. The total inadequacy of Camus' response, intellectually, emotionally and spiritually represents its larger inadequacy in the society: its moral, intellectual and political bankruptcy. In this context of the poetic, Cambridge is clearly no model or inspirational source for the literary arts when all it can offer is this.[23]

'Lycidas' is a deeply moving poem, yet not without its sardonic wit. Camus' verbal inadequacy is one example. The catalogue of flowers is another:

> Bring the rathe Primsore that forsaken dies,
> The tufted Crow-toe, and pale Jessamine,
> The white Pink, and the Pansy freakt with jet,
> The glowing Violet,
> The Musk-rose, and the well-attir'd Woodbine,
> With Cowslips wan that hang the pensive head. (lines 142–7)

It is another commemoration of the English countryside, adapted from the '*Sicilian* muse'. But it is there not as an inert repetition of a tradition, but as a tragically ironic paradox. Lycidas' body is lost at sea so there is no 'Laureate Hearse where *Lycid* lies' (line 151) to strew. It is 'false surmise'. Milton has created literary substance from absence.

The catalogue of flowers, the procession of mourners, the complaint about the failure of divine protection ('Where were ye Nymphs', line 50), the despair at the futility of the struggles of existence ('Alas! What boots it with uncessant care', line 64) are all part of the pastoral elegy whose tradition Theocritus, Moschus, and Bion had established. Milton knows his authorities.[24] But as with his prose polemics, he cites authority yet sets little store by it.[25] These may be the traditional subjects of poetry as practised by the traditional poetic authorities, but in the end the authorities are irrelevant, the tradition is unimportant, the old order has been superseded:

> Weep no more, woeful Shepherds weep no more,
> For *Lycidas* your sorrow is not dead,
> Sunk though he be beneath the wat'ry floor,
> So sinks the day-star in the Ocean bed,
> And yet anon repairs his drooping head.   (lines 165–9)

Christ's nativity has made the classical tradition obsolete. The promise of resurrection has turned the pastoral elegy into elegant but irrelevant fiction. The proper subject of poetry has changed. The final section of the poem draws on the new imagery and the new authority of Christianity:

So *Lycidas*, sunk low, but mounted high
Through the dear might of him that walk'd the waves.

(lines 172–3)

Commentators have remarked on the tension of classical and Christian in the poem, yet it is less a tension than a supersession.[26] Just as the opening poem in the first collection has the old classical divinities leaving the scene – movingly, poetically so, but leaving nonetheless – so here the classical tradition is gradually permeated by and replaced by the Christian. The 'Fountain *Arethuse*' (line 85), inspiration of the classical, is transcended by the mention of 'that strain I heard was of a higher mood' (line 87). Arethuse goes underground and rises again after 'the Pilot of the *Galilean* Lake' speaks: 'Return *Alpheus*, the dread voice is past / That shrunk thy streams; Return *Sicilian* Muse' (lines 132–3). The river Alpheus going underground and arising again as the fountain Arethuse is a prefiguration of the resurrection, however. The classical muses are invoked only to be outclassed by the Christian. The Sicilian muse brings in the beautiful catalogue of flowers but it is a literary token, a fantasy, since there is not a body to strew. That is no problem for the Christian muse. The missing body recalls the empty tomb of Christ's resurrection. 'Weep no more, woeful Shepherds' (line 165). The classical muse remains stuck in despair: the Christian muse continues with triumph. Indeed, we can see this interchange of classical and Christian poetics as a dialogue or debate between the two traditions, in which the Christian inexorably triumphs.

The received image of Milton, and it is not an incorrect one, is of a strong personality. Yet this first volume of poems is strangely impersonal.[27] It is not easy to construct a figure of Milton from it – unlike the figure of Donne or of Herbert that we can construct from their volumes of the 1630s. That idea of Tillyard's that in writing 'Lycidas' Milton was writing about himself is a clever idea but not borne out by a reading of the poem.[28] The title of John Crowe Ransom's essay, 'A Poem Nearly Anonymous', captures the experience more closely.[29] There is a marked absence of the promotion of the personal in these poems. There is a strong concern with poetry, certainly, but not with the individual poet. The poet is the medium transmitting the inspiration of the muses, of the heavenly spirit, not an ego-flaunting author.

But poetry itself is the continual theme. Milton is wrestling with those poetic preoccupations that have been seen as characteristically postmodern, though have surely always been there: poetry created from absence, like 'On Time', which laments the lack of achievement, the lack of substance, and thus creates a poetic substance and achievement; poetry from incompletion and failure, like 'The Passion' where the very inability to replicate or paraphrase Christ's passion is the poem's paradoxical achievement (to have produced a 'successful' poem on the passion would surely have been to have failed, to have been entrapped by hubris and delusion and Satanic pride); and poetry rehearsing the themes of poetry, poetry about the possibilities of poetry, like 'L'Allegro' and 'Il Penseroso', and about the traditions of poetry, like 'Lycidas'. Yet all these preoccupations with the problems and sources and practice of poetry are preoccupations that move outward. Formalist theories are never entertained. The poet has to find the proper subjects and to be open to the inspiration of the heavenly muse to succeed.

NOTES

1 Christopher Hill, *Milton and the English Revolution* (London: Faber and Faber, 1977) is the standard political biography.
2 Louis Martz offers the classic apolitical reading in 'The Rising Poet, 1645', in *The Lyric and Dramatic Milton*, ed. Joseph H. Summers (New York: Columbia University Press, 1965), pp. 3–33.
3 Political readings include Thomas N. Corns, 'Milton's Quest for Respectability', *Modern Language Review* 77 (1982): 769–79; David Norbrook, *Poetry and Politics in the English Renaissance*, (London: Routledge and Kegan Paul, 1984), pp. 235–85; and Michael Wilding, *Dragons Teeth: Literature in the English Revolution* (Oxford: Clarendon Press, 1987), pp. 7–27.
4 Arthur Barker, 'The Pattern of Milton's "Nativity Ode"', *University of Toronto Quarterly* 10 (1940), repr. in *Milton: Modern Judgements*, ed. Alan Rudrum (London: Macmillan, 1968) p. 54.
5 All quotations from *John Milton: Complete Poems and Major Prose*, ed. Merrit Y. Hughes (New York: Macmillan, 1985).
6 I am dealing here only with the English poems, but this concept is explicit in 'Ad Patrem', lines 50–5: 'And now, to sum it all up, what pleasure is there in the inane modulation of the voice without words and meaning and rhythmic eloquence? Such music is good enough for the forest choirs, but not for Orpheus, who by his song – not by his cithara – restrained rivers and gave ears to the oaks, and by his singing stirred the ghosts of the dead to tears. That fame he owes to his song.'
7 Tzvetan Todorov, *The Poetics of Prose* (Ithaca: Cornell University Press, 1977), p. 58.
8 The occasional nature of these poems has been remarked by, amongst others, Mary Ann Radzinowicz, *Toward Samson Agonistes: The Growth of Milton's Mind* (Princeton University Press, 1978), p. 119; Edward W. Tayler, *Milton's Poetry: Its Development in Time* (Pittsburgh: Duquesne University Press, 1979), p. 18; E. A. J. Honigman, *Milton's Sonnets* (London: Macmillan, 1966), p. 31.
9 See William Kerrigan, *The Prophetic Milton* (Charlottesville: University Press of Virginia, 1974); and M. V. Rama Sarma, *Milton and the Prophetic Strain* (New Delhi: Sterling, 1991).
10 It might arguably be claimed both sections are of eight stanzas each. For numerological readings of the poems, see Maren-Sofie Røstvig, 'Elaborate Song: Con-

ceptual Structure in Milton's "On the Morning of Christ's Nativity"' and H. Neville Davies, 'Laid Artfully Together: Stanzaic Design in Milton's "On the Morning of Christ's Nativity"' in Maren-Sofie Røstvig (ed.), *Fair Forms* (Cambridge: D. S. Brewer, 1975), pp. 54–84, 85–118.

11 William Haller, *The Rise of Puritanism* (New York: Columbia University Press, 1972), p. 288.

12 David Shelley Berkeley, *Inwrought with Figures Dim: A Reading of Milton's 'Lycidas'* (The Hague: Mouton, 1984), pp. 33–4.

13 David Daiches, *Milton* (London: Hutchinson University Library, 1957).

14 Catherine Belsey, *John Milton: Language, Gender, Power* (Oxford: Basil Blackwell, 1988), p. 29.

15 *John Milton*, p. 67.

16 'The singing of Orpheus has both purpose and consequence', as Stanley Fish observes,'What It's Like to Read *L'Allegro* and *Il Penseroso*', *Milton Studies* 7 (1975): 93.

17 See Norman B. Council, '*L'Allegro, Il Penseroso*, and "The Cycle of Universal Knowledge"', *Milton Studies* 9 (1976): 203–19.

18 See Kerrigan, *The Prophetic Milton*, pp. 70–82.

19 See Wilding, *Dragons Teeth*, pp. 23–7. A contrary view is expressed in Cleanth Brooks and John Edward Hardy, *Poems of Mr John Milton: The 1645 Edition with Essays in Analysis* (New York: Harcourt Brace and Company, 1951), p. 140.

20 Milton's opposition to the *Book of Sports* is expressed in his *Of Reformation in England* (1641), in *Complete Prose Works of John Milton*, ed. Don M. Wolfe, vol. 1 (New Haven; Yale University Press, 1953), p. 589.

21 See Daiches, *Milton*, pp. 76–92; Belsey, *John Milton*, p. 28.

22 'The Orpheus myth is a displaced return of the repressed, a repetition of the castration complex that the shepherd himself is subjected to.' 'The poem is, finally, a repetition in toto of the castration complex, what amounts to an obsessive poem.' Herman Rapaport, *Milton and the Postmodern* (Lincoln: University of Nebraska Press, 1983), pp. 114, 105.

23 However, David Shelley Berkeley presents 'Cambridge University as a Type of the Heavenly Paradise' in chapter 3 of *Inwrought With Figures Dim*, pp. 85–112.

24 See James H. Hanford, 'The Pastoral Elegy and Milton's *Lycidas*', *PMLA* 25 (1910): 403–27; repr. in *Milton's Lycidas: The Tradition and the Poem*, ed. C. A. Patrides, new and rev. edn (Columbia: University of Missouri Press, 1983), pp. 31–59.

25 See Ernest Sirluck (ed.), *Complete Prose Works of John Milton*, vol. 2 (New Haven: Yale University Press, 1959), pp. 164–5.

26 See *A Variorum Commentary on the Poems of John Milton, Volume Two, The Minor English Poems*, ed. A. S. P. Woodhouse and Douglas Bush (New York: Columbia University Press, 1972) for examples.

27 Cf. Northrop Frye, 'Literature as Context: Milton's *Lycidas*', *Proceedings of the Second Congress of the International Comparative Literature Association*, ed. W. P. Friederich, University of North Carolina Studies in Comparative Literature, no. 23 (1959); repr. in Patrides (ed.), *Milton's Lycidas* p. 272.

28 E. M. W. Tillyard, *Milton* (London: Chatto and Windus, 1930), p. 80.

29 John Crowe Ransom, 'A Poem Nearly Anonymous', *American Review* 4 (1933), repr. in Patrides (ed.), *Milton's Lycidas*, pp. 69–85. See also Stanley E. Fish, 'Lyicdas: A Poem Finally Anonymous,' *Glyph* 8 (1981) repr. in Patrides (ed.), *Milton's Lycidas*, pp. 319–45.

FURTHER READING

Bateson, F. W., *English Poetry: A Critical Introduction* (London: Longman, 1950)

Belsey, Catherine, *John Milton: Language, Gender, Power* (Oxford: Basil Blackwell, 1988)

Brooks, Cleanth and John Edward Hardy, *Poems of Mr John Milton: The 1645 Edition With Essays in Analysis* (New York: Harcourt Brace, 1951)

Burnett, Archie, *Milton's Style: The Shorter Poems, 'Paradise Lost,' and Samson Agonistes* (London: Longman, 1981)

Corns, Thomas N., *Milton's Language* (Oxford: Basil Blackwell, 1990)

Davis, H. Neville, 'Milton and the Art of Cranking', *Milton Quarterly* 23.1 (1989): 1–7

Fish, Stanley E., 'What It's Like to Read L'Allegro and Il Penseroso', *Milton Studies* 7 (1975): 77–99

Fowler, Alastair, *Silent Poetry: Essays in Numerological Analysis* (London, Routledge and Kegan Paul, 1970)

Hill, Christopher, *Milton and The English Revolution* (London: Faber and Faber, 1977)

Hunt, Clay, *Lycidas and the Italian Critics* (New Haven: Yale University Press, 1979)

Leishman, J. B., *Milton's Minor Poetry* (London: Hutchinson, 1969)

Leonard, John, '"Trembling Ears": the Historical Moment of *Lycidas*', *Journal of Medieval and Renaissance Studies* 20 (1991): 59–81

Milner, Andrew, *John Milton and the English Revolution* (London: Macmillan, 1981)

Norbrook, David, *Poetry and Politics in the English Renaissance* (London: Routledge and Kegan Paul, 1984)

Parker, William Riley, *Milton: A Biography*, 2 vols. (Oxford: Clarendon Press, 1968)

Patrides, C. A., (ed.), *Milton's Lycidas: The Tradition and the Poem*, new and rev. edn (Columbia: University of Missouri Press, 1983)

Richmond, Hugh, *The Christian Revolutionary: John Milton* (Berkeley: University of California Press, 1974)

Shawcross, J. T. (ed.), *Milton: The Critical Heritage* (London: Routledge and Kegan Paul, 1970)

   Milton 1732–1801: The Critical Heritage (London: Routledge and Kegan Paul, 1972)

Summers, Joseph H. (ed.), *The Lyric and Dramatic Milton* (New York: Columbia University Press, 1965)

Wilding, Michael, *Dragons Teeth: Literature in the English Revolution* (Oxford: Clarendon Press, 1987)

Wittreich, Joseph A., Jr, *Visionary Poetics: Milton's Tradition and His Legacy* (San Marino, Calif.: Huntington Library, 1979)

12

ANTHONY LOW

Richard Crashaw

Richard Crashaw (1612/13–49) was revived early in the twentieth century as
a 'Metaphysical' poet and as a member of the 'School of Donne'.[1] In some
ways that classification was advantageous to his status, because he gained a
degree of recognition by riding on Donne's coat-tails in the great wave of
popularity inspired by H. J. C. Grierson, T. S. Eliot, F. R. Leavis, I. A. Rich-
ards, William Empson, A. Alvarez, George Williamson, Frank Kermode,
and scores of other famous advocates of metaphysical poetry as a kind of
forerunner of our modern sensibility.[2] The great disadvantage of being
placed this way, however, was that Crashaw was vigorously assailed, by
Leavis, Empson, Robert M. Adams and others, for not being just like
Donne. Indeed, mid-twentieth-century criticism is full of violent (and often
very funny) attacks on Crashaw's poetry as, among other things, neurotic,
perverted, feminine, infantile, 'foreign', extravagant, tasteless, Catholic, and
even cannibalistic.[3] Some central quality in his poetry has consistently out-
raged critical tempers, inspiring otherwise moderate writers to reach for
their purplest prose. One's first reaction to this phenomenon is that a poet
who elicits such strong opposition – yet who continues to be reprinted, read,
enjoyed, and argued about – cannot be all that bad. He must still have
something important to tell us.

A second strand of criticism has viewed Crashaw more as a 'Baroque'
than a 'Metaphysical' poet. Mario Praz and Austin Warren published major
and still fundamental studies setting Crashaw against the larger background
of the European Baroque movement and the Catholic Counter-
Reformation.[4] Such studies of the relationships among literature, art, architecture, music, and religion are hard to conduct persuasively; but if any
English poet may be called 'Mannerist' or 'Baroque', Crashaw is the best
candidate. Critics have found it impossible to resist setting his Teresa poems
against Bernini's statue of the saint in ecstasy, or his poems in general
against such monuments of Baroque art as Bernini's Baldacchino in St
Peter's Basilica.

Crashaw largely escaped the grasp of the most influential study of English devotional poetry, Martz's *Poetry of Meditation*, because (I would argue) he is not primarily a meditative poet.[5] When Barbara K. Lewalski's *Protestant Poetics* appeared (followed by a host of imitators) to challenge Martz's irenic views on the working relationships among continental Catholic and English Protestant devotional traditions, Crashaw was pushed further toward the margins of what is now recognized to be the greatest flowering of English religious poetry.[6] Crashaw has suffered broadly from our modern misgivings about religion and more narrowly from suspicions raised by his conversion to Roman Catholicism. He has also proved less accessible than some of the Protestant religious poets – Sidney, Spenser, Herbert, and Milton especially – to secularization, and thus to recuperation for modernist or postmodernist agendas.[7] There was a short-lived attempt in the 1960s to promote him as a 'psychedelic' poet, because of what a few critics thought to be the chaotic, distorted, and too colourful nature of his imagery; but this move did little to advance either his reputation or that of the drug culture. So Crashaw has been a figure in dispute and partly in eclipse; yet still a poet who has, in spite of established disapproval, engaged the attention of a surprising number of our most prominent critics.

Devotional practices in the seventeenth century were beginning to separate more widely from their connections with church and liturgy among both Catholics and Protestants, growing more private than they had usually been in earlier periods. They still, however, derived support from an evolving framework of technical methodology, laid out in the devotional handbooks, put to use in sermons and private devotions, and often reflected in devotional poetry: a framework nearly as elaborate as the highly sophisticated rhetorical methodology that underlay the century's poetic practice. One would expect Crashaw to fall into some recognizable school of devotion, or (as was customarily the case) to employ some variant or combination of recognizable techniques.

Among the commonly accepted devotional methods of the time were sung hymns and spoken prayers, clearly an important influence on Crashaw; several kinds of meditation, none of which resemble his practice very closely; and contemplation or mystical prayer, with which several critics have associated him.[8] Authorities of his time also speak of a fourth kind of devotion, which they call 'affective' devotion, 'sensible affection', or sometimes 'affective meditation' (when it is combined with meditative techniques). In keeping with the habits of the time, these four kinds of devotion were organized hierarchically, with sung or vocal prayer at the lowest level, contemplation at the highest, and meditation and sensible affection in between, serving as bridges for those who sought to climb the spiritual ladder toward God. In general, Protestants, at least those toward the more radical or Puritan end of the spectrum, were much more suspicious of the possibility of orderly spiritual progress than Catholics. They often borrowed from Catholic devotional treatises but felt free to modify them in accordance with their own ideas about the workings of grace. Crashaw, however, would have been closer to Catholic than to Puritan devotional practices even before his conversion.[9] Paradoxically, as several critics have surmised, he probably first learned to practise devotion in his youth from the large library of Catholic treatises that his Puritan father had assembled in order to refute them.

Many of Crashaw's best poems are hymns or sung devotions, and one of his great strengths is the 'musical' nature of his language. Not only is his poetry often written to be set to music, but he skilfully employs the traditional techniques by which poetry most closely approaches the condition of music, in rhythm, sound, and imagery. Critics have most often associated the singing of hymns and psalms with Protestantism; but it was, of course, an ancient practice of the church (and, even earlier, of pagan antiquity), which found new vitality in the high-church Anglicanism of Crashaw's Cambridge college, Peterhouse, as well as in Counter-Reformation Rome. An early instance of Crashaw's remarkable ability to imitate and to evoke musical effects in his poetry is one of his most notable secular poems, 'Music's Duel'. In its version of the old quarrel between nature and art, it embodies, in brilliantly musical verse, a competition to the death between a nightingale and a human singer, who accompanies himself on the lute:

> Hee amazed
> That from so small a channell should be rais'd
> The torrent of a voyce, whose melody
> Could melt into such sweet variety
> Straines higher yet; that tickled with rare art
> The tatling strings (each breathing in his part)
> Most kindly doe fall out; the grumbling Base
> In surly groanes disdaines the Trebles Grace.[10] (lines 43–50)

The hymns, too, revel in musical effects – as is appropriate to their poetic genre and devotional mode – weaving sound with the other senses: sight, smell, taste, and touch. Crashaw's early hymnology is marked by simple melody, such as that suggested by the regular stanzas, pastoral voices, and humble emotions of 'A Hymn of the Nativity':

> WINTER chidde aloud; and sent
> The angry North to wage his warres.
> The North forgott his feirce Intent;

> And left perfumes in stead of scarres.
> By those sweet eyes' persuasive powrs
> Where he mean't frost, he scatter'd flowrs.   (lines 24–9)

In his later hymns, Crashaw's musical effects range upward to sublimely impassioned rhapsodies, influenced (I think) by the ancient hymns and odes of Hesiod and Pindar as well as by Palestrina and the new recitative style (or *seconda practica*) of Monteverdi. These are the influences – poetic, devotional, and musical – that animate such late, irregular hymns as 'To the Name of Jesus' and 'In the Glorious Epiphany'. The antiphonal responses of the latter offer to scale the mystical heights, in a music less immediately sensuous than that of most of his hymns but all the more remarkable for its energetic rhythmic daring.[11]

> [1.] Thus we, who when with all the noble powres
> That (at thy cost) are call'd, not vainly, ours
>   We vow to make brave way
> Upwards, and presse on for the pure intelligentiall Prey;
>   [2.] At lest to play
>   The amorous Spyes
> And peep and proffer at thy sparkling Throne.   (lines 220–6)

But if music plays an important role throughout Crashaw's major poetry, nonetheless affective or sensible devotion, which has been overlooked by most critics writing on seventeenth-century poetry, is probably the neglected key to a sympathetic entry into his work. I would argue that, in Crashaw's case, it is especially significant that the practice of affective devotion was most often recommended for women. Crashaw was relatively uninterested in what were considered in his time to be active or 'masculine' forms of devotion. In particular, he was uninterested in meditation (whether Ignatian or 'Protestant'), which involves rigorous intellectual analysis and active, even aggressive, searching for God.[12] Instead he gravitated naturally to the form of devotion usually recommended for women: sensible affection. In this form of devotion, which emphasizes feeling rather than intellect and passivity rather than activity – openness to the divine lover – the soul does not actively search, but passively waits. That it should be a form of devotion recommended especially to women is (according to the thinking of the times) connected with the prevalent view that women are more inclined to express their feelings and emotions and less inclined to rely on their intellectual faculties than men. Although such an attitude appears patronizing and demeaning to us – and, indeed, doubtless it often was demeaning – it was not necessarily so. Until the Reformation, contemplation was traditionally thought to be a higher state of life than action. In the long debate concerning which was the higher faculty, intellect or will (in the latter of which *caritas* was thought to inhere), it is far from clear that intellect was always the winner, particularly in spiritual affairs.

As St Francis de Sales writes:

> knowledge having produced holy love, Love doth not staie within the compasse of the knowledge which is in the understanding, but goes forward, and passeth farre beyond it; so that in this life we may have more love, then knowledge of God, whence great S. THOMAS. assures us that often tymes the most simple and women abound in devotion being more ordinarily capable of heavenly love then able and understanding people.[13]

That women should be grouped with 'the most simple' and men (by implication) with the 'able and understanding' is at once both insulting to women and (in view of the context and of the Christian paradox that in the Kingdom of Heaven the last shall be first and the first shall be last) complimentary.[14]

On the subject of 'feminine' love and devotion, St Francis de Sales also recounts an irresistible story about the first Franciscans:

> The Blessed Brother Gilles, one of the first companions of S. FRANCIS, saied one day to S. BONAVENTURE, oh how happie you learned men are, for you understand many things, whereby you praise God: but what can we Idiotes doe? S. BONAVENTURE replied, the grace to love God is sufficient. No, but Father, replied Brother Gilles, can an ignorant man love God, as well as a learned? yes, saieth S. Bonaventure, yea more, a poore sillie woman may love God as well as a Doctour of Divinitie: with this Brother Gilles cried out, falling into a fervour, oh poore simple woman, love thy saviour, and thou shall be as great, as Brother Bonaventure; and upon it, he remained for the space of three houres in a RAPTURE.[15]

There is a nice balance here (though almost as likely to outrage modern feminist principles as to assuage them) between the usual opinion of society – that a woman is less than a man, and an uneducated lay brother less than a priest – and the point of the story (which sends Brother Gilles into a mystical rapture) that the love of God, which was thought to be the highest of human ends, does not depend on any of the usual human preparations or social distinctions.

Even those who practise Ignatian meditation do not practise intellectual analysis or aggressive meditation as ends in themselves, but use them to arouse their feelings and to motivate their wills toward some good resolution or change of heart and life. If women's feelings toward God were by nature already aroused and receptive – which was thought to be more commonly the case with them than with men – it would be unnecessary, even sterile and spiritually harmful, for them to undertake such intellectual exercises.[16] Augustine Baker writes: 'It is a great mistake in some writers who think the exercise of the will to be mean and base in comparison of inventive meditation and curious speculation of divine mysteries.' Some persons with affective natures, he continues, need not be 'driven to the pains and expense of time in finding out reasons and motives to raise their affections to our Lord, but immediately and without more ado suffer the affections to flow'.[17]

Those naturally drawn toward sensible affection did not need to be women, but women provided the usual model. Some spiritual directors of women, such as St Francis de Sales and Augustine Baker, were themselves inclined to a more emotional, less intellectual, form of devotion. In some cases they seem to have learned a great deal from, as well as taught, their charges. Such was clearly the case with Baker and Dame Gertrude More, with whom he was closely associated.[18] Such, too, would seem to have been the case with Crashaw, who was at least informally the spiritual director of several women. Earlier in this century, the 'feminine' nature of his poetry was often vigorously attacked by critics (usually male) who accused him of aberrancy, foreign effeminacy, and bad taste. More recently, it has been reinvestigated and praised.[19]

An extraordinary number of Crashaw's major devotional poems are concerned with women. His last collection, *Carmen Deo Nostro*, includes his epistle offering spiritual advice to the Countess of Denbigh; his poem 'To the Queen's Majesty'; 'Sancta Maria Dolorum', which views the crucifixion through Mary's eyes; 'In the Glorious Assumption of Our Blessed Lady'; 'The Weeper', Crashaw's most vivid exercise in sensible affection; the three poems on St Teresa; the affective-mystical ode on a 'Prayerbook Given to a Young Gentlewoman' with its sequel; and the three complaints of Alexias, wife of St Alexis. In all of these thirteen poems, to one degree or another, Crashaw not only addresses a woman but identifies with her emotionally or speaks directly through her. All of these poems educate the reader in what might be called 'feminine spirituality' – except that Crashaw's point is that men can profit equally from such spirituality. At the centre of this spirituality is Crashaw's central vision of sacred love, which conquers through weakness, suffering, passivity, and submission. Like the martyrs who welcome Christ into the world in 'To the Name of Jesus', each of these spokeswomen exemplify (or are counselled to exemplify) a love that lets divine Love in through its wounds. If there is any element of parody based on the secular love tradition – which there must be, in a love so clearly couched in vivid sexual metaphors – it is a parody not of male but of female experience:

> She never undertook to know
> What death with love should have to doe;
> Nor has she e're yet understood
> Why to show love, she should shed blood
> Yet though she cannot tell you why,
> She can LOVE, and she can DY.
>
> ('A Hymn to ... St Teresa', lines 19–24)

> Leave her that; and thou shalt leave her
> Not one loose shaft but love's whole quiver.
> For in love's feild was never found
> A nobler weapon then a WOUND.
> Love's passives are his activ'st part.
> The wounded is the wounding heart.
>
> ('The Flaming Heart', lines 69–74)

The 'she' of these lines is St Teresa. Yet it might equally well be the poet's soul, also usually called 'she'. Crashaw makes it clear that he knows St Teresa was no passive pushover; like Christ's (her own exemplar), hers is a conquering passivity. She is held up not only for our admiration but for our ardent imitation. Crashaw is, in effect, a feminist who argues, not that women should be more like men and accumulate more power, but that men should be more like women, and learn to suffer, to serve, to give, and to love.[20] The same pattern may be found in a dozen of Crashaw's other major poems, which might be cited at length if they were not already so familiar. It is recognizably a pattern central to all of Crashaw's sacred poetry.

Authorities on devotion remarked that the proper end of sensible affection, as of meditation, was to rise out of the senses into the will and spirit, and ultimately to manifest itself as contemplation or mystical prayer. Indeed, the mystics traditionally borrowed from the Song of Songs to describe their indescribable experience through the same kind of sensuous imagery as was commonly used in sensible devotion. Crashaw could find such a pattern in the mystical writings of St Teresa, who was one of the strongest influences on his later work. Both forms of devotion, affective and mystical, emphasize passivity to the divine lover, both involve a similar use of rapturous, metaphorically sexual language. In Crashaw's 'Prayer: An Ode, which was Prefixed to a little Prayer-book given to a young Gentlewoman', we may see how affective devotion reaches upward toward – or perhaps into – mystical devotion:

> O happy and thrice happy she
> Selected dove
> Who ere she be,
> Whose early love

With winged vowes
Makes hast to meet her morning spouse
And close with his immortall kisses.
Happy indeed, who never misses
To improve that pretious hour,
   And every day
   Seize her sweet prey
All fresh and fragrant as he rises
Dropping with a baulmy Showr
A delicious dew of spices;
O let the blissfull heart hold fast
Her heavenly arm-full, she shall tast
At once ten thousand paradises;
   She shall have power
   To rifle and deflour
The rich and roseall spring of those rare sweets
Which with a swelling bosome there she meets
   Boundles and infinite
   Bottomles treasures
Of pure inebriating pleasures.
Happy proof! she shal discover
   What joy, what blisse,
How many Heav'ns at once it is
To have her GOD become her LOVER.   (lines 97–124)

But if Crashaw's affective devotion aspires to contemplation, it also has its roots below, in secular love, the senses, and sexuality. It is influenced by St Teresa but it also parodies secular love poetry. These connections may be clearly seen in a brief, comparatively less-well-known poem, 'A Song', which follows the three Teresa poems in the 1648 and 1652 collections:

Lord, when the sense of thy sweet grace
Sends up my soul to seek thy face.
Thy blessed eyes breed such desire,
I dy in love's delicious Fire.
   O love, I am thy SACRIFICE.
Be still triumphant, blessed eyes.
Still shine on me, fair suns! that I
Still may behold, though still I dy.

Second part.
   Though still I dy, I live again;
Still longing so to be still slain,
So gainfull is such losse of breath,
I dy even in desire of death.

> Still live in me this loving strife
> Of living DEATH and dying LIFE.
> For while thou sweetly slayest me
> Dead to my selfe, I live in Thee.

G. W. Williams suggests that this poem was 'Perhaps inspired' by St Teresa's *Interior Castle*.[21] If so, the debt is general rather than specific. To live by dying through the intensity of divine love is characteristic of Teresa's spirituality, as it was also characteristic of that of her contemporary, St John of the Cross. A connection is equally clear to Crashaw's own Teresa poems. Even more obviously, as R. V. Young has suggested, the poem is a parody of a thousand Italian love songs and Elizabethan madrigals about dying from the intense experience of love – that is, from the ecstasy of sexual consummation.[22] In support of this parodic connection with secular love songs is an earlier version of Crashaw's text, which survives in manuscript, with a musical setting by an unknown composer. As Louise Schleiner notes, the composer rather heavy-handedly seizes the opportunity to emphasize the phrases 'though still I die' and 'to be still so slain' – just, I would add, as Italian composers so dearly loved to do with '*io moro*' in their love songs.[23] Thus the composer emphasizes what he finds in his text: Crashaw's emphasis on a powerful, killing 'desire', which is – as in St Francis de Sales's *Treatise on the Love of God* – not so much an empty longing for something absent as the intensely amorous experience of present, continuing, superabundant gratification: '[W]e are to have an insatiable desire of Loving God, adding continually love upon love.'[24]

Crashaw's sacred poems are filled with something resembling St Francis's transformed or gratified desire, which is neither a lustful longing – for possession of a person or object, for worldly success, or for sexual conquest – nor an empty longing for something absent; but rather a warm, sometimes fiery, longing for something already enjoyed, for a God who is not absent but, in some deeply satisfying fashion, already present.[25] We see such a desire exemplified in the 'Hymn to ... St Teresa': 'Her weake brest heaves with strong desire' (line 40); in 'The Flaming Heart': 'By all thy brim-fill'd Bowles of feirce desire' (line 99); and in 'Prayer: An Ode': 'setts the house on fire / And melts it down in sweet desire' (lines 73–4). His interest in intensely gratified desire, in a love that is returned and satisfied rather than in the unsatisfied longing of the Petrarchan love tradition, is well exemplified by his youthful translations of love poems by Moschus and Catullus from the Greek and Latin, as well as of several poems from the Italian on the pleasures of mutual sexual fulfilment.[26]

Returning to Crashaw's parody, 'A Song', we find that there is only a hairline's difference between it and its secular exemplars, which in turn had borrowed earlier from the language of sacred devotion. If we change the first word 'Lord' to 'Love', the poem becomes entirely ambiguous. In that case, too, the speaker's sex becomes indeterminable. His basic stance is 'feminine', to the extent that he is acted upon but does not act, dies but does not kill in return, suffers but does not inflict suffering. Aside from the opening word and the context of sacred poetry in which the poem is found, however, we could imagine the speaker to be a man addressing his mistress, a woman addressing her lover, or a suppliant addressing his or her God. This sexual interchangeability is not generally true of English Petrarchan love poetry or, for example, of the devotional poetry of Donne, Herbert, and Vaughan.[27]

That Crashaw's religious poems were admired by some of his contemporaries, despite their differences on points of religion, is evidenced by the well-known comments of writers such as Abraham Cowley. Nevertheless, Crashaw did not have much direct influence with regard to love on the tone or the stance of other English devotional poets. His 'feminine' way of thinking and feeling, in particular, has caused him to seem 'foreign' to most observers (mostly masculine) over succeeding centuries. His introduction of figures like St Teresa and St Mary Magdalene as devotional intermediaries or mediators has seemed attractive to some English-speaking observers, but also rather quaint and foreign – something to wonder at and admire, perhaps, but not to imitate. His passiveness has been troubling. His emphasis on pleasure and on gratification of the senses has offended the sensibilities even of some of his stoutest defenders. He has fed our worst suspicions about the psychological linkages between sex and religion.

I remain persuaded that a true appreciation for Crashaw is determined by one's reaction to the so-called 'worst' cases. It is not enough mildly to enjoy such relatively restrained poems as 'In the Holy Nativity'. We should learn to understand and to sympathize with such odd effects of his practice of sensible devotion as Mary Magdalene's upward-flowing tears in 'The Weeper', which ascend to the Milky Way, and from which 'A brisk Cherub somthing sippes' each morning to make his breakfast and sweeten his song. If we understand the curve of affects in this passage, we may even understand how the flowing fountains of her eyes can become, without undue grotesqueness – but to the distinct displeasure of a hundred critics – 'Two walking baths; two weeping motions; / Portable, and compendious oceans'.

Our present time likes to think itself appreciative of good poetry wherever it finds it, almost regardless of its message. But not many of us are simultaneously and equally responsive to the pleasures of sexual gratification and of religious devotion. Those who, to put it bluntly, admire sexual gratification without guilt and 'androgyny' or 'polymorphous perversity' without conventional self-control may admire Crashaw from one restricted perspective. Those who, to put it equally bluntly, admire a pure and genuine but totally abstract and asexual religious devotion, such as the tradition of English hymnody descending from George Herbert, may admire him from another restricted perspective. (I am not thinking of particular critics, but invoking the straw men of two extremes.) Commerce between the two views is difficult, perhaps even impossible. Nonetheless, it is possible, I think, to negotiate a path that is responsive to Crashaw's poetry and to his views about love as implied by that poetry.

The paradox may be that we are finally in a position, for the first time since the Reformation came into England and into the English-language literary tradition, to begin to understand and to sympathize with a 'feminine' approach to love like Crashaw's. Yet we are less inclined than ever to follow that love in directions he would have wished it to lead us. Not unlike other ages – although the particulars change – we are more easily inclined to empowerment than to sacrifice, to vindication than to sympathy, to material welfare than to transcendence. At our most unselfish and self-congratulatory, we crave the empowerment, vindication, and material welfare of others who lack these perquisites – which are not, however, always wholly beneficial to their possessor. Crashaw preferred to wish that others should, like himself and the female saints he admired, cheerfully offer themselves up, in sacrifice, love, and suffering. It would be hard to argue that he has managed to introduce into our customary attitudes toward love anything that has permanently influenced succeeding ages – or is soon likely to do so. Yet he has often been admired. He has, seemingly, often been on the verge of being understood. And at least he remains a lasting and a remarkable provocation.

NOTES

1 Crashaw, son of Revd William Crashaw (disciple of Perkins and noted anti-Catholic polemicist) was born in London and educated at Charterhouse (1629–31) and at Pembroke College, Cambridge (BA 1634). In 1635 he became a fellow of Peterhouse, a high-church college under the mastership of the prominent Laudian, John Cosin. Crashaw was a friend of Joseph Beaumont and Abraham Cowley, tutored Ferrar Collet, and often visited Little Gidding. By 1639 he was ordained and appointed curate of Little St Mary's, then the college chapel. He left Cambridge in 1642 and was formally ejected in 1644. He travelled to Leyden and to the court of Henrietta Maria in Paris, becoming a convert to Roman Catholicism by 1646. In exile he suffered poverty and illness. In 1647 he entered the service of Cardinal Pallotta, who in 1649 gave him a post at the Shrine of Our Lady in Loretto, where he died. His published volumes were *Epigrammatum Sacrorum Liber* (1634), *Steps to the Temple* (1646; enlarged 1648), and *Carmen Deo Nostro* (Paris, 1652).

2 The rise of the Metaphysicals at the expense of Milton is well described in Patrick Murray, *Milton: The Modern Phase: A Study of Twentieth-Century Criticism* (London: Longman, 1967).

3 On Crashaw's reputation, see essays by Lorraine M. Roberts and John R. Roberts in *New Perspectives on the Life and Art of Richard Crashaw*, ed. John R. Roberts (Columbia: University of Missouri Press, 1990). This collection, together with John R. Roberts's splendid *Richard Crashaw: An Annotated Bibliography of Criticism, 1632–1980* (Columbia, University of Missouri Press, 1985), is a good place to acquaint oneself with the criticism. (The charge of cannibalism – the provenance of which Crashaw would have known to be such anti-Catholic polemics as his own father's – is Empson's.)

4 Mario Praz, *The Flaming Heart: Essays on Crashaw, Macchiavelli, and other Studies* (New York: Doubleday, 1973), from his earlier study in Italian of Donne and Crashaw (1925); Austin Warren, *Richard Crashaw: A Study in Baroque Sensibility* (Ann Arbor: University of Michigan Press, 1939); see also Louis L. Martz, *The Wit of Love* (University of Notre Dame Press, 1969); and Frank J. Warnke, *Versions of Baroque* (New Haven: Yale University Press, 1972). Marc F. Bertonasco, *Crashaw and the Baroque* (University of Alabama Press, 1971), argues that Crashaw belongs to a native English Baroque; R. V. Young, *Richard Crashaw and the Spanish Golden Age* (New Haven: Yale University Press, 1982), sets him against the background of the major Spanish Baroque poets and mystics.

5 Louis L. Martz, *The Poetry of Meditation* (New Haven: Yale University Press, 1954). Martz writes about Crashaw as a Baroque artist, however, in *The Wit of Love*, pp. 113–47.

6 Barbara K. Lewalski, *Protestant Poetics and the Seventeenth-Century Religious Lyric* (Princeton University Press, 1979).

7 On connections between seventeenth-century radical Protestantism and post-modernist ideology, see the two Milton chapters in my forthcoming book, *The Reinvention of Love: Poetry, Politics and Culture from Sidney to Milton* (Cambridge University Press, 1993).

8 The best study of meditation remains Martz's *Poetry of Meditation*, supplemented by Lewalski's *Protestant Poetics*, which adds to the details of English Protestant practice but neglects (by ignoring) connections to the past and to the continent that Martz draws so clearly. On the other devotional techniques and their relation to meditation see Anthony Low, *Love's Architecture: Devotional Modes in Seventeenth-Century English Poetry* (New York University Press, 1978); or his 'Metaphysical Poets and Devotional Poets', in *George Herbert and the Seventeenth-Century Religious Poets*, ed. Mario A. DiCesare (New York: Norton, 1978), pp. 221–32. On mysticism see Young, *Richard Crashaw*, pp. 79–112.

9 On Crashaw's religious views in his Cambridge years (and for the best summary biography), see L. C. Martin's introduction to his standard edition, *The Poems English Latin and Greek of Richard Crashaw*, 2nd edn (Oxford: Clarendon Press, 1957); also Hilton Kelliher, 'Crashaw at Cambridge', in *New Perspectives on Crashaw*, ed. Roberts, pp. 180–214.

10 All quotations from Crashaw are from *The Poems*, ed. Martin; I normalize i, j, u, v, and expand contractions.

11 On Crashaw and music, see Louise Schleiner, *The Living Lyre in English Verse* (Columbia: University of Missouri Press, 1984), pp. 85–101.

12 On meditation as active and masculine, see Martz, 'The Action of the Self: Devotional Poetry in the Seventeenth Century', in *Metaphysical Poetry*, ed. Malcolm Bradley and David Palmer, Stratford-upon-Avon Studies, no. 11 (London: Edward Arnold, 1970), pp. 101–21.

13 Francis de Sales, *Treatise on the Love of God*, trans. Miles Car (Douay, 1630), p. 332 (6.4.1). I have not located this particular remark of St. Thomas's; but see his *Summa Theologica* (trans. Fathers of the English Dominican Province, 2 vols. (New York: Benziger Brothers, 1947), vol. 1, p. 415), part 1, Q. 82, art. 3, p. 415; 'Whether the Will Is a Higher Power Than the Intellect': 'When, therefore, the thing in which there is good is nobler than the soul itself, in which is the idea understood; by comparison with such a thing, the will is higher than the intellect. But when the thing which is good is less noble than the soul, then even in comparison with that thing the intellect is higher than the will. Wherefore the love of God is better than the knowledge of God; but, on the contrary, the knowledge of corporeal things is better than the love thereof.'

14 Similar thinking is found in Erasmus's *Praise of Folly*.

15 *Treatise of the Love of God*, pp. 332–3 (6.4.2).

16 See Low, *Love's Architecture*, pp. 124–58; Augustine Baker, *Sancta Sophia* (Douay, 1657), 3.1.3–5, 3.3.1; St Francis de Sales, *An Introduction to a Devoute Life*, trans. John Yakesley (Rouen, 1614), pp. 126–9; Jean Pierre Camus, *A Spirituall Combat*, trans. Thomas Carre (Douay, 1632), pp. 222–35. On spiritual advisement of women, see also Sister M. St Teresa Higgins, CSJ, 'Augustine Baker', dissertation, University of Wisconsin, 1963.

17 Baker, *Sancta Sophia* 3.2.5.5–8.

18 Edited selections from her writings were published as *The Spiritual Exercises of the Most Vertuous and Religious D. Gertrude More*, ed. Fr Francis Gascoigne (Paris, 1658). Her manuscript writings, collected by Baker as 'Confessiones Amantes', remain unpublished. An abridgement of her life and writings is *The Inner Life and the Writings of Dame Gertrude More*, ed. Dom Benedict Weld-Blundell, 2 vols. (London: R. and T. Washbourne, 1910–11).

19 See Low, *Love's Architecture*; Paul A. Parrish, 'The Feminizing of Power: Crashaw's Life and Art', in *'The Muses Common-Weale': Poetry and Politics in the Seventeenth Century*, ed. Claude J. Summers and Ted-Larry Pebworth (Columbia: University of Missouri Press, 1988), pp. 148–62; Parrish, '"O Sweet Contest": Gender and Value in "The Weeper"'; in *New Perspectives on Crashaw*, ed. Roberts; and Maureen Sabine, *Feminine Engendered Faith: John Donne and Richard Crashaw* (London: Macmillan, 1992).

20 Maureen Sabine, whose book I read in manuscript, presents a far more detailed case for Crashaw's feminism than I can here.

21 *The Complete Poetry of Richard Crashaw*, ed. George Walton Williams (New York: Doubleday, 1970), p. 65n.

22 Young, *Richard Crashaw and the Spanish Golden Age*, pp. 48–50. Young comments cogently on sacred parody in Crashaw and among his Spanish predecessors (pp. 20–50).

23 See Schleiner, *The Living Lyre*, pp. 91–3. She discusses the song qualities of the

poem and reprints the musical setting. The pun on 'dying' is a favourite of twentieth-century expositors.

24 *A Treatise of the Love of God*, p. 760.

25 For a contrasting spiritual longing out of absence and emptiness, see Debora Shuger, *Habits of Thought in the English Renaissance* (Berkeley: University of California Press, 1990), pp. 69–90.

26 See the chapter on Crashaw in Low, *The Reinvention of Love*.

27 On Donne and Herbert, see *ibid*. Although Donne often tries to assume the female role in relation to God – a traditional devotional technique – he has great difficulties, and it would be hard to mistake his voice for a woman's. Herbert, who occasionally assumes the woman's role in the divine courtship, drops it for a child's role when that courtship is about to be consummated. In 'The Night', Vaughan assumes the traditional role of the Beloved from the Song of Songs – but only at night in prayer. During the day he is a busy, distracted man. Of these poets, only Crashaw shows a natural, sympathetic, continuing identification with women – which we may fairly call *habitual*.

FURTHER READING

Crashaw, Richard, *The Poems English Latin and Greek of Richard Crashaw*, ed. L. C. Martin (Oxford: Clarendon Press, 1957)

Low, Anthony, *Love's Architecture: Devotional Modes in Seventeenth-Century English Poetry* (New York University Press, 1978)

Martz, Louis L., *The Poetry of Meditation* (New Haven: Yale University Press, 1954)

  The Wit of Love (University of Notre Dame Press, 1969)

Praz, Mario, *The Flaming Heart: Essays on Crashaw, Machiavelli, and other Studies* (New York: Doubleday, 1973)

Roberts, John R., *Richard Crashaw: An Annotated Bibliography of Criticism, 1632–1980* (Columbia: University of Missouri Press, 1985)

Roberts, John R. (ed.), *New Perspectives on the Life and Art of Richard Crashaw* (Columbia: University of Missouri Press, 1990)

Sabine, Maureen, *Feminine Engendered Faith: John Donne and Richard Crashaw* (London: Macmillan, 1992)

Warnke, Frank J., *Versions of Baroque* (New Haven: Yale University Press, 1972)

Warren, Austin, *Richard Crashaw: A Study in Baroque Sensibility* (Ann Arbor: University of Michigan Press, 1939)

Young, R. V., *Richard Crashaw and the Spanish Golden Age* (New Haven: Yale University Press, 1982)

13

JONATHAN F. S. POST

Henry Vaughan

The American feminist poet, Adrienne Rich, remarks how, as a student in her early twenties, she was led to believe that poetry was 'the expression of a higher world view, what the critic Edward Said has termed "a quasi-religious wonder," instead of a human sign to be understood in secular and social terms'.[1] My starting place is to remark that whatever conditions underlie Rich's sense of the opposition between poetry as transcendental expression and poetry as a sign system to be understood in secular and social terms, the conflict is misleading, although in interesting ways, when applied to a pre-Romantic (who is sometimes thought to be a proto-Romantic) like Vaughan, despite the fact that he is almost always remembered as the signal instance of a seventeenth-century poet who became memorable once he became a poet of transcendence: 'Lord, then said I, *On me one breath, / And let me dye before my death*.'[2]

In beginning this way, I do not mean to suggest that the difference between secular and devotional poety is insignificant to the seventeenth century or to Vaughan. Few poets in the period worked more conscientiously than Vaughan to articulate this difference, a difference central to the Preface to the 1655 collection of *Silex Scintillans*, Vaughan's most significant work, and visible in the overall shape he gave to his career. Nor do I want to suggest that the more distant reaches of the devotional experience – whether those associated with mystical theology or Hermetic lore – are merely imported for what are sometimes thought of as poetic occasions. Vaughan's appeal has always been the appeal of the abrupt: the vertiginous opening of 'The World' ('I saw eternity the other night'), the sublime exodus of 'They are all gone into the world of light', the radical telescoping of time that marks the beginning of 'The Night' in which Nicodemus comes to Christ under a cover of darkness; and even when his poems seem to falter, as they are notorious for doing, their claim on us is not readily demystified. But the opposition noted by Rich is, I think, too stark, too insufficiently dialectical when applied to Vaughan for the simple reason that the further Vaughan moved toward 'quasi-religious wonder', the more completely he betrayed his connections to history. Or to rephrase the issue in contemporary terms, the deeper he sounded a note of 'retreat', the more deeply he entered into a discourse of 'retreat' sounded by his disenfranchized royalist Anglican contemporaries. The language of devotion was also the language of debate.[3]

I think it is important to keep this reactive (and reactionary) paradox in mind not because every utterance of this deeply meditative poet ought to be interpreted as a veiled political allegory but because history in its most personally and institutionally disruptive forms – war, the loss of a younger brother William (perhaps a casualty of the fighting), the beheading of the king, and the disestablishment of the church – provided Vaughan with an imperative of the most elemental kind: to rewrite himself in relation to his immediate culture. In pointed contrast to a number of his contemporaries (Herrick and Lovelace come readily to mind), Vaughan is the prime instance of a poet who discovered his calling during the Civil War and the Interregnum – indeed, perhaps the sole instance for which such a claim might be made. (His closest competitor in this regard is probably Andrew Marvell, whose most celebrated lyrics are generally assumed to belong to the same years; but the very absence of a secure chronology militates against the idea of identifying a 'discovery' in the first place.) At almost the precise moment when Herrick was setting 'His Pillar of Fame' against 'the Kingdom's' overthrow at the end of *Hesperides* (1648) to mark his shift into silence, Vaughan was rethinking his relationship to English poetry through the guiding hand of George Herbert, 'whose holy *life* and *verse* gained many pious *Converts* (of whom I am the least)' (p. 391). While Lovelace was seeking, uncertainly, to continue as 'the Cavalier' into the 1650s, Vaughan was in the process of repudiating, publicly, any connection with 'idle' verse. If Vaughan looked to France with other royalists, it was not to translate court romances but writings from some of the 'primitive' fathers of the church once located there. If he took flight, it was as a lyricist.

The urge to rewrite and the desire for the 'primitive' stem from a similar wish to return blood and bread to his poetry in more ways than one; and I don't think it is at all accidental that the moment when Vaughan first identifies himself with his ancient, warlike clansmen, the Silurists (on the title page of *Silex Scintillans*, 1650), should coincide with his 'regeneration' as a poet under Herbert's tutelage. Both involve quests for a new authority – a new way of speaking to the present circumstances. In his earlier poetry, Vaughan had written as an outsider, as a poet on the fringe of a courtly, royalist tradition. 'I knew thee not' begins his commendatory poem to Fletcher; 'I did but see thee', he remarks at the outset of his verse elegy to Cartwright, although in both cases Vaughan's desire to throw in his lot and join a communal act of royalist commendation and solidarity was sufficient to overcome these hesitations. As a poet on the fringe, he imported heavily. His early amatory verse (*Poems*, 1646) is a tissue of echoes from Donne, Habington, Carew, and Jonson, among others. And he exported, too. As the Swan of the Usk in *Olor Iscanus* (published in 1651 but largely completed by 1647), he wrote as a regionalist, as someone voicing his political views (and loyalist support) from afar as well as recording local goings on – the death of several people killed in action, the appearance of Katherine Philips as a poet, and of festivity and fellowship in Brecknock.

It would be wrong to suggest that these 'secular' poems (as they have come to be called) and the lyrics appearing many years later in *Thalia Rediviva* (1678) are without merit. They show evidence of literary ambition beyond that of much collected in Saintsbury's three-volume edition of *Minor Caroline Poets*.[4] But they still lack a theme or, better yet, a purposive vision – a precise register that will fully differentiate Vaughan from the many gentleman poets of the period. In *Silex*, the act is decisive, but in the process Vaughan became not less but more of an outsider – more of a writer on the margins, as might be said today, so long as we remember that the margins, in this particular case, were also sites of textual and political power. (Recall the Geneva Bible or the role Welsh antiquity played in the formation of England's identity – to say nothing about Herbert's family lineage in nearby Montgomery.) 'I am here in body but not in heart' the poetry and the prose keeps repeating. I am with George Herbert, that 'most glorious true *Saint*' of the British church and 'a *seer*' whose 'incomparable prophetic Poems' predicted the present disasters (*Works*, p. 186); I am with St Paulinus of Nola (in France); I am with the Spanish Jesuit Juan Eusebius Nieremberg; I am with Christ in the Mount of Olives. I am only barely here in body, as the penultimate paragraph to the 1655 Preface, nearly Vaughan's 'final' statement, makes clear; and I am here only because of God's special mercy: 'When I expected, and had (by his assistance) prepared for a *message* of *death*, then did he *answer* me with *life*' (p. 392).

To speak of Vaughan as being only barely present in the body is to see how fully he framed his role as an author in this resisting light. Even if we pass quickly by his militant revision of the Book of Common Prayer (banned by the Westminister Assembly in 1645) that appeared as the first part of his *Mount of Olives* (1652), in which the Laudian practice of bowing at the name of Jesus is remembered, or refuse an explicitly autobiographical reading of his 'Prayer in adversity, and troubles occasioned by Our Enemies' ('Thou seest, O God, how furious and Implacable mine Enemies are, they have not only rob'd me of that portion and provision which thou hadst graciously given me, but they have also washed their hands in the blood of my friends, my dearest and nearest relatives'), there is still the constant call of the wild in Vaughan: the sharp outbursts against the new Puritan authorities for propagating destruction rather than worship (p. 217), against the apparent hypocrisy involved in sectarian sainting ('St Mary Magdalene'), at times even against God, cries that resonate like 'songs in the Night' – to borrow a phrase from the epigram from Job on the title page of the completed *Silex* – with the ubiquitous wish to be elsewhere: in the desert with St Jerome perhaps, or walking the fields of Bethany with the raised Jesus and his disciples, or simply with the many dead, Abel or otherwise.

The calling is most acute in the devotional poetry, as we might expect. 'More of *fashion* then *force*' (p. 391) is how Vaughan characterized Herbert's other followers, but the same cannot be said of him in his desire to be elsewhere. Herbert had led the way in sounding the heart, but always within the imagined realms of an ever-present *via media* incorporating the principal events of worship. His is the story, as he says in 'The Forerunners', of bringing 'lovely enchanting language' to church and making it 'well dressed and clad'. Vaughan is everywhere more woolly. His is the narrative of the exile – of the person who '*stole* abroad' (emphasis mine), as he says at the outset of the opening poem to *Silex*, in search of the dazzling light of divinity:

> Here, I repos'd; but scarse well set,
> A grove descryed
> Of stately height, whose branches met
> And mixt on every side:
> I entred, and once in
> (Amaz'd to see't)
> Found all was chang'd, and a new spring
> Did all my senses greet;
>
> The unthrift Sunne shot vitall gold
> A thousand peeces,
> And heaven its azure did unfold
> Checqur'd with snowie fleeces,
> The aire was all in spice
> And every bush
> A garland wore; Thus fed my Eyes
> But all the Eare lay hush.   ('Regeneration')

As this passage suggests, with its stunningly lush version of a primitive church that resembles an episcopal cathedral, Vaughan's most brilliant verbal effects often have little to do with refashioning courtly discourse and returning it to its heavenly owner. Although there might elsewhere remain a

Jonsonian dimension to his verse in his use of the pentameter line or in the smoother octosyllabics of 'The Retreat', Vaughan is at his most linguistically inventive when nature or the speaker's response to a divinized nature, not the court, is the object of mimesis. In the memorable opening of 'The Waterfall', the exuberant play with liquid sounds and the shifting, cascading rhythms and abrupt enjambments present us with more than a visual hieroglyph of a waterfall (a common enough practice among emblem poets in Vaughan's day). Vaughan has heard and recirculated the 'deep murmurs', as well as the chiding 'call' of water – its alluring force and energy:

> With what deep murmurs through times silent stealth
> Doth thy transparent, cool and watry wealth
> Here flowing fall,
> And chide, and call,
> As if his liquid, loose Retinue staid
> Lingring, and were of this steep place afraid,
> The common pass
> Where, clear as glass,
> All must descend
> Not to an end:
> But quickned by this deep and rocky grave,
> Rise to a longer course more bright and brave. ('The Waterfall')

Given the level of linguistic intensity recorded in these passages, it is perfectly understandable why scholars have not been content to locate Vaughan strictly within Renaissance conventions of the pastoral but have looked to Hermetic texts of the period, especially those produced by Thomas Vaughan, to explain the energizing potential embodied in the representation of nature in the devotional verse (as well as the presence of words with occult inflections like 'ray', 'seed', 'dew', and 'tincture', for instance). As Thomas noted, with an elitism characteristic of the Vaughans more generally, 'the *Peripatetickes* [Aristotelians] look on *God*, as they do on *Carpenters*, who build with *stone* and *Timber*, without any *infusion* of *life*. But the *world*, which is *Gods building*, is full of *Spirit*, *quick*, and *living*.'[5] Quick and living have special meaning for Henry, too, but not only as properties found in the nature identified in his verse. '*Infusions* of *Life*' characterize the very essence of 'sacred ejaculations', as in the celebrated opening of 'The Morning-watch':

> O Joyes! Infinite sweetnes! with what flowres,
> And shoots of glory, my soul breakes, and buds!
> All the long houres
> Of night, and Rest
> Through the still shrouds

> Of sleep, and Clouds,
> This Dew fell on my Breast;
> O how it Blouds,
> And *Spirits* all my Earth! heark! In what Rings,
> And *Hymning Circulations* the quick world
> Awakes, and sings.

In this waking hymn, the level of reciprocity with nature is so intense (even if Vaughan begins by way of a line from Herbert's 'H[oly] Scriptures') that it is all but impossible to distinguish internal from external – the breaking and budding of the speaker's body from nature's, or the '*Hymning Circulations*' in the world from those uttered by the rejuvenated speaker. 'If *Priest* and *People* change, keep thou thy ground', Vaughan noted in 'Rules and Lessons'. Here and elsewhere, the act of keeping is more than an exercise in stoic resolve, just as 'ground' is more than a term in a familiar phrase. Keeping is a matter of absorbing and being absorbed by the landscape – of speaking its language in 'quickening' turns.

To highlight the divinized landscape in Vaughan is to underscore the non-institutionalized (or in the case of 'Regeneration', the fleetingly institutionalized) opportunities for worship repeatedly 'discovered' in *Silex Scintillans* – the traces of God continually glimpsed in animated things that point to their ultimate home: stones, herbs, and birds, and here especially the cock of 'Cock-crowing', in singular possession of a 'Sunnie seed' from above:

> Father of lights! what Sunnie seed,
> What glance of day hast thou confin'd
> Into this bird? To all the breed
> This busie Ray thou hast assign'd;
> Their magnetisme works all night,
> And dreams of Paradise and light.

It is also to note the primitive, shadowy character of Vaughan's landscape to be more like that of Milton's *Masque* (*Comus* was originally staged in nearby Ludlow Castle) than that of the more manicured Herbert: unbounded and sometimes with strange flora in it. Vaughan's most moving elegy, in fact, makes much of a 'poor root' that lies below ground 'but is still trod / By ev'ry wandring clod'; indeed, the action might be said to pivot on a bizarre encounter or recognition scene between a 'warm Recluse' and the speaker, much as the plot of *Comus* turns on the discovery of a 'small unsightly root' on which 'the dull swain /Treads ... daily' (lines 629–35).

But the spirit blows where it lists in *Silex*. To celebrate light in whatever form is to begin to worry over its loss: 'O take it off! make no delay, / But brush me with thy light, that I / May shine unto a perfect day'; to find a poor root in the landscape is immediately to wish to see through it, to view the landscape as but a 'Masque' and shadow leading to a greater reality. As has been recently re-argued, *Silex* 'is much more about the possibility of searching than it is about finding',[6] or more accurately still, about the *problems* of searching, especially in the first part when, in the immediate wake of the Puritan triumph, the rhetoric of retreat is most insistent and Vaughan's sense of displacement from the present most pronounced and profound. An often anthologized poem like 'Religion', for instance, begins as if an ideal devotional retreat is being envisioned:

> My God, when I walke in those groves,
> And leaves thy spirit doth still fan,
> I see in each shade that there growes
> An Angell talking with a man.
>
> Under a *Juniper*, some house,
> Or the coole *Mirtles* canopie,
> Others beneath an *Oakes* greene boughs,
> Or at some *fountaines* bubling Eye.

For a moment the sense of the past belongs entirely to Vaughan. The pun on 'Leaves' hardly diminishes the note of devotional fervour, as the idyllic description continues for another three stanzas and displays what Stephen Greenblatt might call the 'marvellous possessions' of the Old Testament: figures of Jacob dreaming and wrestling with Angels, Abraham being visited by his 'winged guests', and so forth.[7] But these 'possessions', privately imagined and momentarily owned, also come to be seen as signs of loss ('O how familiar then was heaven'), as signs of what the recent disturbances have claimed. 'Is the truce broke?' The question simply hangs there in all its glancing insinuations; then proceeds a long Spenserian allegory describing the gradual degradation of Religion until it is seen to break forth like Duessa: 'And at first sight doth many please, / But drunk, is puddle, or meere slime / And 'stead of Phisick, a disease.' The satire here might be chalked up to Vaughan, the physician, simply leaping into the fray, but the reference to 'first sight' – ours and Vaughan's – suggests, too, the tenuous thread on which even mediated descriptions of faith now hang: how easily, in fact, a vision or reading is sacrificed to present events, how readily the reader is dispossessed of his or her landscape and its marvellous possessions.

The closing prayer attempts specifically to resolve this problem. Vaughan calls for a healing that involves both a critique of Puritan worship (and therefore not a real mediation) and a revivification – a quickening – of the land that will allow angels to talk once more to man – for retreats to be real and idylls not to be idols:

> Heale then these waters, Lord; or bring thy flock,
> Since these are troubled, to the springing rock.
> Looke downe great Master of the feast; O shine,
> And turn once more our *Water* into *Wine*!

The eucharistic allusions are unmistakable; but the biblical inscription that follows suggests, too, that renewal is also linked to the restoration of the church: '*My Sister, my spouse is as a garden Inclosed, as a Spring shut up, and a fountain sealed up.*' Vaughan is not Spenser, much less St George, but he can still thrust a sword from below in an attempt to rescue the true church. Vaughan, we remember, translated Juvenal as well as Boethius.

Still, retreat is never far from Vaughan's thinking (nor is Boethius), even if the subject is often double-edged and double-edged for more than one reason: something eagerly desired because it has been so fully interrupted; something denied and therefore more fully desired. Based in part on the fifth metre of Boethius, his most famous poem, in fact, might be said to worry conventional ideas of retreat (as, say, expressed in Vaughan's own translation of Guevara's *The Praise and Happiness of the Country-Life*) beyond the pale. Rather than a mere anticipation of the glories of childhood eventually perfected in Wordsworth, 'The Retreat' is a poignant hymn of personal displacement:

> Happy those early dayes! when I
> Shin'd in my Angell-infancy.
> Before I understood this place
> Appointed for my second race,
> Or taught my soul to fancy ought
> But a white, Celestiall thought.

As in 'Religion', the controlling scheme is relentlessly temporal: 'before' (or 'when', 'when', 'before' in the remaining paragraph). But with each restatement, the sense of bifurcation between then and now becomes only more deeply etched (as if the act of restating only made Vaughan more aware of the problem of placelessness), until the wish to retreat receives its quintessential expression in a line famously transported from one of Owen Felltham's *Resolves* ('The *Conscience*, the *Caracter* of a *God* stampt in it, and the apprehension of *Eternity*, doe all prove [the soul] a *shoot of everlastingnesse*':

> My gazing soul would dwell an houre,
> And in those weaker glories spy
> Some shadows of eternity;
> Before I taught my tongue to wound
> My Conscience with a sinfull sound,

> Or had the black art to dispence
> A sev'rall sinne to ev'ry sence,
> But felt through all this fleshly dresse
> Bright *shootes* of everlastingnesse.

One is tempted to say that the simple addition of 'bright' makes the poetic difference here, especially when the 'shoot' is 'felt through all this fleshly dresse' and in the alliterative plural. Much of the emotive thrust of the poem, indeed of Vaughan in general, is fused in this wishful couplet. But, as in many of Vaughan's most memorable lines, the brilliance leaves only a deeper yearning in the reader (and the poet) for an afterglow – in this case, if not for a vision of all going into a world of light, then for a view of a luminous past that recedes at a pace faster than the itinerant imagination, as the 'O' of desire gives way to the 'Ah' of defeat:

> O how I long to travell back
> And tread again that ancient track!
> That I might once more reach that plaine,
> Where first I left my glorious traine,
> From whence th'Inlightned spirit sees
> That shady City of Palme trees;
> But (ah!) my soul with too much stay
> Is drunk, and staggers in the way.
> Some men a forward motion love,
> But I by backward steps would move,
> And when this dust falls to the urn
> In that state I came return.

'Search well another world; whose studies this, / Travels in Clouds, seeks *Manna*, where none is' ('The Search'). Peace is in another country far beyond the stars ('Peace'). Here, the flesh is weak: the soul staggers, 'The sons the father kil' ('The Constellation').

If retreat is often as elusive and problematic in *Silex* as it is enchanting, there are still other responses to the difficulties of historical displacement besides melancholy lament or the kind of visionary satire only partially realized in 'The World'. The world that necessitates escape can also be re-turned, re-imagined as a place ripe for transformation itself – perhaps 'healed', as in the end of 'Religion', or more radically altered by calling for the Second Coming itself:

> Ah! what time wilt thou come? When shall that crie
> The *Bridegroome's Comming*! fil the sky?
> Shall it in the Evening run
> When our words and works are done?

> Or wil thy all-surprizing light
>   Break at midnight?   ('The Dawning')

In the face of such possibilities, Vaughan seems almost without defence – already transported by the cry from above and wondering now only about the hour of Christ's arrival. Like a good many writings of the 1650s, including some of Marvell's poems, *Silex* reverberates with a sense of great expectations: two Judgement Day poems, one on the Conversion of the Jews, a strange 'dramatic monologue' based on an episode from Joshua ('The Stone'), and a host of allusions to the day of doom, some appended in the form of biblical inscriptions, others more loosely suggested through a kind of continuous allegory with light and darkness or an occasional reference to a phrase from Revelation itself.

Marvell might tease this theme in many directions,[8] but for Vaughan, apocalypse is most often represented as a solution to corruption, to the dark changes recently brought about, rather than as a response to a belief in the impending possibility of social improvement, in a potential utopian moment:

> Sin triumphs still, and man is sunk below
>   The Center, and his shrowd;
> All's in deep sleep, and night; Thick darkness lyes
>   And hatcheth o'r thy people;
> But hark! what trumpets that? What Angel cries
>   *Arise! Thrust in thy sickle.*   ('Corruption')

Egypt is now; for Vaughan, there is no Psalm 114 (as there was for Milton), but the poet still has an enunciating role in the imagined cosmic drama. As Louis Martz has recently noted, 'hatcheth o'r' means to close over, to form a hatch over, but 'perhaps also with the suggestion of bringing to maturity a hidden process'.[9] If so, it is a hidden process, like the shift from 'hatch' to 'sickle' (without mentioning 'hatchet'), in which the speaker participates; for when he suddenly shifts from narrator to auditor to announcer ('But hark!') and recirculates in the imaginary present the blast of trumpets and the angel's cry from Revelation 14:15, he bears witness to the moment of change itself.

The 'sickle' should form a slant rhyme with 'people' is perhaps the merest coincidence – a flickering sign of the anti-populism that runs through Vaughan's writing. Elsewhere, however, judgement scenes allow for a return of the repressed, for an opportunity to vocalize victimization beyond that hinted at in the elegies. In this regard, 'Abel's Blood' remains one of the most restless and unsettling poems in *Silex*, as the blood of the murdered Abel emerges from the ground to protest the massive slaughter of innocence. From the outset, Vaughan uses 'still' to denote an action that is ongoing without, perhaps, ever ending – at least until the moment of Judgement itself when it will be possible, once again, to regard 'still' in the other sense of meaning quiet:

> Sad, purple well! whose bubling eye
> Did first against a Murth'rer cry;
> Whose streams still vocal, still complain
>   Of bloody *Cain*,
> And now at evening are as red
> As in the morning when first shed.
>   If single thou
> (Though single voices are but low,)
> Could'st such a shrill and long cry rear
> As speaks still in thy makers ear,
> What thunders shall those men arraign
> Who cannot count those they have slain,
> Who bath not in a shallow flood,
> But in a deep, wide sea of blood?
> A sea, whose lowd waves cannot sleep,
> But *Deep* still calleth upon *deep*:
> Whose urgent *sound* like unto that
> *Of many waters*, beateth at
> The everlasting doors above,
> Where souls behinde the altar move,
> And with one strong, incessant cry
> Inquire *How long?* of the most high.

In Herbert, justice is a matter of balancing scales between sinner and maker – of the speaker arriving at a measured understanding of the role of 'merit' at the great day. For Vaughan, justice represents a supreme opportunity to speak out: not merely to 'complain', but to register through the multiplying voices a sense of sheer outrage over the accumulated acts of violence and then to attempt to separate himself from the bloody event of civil war:

>   O accept
> Of his vow'd heart, whom thou hast kept
> From bloody men! and grant, I may
> That sworn memorial duly pay
> To thy bright arm, which was my light
> And leader through thick death and night.

It also represents a supreme test of patience. The passionate cry of '*How long*' runs counter to (perhaps 'into', given the radical shift in argument at the poem's midpoint) the superior command of the 'Almighty Judge! / At whose just laws no just men grudge', including the New Testament 'law' of meekness and peace centred in the Sacrifice:

> May no cries
> From the low earth to high Heaven rise,
> But what (like his, whose blood peace brings)
> Shall (when they rise) *speak better things*,
> Then *Abels* doth!

But even here, while Vaughan can retract the thunder of voices from his poem, the 'urgent *sound* like unto that / *Of many waters*', he cannot fully 'still' the exclamatory violence from his own voice:

> May *Abel* be
> Still single heard, while these agree
> With his milde blood in voice and will,
> *Who* pray'd for those that did him kill!

As the clinch of the final rhyme indicates, the deep still calls upon the deep. 'Will' and 'kill' are difficult to dislodge, except through a superior act of the will.

For that reason, it is easy to understand why Vaughan frequently prayed for 'the patience of the Saints' ('The Palm-tree'). How to walk the straight and narrow ('The Ass', 'The Men of War'), how to keep close counsel ('Righteousness') are frequent themes in the second part of *Silex* when the note of expectation and release is especially strong, a note that receives circumstantial grounding in the various allusions to 'our sad captivity'. They were also prime challenges for Vaughan, as they were for Milton, and therefore attitudes potentially ripe for fashioning into acts of heroic resistance or of sublime secrecy. In the remainder of this essay, I want to concentrate on two of Vaughan's most impressive poems from this angle. Both are from *Silex* 1655, and in both, with their twin concerns with martyrdom and mysticism, the idea of retreat receives something approaching its ultimate expression in Vaughan.

In the case of 'The Proffer', the literature of religious persecution was rich with examples of martyrdom, and the charge to remember them in times of duress was a commonplace in Renaissance England, as the illustrious printing history of Foxe's *Book of Martyrs* makes clear. Vaughan himself cited perhaps the greatest exemplar from late antiquity in his translation of *The Life of Paulinus*: 'it is an observation of the Readers of Saint *Cyprian, quod in ejus scriptis singula prope verba Martyrium spirant*, that through all his writings, almost every word doth breath Martyrdome. His expressions are all Spirit and Passion, as if he had writ them with his blood, and conveyed the anguish of his sufferings into his writings' (p. 346). Whether or not Vaughan had Cyprian in mind at the end of 'The Proffer' when he exhorted himself (and others, by implication) to 'keep the ancient way', he fully imagined the poem from the point of view of the body under siege – attacked by 'black Parasites' and 'poys'nous, subtile fowls! / The flies of hell' that are clearly associated with the Commonwealth. (Hutchinson plausibly suggests that Vaughan might have been made an offer to 'collaborate' with the Puritan authorities.[10]) The poem begins with a powerful denunciation; then as proof of his unbending resistance to temptation, Vaughan offers in the middle a brief 'character' of the holy life that he has struggled to achieve, a self-portrait in which 'every word doth breath Martyrdome':

> Think you these longing eyes,
>   Though sick and spent,
> And almost famish'd, ever will consent
>   To leave those skies,
> That glass of souls and spirits, where well drest
>   They shine in white (like stars) and rest.
>
> Shall my short hour, my inch,
>   My one poor sand,
> And crum of live, now ready to disband
>   Revolt and flinch,
> And having born the burthen all the day,
>   Now cast at night by Crown away?
>
> No, No; I am not he,
>   Go seek elsewhere.
> I skill not your fine tinsel, and false hair,
>   Your Sorcery
> And smooth seducements: I'le not stuff my story
>   With your Commonwealth and glory.

We do not hear the crackle of the pyre that a recent scholar finds in Cyprian's writings, but we find a similar concern with the visceral as part of the defence of the holy way.[11] Famished as it might be, the body serves as symbol of the soul's steely control in the face of temptation. The eyes remain skyward to the end:

> Then keep the antient way!
>   Spit out their phlegm
> And fill thy brest with home; think of thy dream:
>   A calm, bright day!
> A Land of flowers and spices! the word given,
>   *If these be fair, O what is Heaven!*

If 'The Proffer' remains undervalued (and is ripe to be further historic-ized), the poem that has come to seem Vaughan's richest of late 'takes the ancient way' in an altogether different manner.[12] In 'The Night', the potential martyr's fierce resistance melts in the dusky light of the lover's intimate and secret retreat with Christ. Dark, as it were, calls unto the dark, light unto the light. In this strange and beautiful poem, there is a welcome generosity of intent on Vaughan's part, a desire, as Frank Kermode has suggested in a related context while revisiting this poem, 'to have more of the story than was originally offered'[13] in John 3:2 (indeed, much of John is relevant); and it produces a powerful overflow of mysterious meaning – a 'dark conceit' that brings together Nicodemus and Herbert, the language of the Song of Songs and Dionysius the Areopagite, the first moments of Chris-tianity with the last, a hallowing reverence for the quiet of prayer amid the clatter of the present, the Virgin Mary, Mary Magdalene, and the Bride of Christ, the light of midnight associated with the 'Sun' and 'the deep but dazling darkness' that is God.

A poem that has stimulated so many readings need not be reinterpreted again in full, but a few oddities and points of resistance are still worth remarking on. Several appear in the crucial opening stanza:

> Through that pure *Virgin-shrine*,
> That sacred vail drawn o'r thy glorious noon
> That men might look and live as Glo-worms shine,
> And face the Moon:
> Wise *Nicodemus* saw such light
> As made him know his God by night.

On the strength of Vaughan's usual sympathy with nature, a few readers have made the opening conceit more difficult than it is by seeking to draw a parallel between the experience of Nicodemus seeing Christ at night with the habits of glow-worms facing the moon.[14] But Vaughan would seem to be developing the contrast; the association of men with glow-worms in the seventeenth century was often applied contemptuously, as the example (one of several cited by the *Oxford English Dictionary*) from Joseph Hall makes especially clear: 'the world is full of such glow-wormes, that make some show of Spiritual Light from God'. (Given the 1652 date of the work of Hall's in which this phrase appears, it is even conceivable Vaughan had this particular example in mind.)

The contrast helps to throw into sharp relief the special character of Nicodemus' 'wisdom'. He not only saw the light; the light illuminated him with the knowledge that it was '*his* God' (emphasis mine). While others might continue to face the moon, kept from the light of truth by a veil, he saw through the 'pure *Virgin-shrine*' of the moon, a figure that combines chaste Diana with the Virgin Mary, to this other light, 'the glorious noon', the 'Son' of God. The vision is both compelling and unequivocal. If it injects into the poem a conspiratorial note, moreover, involving a plot of the elect that especially sanctions secrecy, the association is one that appears frequently in Vaughan's writings, particularly later on (see 'The Seed Growing Secretly' and *The Life of Paulinus* as well as the earlier 'Love, and Discipline'). It is also a perspective inevitably and often subtly articulated by disenfranchized royalists.[15]

In focussing on Nicodemus, Vaughan stands completely apart from the other devotional poets with whom he is usually associated: Donne, Herbert, Crashaw, and even Milton have no place for Nicodemus in their poetry. And in favouring him, Vaughan goes against strong exegetical evidence to the contrary, perhaps even against Calvin's earlier condemnation of those Protestants as cowardly Nicodemites who chose to go along with Catholic formalities rather than to risk persecution.[16] Nicodemus has been always a questionable figure for the orthodox; but for Vaughan, living in a 'land of darkness and blinde eyes', requiring secrecy under the threat of persecution and yet wishing regeneration, Nicodemus could readily be imagined as a 'kinred' spirit. 'The Night', it should be noted, is next to 'Abel's Blood'.

But something else odd happens in the poem, too, something for which, one can only guess, Vaughan's reading of Nicodemus played a pivotal role as well. *Quem quæritis?* If Nicodemus is the exemplary believer ('Most blest believer he!') who reappears in John 19:39 to help preserve Jesus' body, Vaughan becomes a Mary Magdalene figure looking for the Lord. 'And they say unto her, Woman why weepest thou? She saith unto them, Because they have taken away my Lord, and I know not where they have laid him' (20:13):

> O who will tell me, where
> He found thee at that dead and silent hour!
> What hallow'd solitary ground did bear
> So rare a flower,
> Within whose sacred leafs did lie
> The fulness of the Deity.

Mary's lament for Jesus becomes braided into Vaughan's for a vision comparable to Nicodemus', a fusion in which the worry of loss, concentrated in the word 'dead', is gradually transformed into an experience of wonder by the image of 'the fulness of the Deity' emerging from 'so rare a flower'. There is nothing shocking here, as there is in 'I Walked the Other Day', when the 'warm Recluse' delivers its startling message of loss and renewal.

Rather, the moment of solitude – Nicodemus', Mary's, Vaughan's, the reader's – is hallowed, the ground sanctified, as it were, by the view of Jesus alone, observed only by nature and by us:

> No mercy-seat of gold,
> No dead and dusty *Cherub*, nor carv'd stone,
> But his own living works did my Lord hold
> And lodge alone;
> Where *trees* and *herbs* did watch and peep
> And wonder, while the *Jews* did sleep.

'My Lord': and from here, we move from one imaginary garden to another, as the voice migrates into that of the bride in the Song of Songs: 'I am come into my garden ... I sleep, but my heart waketh; *it is* the voice of my beloved that knocketh, *saying*, Open to me, my sister, my love, my dove, my undefiled: for my head is filled with dew, *and* my locks with the drops of the night' (5:1–2). We might remember how Vaughan represented the Bride as Church in the 'The British Church' lamenting its forced separation from Christ, its head. But in this night of nights, things are different; now the body muses over an amorous return of the head in a moment of near perfect stillness:

> Dear night! this worlds defeat;
> The stop to busie fools; cares check and curb;
> The day of Spirits; my souls calm retreat
> Which none disturb!
> *Christs* progress, and his prayer time;
> The hours to which high Heaven doth chime.
>
> Gods silent, searching flight:
> When my Lords head is fill'd with dew, and all
> His locks are wet with the clear drops of night;
> His still, soft call;
> His knocking time; The souls dumb watch,
> When Spirits their fair kinred catch.

In the allusion to 'my Lords head' and to Christ's kingly 'progress, and his prayer time', we might be tempted to fantasize momentarily about the other, decapitated, king, whose habits of private prayer had been made available for all England to witness in the frontispiece to *Eikon Basilike* (1649). But the licence for a lover's intimacy belongs to scripture and to Herbert: the chime of 'Prayer (I)' as part of the stanzaic 'background' incorporating the 'still, soft call' reminds us that the most intimate moment of communion in Vaughan could be fully realized only in company with Herbert. Still, the

final enactment of 'this worlds defeat' lies elsewhere – in the great concluding stanza:

> There is in God (some say)
> A deep, but dazling darkness; As men here
> Say it is late and dusky, because they
> See not all clear;
> O for that night! where I in him
> Might live invisible and dim.

Vaughan is not 'there' yet; and were he to arrive, moreover, there would be
no means of measuring his desire to be elsewhere – of defeating the world.
But the wish has taken him to the farthest outpost of the imagination: to a
deep but dazzling darkness so powerful and remote that all thoughts of
living – whether with Herbert or Paulinus, Jesus, Nicodemus, or Mary – are
willingly exchanged in favour of becoming altogether invisible in God. Here,
at the end of 'The Night', the distance between militancy and devotion
approaches zero.

NOTES

1 Adrienne Rich, *Blood, Bread, and Poetry: Selected Prose, 1979–1985* (New York:
W. W. Norton, 1986), p. 170.
2 Quoted from 'Regeneration', p. 397. Further quotations of Vaughan's writings
are from *The Works of Henry Vaughan*, ed. L. C. Martin, 2nd edn (Oxford:
Clarendon Press, 1957). Serious students of Vaughan will also want to consult
the more recent, annotated editions by Alan Rudrum (Harmondsworth: Penguin,
1976) and Louis Martz (Oxford University Press, 1986). When quoting from the
Bible, I have chosen the King James version, but it should be noted that Vaughan
was familiar with the Geneva Bible as well.
3 Although there is much criticism on the subject of retreat and retirement in the
seventeenth century, my most immediate debt is to Lois Potter, *Secret Rites and
Secret Writings: Royalist Literature, 1641–1660* (Cambridge University Press,
1989).
4 See James D. Simmonds, *Masques of God: Form and Theme in the Poetry of
Henry Vaughan* (University of Pittsburgh Press, 1972); and my *Henry Vaughan:
The Unfolding Vision* (Princeton University Press, 1982). For interesting
treatments of *Thalia Rediviva*, focussing on 'Daphnis: An Elegiac Ecologue', see
Cedric C. Brown, 'The Death of Righteous Men: Prophetic Gesture in Vaughan's
"Daphnis" and Milton's *Lycidas*', *The George Herbert Journal* 7 (1983–4) 1–25;
and Graeme J. Watson, 'Political Change and Continuity of Vision in Henry
Vaughan's "Daphnis: An Elegiac Ecologue"', *Studies in Philology* 83 (1986:
158–81.
5 Quoted from *Anthroposophia Theomagica* in *The Works of Thomas Vaughan*,
ed. Alan Rudrum (Oxford: Clarendon Press, 1984), p. 52. Important discussions
of Vaughan's hermeticism date from Elizabeth Holmes's *Henry Vaughan and the*

Hermetic Philosophy (Oxford University Press, 1932) and include several valuable articles by Alan Rudrum: 'The Influence of Alchemy in the Poems of Henry Vaughan', *Philological Quarterly* 49 (1970): 469–80; and 'An Aspect of Vaughan's Hermeticism: The Doctrine of Cosmic Sympathy', *Studies in English Literature* 14 (1974): 129–38. The best general discussion of Vaughan and pastoral belongs to Georgia B. Christopher, 'In Arcadia, Calvin . . . A Study of Nature in Henry Vaughan', *Studies in Philology* 70 (1973): 408–26.

6 John N. Wall, *Transformations of the Word: Spenser, Herbert, Vaughan* (Athens: University of Georgia Press, 1988), p. 301. The seminal article on the subject of searching in Vaughan is by Louis Martz, 'Henry Vaughan: The Man Within', *PMLA* 78 (1963): 40–9.

7 Stephen Greenblatt, *Marvelous Possessions: The Wonder of the New World* (University of Chicago Press, 1992), especially chapter 2.

8 See, for example, Joseph H. Summers, 'Some Apocalyptic Strains in Marvell's Poetry', in *Tercentenary Essays in Honor of Andrew Marvell*, ed. Kenneth Friedenreich (Hamden, Conn.: Archon Books, 1977), pp. 180–203.

9 *George Herbert and Henry Vaughan*, ed. Louis L. Martz (Oxford University Press, 1986), p. 504.

10 F. E. Hutchinson, *Henry Vaughan: A Life and Interpretation* (Oxford: Clarendon Press, 1947), pp. 124–5.

11 Peter Brown, *The Body and Society: Men, Women, and Sexual Renunciation in Early Christianity* (New York: Columbia University Press, 1988), pp. 193–5.

12 Two recent articles, from very different angles, will give the reader a spectrum of interpretive possibilities elicited by this poem. See Graeme J. Watson, 'The Temple in "The Night": Henry Vaughan and the Collapse of the Established Church', *MP* 84 (1986): 144–61; and Geoffrey Hill, 'A Pharisee to Pharisees: Reflections on Vaughan's "The Night"', *English* 38 (1989): 97–113.

13 Frank Kermode, *The Uses of Error* (London: Collins, 1990), p. 431. See also his earlier, influential essay, 'The Private Imagery of Henry Vaughan', *RES* ns 1 (1950): 206–25.

14 See, for instance, Alan Rudrum, 'Vaughan's "The Night": Some Hermetic Notes', *Modern Language Review* 64 (1969): 14–15. In his 1976 Penguin edition of Vaughan's poetry, Rudrum attempts to fortify this position further (and in turn a Behmenist reading of 'The Night') while nonetheless citing *OED*'s authority to the contrary. His reasoning seems to be that since Vaughan often views creatures sympathetically, it is therefore 'typical of Vaughan that he should refuse to adopt a convention of speech which would imply contempt of one of God's humbler creatures'. But Vaughan could occasionally view the creatures contemptuously in order to indicate his criticisms of man (see 'Idle Verse', for instance, or the 'mole' in 'The World'), and he seems to have done so on this occasion. It is perhaps indicative of the shaky argument that Rudrum introduces his gloss with a 'perhaps'. Pettet's remarks (also cited) would not seem to support this position either since Pettet, somewhat illogically, is speaking of a 'worm' rather than of a 'glow-worm' in the gloss he produces from Psalm 22 ('But I am a worm, and no man.')

15 Potter, *Secret Rites and Secret Writing*, p. 133. See also the particularly interesting essay by Janet E. Halley, 'Versions of the Self and the Politics of Privacy in *Silex Scintillans*', *The George Herbert Journal* 7 (1983–4): 51–71.

16 Watson, 'The Temple in "The Night"', pp. 154–5, takes up the issue of persecution in some detail. For Calvin's place in this debate, see Carlos M. N. Eire, *War Against the Idols: The Reformation of Worship from Erasmus to Calvin* (Cambridge University Press, 1986), chapter 7.

FURTHER READING

Calhoun, Thomas O., *Henry Vaughan: The Achievement of Silex Scintillans* (Newark: University of Delaware Press, 1981)

Durr, R. A., *On the Mystical Poetry of Henry Vaughan* (Cambridge, Mass.: Harvard University Press, 1962)

Garner, Ross, *Henry Vaughan: Experience and the Tradition* (University of Chicago Press, 1959)

Hammond, Gerald, 'Henry Vaughan's Verbal Subtlety: Word Play in *Silex Scintillans*', *Modern Language Review* 79 (1984): 526–40

Hill, Christopher, 'Henry Vaughan', in *Collected Essays*, 3 vols. (Sussex: Harvester Press, 1985), vol. 1, pp. 207–25

Lewalski, Barbara K., *Protestant Poetics and the Seventeenth-Century Religious Lyric* (Princeton University Press, 1979)

Mahood, M. M., *Poetry and Humanism* (1950; rpr. New York: W. W. Norton & Co., 1970)

Marilla, E. L., 'The Secular and Religious Poetry of Henry Vaughan', *Modern Language Quarterly* 9 (1948): 394–411

Martz, Louis L., *The Poetry of Meditation: A Study in English Religious Literature of the Seventeenth Century* (New Haven: Yale University Press, 1954)

Pettet, E. C., *Of Paradise and Light: A Study of Vaughan's Silex Scintillans* (Cambridge University Press, 1960)

Poetry Wales: A Henry Vaughan Number, no. 11 (1975)

Rudrum, Alan, *Henry Vaughan* (Cardiff: University of Wales Press, 1981)

'Henry Vaughan, the Liberation of the Creatures, and Seventeenth-Century English Calvinism', *The Seventeenth Century* 4 (1989): 33–54

Rudrum, Alan (ed.), *Essential Articles for the Study of Henry Vaughan* (Hamden, Conn.: Archon Books, 1987)

Seelig, Sharon, *The Shadow of Eternity: Belief and Structure in Herbert, Vaughan, and Traherne* (Lexington: University of Kentucky, 1981)

Skulsky, Harold, 'The Fellowship of the Mystery: Emergent and Exploratory Metaphor in Vaughan', *Studies in English Literature* 27 (1987): 89–107

Summers, Joseph H., *The Heirs of Donne and Jonson* (Oxford University Press, 1970)

14

DONALD M. FRIEDMAN

Andrew Marvell

'Climacteric' (from the Greek for 'ladder') as a word and concept appears first in English at about the end of the sixteenth century. It identifies a critical moment in the life of an individual or a nation, so it is not surprising that it should come into currency around the death of Queen Elizabeth I, and become a familiar usage as the course of the Stuart dynasty moves toward armed rebellion and civic upheaval.[1] In 'An Horatian Ode upon Cromwell's Return from Ireland' Marvell predicts that 'to all States not free' Cromwell will '*Clymacterick* be'[2] (lines 103–4), that the same overwhelming military prowess Cromwell has displayed in subduing the Irish rebellion may be deployed against the remaining monarchic states of Europe. He implies that the triumphant Protestant general embodies the force of change that marks a crucial moment of history. The occasion for his writing the 'Ode' is also a climacteric moment in the poet's own development.

Andrew Marvell's twenty-ninth birthday fell in March of 1650; less than two months later the event occurred that led him to write the poem that marks his climacteric moment: the return of Oliver Cromwell from a successful, and memorably brutal, campaign in Ireland. Not only for Marvell, but for the entire English nation, Cromwell's entry into London marked a point of poised, breathless, precarious, expectant, suspended potential for change. A year earlier Parliament had brought Charles I to trial, convicted him of high treason for making war 'upon the people of his kingdom', and had beheaded him on a scaffold beside the Banqueting Hall of the palace of Whitehall, the site of the elaborate allegorical masques which had been the distinctive art form of the Caroline court. Since that time Parliament had ruled as the sole governing power in the country; but divisions within Parliament, over questions of the religious settlement of the new national church, over economic policies, and over political relations with the army, had already begun to appear. Lord Thomas Fairfax, commander of the Parliamentary army, expressed his strong reservation, tantamount to revulsion, at the thought of invading Scotland, which he regarded as a partner in the

Solemn League and Covenant, despite the threat of concerted aggression against England by the Scots and Charles Stuart, the king's son and heir. Fairfax resigned his commission, and Cromwell was appointed by Parliament to assume command of the army and lead the campaign against the Scots. The Lord General eventually retired to his estate at Nunappleton in Yorkshire, and Cromwell embarked on the military venture which led to yet another victory and his eventual elevation to the position of Lord Protector, as titular head of state. Shortly after these events Marvell accepted a position as tutor to Fairfax's daughter Mary, and lived at Nunappleton for several years.

The 'Horatian Ode' appears to have been written between Cromwell's arrival in London on 1 June and his departure for the north on 28 June. Marvell responded to the occasion for his poem in a way that expanded its significance, to encompass not only the poet's understanding of his relation to the event, but also the place of the event in a larger and more shadowy national history. The summoning of the Long Parliament in 1640 had released a tide of feeling calling for the completion of the reformation begun in the previous century, and asserting the providential role of the English people in that work of reformation. Millennial prophecies of radical religious sects made consort with the most visionary designs for political change; the moment of 'new heaven, new earth' seemed to be imminent.

It was in this atmosphere of expectation and uncertainty that Marvell was impelled to give form to his thoughts about the killing of the king and the emergence of a new military leader.[3] The choice of genre was always crucial for Marvell; he showed both precise knowledge of and intense critical interest in literary genres.[4] In choosing to write an 'Horatian' ode, Marvell was making several implicit statements about his approach to the subject of Cromwell's entrance onto the political scene. The ode itself was not yet a fully naturalized form in English poetry; Ben Jonson was its only true master during the early decades of the seventeenth century, and he had converted its elevated language and episodic structure, in some cases, to personal and polemic uses.[5]

Marvell's choice of the ode was made, inevitably, in the shadow of this Jonsonian enterprise. Marvell understood Jonson's explicit and implicit claims to give voice to the fundamental standards of a civilization, to instruct its leaders, and to maintain that role and those values as they are challenged by innovation and change. But he also went further, in designating his poem 'Horatian', and invoked both the perspective and the historical circumstances of Horace, a supporter of the Roman republic who became the poet of empire by creating a mode that could celebrate and criticize at the same time, in the service of an ideal of humane conduct. To be 'Horatian', in this understanding, was to cultivate the cooperative powers of perception, analysis, and evaluation, to preserve a sense of personal integrity by maintaining distance from the events that provided the occasion for public utterance, and to insist on the interdependence of the poet's privilege and responsibility to speak truth to power. It did not escape Horace that to the extent that he succeeded in establishing his title as defender of Roman civilization and culture he also established his independent power to designate and celebrate the heroes of that culture. The creation of Augustus' reputation for the virtuous exercise of supreme power entailed the regime's dependence on its creator. Something of this reflexive process must have been apparent to Marvell, however private his meditations on it proved to be.

To begin to understand the action of 'An Horatian Ode' some consideration must be given to the course of Marvell's career until 1650, and to the development of his political thinking. Born in Yorkshire, he maintained a lifelong connection with that complex and turbulent region, almost a country to itself in its traditions and institutions. He was probably educated at Hull Grammar School, and in 1633 matriculated at Trinity College, Cambridge, where he took his BA and stayed until 1641. Apart from a legendary flight to London during his student days to join the Jesuits (from which his father, a sternly Calvinist minister, retrieved him quickly) and the publication of a Latin poem (adapted from one of Horace's odes to Augustus) and one in Greek in a volume of student congratulations to King Charles I on the birth of a daughter in 1637, Marvell's time at Cambridge appears to have been uneventful. But academic records cannot convey the significance of the presence of undergraduate poets like Richard Crashaw and Abraham Cowley, and the preaching of latitudinarian divines like Benjamin Whichcote (one of the founders of the school of philosophers and theologians who became known as Cambridge Platonists).

Documentation of the years that follow is sparse; but it seems that Marvell left England for travel and employment as a tutor on the European continent. In 1653, Milton, writing to recommend Marvell for a position in the Commonwealth bureaucracy, notes that he 'spent four years abroad in Holland, France, Italy, and Spain to very good purpose', including mastery of their languages. By 1648 he had returned to England, and in a short time published two or three poems which, by implication, ally him to the royalist party, or at least suggest his sympathy for the monarchy.

What these poems reveal most clearly is a student of language, already adept in the styles of classicizing poetry, and nervously sensitive to the filiations between standards of rhetoric and standards of civic morality. The values that illumine his imagination at this point are those of political stability, cultural continuity, inherited and customary rights and principles, and the complete implication of language in the moral life of individuals and communities. He might with justice be called an absolute humanist, but not, perhaps, a member of 'the king's party'.

The decision to write the 'Ode', however, is characteristic both of Marvell and of a current in reformist thought of the period, in that it implies the drive to understand the shape of providential history, and the equally importunate need to bring individual will into conformity with the divine will. To try to understand God's design became not only an all-embracing moral duty but also a crucial task of introspection, analysis, and discipline by which to determine the choices of life; Marvell's telling phrase for that discipline occurs in 'Upon Appleton House, to my Lord Fairfax', where he looks forward to the time when the Fairfax family will 'make their *Destiny* their *choice*', (line 744).[6] The trial and execution of Charles seem not to have elicited from Marvell at the time a response strong enough to move him to poetry; but the emergence of Cromwell, taken together with the resignation of Fairfax and the consequent likelihood of a radical change in the temper and plans of the new government, presented a challenge peculiarly attuned to his habits of mind.

It is an intensely self-conscious mind, that of an observer of the process of thought itself. It reveals itself in a persistent diffidence about categorical statement, a sense of the incompleteness of any verbal formulation of complex truth, scepticism about the ties between motive and declaration, the frequent resort to puns and plays on words that suggest the implication of apparently opposed meanings with each other, and in what might be called a rhetorical rhythm, a systole and diastole of evaluation and decision. Marvell's has been called a poetry of judgement, in recognition of its intellectual balance, personal reserve, and moral austerity. It might be more accurate to say that it does not judge, but rather selects, crystallizes, and presents the materials necessary for judgement.

Marvell devised a metrical pattern for the 'Ode' that he never repeated;[7] its alternation of tetrameter and trimeter couplets is brilliantly suited to the poems' general rhythm of thinking and rethinking, concluding and then revising, proposing and qualifying, moving through a series of powerfully expressive images that argue their significance with each other, yet always reminding the reader (and the mind which is doing the reminding) of the obligation to find what can be said 'if we would speak true' (line 27).

The habit of mind that leads Marvell to begin so meditative a poem as 'The Garden'[8] with a tangle of puns – 'How vainly men themselves amaze' (line 1) – is fully present in the opening lines of the 'Horatian Ode', as he thinks about what Cromwell's return means for those who witness it. As

Herbert addressed 'The Church-porch' and, presumably, all the poems of
The Temple to a putative 'sweet youth' who stood most in need of spiritual
guidance, so Marvell moves to the foreground the 'forward Youth that
would appear'. The adjective and the conditional verb epitomize one of the
structural dilemmas of the poem: is to be 'forward' to intuit the direction of
an emergent age, or is it to anticipate the times out of ambition and self-
regarding desire? Whichever is the case, Marvell suggests, the choice to
abandon one way of life to pursue the possible rewards of another remains
open; even a forward youth must *choose* to 'appear'. But if he does so, the
couplet informs him relentlessly, he *must* 'forsake his *Muses* dear' (line 2).[9]
But any hesitation or regret in the opening lines is modulated by the vision
of the youth serving his muses 'in the Shadows', singing in 'Numbers languishing' (lines 3–4), a scene of idle or ignoble retreat and indulgent feeling,
and by the firm assertion that ''Tis time to leave the Books in dust' (line 5).
With equal firmness the next tetrameter couplet declares, 'So restless
Cromwel could not cease / In the inglorious Arts of Peace' (lines 9–10).
Although the 'Arts of Peace' are arts still, they have been rendered 'inglorious' by the decision to 'oyl th'unused Armours rust' (line 6). But questions
flock around the seemingly flat declaration like the ghosts around Aeneas: is
'inglorious' dismissive or descriptive? is it a judgement, or an observation
that the arts of peace lack the 'glory' of war? and in either case, in whose
mind is this so? Cromwell's? the youth's? Marvell's? Those questions raise
more questions: what happens to ideas of the value of the arts of peace
when they are thrust aside by the exigencies and the transvaluations of the
time of war? what becomes of what is forsaken?

To write in tetrameters is to accept the limitations of a restricted line
and its potential to create a song- or dance-like rhythm even where it risks
being inappropriate. Marvell meets that challenge in part by the extraordinary precision of his diction. As he comments reflectively on the image
of supernaturally destructive Cromwell – ''Tis Madness to resist or blame /
The force of angry Heavens flame' (lines 25–6) – he spans possible reac-
tions to acts of revolutionary power in naming resistance (or denial) and
the displacement of responsibility by placing blame, a responsibility he
foreshadows by naming 'angry Heavens'. If Cromwell is the agent of a
punitive divinity, then his restlessness, his fiery urgency, are not merely his
own, but act to further a providential plan. To resist him, then, would be
impious as well as pointless. But Marvell calls it 'Madness', and leaves it to
be decided whether he means actual overthrow of reason, or the wilful
madness of futile opposition. As if he himself is poised between resistance
and blame, and struck by the fearful glamour of the image he has created
of Cromwell 'burning through the Air', he muses that 'Much to the Man is

due' (lines 21, 28) – due from his admirers and his detractors, as well as to his deeds.

What Marvell admires is Cromwell's ascent from 'his private Gardens' (line 29) to his present eminence;[10] he attributes his success to 'industrious Valour', a phrase as oxymoronic in normal usage as 'Urged his active Star' (lines 33, 12). But Marvell is trying to define the nature of Cromwell's 'Courage high' (line 17), which is distinguished from ordinary heroic valour by its controlled and even calculating discipline. The times have forced upon England the choice between the stability of custom and the opportunity afforded by the new vision of a sovereign figure who defines himself without the symbolic language of tradition.

The poem (so to speak) still wants to believe that the choice is eternally before us; but the iron need to 'speak true' demands that the situation in 1650 be confronted squarely:

> Though Justice against Fate complain,
> And plead the antient Rights in vain:
> But those do hold or break
> As Men are strong or weak.　　　　(lines 37–40)

Justice is still named justice, and the ancient rights are still rights (every party to the civil disputes of the 1630s and 1640s claimed to be defending the ancient rights of Englishmen); but the strength of their claims is embodied in the moral strength of those who support them. As Cromwell has shown that Caesars are not really protected by their symbolic laurel wreaths, so the events of the civil wars prove that a society's ideals, like its religious truths, must be incarnated if they are to sustain faith. The poem thus turns to Cromwell with a finer focus on his abilities, and, reflexively, on the dilemma of evaluating them. Marvell's praise of Cromwell's military prowess –

> What Field of all the Civil Wars
> Where his were not the deepest Scars?　　　　(lines 45–6)

– apart from putting before us the self-contradictory phrase, 'Civil Wars', makes it impossible to distinguish between the scars Cromwell has suffered from those he has given – which is Marvell's point: the costs are commensurable with the achievements.

In moving from Cromwell's battlefield ability to his political acumen, or 'wiser Art' (line 48), Marvell revives the tale that Charles's escape from Hampton Court was engineered to bring him more closely under the army's control. The larger argument is, however, that even this matching of wiles was part of an impersonal design; Charles's flight and capture occurred:

> That thence the *Royal Actor* born
> The *Tragick Scaffold* might adorn.　　　　(lines 53–4)

Charles was carried to the scaffold to perform the role he was born to act. His consummate action is to personate a king; and this he did superbly. It is perfect in its self-enclosed definition, but hollow in its display of 'helpless Right' (line 62). It is indeed a 'memorable Scene' (line 58), fixed in memory because frozen out of the current of time, a static 'scene' comparable to the symbolic masque; but it is transformed into a 'memorable Hour' (line 65) by the fall of the axe, which marks the resumption of historical process. The accents of surrender are unmistakable in the broken rhythm of:

> But bow'd his comely Head,
> Down as upon a Bed. (lines 63–4)

The nostalgic sympathy and distanced aesthetic appreciation that illumine this passage generate, in Marvell's paradoxical pattern, the strong, regular, almost martial pronouncement that follows:

> This was that memorable Hour
> Which first assur'd the forced Pow'r. (lines 65–6)

'Was' places the scene in memory, and forever in the past; the hours move on.

The Irish campaigns are drawn upon for testimony to Cromwell's abilities; and predictions of his triumphs in Scotland and ultimately abroad balance the implications of:

> Nor yet grown stiffer with Command,
> But still in the *Republick's* hand. (lines 81–2)

No longer a blazing force of angry divinity Cromwell now shows as a bird of prey which kills on command, only to return to 'the next green Bow', where 'The Falckner has her sure' (lines 94, 96). The man who in subduing the Irish has shown how much he can do 'That does both act and know' (line 76), in contradistinction to the king whose supreme moment was to act, has become a female predator, submissive to her handler's 'lure'.

An ode must combine celebration and prophecy, must extrapolate from past actions to future promise. Marvell reminds Cromwell that his dynasty consists entirely of being 'the Wars and Fortunes Son'. He must 'March indefatigably on' (lines 113, 114) and keep his sword erect; nothing lies beneath or behind the ruler but his native ability, since he has demonstrated the hollowness of mysteries of state and the myths and symbols that surround an anointed monarch. Having abandoned 'the inglorious Arts of Peace', Cromwell has made himself the child of the '*Arts* that did *gain* / A *Pow'r*' (lines 119–20); the man who appeared first as a flame in the skies goes out of the poem as a lonely figure marching into the darkness, holding a sword with which to frighten 'The Spirits of the shady Night' (line 118).

Within that rhetorical arc Marvell has registered a movement not only of historical actuality, but of the modes of understanding of the individual consciousness in the stream of time. Many have thought that in doing so he marked a clear moment of transition from one way of thinking about and figuring providential purpose to what we think of as the modern way of imagining our relation to history.

Marvell's thinking in poetry is typically alert to the reciprocities of imaginative activity. The 'Horatian Ode' meditates on the arena of political conflict, but it begins by 'appear[ing]' out of the muses' 'shadows', the retired place of poetic creativity. He associated that place with the mode of poetic figuration we call 'pastoral'. Throughout most of its polymorphous literary history, pastoral has been rooted in the need for sophisticated members of complex societies to try to understand their relationship to the created world. The need arises from the consciousness that we are at the same time creatures like all others and different from all others in that we have devised the distinction between the creatures and ourselves.

The idea of a golden age is part of the genetic code of western pastoral literature, and one of the reasons why it blended so gratefully into the biblical mythology of Eden and the fall from perfect humanity into corruption and decline. Prelapsarian life in the garden of Eden is recognizably akin to the earliest and latest classical versions of the myth of original perfection, from Hesiod to Ovid. The fundamental circumstance of our lost paradise was that human beings were the centre and beneficiaries of a bounteous and benevolent nature, unperturbed by changes of season or extremes of temperature, fed and clothed by plants and animals who existed to provide for their necessities. Where all was freely given there could be no concept of property; therefore there was neither greed, envy, anger, nor ambition, no cause for gluttony, no meaning to sloth, and no basis for pride.

Marvell's interest in the meanings of pastoral tropes, however, is not limited to these conventions. Marvell takes us closer to the unspoken premises of the myth of the garden, the assumption that in the original microcosm of creation, the human mind was fitted intrinsically to the structure of the world it perceived. The idea survives in the biblical scene of Adam naming the animals because he was able to know their essences directly – and in the Mower Damon's plangent claim, 'My Mind was once the true survey / Of all these Medows fresh and gay.'[11] What in Adam is a sign of power over subordinate nature is in Marvell's rereading of Genesis a hypothesis about the ways in which consciousness and the world that we believe to be independent of it nevertheless interact and depend on each other. 'Survey' is both transitive and passive, a map and an act of intellectual structuring.

Marvell's Mower is intimately involved in the glossing of the biblical phrase, 'all flesh is grass'. Characteristically,[12] Marvell presses the metaphor toward its root or hidden meaning, and identifies the Mower with the grass as an emblem, not simply of mortality, but of the primeval unity of mind and nature which has been ruptured by consciousness itself and its power to produce metaphor, symbols, and other kinds of abstract representations of reality. He drives the point home with grim irony as he comments on the fallen hero in 'Damon the Mower,[13] 'Death thou art a Mower too.' (line 88).

Only three of what have come to be called 'the Mower poems' present Damon as their central concern; he speaks in his own voice in 'The Mower's Song' and in 'The Mower to the Glow-worms',[14] but his verses in 'Damon the Mower' are introduced in mock-heroic style ('Heark how the Mower *Damon* Sung', line 1). Damon is consistently aware of Juliana's power to destroy the pre-existent harmony of his mind and the fields he tends. What is unusual is the poems' concentration on the mind as the centre of feeling, passion, conscious identity. Damon puts his understanding most poignantly and characteristically when he tells the glow-worms that their 'courteous Lights' are useless, 'For She my Mind hath so displac'd / That I shall never find my home' (lines 13, 15–16).

'The Mower against Gardens' may be Damon, but if so he is a more sophisticated Damon indeed, for the burden of his attack is the ancient debate over the relation of conscious art to the objects it imitates or shapes. A number of passages in Marvell's poems and prose indict 'the architects' who 'square and hew, / Green Trees that in the Forest grew'; but it is the Body in 'A Dialogue between the Soul and Body'[15] that makes that charge, and we need to recall that architecture is, etymologically, the master skill, the fundamental power of design, the human art of creation in its original form. The Mower who inveighs against gardens speaks for a purist vision of a nature untainted by human intention; for him man is 'Luxurious', and gardens a sign of his limitlessly arrogant drive to reform nature in his own image. Marvell's Mower is engaged in a philosophical debate about the nature of the mind's contact with the world it knows and names; it is a question central to his idea of the poetic act.

The title itself of 'The Garden'[16] hints at the audacity of the poem, in suggesting that it intends to incorporate the immense history and range of meaning that have accrued to that word. It promises to image the lost paradise of Genesis 1–3, and also the garden of Canticles, the *hortus mentis* of the philosophers, the *hortus conclusus* of the cults of the Virgin, the green retreats of stoic moralists, the gardens in which Renaissance mistresses walked and Marvellian mowers complained, and, in sum, all the wild and cultivated places of tranquil solitude in which the mind can recreate itself and perform its native act of contemplation. For the other great theme of pastoral literatures which rings in Marvell's consciousness is the ancient argument over the competing virtues of active engagement in the affairs of the polis and the disinterested attempt to understand the worlds of men and nature, to realize the unique gift of rationality, in the cloister, the study – or the garden.

In order to think about these things, Marvell characteristically takes us *into* the garden, for he is interested not so much in traditional ideas of the experience of gardens as in experiencing the creation of those ideas. Marvell is as careful here to ambiguate the nature of his poem's speaker as he was in presenting the 'forward youth' of the 'Horatian Ode'. The habit of conceiving his nonce voice as in some sense distinguishable from his own opinion-holding mind is deeply implicated in Marvell's rhetorical world view.

The speaker of 'The Garden' places himself in a felicity earned by having abandoned 'the busie Companies of Men', who are mocked for striving mightily to win a 'crown' (lines 12, 4) woven from the leaves of one of the canonical trees of victory: the palm of the triumphant general, the oak of the public leader, the bays of maker of poems. But it is not enough to criticize the futile labours of *negotium*; Marvell invents the 'Garlands of repose' (line 8), the reward for *in*activity, and inverts the motif of passionate pursuit of the symbols of conquest by comparing the 'short and narrow verged Shade' (line 5) with which the trees of the active life 'upbraid' their hectic suitors, with the broad shadow of 'delicious Solitude' formed by the sensuous 'closing' of 'all Flow'rs and all Trees' (lines 6, 16, 7).

The poem works by overturning conventional views of the purpose of effort – or, more properly, by turning them inside out, transforming them. The green of the trees of the garden is more 'amorous' than the whites and reds of the landscape of love poetry; the speaker will not reject, but strike to the essence of, the lover's gesture of carving the beloved's name in bark: he will, of course, carve only the name of the tree.[17] What the garden does, above all, is to clarify the mind's view of its desires and purpose; it accomplishes this task by revealing the true motives underlying our acts, and the stories we inherit and go on telling ourselves. In the pastoral mode the most important stories are those of failed ambition and frustrated love; and so Marvell moralizes Ovid anew by discovering that:

> Apollo hunted Daphne so,
> Only that She might Laurel grow.
> And Pan did after Syrinx speed,
> Not as a Nymph, but for a Reed.[18]   (lines 29–32)

The master-plot of the sublimation and metamorphosis of sexual passion leads, in the garden, to the creation of the arts of poetry and song. But the main point of the stanza is to argue that 'Love hither makes his best retreat', that the garden is the natural resort of those who have run their 'Passions heat' (lines 25–6), the place where appetite is allayed, and the desire for the other is met by the generative power of art. The conclusive proof of this hypothesis is 'The *Gods*, that mortal Beauty chase, / Still in a Tree did end their race' (lines 27–8); the restless energy of the pagan deities here is stilled in the laurel and the reed, and the 'race' of gods finds its end in the 'tree' of Calvary.

As he surrenders to the actualities of the garden, the 'wondrous life' he describes enacts the very sensations of the lost golden age, as the fruits press themselves upon him in amorous benevolence. His fall on grass, 'Stumbling' and 'Insnard' (lines 33, 39–40) as it may be by the bounteous flora, is harmless. From this acme of innocent sensuous pleasure, there is nevertheless an ascent – or, at least, a change – from the pleasures now seen as 'less' from the perspective to which the mind 'withdraws'. Like the asymmetrical couplets of the 'Horatian Ode', the successive couplets of 'The Garden' mark stages of understanding, as each assertion is further qualified, each achievement refined and superseded. The mind, at first proclaimed as 'that Ocean' that contains 'each kind' found in the world of the garden,[19] goes further in its generative powers:

> Yet it creates, transcending these,
> Far other Worlds, and other Seas,
> Annihilating all that's made
> To a green Thought in a green Shade.   (lines 45–8)

Marvell's lines seem to applaud the mind's transcendent creative faculties; but does transcendence lose touch with the world we live in, and what are those 'other Worlds' to the ones we know? Is annihilation a process of artistic distillation, clarifying and intensifying the meanings of the things of the world, or is it self-aggrandizing, narcissistic, and destructive? Is a 'green Thought in a green Shade' admirable for its imaginative wholeness, its undistracted concentration? Or is the phrase meant to suggest the self-enclosure of imaginative activity, the indistinctness of its forms, its inclination to reduce complexity to the simplicities of the willed? At the centre of the garden, the traditional symbol of the place where such thoughts are indigenous, Marvell's denizen thinks about his mind thinking about its own greenness.

He can think about it because 'he' now watches his soul, disembodied, take on the ancient emblematic shape of a bird, singing its 'unexpressive' song (perhaps this poem?) and poised, as it 'Waves in its Plumes the various Light', for the 'longer flight' (lines 55–6) that may be the expected journey to its neo-platonic origins, or the greater work of art which should follow from the garden ecstasy – or perhaps finally, and only, the rest of life, for which the imagination of mental existence before the Fall is preparation.

The tripartite metamorphosis ends abruptly as we find ourselves outside the garden, looking back or in. The experience we have undergone was not a representation, but transformed time; and 'such was that happy Garden-state' (line 57) marks not only the story of Eden but the utterance we have just listened to and mistaken for a version of Eden. The continuity that holds one time to the other is insistence on the purity of solitude and on the disruption caused by passion (as in the Mower's laments). The discontinuity that holds them together is the newly imagined floral sundial, present to sight, touch, and smell, and therefore more 'real' in the poem than the remembered glories of 'that happy Garden-state'. Hours may be the invention of the human mind to mark its passage through the universe; but the sun runs through this 'fragrant Zodiack' as well as through its heavenly one; and the bee 'Computes its time as well as we' (lines 68, 70), teaching, all unknowing, modesty and practicality at the same time that it honours and uses the work of the 'skilful Gardner', who in this case may have been working on a model provided by the poet who would prefer to live within his created garden, but who can recognize a reasonable facsimile when he sees one.

Within a very few months after exercising the scruples of the 'Horatian Ode' Marvell became a member of the household of a military hero of national (and international) stature, but one who, in sharp contradistinction to Cromwell, had yielded up his uncontested powers and returned quietly to one of his ancestral estates. He thus posed for Marvell the dilemma between active political engagement or moral and aesthetic detachment, in an unusually stark and immediate form.

The evidence of the relationship between poet and patron lies largely in a few formal compliments: 'Upon the Hill and Grove at Billborough to the Lord Fairfax' and a Latin epigram on the 'mountains' of Almscliff and Bilbrough, both politico-topographical effusions on the Fairfacian virtues of humility and traditional ties to place; but primarily the ambitious and problematic 'Upon Appleton House', whose structure and genre have caused much debate.[20] Although it is clearly in the direct line of descent from such works as Jonson's 'To Penshurst' and Carew's 'To Saxham', in that it praises Fairfax by means of a compliment to his house and observes many of the conventions of the genre, it is not in any simple sense a 'country-house poem'.[21] Characteristically, it examines and tests those conventions, submitting them to the acute and sceptical scrutiny of the poet's 'slow Eyes' (line 81) as he draws his 'survey' of the emblematic landscape of Fairfax's retreat, moving with 'pleasant footstep' through its 'fragrant Gardens, shaddy Woods, / Deep Meadows, and transparent Floods' (lines 78–82), the catalogue clearly marking out the divisions of the poem.

It begins with an apotheosis of the house itself,[22] which introduces a major theme of all of Marvell's meditations: the proper relationship, or proportion, between created nature and the constructions of the intellect and the imagination. The passage also demonstrates his innate habit of identifying the subject of his poetry and the art of its making, and his understanding that the central concept of 'the house' includes not only the building but its history and the history, past and to come, of the family that inhabits it. Marvell alerts his reader (certainly, in this case, the family which is the poem's formal cause) to 'Within this sober Frame expect / Work of no Forrain *Architect*' (lines 1–2), recalling Jonson's praise of Penshurst for eschewing 'envious show', and calling attention to the simple structure of his own stanza of eight lines of eight syllables, a 'frame' that in its imitation of the square becomes a speaking image of stability, rectilinear virtue, and the 'straightness' of the moral architecture it proceeds to outline. The form of the poem, like the form of Appleton House, is fitted to its subject, as 'The Beasts are by their Denns exprest' (line 11). In contradistinction, men 'unruled' 'unproportion'd dwellings build' (lines 9–10); as Marvell insists, '*Humility* alone designs / Those short but admirable Lines, / By which, ungirt and unconstrain'd, / Things greater are in less contain'd' (lines 41–4). Upon this physical and metaphysical paradox this long, meandering, and epic investigation of changing scenes and multiple perspectives is firmly based; for it is Marvell's hypothesis that Fairfax's decision to leave the world of power for the content of his Yorkshire seat is to be understood as part of an ancestral and providential design, a design that demonstrates the counterintuitive truth that the restrictions of disciplined shape are liberating, and that metaphor can capture meanings too large and elusive for discursive statement.

The first integral movement of the poem is devoted to the history of Isabella Thwaites, rapt from the nunnery where she had been confined by her guardian, the Prioress, by William Fairfax, the Lord General's ancestor. Marvell transforms a tale of the struggle for landed inheritance into a fable of the overthrow of the seductions of the cloister by Protestant heroism, impelled by its destined fulfilment in the marriage of the Lord General's only child, and by implication in the restoration of England, 'The Garden of the World ere while' (line 322), to its original, unfallen state.

Thus energy, daring, dynastic sexuality, and intrinsic commitment to the

course of providence conquer narcissistic sensuality, contemplative withdrawal, and the monastic ideal; this is the foundation of the 'house of
Fairfax'. But as the past is refigured as a prophetic explanation of the
present, the present becomes a commentary on the meanings of the past.
Stanza 41 breaks out with a lament for the 'dear and happy Isle', and asks
plangently, 'What luckless Apple did we tast, / To make us Mortal, and The
Wast?' (lines 321, 327–8). War, and the deep causes that led to it, have
changed ploughshares into swords; and Fairfax's retirement has done the
same, on the level of symbol, so that now 'We Ord'nance Plant and Powder
sow' (line 344). Civil war, in short, reverses identities and clashes categories
which are naturally incommensurable.

At this point Marvell confronts the implications of his own dialectic; he is
in the house of the man who is in some measure responsible for the loss he
mourns:

> And yet there walks one on the Sod
> Who, had it pleased him and *God*,
> Might once have made our Gardens spring
> Fresh as his own and flourishing. (lines 345–8)

That possibility was cut off by Fairfax's choice to '*Ambition* weed, but *Conscience* till' (line 354). The *agon* between the virtues of immersion in the
world of action and the lure of detachment and pure integrity is played out
again and again in Marvell.

The interest of the poem is as much in its rendering of the mental act of
perspective vision as it is in its transmutation of the Fairfax estate into a set
of moving images of the poet's preoccupations. The meadow becomes an
unsoundable sea, like the mind's ocean or Damon's reflexive fields. The
mowers are at once Israelites crossing the Red Sea[23] and then mimes of the
recent wars, so that the mown meadow seems 'A Camp of Battail newly
fought' and the field of haystacks 'Lyes quilted ore with Bodies slain' (lines
420, 422). The poetic mode is metamorphic, but what the rapid shifts of
scene[24] allude, or are connected, to is the succession of thoughts in the
poet's imagination.

The poem moves in great, sudden, changes of his mind, although its pace
sounds stately and even aimless. The flood that drowns 'The River in it self'
(line 471) in stanza 59 opens the gate of paradox so wide that the poet retires
and takes 'Sanctuary in the Wood', there to 'imbark / In this yet green, yet
growing Ark' (lines 481–3). There he comes to the centre of his moral laby-
rinth: 'Dark all without it knits; within / It opens passable and thin.'[25] It
opens so easily because this is the landscape that answers to his version of
pastoral.

His delight comes in part from being in this place an '*easie Philosopher*', convinced that he is but 'an inverted Tree', and that he can speak in the 'most learned Original' language of the birds (lines 561, 568, 570). He believes that 'What *Rome, Greece, Palestine*, ere said / I in this light *Mosaick* read', and that he has learned the language of '*Natures mystick Book*' (lines 581–4).

What draws him from this comic idyll is the thought of the flooded meadow and the river Wharfe, now receded, that runs through it:

> See in what wanton harmless folds
> It ev'ry where the Meadow holds;
> And its yet muddy back doth lick,
> Till as a *Chrystal Mirrour* slick,
> Where all things gaze themselves, and doubt
> If they be in it or without.
> And for his shade which therein shines,
> *Narcissus* like, the *Sun* too pines.   (lines 633–40)

In manner – poised, witty, observant and quirky – this is fairly typical of 'Upon Appleton House', and of its mode of proceeding by free-standing commentaries as the poet's figure moves through the landscape. Marvell's ingenious visual metaphors challenge the ancient systems of correspondence typified by theories of microcosm/macrocosm relationship; and they raise, in different form, the persistent question of retirement from the world of active strife. Even the sun 'pines' to be united with its 'shade', the dark, subaqueous image of its glorious self.

Marvell disarms such speculation by picturing himself 'Abandoning my lazy Side' while the fishes 'twang' at his lines, only to be startled back into his task of celebration by the introduction of the '*young Maria*' (lines 643, 648, 651).[26] Like many of the young women who walk through the gardens of seventeenth-century lyric poetry, Mary is presented as the epitome of beauty and potential fruitfulness. Mary is '*She* that to these Gardens gave / That wondrous Beauty which they have' / *She* streightness on the Woods bestows; / To *Her* the Meadow sweetness owes' (lines 689–92); in short, she is cast as the ordering principle that gives form to inchoate nature. She is implicated in the destiny of the house and the family; Marvell compares her to 'a *sprig of Misleto*' that 'On the *Fairfacian Oak* does grow', nor does he balk at the realization that to fulfil her fated obligations 'The *Priest* shall cut the sacred Bud' (lines 739–40, 742). The costs are counted with the achievement; and in the light (or shade) of that acceptance the chastened tutor places both praise and prophecy in a subdued and qualified final perspective:

> 'Tis not, what once it was, the *World*,
> But a rude heap together hurl'd,
> All negligently overthrown,
> Gulfes, Deserts, Precipices, Stone.
> Your lesser *World* contains the same,
> But in more decent Order tame;
> *You Heaven's Center, Nature's Lap.*
> *And Paradice's only Map.* (lines 761–8)

Nunappleton and the greater cosmos are indeed made of the same stuff, but it is a stuff of pain and peril; the best that can be said is that the world that Fairfax has shaped and passed on to the promise of his daughter upholds a 'decent Order tame'. Having understood so much, Marvell re-enters the realm of history and consequential action, but not without remarking on the darkening '*Hemisphere*' of the evening sky, and urging the value of prudence and patience: 'Let's in' (line 775).

Marvell left Fairfax's service after two years or so. When Milton's recommendation failed to obtain for him a government post,[27] he found employment as a tutor to Cromwell's ward. The development of his relationship with the Lord Protector, the title Cromwell assumed in 1653, is marked by his poem on 'The First Anniversary of the Government under O. C.',[28] and by 'A Poem upon the Death of O. C.'[29] In the later Cromwell poems Marvell continues and revives themes and metaphors first encountered in the 'Horatian Ode'. Once again, Cromwell dominates rather than being caught in the music of time, urging his active star rather than merely responding to events. Marvell sharpens this point by associating it with the millennial intimations that developed within religious sectarianism between 1640 and 1660.[30] He argues that if lesser lands could but recognize Cromwell's virtues, 'How might they under such a Captain raise / The great Designes kept for the latter Dayes!' (lines 109–10) and recounts his own hope that if 'High Grace should meet in one with highest Pow'r' 'Foreshortned Time its useless Course would stay, / And soon precipitate the latest Day' (lines 132, 139–40).

What is emerging from the partially clouded vision of 1650 is the shape of a new form of government, in which hereditary monarchy is replaced by the architectural skills of the leader whose authority is derived from his willed submission to the destiny of the state. In 'The First Anniversary' Marvell struggles to reconcile his allegiance to republican virtue with his perception of the providential significance of Cromwell, the particular, timebound individual.[31]

The hopes that surrounded Cromwell's rule collapsed at his death in 1658; and in 1659 the utter failure of his son, Richard, as his successor brought on the restoration of Charles II.[32] In the same year Marvell was elected as Member of Parliament for Hull, and served in that capacity until his death in 1678. During that time he wrote primarily satirical poems on the state of domestic and international politics under the Restoration monarchy, many of them published anonymously, obviously because of the oppositional stance they assumed toward the government.

But there is a large group of poems, appearing for the first time posthumously in *Miscellaneous Poems*, that speak for interests equally important to a full appreciation of Marvell's mind and art, and that cannot be assigned a date with any assurance.[33] They are poems about the quarrel between the allure of the goods of the world and the commands of the life of the spirit. Typically, Marvell transforms the traditional genre of the moral debate[34] into a dialogue, creating voices for what in religious tracts and philosophical treatises are more properly epistemological and ontological points of view.[35] Their contest is sharpened in 'A Dialogue between the Soul and Body',[36] as Marvell redacts both Christian and neo Platonic dualism by focussing on the inextricable implication of spiritual consciousness with fleshly sensitivity. As the spirit has been taught by scripture and tradition that it is imprisoned in a rebellious body, so the flesh is made aware of its mortal flaws only because it has been made so by consciousness. Each complains, in effect, that it has been made what it is by the other; and each imagines a state of being in which it would be freely and independently itself, reminding us both of the yearning for single prelapsarian blessedness in the visionary 'Garden', and of the acceptance of its impossibility. Thus the Soul finds itself 'manacled in Hands', constrained by the senses that give its access to the world; and the body complains of the soul that it 'stretcht upright, impales me so, / That mine own Precipice I go' (lines 4, 13–14). The body wants only to 'rest', the soul to gain the 'Port' from which it has been kept by being 'Shipwrackt into Health' (lines 19, 29–30) by the body. Each desires surcease, and imagines it in the separation that cannot be, in that their dilemma – and the dialogue – exist only because of their understood union. The body is given the last word (in the text as we have it) in lines that are shaped by Marvell's sustained speculation on the poetics of human creativity:

> What but a Soul could have the wit
> To build me up for Sin so fit?
> So Architects do square and hew,
> Green Trees that in the Forest grew.   (lines 41–4)

The Body is as certain as the Mower against gardens that 'Green Trees' are best left in the forest; but the Marvell who celebrated 'The First Anniversary of … O. C.' is more willing to entertain the costs of shaping nature to a moral or spiritual purpose.

The one poem of Marvell's that deserves inclusion in any anthology of seventeenth-century devotional verse, 'The Coronet',[37] is also unusual in that Marvell speaks directly here about poetry, and presents himself as a converted pastoralist. Devotional poetry, he suggests, begins in a sense of sin, and with a desire to 'redress that Wrong' (line 4). But with his familiar cultivated naivety, the repentant shepherd takes that notion too literally, fallibly trying to re-dress Christ's wounded head with a 'Chaplet' woven from the flowers 'That once adorn'd' the 'Shepherdesses head' (lines 11, 8).[38] But the fulcrum for the turn in his spiritual renovation is the discovery of the 'Serpent old' and his 'wreaths of Fame and Interest' (lines 13, 16) deeply involved in the new garlands he has woven from his superseded pastoral fictions. Whereas Herbert, in the two 'Jordan' poems, is concerned primarily with the false choice of *language* with which to honour God and his own purpose, Marvell cuts deeper into the moral tangle that holds the impulse of the creator toward perfection of the creation. Even as he asks that Christ either 'his slipp'ry knots at once untie' – the knots that interweave the poet's skill and the serpent's wiles – or 'shatter too with him my curious frame' (lines 20, 22), the metaphors declare the 'intrinsicate'[39] relationship between the author and his poem (both are described in 'my curious frame'). While he calls for their destruction he cannot keep from reminding Christ that those inadequate garlands were nevertheless 'set with Skill and chosen out with Care' (line 24). Once again, the alternatives are posed as complicit immersion in the flowery world of 'languishing numbers' or the destruction of self through commitment to the larger sphere of virtue, political, or, in this case, moral.

Such a formulation, however, pays insufficient attention to a quality in Marvell that often goes without proper notice: audacity. It is exhibited perhaps most clearly in his treatment of literary genres, in his trenchant interest in the assumptions of rhetorical strategy that underlie them, and in his almost obstinate insistence on driving conventional locutions back towards their origins by literalizing their metaphors. One example of these attitudes both learnedly respectful and sceptically adventurous, is 'The Definition of Love'.[40] The genre to which it belongs has been identified (and debated).[41] The challenge it presents is evident in its title alone: how does one set the limits to a boundless emotion, how does one *define* love? A possible answer is that one writes a poem about it, because this purports to be '*The*' definition of love, not one among many; that is, the poem itself enacts the process of definition, or of confining love within its own verbal limits. Marvell draws upon cosmology and mathematics; 'Loves *oblique*' are compared to geometric figures, and described as able 'Themselves in every Angle [to] greet'.[42] The loves defined by this poem, however, 'so truly

Paralel, / Though infinite, can never meet.' (lines 25–8) Therefore, the fulfilment of love can take place only at infinity, where parallel lines meet, but not in the world of common obliquity. Love is always and only 'the Conjunction of the Mind, / And Opposition of the Stars (lines 31–2).' So rigorous is 'The Definition of Love' in its philosophical self-denial that neither woman nor man appears; its 'object' remains simply that, definable only within a set of relations. Marvell has created a geometry of passion.

This penchant for attempting to control passion by ratiocination is seen here at its most schematic, but it provides the formal motivation for a number of other poems. To fashion poems – or houses, or metaphors, images, stanzas – in which 'things greater are in less contained' is to imitate in the practices of art the 'greater' versions of this same act that are found in the creation of political institutions or in the foundational paradoxes of Christianity. In each case the creator – poet, ruler, God – embodies and constrains the ineffable within a discrete entity, so that an 'idea' can be seen, witnessed, read, understood. History and the divine work in the same way – revealing themselves in earthly, comprehensible singularities, while speaking of the reality that, we suspect, transcends them.

Marvell's way with poetic genres is energized by his awareness of the relation of each manifestation of a kind of poem to the kind (or genre) that identifies it, even as the new exemplum departs from and changes the terms of that definition. 'To his Coy Mistress',[43] with 'The Garden' perhaps his best-known lyric, is clearly intended both to exemplify and to comment on an interrelated set of love lyrics, more particularly those that Renaissance poets revived from classical and medieval predecessors: the invitation to love; the blazon of the beloved lady; the poem of *carpe diem*, passion's animadversion on inevitable mortality. Their common premiss is the power of desire and its struggle against extinction. Their manners include courtly praise, lover's complaint, and philosophic defiance. As T. S. Eliot pointed out in his influential essay, Marvell includes (or alludes to) all of these poetic discourses, but contains them in a deceptively rigid syllogistic frame of argument, whose lineaments appear in the logical hinge-words of the three stanzas: 'Had we ...'; 'But ...'; 'Now, therefore ...' (lines 1, 21, 33).[44]

Both this structure and its tone differ obviously and crucially from the paradigmatic 'Gather ye rosebuds while ye may, / Old time is still a-flying'. Herrick's combination of insouciance and indulgence is as far from Marvell's knowing, tight-lipped impatience as is 'Old time' from 'Times winged Charriot' (line 22) heard hurrying behind the speaker's back. 'To his Coy Mistress', in fact exists only because there is not 'World enough, and Time' (line 1). Its counterfactuality is the ground of its utterance; and Marvell's carefully exaggerated reckoning of the time he *would* devote to each

part of his beloved's blazon is conducted in the deep shadow of the knowledge that any time at all would be inadequate, that hyperbolic Petrarchan
praise is itself a futile gesture of denial and protest against the oncoming
darkness. Braced by this knowledge he can magnanimously apportion 'An
hundred years . . . to praise / Thine eyes', and, in summary haste, 'But thirty
thousand to the rest' (lines 13–14, 16).

If the lady 'deserve[s] this State' and the speaker would not love 'at lower
rate' (lines 19–20), all this counting and accounting is carried on in a world
in which time is not simply hurrying toward them, but hurrying toward an
apocalypse.[45] The 'last Age' (line 18), in Marvell's phrase, combines the
climax of the tradition of erotic epideixis and the moment when all shall be
changed, when poems like this one will lose their purpose, as will the lover.

So, while he expands (like his 'vegetable Love' in line 11) his account of
what he would do if only he could, Marvell's speaker drives toward his
explanation of impossibility. Caught between the deathly chariot winging
toward him and the bleak and empty prospect of eternity, limitless in extension and duration (in this instance holding no promise of immortality), he
abandons the tropes of distant adoration for figures that reverse the process
of transformation which conventionally governs the genre. His 'ecchoing
Song' will be silent, 'Worms shall try / That long-preserv'd Virginity', and
all his 'Lust' will be turned to ashes (lines 27–8, 30).

These are, nevertheless, still versions of a reality within the poet's control,
not facts of fate to be yielded to. 'To his Coy Mistress' is, after all, an act of
persuasion, and persuasion depends as much on ethos as it does on logic.
When the impatient lover points out that:

> The Grave's a fine and private place,
> But none I think do there embrace   (lines 31–2)

it is the interposed 'I think' that simultaneously subverts and intensifies the
argument that sterility is the price of coyness, the 'sweet reluctant amorous
delay'[46] that poets who write such poems require of their subjects. Marvell
knows better, but admits with deliberately disarming modesty that he can't
quite be sure.

Nor can he stay to find out. 'Now therefore'; the heavily stressed, trun-
cated trochee turns the poem around its ultimate corner of haste and desire.
Politesse falls away as the menacing images of time and the grave work their
way into the 'Lady's consciousness (and the speaker's – in persuading he
also strengthens his own conviction). Moving ever further from the starched
formalities of the blazon of praise, the putative lovers become predatory
birds, devouring an enemy which is also an element of their very selves. The
solution to the problem posed at the outset, the only possible plan to evade

the poles of impossibility that contain the poem's syllogistic structure, combines the fusion of opposites, the dissolution of identities, the substitution of violence for sensuality, the creation of pleasure out of pain and difficulty. While all such calculated transformations may be read in a sexual register, they also bespeak an attack on limitation and definition by evasion, and by the poet's power of renaming. The imagined world whose cosmology Petrarch developed and articulated from models inherited from, among others, Catullus and Dante, Marvell has invoked and undermined, as is his habit, by taking its essential artefacts (artificialities?) seriously, and clashing them against equally powerful cultural constructs, like the intimation of apocalypse.

The sound of that clash is the tone of 'To his Coy Mistress', the sad mockery of the interpolated 'Lady', the delayed, subdued qualifier, 'and more slow' (line 12), and the concluding concessive-triumphant claim:

> Thus, though we cannot make our Sun
> Stand still, yet we will make him run.   (lines 45–6)[47]

The conclusion toward which the mortal syllogism drives is one in which both the forms and the concepts indigenous to the poem of *carpe diem* are escaped from, transcended, by an imaginary act of overgoing. If the sun cannot be made to stand still, as Joshua made it do, and as Ovid and Marlowe's Faustus pleaded unsuccessfully that it do, Marvell's lover will blunt the threat of time by making it run faster, loosening its grip by interrupting its relentless rhythm with human intensity. A poem that begins in the traps of convention implodes into a sphere of defiant consciousness. It is a traverse that Marvell follows often.

The primary reason for the widely held opinion that Marvell abandoned lyric poetry when he turned his hand to political satire after the restoration of the monarchy is that the satires are pointedly and precisely topical and so can be dated with confidence, unlike most of the poems that have won Marvell his stature in the twentieth century, such as 'The Garden' and 'To His Coy Mistress'. The obverse of the received idea that Marvell wrote no more lyrics when he began to write satires has no stronger basis in bibliographical fact, for that matter. 'Flecknoe, an English Priest at Rome', 'Tom May's Death', and 'The Character of Holland' demonstrate that topical satire in pentameter couplets was part of Marvell's poetic repertoire during the years when he is most likely to have written his consummate pastorals and meditative lyrics.

Apart from a long sojourn in Holland, and service in embassies to Russia, Sweden, and Denmark during the years 1662–5, Marvell spent those years engaged in three absorbing activities: he represented his home town of Hull and its commercial interests with unflagging dedication, reporting to its governors often several times a week in letters of such extensive detail that they remain among the richest resources of historical documentation for the reign of Charles II; he criticized and characterized in satirical verse the major events and political figures of the time, developing the poetic genre of 'advice to a painter' and extending his personal exploration of the demands and possibilities of representing the process of moral argument leading to rational commitment; and he wrote a number of prose tracts devoted primarily to the defence of toleration in religion, and also to the definition of reasonable and effective modes of debate.

The prose writings of his Parliamentary years are almost all interventions in religious debates, and almost always on behalf of a policy of toleration for nonconformist beliefs and observance. Marvell's position changed from support of the monarch to agreement with Parliament as the political currents swirled around the issue of toleration; but he remained entirely consistent in his defence of freedom of conscience and observance for nonconforming Protestants; he was of his time in that Roman Catholicism (or 'popery', as it was known) marked the limits of commitment to religious toleration.

If his various attempts to see through to the inner processes of history have led ultimately to this almost quietistic acceptance of its power to achieve its ends, Marvell remained throughout his life fascinated by but ambivalent about the nature of his own art, particularly with respect to the relation between the mysteries of craft and the ethical responsibilities they bear. He does not often treat the act of writing directly in his poems, but rather relies on traditional symbols (such as the soul as a singing bird) and allegorical figures (like Amphion or 'the architect') to examine the creative sources of speech and representation, and to pose questions about the work of reasoning and judging in expressive form. His taciturnity seems in some measure a trait of character, connecting his apparent reluctance to circulate his poems and his reputation for guardedness, even secrecy, in political life. In venturing on polemic prose he clearly recognizes the practical dangers of opposing a powerful monarchic government, but acknowledges, too, the political and ethical vulnerability to criticism of any author who addresses the public on contested issues.

Beyond even these considerations, Marvell exhibits a concern with the fundamental reliability of language in shaping images of thought that can both express the mind that imagines them and affect the minds of others. The pervasive scepticism of his writing is a different aspect of the characteristics of his verse that criticism has always regarded as essential: wit, wordplay, and ambiguity. The play on words is the embodiment of Marvell's awareness of the multiple possibilities of meaning intrinsic to most speech; it parallels his fondness for dialogue form, his interest in the mutual incomprehensions of flesh and spirit, incarnate but divided in consciousness. This sense of a gap between the written word as a concrete object and the numinous 'thing' it stands for – an idea or a feeling – marks all of Marvell's writing, even in the reticences of his letters to the Hull Corporation.

It impinges clearly on the considerations of what may be his last non-satiric composition in verse, 'On Mr Milton's *Paradise Lost*', printed in the second edition of the epic in 1674.[48] Marvell confesses to doubts about the epic undertaking, both because of the 'vast Design' that encompasses, as he says simply, 'All', and from fear that Milton, like his own Samson, is driven to 'ruine ... the sacred Truths' 'to revenge his Sight' (lines 2, 5, 7–8, 10). These suspicions are replaced, as Marvell comes to understand the scope and propriety of the poem's plan, by uneasiness that Milton's merely human capacities will lead him to 'perplex' what should be made clear, and thus defeat understanding.[49]

As he reads he discovers that the poet has 'not miss'd one thought that could be fit' (line 27), but that his greater achievement is to have touched the radically distant notes on the scale of imagination that alone could give voice to this vision:

> At once delight and horrour on us seize,
> Thou singst with so much gravity and ease;
> And above humane flight dost soar aloft,
> With Plume so strong, so equal, and so soft.   (lines 35–8)

Not only has Milton met the challenge he set himself in the opening lines of Book 1, to 'soar / Above the Aonian Mount' in his 'adventrous song', but he has mastered the combination of strong and soft that has teased Marvell in his dialogues, in 'To his Coy Mistress', in 'Upon Appleton House', and, in different form, in the political poems.

Marvell's admiration is laced through with the kind of envy that arises from sympathetic understanding of accomplishment. Although the poem concludes with a self-effacing comment on 'tinkling Rhime', and Milton's magisterial refusal to rely on its attractions,[50] it points ironically to the fact that his compliment is composed in rhyming couplets. Marvell observes that:

> I too transported by the *Mode* offend,
> And while I meant to *Praise* thee, must Commend.
> Thy verse created like thy *Theme* sublime,
> In Number, Weight, and Measure, needs not *Rhime*.
>
> (lines 51–4)

Marvell here demonstrates that rhyme can provide more than trivial musical pleasure: it can create the subtlest nuances of social exchange, and act as an element in a complex ideological argument. The intent to praise is displaced by the demands of a couplet rhyme; but to 'commend' is to acknowledge the excellences of *Paradise Lost* from a position of informed judgement rather than subordinate admiration. Furthermore, the praise comes from a poet who at the same time displays his ability to transform a self-imposed limitation into an inevitable trope; that is, the act of self-denigration is itself a performance that proves Marvell's skill, and therefore his title to offer praise worthy of Milton's acceptance.

The poetic themes and historical issues that occupied Marvell's private and public existences are clear enough: the tension between participation and withdrawal; the relative moral positions of the creative human mind and the natural world it operates upon; the sources of civil power and the place of religious belief in authorizing it; the rights of the flesh and the spirit in the government of man's lesser state; the relation of tradition to innovation in the creation of art; the status of images with respect to what the mind makes of them. One can trace changes in his allegiances, or at least shifts in emphasis as he engaged pressing political conflicts or indulged speculative freedom in a time torn by absolutisms of many sorts. He has come to be known in our century as the poet of witty, impassioned scepticism and of strangely impersonal lyric flights; but there is some truth that needs to be recovered in his long-standing reputation as a defender of individual liberties, most profoundly those of inner, perhaps inaccessible, vision.

NOTES

1 In Shakespeare's sonnet 107 ('Not mine own fears, nor the prophetic soul / Of the wide world'), line 5, 'The mortal moon hath her eclipse endured', has been glossed as a reference to the climacteric of the Queen, and thus with her death in 1603. Received numerological beliefs associated the climacteric with multiples of seven, or the odd multiples of seven, or multiples of nine; the fact that Elizabeth I died at the age of sixty-three (the product of seven and nine) seemed therefore all the more significant.

2 *The Poems and Letters of Andrew Marvell*, ed. H. M. Margoliouth, 2 vols., 3rd edn, rev. P. Legouis, with E. E. Duncan-Jones (Oxford: Clarendon Press, 1971) pp. 91–4. All quotations of Marvell's poetry hereafter are from this edition.

3 Marvell's intent in this poem has been associated with a variety of political positions, ranging from the celebration of Cromwell's ascent to supreme power, to qualified support of the republican government and the Commonwealth, to ironic criticism of Cromwell and lamentation for the collapse of the monarchy. See John M. Wallace, *Destiny His Choice: The Loyalism of Andrew Marvell* (Cambridge University Press, 1968); Joseph A. Mazzeo, 'Cromwell as Davidic

King', in *Reason and the Imagination* (New York: Columbia University Press, 1962), pp. 229–55; and the passages about the poem in the standard works of Patterson, Colie, and Chernaik cited in the bibliography below. The exchange between Cleanth Brooks and Douglas Bush can be followed in *English Institute Essays*, (1946): 127–58; *Sewanee Review* 60 (1952): 363–76; and *Sewanee Review* 61 (1952): 129–35. The 'Horatian Ode' has served as a nexus, in Marvell criticism, for the received opinion that he is inherently and temperamentally reluctant to take definite positions, and given to reserve, irony, ambivalence, and even time-serving. The most eloquent, if not the most illuminating, formulation of this view is perhaps T. S. Eliot's well-known remark that Marvell's characteristic wit includes, 'probably, a recognition, implicit in the expression of every experience, of other kinds of experience which are possible' ('Andrew Marvell', in *Selected Essays* (London: Faber and Faber, 1932)). The cumulative critical history of this poem suggests that it cannot be reduced to a definitive political position, and thus perhaps that Marvell's stance had more to do with trying to grasp the meaning of the events surrounding him than to urge a particular action in response to them. There is only speculative evidence that the poem was published or circulated privately; an argument as to its rhetorical purpose, then, is difficult to construct.

4 Rosalie Colie is the best guide to this aspect of Marvell's poetic; see *'My Ecchoing Song:' Andrew Marvell's Poetry of Criticism* (Princeton University Press, 1970), passim.

5 See, for example, 'Ode to Himself'.

6 *Poems and Letters*, 1.62–86. Perhaps the most intense expression of Protestant feeling about the relation between individual choice and providential purpose is to be found in Milton's sonnet on his 'three and twentieth year' and the sonnet written some twenty years later, in his blindness, in which his despair that his 'one talent' has been rendered 'useless', is answered by a personified Patience with the reassurance that 'they also serve who only stand and wait'.

7 The same metre was employed by Sir Richard Fanshawe in his translation of Horace, completed by 1647 but not published until 1652. Thomas Stanley, a contemporary of Marvell's at Cambridge, used the same metre, although to much different effect, in a translation of Johannes Secundus's *Basia* published in 1651; it is possible that his choice was determined by Marvell's poem.

8 *Poems and Letters*, 1.51–3.

9 While 'forsake' means primarily to 'leave', it inevitably carries connotations from erotic poetry, of abandoning a lover coldly. The poet in 'Tom May's Death' 'fights forsaken Vertues cause' (line 66).

10 This is to some extent a pastoral fiction; Cromwell had years earlier shown himself an able and vigorous public figure as an MP.

11 'The Mower's Song', *Poems and Letters*, 1.48–9, line 1.

12 As Rosalie Colie has shown, calling the technique 'unmetaphoring'. See *'My Ecchoing Song'*, p. 79, and the index entry for 'unmetaphoring'.

13 *Poems and Letters*, 1.44–7.

14 *Ibid.*, 1.48–9, 47–8.

15 *Ibid.*, 21–3, lines 43–4.

16 *Ibid.*, 1.51–3.

17 The 'serious' aspect of this joke is its distant allusion to the concept of a natural

language, the language spoken by Adam and Eve before the Fall, the language in which the name was equivalent to the identity of the thing named. When Ben Jonson sought to describe his ideal woman, his muse could give him no better advice than to 'Bedford write, and that was she' (Epigrams, 76, 'On Lucy, Countess of Bedford').

18 'Only' and 'that' leave it open to conjecture whether Marvell does or does not imply intent on the part of the gods; it may be, too, that in keeping with the poem's overall sense of irony, Apollo and Pan did not fully grasp their own implicit motives.

19 Marvell's syntax allows, too, for the possibility that in the mind each 'kind' finds 'its own resemblance'; i.e., that the mental world is one of replicas and mirrorings, like the phenomena of the flooded meadow in 'Upon Appleton House', or the dewdrop and the soul, or 'Eyes and Tears'. This in turn allows the implication that 'its happiness' lies in contemplating the endlessly proliferating images of its own creations.

20 Poems and Letters, 1.62–86. See Colie, 'My Ecchoing Song', pp. 181–294; M. J. K. O'Laughlin, 'This Sober Frame: A Reading of "Upon Appleton House"', in Andrew Marvell: A Collection of Critical essays, ed. G. deF. Lord (Englewood Cliffs, N.J.: Prentice-Hall, 1968), pp. 120–42.

21 Modern critical discussion of the genre begins with G. R. Hibbard, 'The Country House Poem of the Seventeenth Century', JWCI 19, 1–2 (January–June, 1956): 159–174, which remains useful. Like Jonson's 'Inviting a Friend to Supper', the genre represents the absorption of Augustan forms into contemporary rhetorical strategies. In this instance, the praises of moderation, friendship, and detachment from urban vices and ambitions to be found in the images of Horace's retreat and the Baian villa of Martial are fused with the Jacobean policy of attempting to re-establish 'housekeeping' and the influence of the crown in the provinces by urging the aristocracy to spend more time at their country estates.

22 These is some debate about the actual building described in the poem, because Fairfax was engaged in an ambitious rebuilding project at this time; see letters in the Times Literary Supplement for November 1971; 28 January, 11 February, and 31 March 1972.

23 Puritan 'saints' of the era often spoke of themselves as Israelites, in that they felt called especially to do God's work.

24 Numerous critics of the poem have commented on apparent allusions to the scenic effects so prominent in the court masques of Inigo Jones and others.

25 Marvell may be recalling the description of the entrance to the wood of Error in The Faerie Queene, 1.1.

26 Fairfax had departed from tradition, and angered his grandfather the first Lord Fairfax, by breaking the entail on the Nunappleton estate to allow Mary to inherit. His hopes of sustaining the dynasty were frustrated by her unhappy and ruinous marriage to the dissolute Duke of Buckingham; they had no children.

27 He did not achieve this until 1657, when he became Latin Secretary, the position Milton had filled earlier.

28 Published in that year in a quarto, this poem, like the two others on Cromwell, was cancelled from all but two copies of Miscellaneous Poems when that volume appeared posthumously in 1681.

29 Marvell also wrote two songs for an entertainment on the occasion of the marriage of Cromwell's daughter Mary in 1657 (shortly after the wedding of Mary Fairfax, which Cromwell opposed on political grounds).

30 Margarita Stocker, *Apocalyptic Marvell: The Second Coming in Seventeenth-Century Poetry* (Brighton: Harvester Press, 1986), offers the most thorough and imaginative commentary on these matters; but Christopher Hill's work on the subject, especially in *The World Turned Upside Down*, is invaluable. One of the reasons advanced for Cromwell's support of the readmission of Jews to England, from whence they had been expelled in the thirteenth century, was that it was a necessary preliminary to their conversion, which was understood to be one of the signs of an imminent millennium. In 'To his Coy Mistress', 'the Conversion of the *Jews*' (line 10) marks the approach to the end of time.

31 Not surprisingly, there is some disagreement about the political agenda of 'The First Anniversary'; Joseph Mazzeo sees it as a plea by Marvell for Cromwell to accept the crown that was offered to him in 1653, while Nicholas Guild argues that the poem's praise of Cromwell's ability does not extend to a desire for a renewed monarchy. See 'Marvell's "The First Anniversary of the Government Under O. C."', in *Papers on Language and Literature* 11 (Summer 1975): 242–53.

32 Fairfax was instrumental in supporting the recall of Charles to the throne.

33 Compared with the manuscript circulation of Donne's poems, there is very little evidence of Marvell's having sent copies of his work to friends or associates; the reserve which was justified by the political climate of the 1660s and 1670s may have been a trait of his temperament, as John Aubrey suggests when he says of Marvell, 'he was in his conversation very modest, and of very few words. Though he loved wine he would never drink hard in company; and was wont to say, "that he would not play the good-fellow in any man's company in whose hands he would not trust his life".'

34 See R. Osmond, *Mutual Accusation, Seventeenth-Century Body and Soul Dialogues in Their Literary and Theological Context* (University of Toronto Press, 1990), pp. 3–83 and passim.

35 Although when Dryden criticized Donne for 'affecting the metaphysics' in his erotic poetry (thus providing the basis for the critical label, 'Metaphysical' poet), he referred primarily to the use of philosophical *terminology* in what he regarded as an inappropriate context, I would argue that many of Marvell's poems are genuinely metaphysical in that they dramatize and examine problems such as the relationship of body to spirit *as problems*, rather than as analogies to other, conventional poetic concerns.

36 *Poems and Letters*, 1.21–3.

37 *Poems and Letters*, 1.14–15. 'The Coronet' should be compared closely with George Herbert's 'Jordan (II)'.

38 It is germane that 'flowers' was a term for rhetorical figures and graces.

39 *Antony and Cleopatra*, 5.2.304.

40 *Poems and Letters*, 1.39–40.

41 See F. Kermode, 'Definitions of Love', *RES* ns 7, 26 (April 1956): 183–5.

42 Ben Jonson called such erotic experience 'making a little winter-love in a dark corner', in *Discoveries*.

43 *Poems and Letters*, 1.27–8.

44 T. S. Eliot, 'Andrew Marvell', in *Selected Essays*.

DONALD M. FRIEDMAN

45 The 'Conversion of the *Jews*' (line 10), traditionally, was to be one of the signs of the Second Coming, and would thus figure normally the long-expected, but distant, end of time. But in the agitated religious atmosphere of the 1640s and 1650s several radical sects proclaimed the imminence of the Last Days.

46 Milton, *Paradise Lost*, 4.311.

47 Note how the enjambment tends to make the sun 'Stand still' at the end of line 45.

48 *Poems and Letters*, 1.137–9.

49 The 'less skilful hand' Marvell fears might turn the epic into a play or masque (lines 18–22) may be Dryden's. Aubrey reports that he made such a request of Milton, and that Milton acceded to it.

50 Marvell's poem appeared in the 1674 volume immediately before Milton's note on 'The Verse', in which he describes the 'modern bondage of Riming' as 'trivial and of no true musical delight'.

FURTHER READING

Brett, R. L. (ed.), *Andrew Marvell: Essays on the Tercentenary of his Death* (Oxford University Press, 1979)

Carey, John (ed.), *Andrew Marvell* (Harmondsworth: Penguin Books, 1969)

Chernaik, Warren, *The Poet's Time: Politics and Religion in the Work of Andrew Marvell* (Cambridge University Press, 1983)

Colie, Rosalie, *'My Ecchoing Song': Andrew Marvell's Poetry of Criticism* (Princeton University Press, 1970)

Duncan-Jones, E. E., 'Marvell: A Great Master of Words,' *Proceedings of the British Academy* no. 61, 1975 (Oxford University Press, 1976) pp. 267–90

Empson, Sir William, *Some Versions of Pastoral* (London: Chatto and Windus, 1935)

Seven Types of Ambiguity, rev. ed. (London: Chatto and Windus, 1947)

Using Biography (London: Chatto and Windus, 1984)

Everett, Barbara, 'The Shooting of the Bears: Poetry and Politics in Andrew Marvell', in *Poets in Their Time* (London: Faber and Faber, 1986), pp. 32–7

Friedenreich, Kenneth (ed.), *Tercentenary Essays in Honor of Andrew Marvell* (Hamden, Conn.: Archon Books, 1977)

Friedman, Donald, *Marvell's Pastoral Art* (London: Routledge and Kegan Paul, 1970)

Hodge, R. I. V., *Foreshortened Time: Andrew Marvell and Seventeenth Century Revolutions* (Cambridge: D. S. Brewer, 1978)

Legouis, Pierre, *Andrew Marvell. Poet, Puritan, Patriot* (Oxford: Clarendon Press, 1965)

McKeon, Michael, 'Pastoralism, Puritanism, Imperialism, Scientism: Andrew Marvell and the Problem of Mediation', *Yearbook of English Studies* 13 (1983)

Patrides, C. A., *Approaches to Andrew Marvell: The York Tercentary Lectures* (London: Routledge and Kegan Paul, 1978)

Patterson, Annabel, *Marvell and the Civic Crown* (Princeton University Press, 1978)

Scoular, Kitty, *Natural Magic: Studies in the Presentation of Nature in English Poetry from Spenser to Marvell* (Oxford: Clarendon Press, 1965)

Stocker, Margarita, *Apocalyptic Marvell: The Second Coming in Seventeenth Century Poetry* (Brighton: Harvester Press, 1986)

Wallace, John M., *Destiny His Choice: The Loyalism of Andrew Marvell* (Cambridge University Press, 1968)

Wilding, Michael, *Dragons Teeth: Literature in the English Revolution* (Oxford: Clarendon Press, 1987)

INDEX